해양경찰공무원 시험

해사영어

기본이론+기출문제

임하람 저

꼭! 읽어야 하는 기본이론을 균형있게 정리
과거부터 최신까지의 기출문제를 단원 별로 구성
이해를 위해 저자가 직접 그린 그림 다수 수록
2022년 2차 채용 필기시험 문제 및 해설 수록

PREFACE

본서는 해양경찰 시험 과목 중 '해사영어'시험의 최신 기출 문제(22년도 해경시험)를 바탕으로 제작되었습니다. 또한 실제 선박에 비치되어 많은 항해사들이 참고하는 국제협약의 본문과 해당 해석문을 바탕으로 제작하였으며 책의 구성은 해당 파트의 기본개념을 이해한 후 해당 부분의 기출 경향이 어떠한지 즉시 판단하고 공부 할 수 있게끔 되어있습니다.
개념의 이해를 돕기 위해 저자가 직접 제작한 그림도 많이 첨부하였습니다.
20년 3차 순경 시험을 기점으로 점차 출제 범위가 지엽적이라 여겨졌던 파트까지 확대 된 경향을 반영하여 앞으로의 예상 문제에도 최대한 대비할 수 있게끔 핵심파트와 지엽적 파트를 균형 있게 구성했습니다.

해사영어를 처음 공부하는 학생들에게...

해사영어 시험공부의 핵심은 반복과 암기입니다. 많은 학생들이 해사영어를 마주하자마자 고등학교, 대학교 시절 지겹도록 씨름하던 수능영어나 토익을 떠올리곤 합니다. 얘들은 해사영어와는 완전히 다른 유형의 시험입니다. 학생에게 요구하는 목표 자체가 달라요. 수능영어와 토익영어는 '영어능력' 테스트 시험입니다. 예측할 수 없는 여러 분야의 폭넓은 지문들을 랜덤으로 풀게 해 학생의 영어 능력을 검증하는 시험인 겁니다. 해사영어는 다릅니다. 해사영어에서 물어보는 핵심은 '해기지식'입니다. 단지 문제와 지문이 영어로 나오는 것뿐이죠.
공부의 방향성을 이렇게 잡읍시다.

PREFACE

첫 번째, 해야 할 것은 각 단원의 내용을 100퍼센트 숙지하는 일입니다. 물론 영어가 아닌 한글로요. 많은 학생들이 책을 펴자마자 영어 단어부터 해석하려고 합니다. 영어로 말하고자하는 해기지식이 무엇인지는 알지도 못한 채 말이에요. 이건 순서가 바뀐 겁니다. 먼저 내가 가장 익숙한 언어로 해당 단원의 내용을 이해하세요.

두 번째, 내용에 대한 이해가 어느 정도 이루어졌다면 내가 이해한 내용을 영어로는 뭐라고 하는지가 궁금해 져야합니다. 예를 들어 이런 거죠. COLREG라는 국제협약 파트를 보면, 좁은 수로(땅으로 치면 골목길 같은거에요)에서 항해하는 경우 바깥 경계의 우측으로 붙어서 항해하라고 합니다. 좁은 수로 = 우측통항 이라는 내용이해가 100퍼센트 되어 있다면 바로 이런 궁금증이 생겨야 해요. "해사영어에서 좁은 수로는 뭐라고 하고, 우측은 뭐라고 하지?" 이게 핵심입니다. 이제 좁은 수로가 Narrow channel, 우측이 starboard 이라는 사실을 공부하는 겁니다. 이걸 보고 단어 암기라고 하는거에요.

세 번째, 그럼 이런 내용을 시험에서는 어떻게 문제로 내는지를 파악하고 풀이 요령도 익혀야 합니다. 풀이 요령, 꿀 팁, 키워드 이런 건 아무래도 강사의 역량이라 볼 수 있겠네요.

위와 같은 세 가지 단계로 꾸준히 반복해서 공부하시면 반드시 고득점을 받으실 수 있을 겁니다. 근면과 성실은 공무원 시험 분야에선 마법의 비법서 같은 겁니다. 두 가지를 지키기만 하면 이 두 친구는 여러분을 절대 배신하지 않습니다. 확신합니다!

저자 임하람

CONTENTS

PART 01 | SMCP (표준해사통신영어)

CHAPTER • 01 선박의 기본 구조 ·· 14

CHAPTER • 02 INTRODUCTION 소개 ·· 15

CHAPTER • 03 SMCP GENERAL 일반 원칙 ································ 16

CHAPTER • 04 GLOSSARY 용어 ··· 30

CHAPTER • 05 Message Marker 통신부호 ································· 66

CHAPTER • 06 Standard Wheel Orders ···································· 74

CHAPTER • 07 Standard Engine Order ····································· 78

CHAPTER • 08 VHF Standard GMDSS Message 표준 GMDSS 통신문 ··············· 80

CHAPTER • 09 Guide lines on the use of VHF at sea 해상에서의 VHF 사용 지침 ·· 83

CHAPTER • 10 조난 통신의 예시 ·· 90

CHAPTER • 11 On-Board Communication Phrases ················· 96

CONTENTS

CHAPTER — 12 Log Book 항해일지 ··· 113

CHAPTER — 13 Safety on board 선내 안전 ··· 123

CHAPTER — 14 자주 나오는 SMCP 표현 ·· 129

CHAPTER — 15 다양한 SMCP 심화형 문제 ·· 136

PART 02 UNCLOS (United Nations Convention on the Law of the Sea)

CHAPTER — 01 Preamble 서문 ··· 144

CHAPTER — 02 Use of terms and scope 용어의 사용과 적용 범위 ············· 146

CHAPTER — 03 Baseline 영해기선 ·· 148

CHAPTER — 04 Internal Water 내수 ·· 150

CHAPTER — 05 Territorial Sea 영해 ··· 151

CHAPTER — 06 Contiguous zone 접속수역 ·· 157

CHAPTER — 07 Exclusive Economic Zone 배타적 경제 수역 ························· 158

CONTENTS

CHAPTER • 08 High Seas 공해 ·· 160

CHAPTER • 09 Right of innocent passage 무해통항권 ················ 162

CHAPTER • 10 Right of Visit 임검권 ··· 171

CHAPTER • 11 Right of Hot Pursuit 추적권 ······························ 173

CHAPTER • 12 Archipelagic State 군도국가 ······························ 177

CHAPTER • 13 Nationality and Status of ships 선박의 국적과 지위 ·· 179

CHAPTER • 14 Criminal Jurisdiction 형사적관할권 ···················· 180

CHAPTER • 15 Transit Passage 해협에서의 통과 통항 ················ 181

CHAPTER • 16 Continental Shelf 대륙붕 ··································· 187

CHAPTER • 17 UNCLOS의 다양한 규정 ···································· 188

PART 03 ▌IAMSAR(International Aeronautical and Marine Search and Rescue manual)

CHAPTER • 01 Glossary 용어 ··· 192

CONTENTS

CHAPTER — 02 구명용품 용기의 색깔 ··· 205

CHAPTER — 03 Distress 조난 ··· 207

CHAPTER — 04 Search Pattern ··· 211

CHAPTER — 05 인명구조법 ··· 220

CHAPTER — 06 Rescue or assistance by aircraft ······················· 225

CHAPTER — 07 On- Scene Co -ordination 현장 조정 ················· 229

CHAPTER — 08 Man Overboard ·· 231

PART 04 ┃ COLREG(International Regulations for preventing Collision at Sea.)

■ Part A – General ··· 236

■ Part B – Steering and sailing rules ··· 244

■ Part C – Light and shapes ··· 273

■ Part D – Sound and light signals ··· 301

■ Part E – Exemptions ·· 314

CONTENTS

PART 05 ▎SOLAS (International Convention for the Safety of Life at Sea)

CHAPTER • 01 Definitions 정의 ··· 318

CHAPTER • 02 Exceptions 적용제외 ·· 325

CHAPTER • 03 안전 증서 ··· 327

CHAPTER • 04 SOLAS 규정 ·· 328

CHAPTER • 05 SOLAS의 아직 출제되지 않은 규정 ··· 340

PART 06 ▎ISPS (International Code for the Security

CHAPTER • 01 ISPS의 목적과 용어 ·· 344

CHAPTER • 02 SSAS(The Ship Security Alert System) ································· 347

CHAPTER • 03 보안에 대한 당사국의 조치 ··· 349

CHAPTER • 04 Verification and Certification for Ship 선박의 검사 및 증명서 ······ 351

CHAPTER • 05 ISPS 적용 선박 ··· 352

CONTENTS

PART 07 — STCW(International Convention on Standard of Training, Certification and Watchkeeping for Seafarers)

- CHAPTER 01 용어 ········· 354
- CHAPTER 02 승무원 자격 ········· 356
- CHAPTER 03 당직임무에 대한 적합성 ········· 358
- CHAPTER 04 Voyage planning 항해계획 ········· 360
- CHAPTER 05 Watchkeeping at Sea 항해 중 당직근무 ········· 361
- CHAPTER 06 여러 조건과 수역에서의 당직근무 ········· 370

PART 08 — MARPOL(International Convention for the Prevention for Marine Pollution from Ship)

- CHAPTER 01 MARPOL 부속서의 종류 ········· 374
- CHAPTER 02 용어 정의 ········· 375
- CHAPTER 03 기름(Oil)의 배출 ········· 380

CHAPTER	04	Oil filtering equipment & ODME	383
CHAPTER	05	유해액체물질(noxious liquid substances in bulk)의 배출	384
CHAPTER	06	하수(Sewage)의 배출	387
CHAPTER	07	폐기물(Garbage)의 배출	389
CHAPTER	08	각종 문서 및 기록부	391

PART 09 ❙항해, 일반

CHAPTER	01	항해의 기초	394
CHAPTER	02	Geo-Navigation(지문항법)	398
CHAPTER	03	Bearing and Course(방위와 침로)	401
CHAPTER	04	수로도지	404
CHAPTER	05	Aids to navigation (항로표지)	408
CHAPTER	06	Tide(조석)	412
CHAPTER	07	RADAR	416

CONTENTS

CHAPTER — 08 Navigation Equipment(항해 장비) ·· 423

CHAPTER — 09 해양 기상 ·· 427

CHAPTER — 10 선박 개요 ·· 434

CHAPTER — 11 선박의 구조 ·· 436

CHAPTER — 12 선박 설비 ·· 441

CHAPTER — 13 선박에 작용하는 힘 ·· 445

CHAPTER — 14 Stability(복원성) ··· 451

CHAPTER — 15 Turning circle(선회권) ·· 455

CHAPTER — 16 Tonnage(톤수) ·· 457

CHAPTER — 17 기관 ·· 459

CHAPTER — 18 선박 화재 ·· 461

CHAPTER — 19 기타 항해, 일반 문제 통암기 ·· 464

PART 10 부록

CHAPTER — 01 2022년 2차 채용 해경필기시험 해사영어 기출 ················ 470

해사영어 기본이론 임하람

PART 01 SMCP(표준해사통신영어)

Chapter 1	선박의 기본 구조
Chapter 2	INTRODUCTION 소개
Chapter 3	SMCP GENERAL 일반 원칙
Chapter 4	GLOSSARY 용어
Chapter 5	Message Marker 통신부호
Chapter 6	Standard Wheel Orders
Chapter 7	Standard Engine Order
Chapter 8	VHF Standard GMDSS Message 표준 GMDSS 통신문
Chapter 9	Guide lines on the use of VHF at sea 해상에서의 VHF 사용 지침
Chapter 10	조난 통신의 예시
Chapter 11	On-Board Communication Phrases
Chapter 12	Log Book 항해일지
Chapter 13	Safety on board 선내 안전
Chapter 14	자주 나오는 SMCP 표현
Chapter 15	다양한 SMCP 심화형 문제

chapter 01 선박의 기본 구조

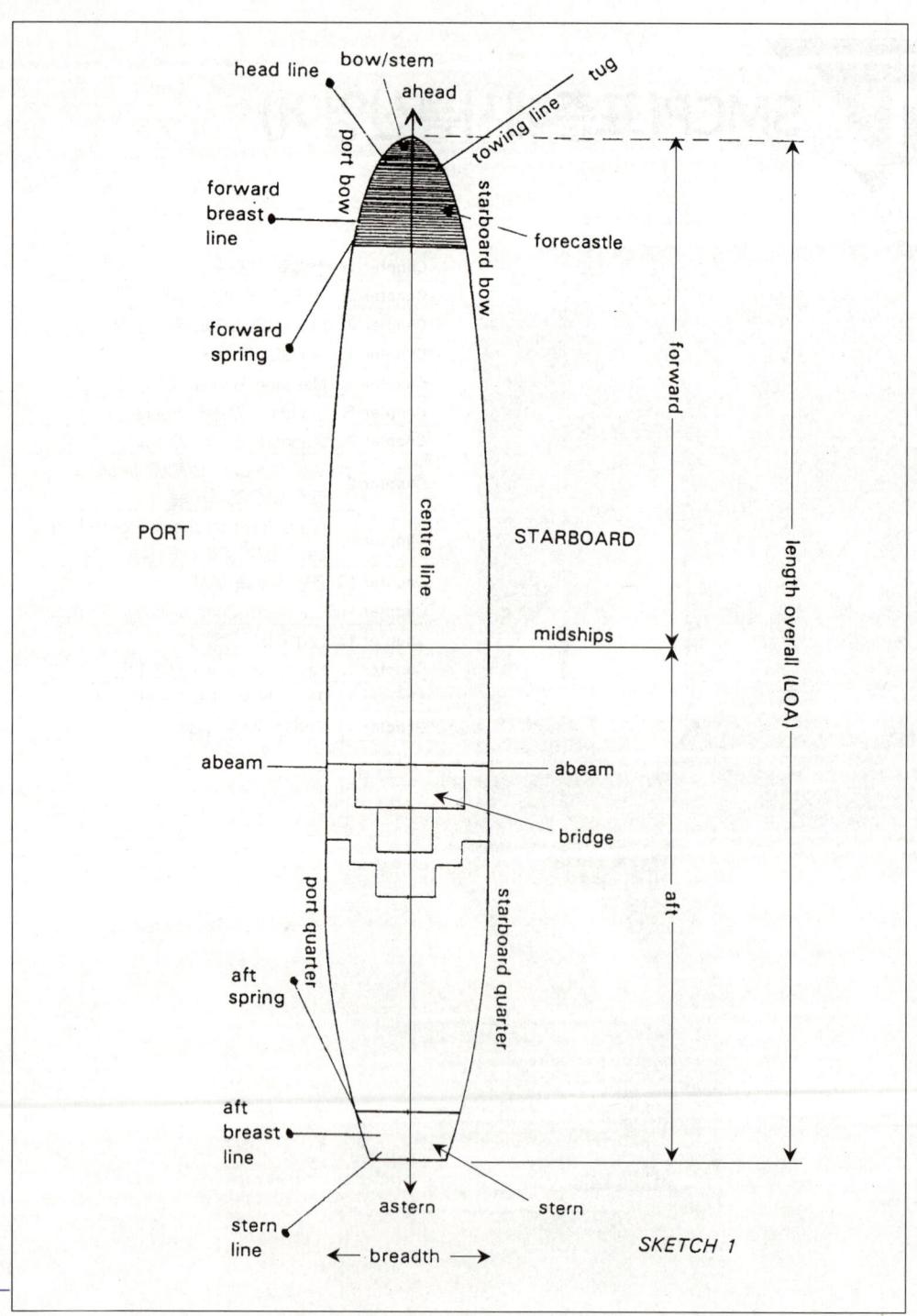

SKETCH 1

chapter 02 INTRODUCTION 소개

01
forward

The SMCP is divided into External Communication Phrases and On-board Communication Phrases as far as its application is concerned, and into PART A and PART B as to its status within the framework of the STCW, 1978, as revised.

As navigational and safety communications from ship to shore and vice versa, ship to ship, and on board ships must be **precise, simple, unambiguous**, so as to avoid confusion and error, there is a need **to standardize the language used**.

02
Position of the SMCP in maritime practice

The Standard Marine Communication Phrases (SMCP) has been compiled:
- to assist in the greater safety of navigation and of the conduct of the ship,
- to standardize the language used in communication for navigation at sea, in port-approaches, in waterways, harbours and on board vessels with multilingual crews, and
- to assist maritime training institutions in meeting the objectives mentioned above.

01 도입
SMCP는 그 적용과 관련하여 외부 통신용어와 선내 통신용어로 나누어져 있고, 개정된 1978년 STCW 협약의 관점에서 그 지위에 따라 A편과 B편으로 나누어져 있다.
선박과 육상간, 육상과 선박간, 선박과 선박간, 그리고 선내의 항해 및 안전 통신은 혼동과 오류를 피하기 위해서 정확하고, 간단하고, 모호하지 않아야 한다. 또한 사용하는 언어를 표준화할 필요가 있다.

02 SMCP의 지위
SMCP는 편집 되었다.
- 선박의 동정과 항행 안전을 보다 더 도모하기 위해
- 항해 중, 입항 중, 수로 상. 항구에서, 그리고 다국적 선원들로 구성된 선박에서의 선박 간 통신을 표준화하기 위해서.
- 위에서 언급한 목적에 맞는 해양 훈련기구에 도움을 주기 위해

▌기출문제

01. 다음 중 표준해사통신영어(SMCP)의 목적으로 가장 옳은 것은? [2021년 상반기]

① To supplant international Regulations for Preventing Collision at Sea
② To supresede the International Code of Signals
③ To contradict special rules or recommendations made by IMO concerning ship's routing
④ assist in the greater safety of navigation and of the conduct of the ship.

해설 SMCP의 편집 목적은 항해상(navigation)의 그리고 선박 운항(conduct of the ship) 상의 보다 나은 안전(greater safety)을 도모(assist)하기 위함이다.

답 ④

chapter 03 SMCP GENERAL 일반 원칙

01 절차

표준해사통신용어를 사용하여 교신하고자 한다는 것을 나타낼 필요가 있는 경우에는 다음과 같은 통신문을 송신한다.
"IMO 표준해사통신용어를 사용하시오."
"IMO 표준해사통신용어를 사용하겠습니다."

01

Procedure

When it is necessary to indicate that the SMCP are to be used, the following message may be sent:
"Please use IMO Standard Marine Communication Phrases."
"I will use IMO Standard Marine Communication Phrases."

02

Spelling

Letter	Code	Letter	Code
A	Alfa	N	November
B	Bravo	O	Oscar
C	Charlie	P	Papa
D	Delta	Q	Quebec
E	Echo	R	Romeo
F	Foxtrot	S	Sierra
G	Golf	T	Tango
H	Hotel	U	Uniform
I	India	V	Victor
J	Juliet	W	Whisky
K	Kilo	X	X-ray
L	Lima	Y	Yankee
M	Mike	Z	Zulu

Number	Spelling	Pronunciation
0	zero	ZEERO
1	one	WUN
2	two	TOO
3	three	TREE
4	four	FOWER
5	five	FIFE
6	six	SIX
7	seven	SEVEN
8	eight	AIT
9	nine	NINER
1,000	thousand	TOUSAND

기출문제

01. 다음은 해사통신에 사용되는 글자의 철자이다. 옳은 것은 모두 몇 개인가?

18년 3차

	㉠	㉡	㉢	㉣	㉤	㉥
Letter	F	K	R	S	V	Y
Code	Fox	Kilo	Radio	Sierra	Victory	Yankee

① 2개 ② 3개
③ 5개 ④ 6개

해설 ㉠ F - Foxtrot, ㉢ R - Romeo, ㉤ V - Victor

답 ②

02. 표준해사통신용어(Standard Marine Communication Phrases)상 사용되는 글자의 철자이다. 옳지 않은 것은 모두 몇 개인가?

19년 1차

	ⓐ	ⓑ	ⓒ	ⓓ	ⓔ
Letter	B	D	O	V	Z
Code	Beta	Delta	Oscar	Victor	Zoo

① 1개 ② 2개
③ 3개 ④ 4개

해설 ⓐ B - Bravo, ⓔ Z - Zulu

답 ②

03. 다음은 표준해사통신영어(Standard Marine Communication Phrases)에 사용되는 글자의 철자이다 옳지 않은 것은 모두 몇 개인가?

20년 3차

	Letter	Code
㉠	T	Tango
㉡	F	Foxtro
㉢	R	Radar
㉣	V	Vector
㉤	S	Sierra
㉥	J	Julu

① 2개 ② 3개
③ 4개 ④ 5개

해설 ㉡ F- Foxtrot, ㉢ R- Romeo, ㉣ V- Victor, ㉥ J- Juliet

답 ③

03
Message Markers

In shore-to-ship and ship-to-shore communication or radio communication in general, the following eight Message Markers may be used (also see "Application of Message Markers" given in PART AI/6 "Vessel Traffic Service (VTS) Standard Phrases"):

(i) Instruction
(ii) Advice
(iii) Warning
(iv) Information
(v) Question
(vi) Answer
(vii) Request
(viii) Intention

04
Responses

4.1 When the answer to a question is in the affirmative, say:
"Yes, ..." - followed by the appropriate phrase in full.

4.2 When the answer to a question is in the negative, say:
"No, ..." - followed by the appropriate phrase in full.

4.3 When the information requested is not immediately available, say:
"Stand by" - followed by the time interval within which the information will be available.

4.4 When the information requested cannot be obtained, say:
"No information."

4.5 When an INSTRUCTION (e.g. by a VTS-Station, Naval vessel or other fully authorized personnel) or an ADVICE is given, respond if in the affirmative:

"I will/can ..." - followed by the instruction or advice in full; and, if in the negative, respond:

"I will not/cannot ..." - followed by the instruction or advice in full. Example : "ADVICE. Do not overtake the vessel North of you."

Respond : "I will not overtake the vessel North of me."

4.5 지시(VTS, 해군함정 또는 완전한 권한이 주어진 사람에 의한)나 권고가 통보되었을 때
긍정적인 응답을 하고자 할 경우 : "I will/can …"이라 하고, 뒤에 지시나 권고의 내용을 생략하지 않고 반복한다.
부정적인 응답을 하고자 할 경우 : "I will not/cannot …"이라 하고, 뒤에 지시나 권고의 내용을 생략하지 않고 반복한다.

4.6 Responses to orders and answers to questions of special importance both in external and on-board communication are given in wording in the phrases concerned.

4.6 외부 통신이나 선내 통신에 있어서, 명령에 대한 응답이나 특별히 중요한 내용의 질문에 대한 대답을 할 경우 관련된 문구에 포함된 용어를 쓴다.

기출문제

04. If information is not ready for a short time, what will you say to listener?

09년 3차

① Out   ② Proceed
③ Go ahead   ④ Stand by

해설 정보(information)가 잠깐 준비가 되지 않았으므로 대기를 하라는 Stand by가 사용된다.

답 ④

05 조난, 긴급, 안전신호

05 Distress, urgency and safety signals

5.1 조난메시지 전송 시 사용.

5.1 **MAYDAY** : to be used to announce a **distress** message.

5.2 긴급 메시지 전송 시 사용.

5.2 **PAN-PAN** : to be used to announce an **urgency** message.

5.3 안전 통신을 알릴 때 사용.

5.3 **SECURITE** : to be used to announce a **safety** message

▮ 기출문제

05. "Urgent messages"이다. 다음 중 빈 칸에 들어갈 단어로 가장 옳은 것은? 〔17년 1차〕

(A) [repeat three times] is to be used to announce a Urgency signals.
(B) [repeat three times] is to be used to announce a Distress signals.
(C) [repeat three times] is to be used to announce a Safety messages.

	A	B	C
①	MAYDAY	PAN PAN	SECURITE
②	SECURITE	MAYDAY	PAN PAN
③	PAN PAN	MAYDAY	SECURITE
④	MAYDAY	SECURITE	PAN PAN

해설 Distress signal : MAYDAY
Urgency signal : PAN PAN
Safety message : SECURITE

답 ❸

06. 다음 중 통신의 우선순위대로 가장 올바르게 나열한 것은? 〔21년 하반기〕

㉠ Distress   ㉡ Safety
㉢ Radio direction finding   ㉣ Urgency

① ㉠ > ㉡ > ㉢ > ㉣
② ㉠ > ㉣ > ㉢ > ㉡
③ ㉢ > ㉠ > ㉣ > ㉡
④ ㉠ > ㉣ > ㉡ > ㉢

해설 무선통신은 ㉠ 조난통신(Distress)> ㉣ 긴급통신(Urgency)> ㉡ 안전정보(Safety)> ㉢ 무선방향 탐지(Radio direction finding)의 우선순위를 갖는다.

답 ❹

06
Standard organizational phrases

6.1 "How do you read (me)?"

6.1.1 "I read you …"

bad/one	with signal strength one (i.e. barely perceptible)
poor/two	with signal strength two (i.e. weak)
fair/three	with signal strength three (i.e. fairly good)
good/four	with signal strength four (i.e. good)
excellent/five	with signal strength five (i.e. very good)

06 표준 구성 문구

6.1 "(이쪽) 신호는 잘 들립니까?"

6.1.1 "그쪽 신호의 감도는…"

…매우 좋지 않습니다/1
감도1(거의 들리지 않습니다.)

…좋지 않습니다/2
감도2(신호가 약합니다.)

…보통입니다/3
감도 3(보통입니다)

…좋습니다/4
감도4(좋습니다)

…매우 좋습니다/5
감도5 (매우 좋습니다)

기출문제

07. ⟨Standard Marine Communication Phrases⟩에서 VHF통신 감도를 묻는 질문에 상대방이 다음과 같이 대답했다면 어느 정도의 감도인가? 〔19년 3차〕

> I read you with signal strength three .

① I read you poor
② I read you fair
③ I read you good
④ I read you excellent

해설 강도 3은 보통(fair) 세기의 감도를 숫자로 표현한 것이다.

답 ❷

6.2 VHF채널/ 주파수에 머무는 것이 권고된다면 말하라 : "VHF채널.../주파수...에서 대기 하시오."	6.2 When it is advisable to remain on a VHF Channel / frequency say : "Stand by **on** VHF Channel ... / frequency ..."
6.2.1 지시된 VHF채널/주파수에 대기하는 것을 수락한다면 말하라 : "VHF채널.../주파수...에서 대기하겠음."	6.2.1 When it is accepted to remain on the VHF channel / frequency indicated, say : "Standing by **on** VHF Channel ... / frequency ..."
6.3 VHF채널/주파수로 변경하는 것이 권고된다면 말하라 : "VHF채널.../주파수...로 옮길 것을 권고한다. " "VHF채널.../주파수를 사용하시오."	6.3 When it is advisable to change to another VHF Channel / frequency, say : "Advise (you) **change to** VHF Channel ... / frequency ... ." "Advise(you) try VHF Channel .. / frequency... ."
6.3.1 VHF채널/주파수의 변경을 수락한다면 말하라 : "VHF채널.../주파수...로 변경했음."	6.3.1 When the changing of a VHF Channel / frequency is accepted, say : "**Changing to** VHF Channel ... / frequency ... ."

▌기출문제

08. 다음 빈칸에 들어갈 말로 가장 적합한 것은? 〔17년 2차〕

Attention all vessel. This is Tongyeong VTS. Navigational information follow ( ) VHF CH.69.

① to   ② with
③ of   ④ on

해설 VHF 채널 앞의 전치사는 on을 사용한다. 다만, 앞에 change가 붙을 때에만 to를 사용한다.

답 ④

07
Corrections
When a mistake is made in a message, say :
"Mistake..." followed by the word :
"Correction..." plus the corrected part of the message.
Example : "My present speed is 14 knots - mistake. Correction, my present speed is 12, one-two, knots."

08
Readiness
"I am / I am not ready to receive your message".

09
Repetition
9.1 If any part of the message are considered sufficiently important to need safeguarding, say :
"Repeat..." followed by the corresponding part of the message.
Example : "My draft is 12.6 repeat one-two decimal 6 metres."
"Do not overtake - repeat - do not overtake."

9.2 When a message is not properly heard, say :
"Say again (please)."

10
Numbers
Numbers are to be spoken in separate digits : "One-five-zero" for 150
"Two decimal five" or Two point five" for 2.5
Note : Attention! When rudder angles e.g. in wheel orders are given, say :
"Fifteen" for 15 or "Twenty" for 20 etc..

---

07 정정
메시지에서 실수를 했을 때, 말하라 :
"Mistake..." 단어가 뒤따라 나옴
"Correction..." 메시지의 수정한 부분을 더한다.
예시 : 본선의 현재 속력은 14노트이다. - mistake, Correction, 본선의 현재 속력은 12노트이다, 12노트이다.

08 준비
"나는 메시지를 수신할 준비가 됐다/안됐다"

09 반복
9.1 통보 사항 중의 어떤 부분이 특히 중요하다고 여겨 보호할 필요가 있을 경우
"반복 …" 이후 메시지 중의 해당 부분을 말한다.
Example"본선의 흘수는 12.6 반복 12.6미터입니다."
"추월하지 마시오. 반복 추월하지 마시오."

9.2 통보 사항이 잘 들리지 않을 경우
"다시 말해 주십시오."

10 숫자
수는 한 자씩 분리된 숫자로 말한다.
150 : "one-five-zero"
2.5 : "Two decimal five" 또는 "Two point five"
주의! 타각(조타 명령) 을 할 때는 15는 "Fifteen", 20은 "Twenty"등으로 붙여 말한다.

11
Positions

11 위치

11.1 위도와 경도를 사용하고자 할 때는 도와 분(필요하면 분의 소수) 및 적도에서 북위와 남위, 본초자오선에서 동경과 서경으로 나타낸다.

Example "경고. 북위15도 34분, 서경 061도 29분에 위험한 난파선이 있음."

11.2 표지와 관련지어 위치를 나타내고자 할 경우, 그 표지는 해도상에서 확실히 확인할 수 있는 것이어야 한다. 방위는 진북을 기점으로 하여 360도 표기법으로 나타내고 표지로부터 위치를 바라본 방위를 표시한다.

Example "그쪽의 위치는 Big Head 등대로부터 137도, 거리 2.4해리 지점임."

11.1 When **latitude and longitude** are used, these shall be expressed in degrees and minutes (and decimals of a minute if necessary), North or South of the Equator and East or West of Greenwich.

Example : "WARNING. Dangerous wreck in position 15 degrees 34 minutes North, 061 degrees 29 minutes West."

11.2 When the position is related to a **mark**, the mark shall be a **well-defined charted object.** The bearing shall be in the 360 degrees notation from true north and shall be that of the position **FROM** the mark.

Example : "Your position bearing 137 degrees from Big Head lighthouse distance 2.4 nautical miles."

기출문제

09. 아래 문장에서 빈칸에 공통으로 들어갈 IMO 표준해사 통신용어로 가장 적절한 것은? [16년 일반직]

A : What is your ( )?
B : My ( ) is 34-14.5N, 125-10.2E

① speed
② position
③ course
④ bearing

해설 위치는 위도와 경도로 나타낸다.

답 ❷

12

Bearings

The bearing of the mark or vessel concerned, is the bearing in the 360 degree notation from north (true north unless otherwise stated), except in the case of relative bearings. Bearings may be either **FROM** the mark or **FROM** the vessel.

Examples : "Pilot boat is bearing 215 degrees from you."
Note : Vessels reporting their **position** should always quote their bearing **FROM** the mark, as described in paragraph 11.2 of this section.

12.1 Relative bearings

Relative bearings can be expressed in degrees relative to the **vessel's head.** More frequently this is in relation to the port or starboard bow.

Example : "Buoy 030 degrees on your port bow."
(Relative D/F bearings are more commonly expressed in the 360 degree notation.)

12 방위

관련된 표지나 선박의 방위는 상대방위로 표시하는 경우를 제외하고는 북쪽(다른 언급이 없는 한 진북)을 기점으로 360도 표기법으로 표시한다. 방위는 표지나 선박 중 어느 쪽으로부터의 방위로 표시해도 상관없다.

Example "도선선은 귀선으로부터 215도 방향에 있음."
Note : 선위통보를 하는 선박은 11.2에서 설명한바와 같이 항상 방위를 물표로부터 언급한다.

12.1 상대방위

상대방위는 선수를 기준으로 한 각도로 표시하고, 선수 좌현 혹은 선수 우현 몇 도라고 표시하는 경우가 많다.

Example "부표는 귀선의 선수 좌현 030도 방향에 있음."

기출문제

10. 다음 괄호 안에 들어갈 가장 알맞은 말은 무엇인가? 18년 3차

( ) can be expressed in degrees relative to the vessel's head or head bow. More frequently this is in relation to the port or starboard bow.

① Position ② Bearing(s)
③ Course(s) ④ Relative bearing(s)

해설 상대방위는 선수를 기준으로 한 각도로 표시하고, 선수 좌현 혹은 선수 우현 몇 도라고 표시하는 경우가 많다.

④

13

Courses

Always to be expressed in 360 degree notation from north (true north unless otherwise stated). Whether this is to **TO or FROM** a mark can be stated.

14

Distances

Preferably to be expressed in **nautical miles** or **cables** (tenths of a mile) otherwise in kilometres or metres, **the unit always to be stated.**

15

Speed

To be expressed in **knots** :

15.1 without further notation meaning **speed through the water;** or,

15.2.1.1 "ground speed" meaning **speed over the ground.**

16

Times

Times should be expressed in the 24 hour **UTC** notation; if **local time** will be used in ports or harbours it should clearly **be stated.**

17

Geographical names

Place names used should be those on the chart or in Sailing Directions in use. Should these not be understood, latitude and longitude should be given.

기출문제

11. 다음 중 빈칸에 들어갈 단어로 가장 옳은 것은? [20년 3차]

> In the general principles for using the IMO SMCP, ship's speed is to be expressed in case there is no further notation in ship's speed, for example "My ship's present speed is 12 knots.", the present speed means the speed (   ).

① over the ground
② made actually over the ground
③ at the average
④ through the water

해설 선속은 특별한 언급이 없는 한 대수속력(through the water)을 나타낸다.

답 ④

12. 다음은 해사표준통신용어(Standard Marine Communication Phrases)를 사용하는 일반적 원칙에 대한 내용이다. 옳은 것은 모두 몇 개인가? [20년 1차]

> ㉠ If the geographical names on the chart or in Sailing Direction are not understood, latitude and longitude should be given.
> ㉡ Speed is to be expressed in knots. Without further notation meaning speed through the water; or, "ground speed" meaning speed over the ground.
> ㉢ Distance is preferably to be expressed in nautical miles or cables, and the unit may be omitted in case it is understood each other.
> ㉣ The numbers are to be spoken in separate digits except when rudder angles are given.
> ㉤ When the position is related to a mark, the mark shall be a well-defined charted object. The bearing shall be in the 360 degrees notation from true north and shall be that of the position FROM the mark.

① 2개
② 3개
③ 4개
④ 5개

해설 ㉢ To be expressed in nautical miles or cables (tenths of a mile), the unit always to be stated. 거리는 해리나 케이블(0.1해리)로 표시하며, 단위를 반드시 명시하여야 한다.

답 ③

18 모호한 어구

영어에서 어떠한 단어는 그들이 쓰이는 문장에 따라 의미를 달리 가지고 있다. 이러한 오해가 자주 발생하여(특히 VTS 통신에서) 사고를 발생시켰다. 그러한 단어에는 다음이 있다.

18.1 "May", "Might", "Should" 및 "Could"와 같은 가정 어구

May

말하지 마라 : "항로에 들어가도 되는가?"

말하라 : "Question, 항로 진입을 허가하는가?"

말하지 마라 : "귀선은 항로로 들어가도 된다."

말하라 : "Answer, 귀선은 항로로 들어가도록 허가 받았다."

Might

말하지마라 : "항로로 들어갈 지도 모른다."

말하라 : "Intention 본선은 항로에 진입하겠다"

Should

말하지마라 : "묘박지 B3에 투묘하는 것이 좋다."

말하라 : "Advice, 묘박지 B3에 투묘하라."

Could

말하지 마라 : "위험물 쪽으로 향할 수 있다."

말하라 : "Warning, 귀선은 위험물 쪽으로 향하고 있다."

18 Ambiguous words

Some words in English have meanings depending on the context in which they appear. Misunderstandings frequently occur, especially in VTS communications, and have produced accidents. Such words are :

18.1 The Conditionals "May", "Might", "Should" and "Could".

May

Do not say : "May I enter the fairway?"

Say : "QUESTION. Do I have permission to enter the fairway?"

Do not say : "You may enter the fairway."

Say : "ANSWER. You have permission to enter the fairway."

Might

Do not say : "I might enter the fairway."
Say : "INTENTION. I will enter the fairway."

Should

Do not say : "You should anchor in anchorage B 3."

Say : "ADVICE. Anchor in anchorage B 3."

Could

Do not say : "You could be running into danger."

Say : "WARNING. You are running into danger."

18.2 The word "Can"

The word "Can" either describes the possibility or the capability of doing something. In the SMCP the situations where phrases using the word "Can" appear make it clear whether a possibility is referred to. In an ambiguous context, however, say, for example :

"QUESTION. Do I have permission to use the shallow draft fairway at this time?",
do not say : "Can I use the shallow draft fairway at this time?", if you ask for a permission. (The same applies to the word "May")

Note : In all cases the radiotelephone procedures as set out in the ITU - Radio Regulations have to be observed.

18.2 "Can"이라는 단어

"Can"이라는 단어는 어떤 일의 실현 가능성이나 할 수 있는 능력을 나타낸다. SMCP에서는 "Can"을 쓰는 어구가 나타나는 상황에서는 그것이 실현 가능성에 대하여 말하고 있는지를 명확하게 밝힌다. 그러나 애매한 문맥에서 허락을 요청할 경우 사용하는 예와 사용하지 않는 예는 다음과 같다.

"QUESTION. Do I have permission th use the shallow draft fairway at this time?"
말하지 마라 : "Can I use the shallow draft fairway at this time?"
이는 "May"라는 단어에도 동일하게 적용된다.

주의 : 모든 경우에 ITU무선통신규정에서 정하는 대로 무선전화의 절차를 따라야만 한다.

기출문제

13. 다음에 들어갈 적절한 단어는?   `04년 5차`

May I ( ) the traffic lane?

① get   ② overtake
③ have   ④ enter

해설 traffic lane(통항로)가 목적어 이므로 통항로에 입장하다(enter)가 적절하다. 주의 할 점은 해당 문장은 SMCP에서 지양해야하는 표현 방법중 하나로 실제로 사용되어야 하는 표현은 "Question, do I have permission to enter the fairway"가 된다.

답 ④

chapter 04
GLOSSARY 용어

01
VTS 특수 용어

Fairway 항로	Navigable part of a waterway.	수로의 항행 가능한 부분
Fairway speed 항로내 제한속력	Mandatory speed in a fairway.	항로 내에서 강제적으로 지켜야 할 속력
Manoeuvring speed 조종 속력	A vessel's reduced speed in circumstances where it may be required to use the engines at short notice.	기관을 즉시 사용하게 될 수도 있는 상황에서도 감소된 선박 속력
Receiving point 지시 수령점	A mark or place at which a vessel come under obligatory entry, transit, or escort procedure.	선박의 진입, 통과, 호송작업에 있어서 강제인 절차를 따르기 시작하는 지점 또는 그 지점을 나타내는 표지
Reference line 참조선	A line displayed on the radar screens in VTS Centres and/or electronic sea-charts separating the fairway for inbound and outbound vessels so that they can safely pass each other.	VTS 본부의 레이더 화면이나 전자해도상에 표시되어 입항선과 출항선의 항로를 분리함으로서, 그들의 상호 간에 안전하게 항과할 수 있도록 해주는 선
Reporting point 보고지점	A mark or position at which a vessel is required to report to the local VTS-Station to establish its position.	어떤 선박이 위치를 확인해 주기 위하여 지역의 VTS국에 보고해야 하는 항해표지나 지점
Traffic clearance 통항 허가	VTS authorization for a vessel to proceed under conditions specified.	선박으로 하여금 명시된 조건에서 항진하도록 VTS가 허가하는 것
VTS	Vessel Traffic Services : Services, designed to improve safety and efficiency of vessel traffic and to protect the environment.	선박 통항 관제 업무 : 선박 통항의 안전성, 효율성을 향상시키고 환경을 보호하기 위하여 설정된 업무
VTS-area	Area controlled by a VTS-Centre or VTS-Station.	VTS본부나 VTS국의 통제를 받는 구역

기출문제

01. "Fairway speed is 7 knots." 에서 밑줄 친 부분의 의미는?   `15년 일반직`

① reduced speed in a fairway
② moderate speed in fairway
③ mandatory speed in a fairway
④ slow speed in a fairway

해설 Fairway speed란 'Mandatory speed in a fairway' 항로 내에서 강제적으로 지켜야할 속력이다. 항로내 제한속력이 7노트라면, 항로 안에서는 7노트 이내의 속력을 유지해야 한다.

답 ③

02. 국제 해상교통관제(VTS) 관련 다음 빈 칸에 들어갈 말로 가장 적절한 것은?   `15년 일반직, 18년 3차`

> A service implemented by a competent authority, VTS is designed to improve the (   ) and (   ), safety of life at sea and the protection of the marine environment.

① urgent, distress
② distress, urgent
③ safety, efficiency of navigation
④ safety, efficiency of marine communication

해설 VTS란, 'Services, designed to improve safety and efficiency of vessel traffic and to protect the environment.' 즉, 선박 통항의 안전성, 효율성을 향상시키고 환경을 보호하기 위하여 설정된 업무를 의미한다.
두 번째 빈칸의 경우, 'efficiency of vessel traffic'이 교통의 효율성으로 'efficiency of navigation'으로 쓰였다.

답 ③

02

Ship routing system

Routing system 항로지정방식	Any system of one or more routes or routing measures aimed at reducing the risk of casualties. It includes traffic separation schemes, two-way routes, recommended tracks, areas to be avoided, inshore traffic zones, roundabouts, precautionary areas and deep-water routes.	해난의 위험감소가 목적인 한 개 이상의 항로체계 또는 항로지정 방법 체계. 이것은 통항 분리방식, 대면항로, 추천항로, 피항해역, 연안통항대, 원형교차점, 경계해역 및 심수심 항로를 포함한다.
Traffic separation scheme 통항분리방식	A routing measure aimed at the separation of opposing streams of traffic by appropriate means and by the establishment of traffic lanes.	통항로를 설정 하거나, 적당한 수단을 통해서 마주오는 교통의 흐름을 분리시키는 것을 목적으로 하는 항로지정방법의 하나이다.
Separation zone or line 분리대/분리선	A zone or line separating the traffic lanes in which ships are proceeding in opposite or nearly opposite directions; or separating a traffic lane from the adjacent sea area; or separating traffic lanes designated for particular classes of ship proceeding in the same direction.	반대방향 혹은 거의 반대방향으로 항진하는 선박의 통항로들을 분리하거나, 한 통항로와 인접한 연안통항대를 분리하고 있는 구역 또는 선이다.
Traffic lane 통항로	An area within defined limits in which one-way traffic is established. Natural obstacles, including those forming separation zones, may constitute a boundary.	그 내측에서는 한방향의 통항이 정해져 있는 한정된 해역. 자연 장애물(분리대를 형성하고 있는 경우도 포함)이 경계를 구성할 수 있다.
Roundabout 원형교차점/로터리	A routing measure comprising a separation point or circular separation zone and a circular traffic lane within defined limits. Traffic within the roundabout is separated by moving in a counterclockwise direction around the separation point or zone.	한정된 해역에서 분리점 또는 원형분리대 및 원형통항로로 이루어진 항로지정방법의 하나. 원형교차점 내의 교통은 분리점 또는 분리대의 반시계 방향 움직임에 인해 분리된다.
Inshore traffic zone 연안통항대	A routing measure comprising a designated area between the landward boundary of a traffic separation scheme and the adjacent coast, where local special rules may apply, and normally not to be used by through traffic.	항로지정방법의 하나로 분리통항대의 육지 쪽의 경계와 인접한 해안 사이의 지정해역을 말하며, 보통 통항교통에는 사용되지 않고, 해당 지역 특별 규정이 적용 될 수 있다.
Two-way route 상호통항로/교행항로	A route within defined limits inside which two-way traffic is established, aimed at providing safe passage of ships through waters where navigation is difficult or dangerous.	항행이 곤란하거나 위험한 해역을 통항하는 선박에게 안전한 통행을 제공하는 것을 목적으로 하는 서로 방향이 다른 통항이 실시되고 있는 한정된 범위의 항로

Recommended track 추천항로	A route which has been specially examined to ensure so far as possible that it is free of dangers and along which ships are advised to navigate.	위험물에 대해서 안전하다는 것을 가능한 한 보장하기 위해서 특별 조사를 실시하고, 선박이 항행하도록 추천하고 있는 항로
Deep water route (DW) 심수심항로	A route within defined limits which has been accurately surveyed for clearance of sea bottom and submerged obstacles as indicated on the chart.	해도에 표시된, 해저 혹은 수중 장애물까지의 수심을 정확히 측량한 한정된 범위의 항로
Precautionary area 경계해역	A routing measure comprising an area within defined limits where ships must navigate with particular caution and within which the direction of traffic flow may be recommended.	항로지정방법의 하나로, 선박이 특별한 주의를 하면서 항행해야 하고, 그 해역 내에서 교통의 흐름의 방향을 권고 받을 수 있는 한정된 범위의 해역
Area to be avoided 피항수역	A routing measure comprising an area within defined limits in which either navigation is particularly hazardous or it is exceptionally important to avoid casualties and which should be avoided by all ships, or certain classes of ship.	항로지정방법의 하나로, 해당 해역 내에서는 항행이 특히 위험하거나, 혹은 해난사고를 피하는 일이 매우 중요하여 모든 선박 혹은 특정 종류의 선박이 피해야 하는 한정된 해역
Established direction of traffic flow 설정통항방향	A traffic flow pattern indicating the directional movement of traffic as established within a traffic separation scheme.	교통의 흐름의 한 형태로 통항분리 방식 내에 설정되어 있는 것과 같이 통항 방향을 지시하는 것
Recommended direction of traffic flow 권고통항방향	A traffic flow pattern indicating a recommended directional movement of traffic where it is impractical or unnecessary to adopt an established direction of traffic flow.	교통의 흐름의 한 형태로, 설정통항방향을 채택하기엔 비실용적이거나 불필요한 경우, 특정 통항방향을 권고하는 것

기출문제

03. Choose the correct one for the blank.　　18년 1차

A routing measure comprising an area within defined limits in which either navigation is particularly hazardous or it is exceptionally important to avoid casualties and which should be avoided by all ahips, or certain classes of ship is called (　　).

① Roundabout　　② Area to be avoided
③ Precautionary area　　④ Inshore traffic zone

해설　피항해역(Area to be avoided)에 대한 설명이다.

답 ❷

기출문제

04. 아래에서 설명하고 있는 것은 무엇에 대한 설명인가? `15년 일반직`

> A routing measure aimed at the separation of opposing stream of traffic by appropriate means and by the establishment of traffic lanes.

① Separation zone or line
② Inshore traffic zone
③ Traffic separation scheme
④ Traffic lane

해설 분리통항방식(Traffic separation scheme)에 대한 설명이다.

답 ❸

05. Choose the best one for the blank. `15년 2차`

> A routing measure comprising an area within defined limits in which either navigation is particularly hazardous or it is exceptionally important to avoid casualties and which should be avoided by all ships, or certain classes of ship is called (　　　　).

① roundabout
② area to be avoided
③ precautionary area
④ inshore traffic zone

해설 피항해역(area to be avoided)에 대한 설명이다.

답 ❷

06. 다음은 「IMO SMCP(표준해사통신언어)」상 용어의 정의이다. 가장 옳은 것은? `18년 일반직`

> An area within defined limits in which one-way traffic is established.

① Traffic lane
② Traffic clearance
③ Reference line
④ Fairway

해설 통항로(traffic lane)에 대한 설명이다.

답 ❶

기출문제

07. 다음은 통항분리방식의 용어에 관한 설명이다. 옳은 것은 몇 개인가? `13년 2차`

ⓐ Separation zone or line - A zone or line separating the traffic lanes in which ships are proceeding in opposite or nearly opposite direction, or separating a traffic lane from the adjacent inshore traffic zone.
ⓑ Roundabout - A routing measure comprising a separation point or circular traffic lane within defined limits.
ⓒ Inshore traffic zone - A routing measure comprising a designated area between the landward boundary of a traffic separation scheme and the adjacent coast, intended for local traffic.
ⓓ Precautionary area - A route which has been specially examined to ensure so far as possible that it is free of dangers and along which ships are advised to navigate.
ⓔ Recommended track - A routing measure comprising an area within defined limits where ships must navigate with particular caution and within which the direction of traffic flow may be recommended.

① 1개   ② 2개
③ 3개   ④ 4개

해설 ⓓ Recommended track에 대한 설명이다.
ⓔ Precautionary area에 대한 설명이다.

답

08. 다음은 항로지정에 사용되는 용어이다. 내용으로 옳은 것은 모두 몇 개인가? `21년 하반기`

㉠ Traffic Separation Scheme : A scheme which separates traffic proceeding in opposite or nearly opposite direction by the use of a separation zone or line, traffic lanes or by other means
㉡ Recommended Track : A routing measure comprising an area within defined limits where ship must navigate with particular caution and within which the direction of traffic flow may be recommended
㉢ Separation Zone or Line : An area within defined limits inside which one-way traffic is established. Natural obstacles, including those forming separation zones, may constitute a boundary

① 없음   ② 1개
③ 2개   ④ 3개

해설 ㉡은 Precautionary area에 대한 설명이다.
㉢은 Traffic lane에 대한 설명이다.

답

I 기출문제

09. 다음은 항로지정에 사용되는 용어들에 관한 설명이다. 틀린 것은 몇 개인가? `18년 1차`

ⓐ Recommended Track : A route which has been specially examined to ensure so far as possible that it is free of dangers and along which ships are advised to navigate.
ⓑ Precautionary area : A routing measure comprising an area within defined limits where ships must navigate with particular caution and within which the direction of traffic flow may be recommended.
ⓒ Separation zone or line : A zone or line separating the traffic lanes in which ships are proceeding in opposite or nearly opposite direction, or separating a traffic lane from the adjacent inshore traffic zone.
ⓓ Traffic Lane : An area within defined limits in which one-way traffic is established. Natural obstacles, including those forming separation zones, may constitute a boundary.
ⓔ Routing System : A scheme which separates traffic proceeding in opposite or nearly opposite direction by the use of a separation zone or line, traffic lanes or by other means.

① 0개(없음) ② 1개
③ 2개 ④ 3개

해설 ⓔ Traffic Separation Scheme에 대한 설명이다.

답 ❷

10. 다음 지문에서 설명하는 것으로 가장 옳은 것은? `20년 3차`

A routing measure comprising a separation point or circular separation zone and a circular traffic lane within defined limits.

① Roundabout ② Inshore traffic zone
③ Traffic lane ④ Separation zone

해설 원형교차로(roundabout)에 대한 설명이다.

답 ❶

11. 표준해사통신용어(Standard Marine Communication Phrases)상 아래 문장이 의미하는 것으로 가장 옳은 것은? `19년 1차`

A routing measure comprising a designated area between the landward boundary of a traffic separation scheme and the adjacent coast, intended for that traffic.

① ITZ ② VTS
③ TSS ④ Traffic lane

해설 연안통항대(Inshore Traffic Zone, ITZ)에 대한 설명이다.

답 ❶

기출문제

12. 〈Standard Marine Communication Phrases〉상 각각의 빈칸에 들어갈 말로 가장 옳은 것은?

19년 3차

- Two-way route : A route within defined limits inside which two-way traffic is established, aimed at (　　　) of ships through waters where navigation is difficult or dangerous.
- (　　　　　) : A route which has been specially examined to ensure so far as possible that it is free of dangers and along which ships are advised to navigate.

① providing safe passage, Recommended track
② providing fast passage, Precautionary area
③ providing safe passage Precautionary area
④ providing fast passage, Recommended track

해설 - Two-way route(상호통항로) : 항행이 곤란하거나 위험한 해역을 통항하는 선박에게 안전한 통로를 제공 (providing safe passage)하는 것을 목적으로 서로 방향이 다른 통항이 실시되고 있는 한정된 범위의 항로
- Recommended track(추천항로) :
위험물에 대해서 안전하다는 것을 가능한 한 보장하기 위해서 특별 조사를 실시하고, 선박이 항행하도록 추천하고 있는 항로

답 ❶

13. 다음은 표준해사통신영어(Standard Marine Communication Phrases)상 Ships Routing System에 대한 설명이다. 가장 옳지 않은 것은?

20년 3차

① Two-way route : A route within defined limits inside which two-way traffic is established, aimed at providing safe passage of ships through waters where navigation is difficult or dangerous
② Recommended track : A route which has been specially examined to ensure so far as possible that it is free of dangers and along which ships are advised to navigate
③ Inshore traffic zone : A designated area between the landward boundary of a traffic separation scheme and adjacent coast, intended for local traffic
④ Precautionary area : An area within defined limits in which either navigation is particularly hazardous or it is exceptionally important to avoid casualties and which should be avoided by all ships, or by certain classes of ships

해설 ④는 Area to be avoided에 관한 설명이다.

답 ❹

03
SMCP용어

Abandon vessel 퇴선	To Evacuate crew and passengers from a vessel following a distress	조난으로 인하여 승무원과 여객을 선박으로부터 대피시킴
Accommodation ladder 현문사다리	Ladder attached to platform at vessel's side with flat steps and handrails enabling person to embark/disembark from water or shore	현측 발판에 취보된 사다리로서 평평한 계단과 난간이 설치되어서 사람이 수면이나 육상으로부터 승/하선할 수 있도록 해주는 것
Adrift 표류	Uncontrolled movement at sea under the influence of current, tide or wind	해상에서 해류, 조류, 바람의 영향으로 제어되지 않고 떠다니는 것
Air draft 에어 드라프트	The height from the waterline to the highest point of the vessel	수면으로부터 선체의 가장 높은 부분까지의 높이
Assembly station 집합장소	Place on deck, in mess rooms, etc. assigned to crew and passengers where they have to meet according to the muster list when the corresponding alarm is released or announcement made	구령이 발령되거나 해당 비상신호가 울렸을 때, 부서 배치표에 정하여진 바대로 승무원과 여객이 집합하도록 할당된 갑판상의 장소, 식당 등
Backing (of wind) (풍향)반전	Shift of the wind direction in an anticlockwise manner, for example from north to west; opposite of veering	풍향이 반시계방향, 예를 들면 북풍으로부터 서풍으로 변하는 것 ↔ 풍향순전
Beach (to) 좌안	To run a vessel up on a beach to prevent its sinking in deep water	수심이 깊은 곳에 선박이 침몰하는 것을 방지하기 위하여 배를 해변에 끌어 올려 놓음(임의 좌초)
Berth 1. 여유수면 2. 정박지	1. A sea room to be kept for safety around a vessel, rock, platform, ect. 2. The place assigned to a vessel when anchored or lying alongside a pier, etc.	1. 선박, 바위, 플랫폼의 주위에 안전을 위하여 확보해야 할 해상 여유 공간 2. 어느 선박의 투묘나 부두 계류 등을 위하여 할당된 장소
Blast 기적신호	A whistle signal made by the vessel	선박에서 만들어지는 음향 신호
Blind sector 맹목구간	An area which cannot be scanned by the ship's radar because it is shielded by parts of the superstructure, masts, ect	선박의 상부 구조물, 마스트 등으로 인하여 차폐되어 선박의 레이더로 탐지 할 수 없는 구역
Boarding arrangements 승선 설비	All equipments, such as pilot ladder, accommodation ladder, hoist, etc, necessary for a safe transfer of the pilot	도선용 사다리, 현문 사다리, 호이스트 등 도선사의 안전한 승/하선을 위하여 필요한 모든 장비
Boarding speed 승선 속력	The speed of a vessel adjusted to that of a pilot boat at which the pilot can safely embark/disembark	도선사가 안전하게 승/하선할 수 있도록 도선선의 속력에 맞춰 조정된 본선의 속력
Bob-cat 보브캣	A mini-caterpillar with push-blade used for the careful distribution of loose goods in cargo holds of bulk carriers	산적 화물선의 화물창에 있는 산적 화물을 주의 깊게 배치하기 위하여 사용되는 푸시블레이드가 장치된 소형 무한궤도 차

Briefing 상황설명	Concise explanatory information to crew and/or passengers	승무원과 승객에 대한 간단한 설명적 통보
Cable 케이블	1. Chain connecting a vessel to the anchor(s) 2. Wire or rope primarily used for mooring a ship 3. (measurement) One hundred fathoms or one tenth of a nautical mile	1. 닻과 선체를 연결하는 사슬 2. 선박을 계류하는 데 주로 사용되는 와이어나 밧줄 3. (치수) 100패덤 즉, 0.1해리
Capsize 전복	To turnover	상하가 전도되는 것
Cardinal buoy 방점부표	A seamark, i.e. a buoy, indicating the North, East, South or West, i.e. the cardinal points from a fixed point such as a wreck, shallow water, banks, etc.	난파선, 여울, 사주 등 정해진 지점의 북·동·남·서 즉 방점을 표시하는 항로표지 (방위표지)
Cardinal points 방점	The four main points of the compass : north, east, south and west	나침반의 네 개의 주요 방위, 즉 북·동·남·서
Casualty 사고	Case of death in an accident or shipping disaster	사고나 해난으로 인한 사망사고를 말함
Check (to) 1. 점검 2. 억제	1. To make sure that equipment etc. is in proper condition or that everything is correct and safe 2. To regulate motion of a cable, rope or wire when it is running out too fast	1. 장비 등이 적절한 상태에 있는지, 또는 모든 것이 제대로 되어 있고, 안전한지를 확인하는 것 2. 닻줄, 밧줄, 와이어 등이 너무 빨리 풀려 나갈 때 그 움직임을 억제하는 것
Close-coupled towing 밀접결합 예인	A method of towing vessels through polar ice by means of icebreaking tugs with a special stern notch suited to receive and hold the bow of the vessel to be towed	피예인선의 선수를 받아들여 잡아맬 수 있도록 선미에 특별한 홈이 설치된 쇄빙 예인선을 사용하여 수행하는 극지방 빙해역에서의 선박 예인 방법
Close up (to) 접근	To decrease the distance to the vessel ahead by increasing one's own speed	자선의 속력을 증가시켜 전방의 선박과의 거리를 좁히는 것
Compatibility (of goods) 격리 특성	States whether different goods can be safely stowed together in one cargo space	서로 다른 화물을 한 화물 공간에 같이 안전하게 적부할 수 있는지의 여부
Convoy 호송 선단	A group of vessels which sail together, e.g. through a canal or ice	운하나 빙하를 함께 항해하는 한 떼의 선박들
Course 침로	The intended direction of movement of a vessel through the water	수면을 기준으로 한, 어느 선박이 이동하고자 하는 방향
Course made good 대지 침로	That course which a vessel makes good over ground, after allowing for the effect of currents, tidal streams, and leeway caused by wind and sea	해류, 조류, 바람과 파도에 의한 풍압편위 등의 영향을 고려하여 대지를 기준으로 한 침로

Term	Definition (English)	Definition (Korean)
COW 원유세정법	Crude Oil Washing : A system of cleaning the cargo tanks by washing them with the cargo of crude oil during discharge	원유 양하 후에 화물인 원유로 화물탱크를 세척하는 시스템
CPA/TCPA	Closest Point of Approach/Time to Closest Point of Approach : limit as defined by the observer to give warning when a tracked target or targets will close to within these limits	최접근점(거리) : 추적하고 있던 표적이 그러한 한계 이내로 접근하게 되면 정보를 발하도록 관측자가 설정한 최접근 한계에 표적이 도달하는 시간
Crash-stop 비상 긴급 정지	An emergency reversal operation of the main engine(s) to avoid a collision	충돌을 피하기 위하여 주기관을 비상 역전시키는 작업
Damage control team 손상제어반	A group of crew members trained for fighting flooding in the vessel	선내의 침수 방지에 대한 훈련을 받은 승무원 집단
Datum 1. 추정 기점 2. 기본수준면	1. The most probable position of a search target at a given time 2. The plane of reference to which all data as to the depth on charts are referenced.	1. 주어진 시각에 있어서 목표물을 발견할 가능성이 가장 높은 위치. 2. 해도상의 수심에 관한 모든 자료의 기준이 되는 기준면
Derelict 유기선	Vessel still afloat, abandoned at sea	해상에 버려진 떠 있는 선박
Destination 목적항	Port where a vessel is bound for	어떤 선박이 향하는 목적 항구
Disabled 파손 선박	A vessel damaged or impaired in such a manner as to be incapable of proceeding on its voyage	항해를 계속할 수 없을 정도로 파손되거나 장애가 있는 선박
Disembark (to) 하선	To go from a vessel	선박으로부터 내려옴
Distress alert (GMDSS) 조난경보	A radio signal from a distressed vessel automatically directed to an MRCC giving position, identification, course and speed of the vessel as well as the nature of distress	조난선으로부터 자동적으로 해상구조조정본부(MRCC)에 보내지는 위치, 식별부호, 침로, 속력 및 조난의 성질 등을 포함하는 무선 신호
Distress/Urgency traffic 조난/긴급 통화	The verbal exchange of information on radio from ship to shore and/or ship to ship/aircraft about a distress/urgency situation as defined in the relevant ITU Radio Regulations	ITU의 관련 무선 규칙에 정의된 조난/긴급 상황에 대한 선박과 육상 간/선박과 선박 간/선박과 항공기 간의 무선 음성정보 교환
Draft 흘수	Depth in water at which a vessel floats	물에 뜬 선체의 깊이
Dragging (of anchor) (닻의) 주묘	Moving of an anchor over the sea bottom involuntarily because it is no longer preventing the movement of the vessel	닻이 선체의 이동을 더 이상 저지하지 못하여 어쩔 수 없이 해저를 따라 끌리고 있는 상태

Dredging (of anchor) 인묘, 예묘, 용묘	Moving of an anchor over the sea bottom to control the movement of the vessel	선체의 운동을 제어하기 위하여 해저를 따라서 닻을 이동시키는 것
Drifting 표류	Being driven along by the wind, tide or current	바람, 조류, 해류에 의하여 떠내려가게 하는 것
Drop back(to) 뒤처짐	To increase the distance to the vessel ahead by reducing one's own speed	자선의 속력을 낮춤으로써 앞에 있는 선박과의 거리를 넓힘
DSC	Digital Selective Calling (in the GMDSS system)	(GMDSS 시스템 내의) 디지털 선택 호출
Embark (to) 승선	To go aboard a vessel	선박에 탑승함
EPIRB	Emergency Position Indicating Radio Beacon	비상 위치 표시용 무선 비이콘
Escape route 탈출로	A clearly marked way in the vessel which has to be followed in case of an emergency	선박에서 비상사태가 발생하는 경우 따라가야 할 대피 통로로서 명확하게 표시된 길
Escort 호송	Attending a vessel, to be available in case of need, e.g. ice-breaker, tug, etc.	필요한 경우 이용할 수 있도록 어떤 선박에 동행함, 예를 들어 쇄빙선, 예인선 등
ETA	Estimated Time of Arrival	도착 예정 시간
ETD	Estimated Time of Departure	출발 예정 시간
Fathom	A measure of 6 feet in length	6피트 길이의 수심의 단위
Fire patrol 화재순찰자	A member of the watch going around the vessel at certain intervals so that an outbreak of fire may be promptly detected; mandatory in vessels carrying more than 36 passengers	화재의 발생을 조기에 탐지할 수 있도록 일정 간격으로 선내를 순찰하는 당직원; 36인 이상의 여객을 수송하는 선박에서는 강제 사항이다.
Flooding 침수	Major uncontrolled flow of seawater into the vessel	제어되지 않고 대량으로 선내에 유입되는 해수의 흐름
Fire monitor 소화 모니터	Fixed foam/powder/water cannon shooting fire extinguishing agents on tank deck, manifold, etc.	탱크의 갑판이나 매니폴드 등에 소화 약제를 발사하는 고정식의 포말·분말·소화수 발사기
Foul (of anchor) (닻)엉킴	Anchor has its own cable twisted around it or has fouled an obstruction	닻이 닻줄에 감기거나 장애물에 걸림
Foul (of propeller) (프로펠러)엉킴	A line, wire, net etc., is wound around the propeller	밧줄, 와이어, 그물 등이 프로펠러에 엉킴
Full speed 전속력	Highest possible speed of a vessel	어떤 선박의 가장 빠른 속력
Fumes 유해가스	Often harmful gas produced by fires, chemicals, fuel, etc.	화재, 케미컬, 연료 등에 의해서 생기는 해로운 가스
General emergency alarm 일반비상경보	A sound signal of seven short blasts and one prolonged blast given with the vessel's sound system	선박의 기적신호 장치로 발생시키는 단음 7회, 장음 1회로 이루어진 음향신호

Give way 피항	To keep out of the way of another vessel	다른 선박의 진로로부터 길을 내어줌
GMDSS	Global Maritime Distress and Safety System	전 세계 해상 조난 및 안전 체계
(D)GPS	(Differential) Global (satellite) Positioning System	전 세계 (위성) 위치 결정 시스템
Half cardinal points 우점	The four main points lying between the cardinal points; north east, south east, south west and north west	방점 사이에 있는 네 주요점 : 북동, 남동, 남서, 북서
Hampered vessel 조종제한선	A vessel restricted by her ability to manoeuvre by the nature of her work	작업의 성격상 조종성능이 제한받고 있는 선박
Hatchrails 해치레일	Ropes supported by stanchions around an open hatch to prevent persons from falling into a hold	사람이 화물창 안으로 추락하는 것을 방지하기 위하여 개방된 해치 주위에 지주로 지지하여 설치되는 줄
Heading 선수 방위	The horizontal direction of the vessel's bows at a given moment measured in degrees clockwise from north	어느 해당 순간에 선수의 방향을 북쪽으로부터 시계방향으로 측정한 수평 방향
Hoist 호이스트	A cable used by helicopters for lifting or lowering persons in a pick-up operation	헬리콥터에서 인양 작업 중 사람을 들어 올리거나 내릴 때 사용하는 밧줄
Icing 착빙	Coating of ice on an object, e.g. the mast or superstructure of a vessel	선박의 마스트, 상부구조물과 같은 물체에 얼음이 얼어서 덮이는 것
IMO-Class IMO 등급	Group of dangerous or hazardous goods, harmful substances or marine pollutants in sea transport as classified in the International Maritime Dangerous Goods Code (IMDG Code)	해상으로 운송되는 위험화물, 유해물질, 해양오염 물질을 분류한 것으로, IMDG Code로 분류된다.
Inert (to) 불활성화	To reduce the oxygen in a tank by inert gas to avoid an explosive atmosphere	불활성 기체를 탱크에 주입하여 산소를 줄임으로서 폭발을 방지하는 것
Initial course 최초 침로	Course directed by the OSC or other authorized person to be steered at the beginning of a search	현장 지휘자나 다른 권한 있는 자가 지시한 수색개시 당시의 조타 침로
Inoperative 작동되지 않는	Not functioning	작동되지 않는
Jettison (to) (of cargo) (화물의 고의적) 투하	Throwing overboard of goods in order to lighten the vessel or improve its stability in case of an emergency	비상시에 선박을 가볍게 하거나 복원성을 향상시키기 위하여 화물을 선외로 고의적으로 버리는 것
Launch (to) 진수	To lower, e.g. lifeboats to the water	구명정을 수면에 하강시킴

Leaking 누출	Escape of liquids such as water, oil, etc., out of pipes, boilers, tanks, etc., or a minor inflow of seawater into the vessel due to damage to the hull	물, 유류 등의 액체가 파이프, 보일러, 탱크 등으로부터 누출되는 것, 또는 선체의 손상으로 인하여 소량의 해수가 선내로 유입되는 것
Leeward 풍하측	On or towards the sheltered side of a ship; opposite of windward	선체에 의하여 바람으로부터 차폐되는 방향 또는 그쪽 현; 풍상측과 반대이다.
Leeway 풍압차	Vessels sideways drift leeward of the desired course	선박이 의도하는 침로로부터 바람이 불어가는 쪽으로 밀리는 것
Let go (to) 투묘	To set free, let loose, or cast off (of anchors, lines, etc.)	자유롭게 하다, 느슨하게 하다, (닻. 계류삭 등을) 풀다
Lifeboat station 구명정 부서	Place assigned to crew and passengers to muster before being ordered into the lifeboats	구명정에 탑승하도록 지시받기 전에 승무원과 여객이 모일 장소로 할당된 공간
List 횡경사	Inclination of the vessel to port side or starboard side	좌현쪽이나 우현쪽으로 선박이 경사함
Located 위치 확인	in navigational warnings : Position of object confirmed	항해의 경고사항에서 : 목표물의 위치를 확인함
Make water (to) 누수	Seawater flowing into the vessel due to hull damage or hatches awash and not properly closed	선체의 손상이나 해치가 적절히 밀폐되지 못하여 물에 잠겨서 해수가 선내로 흘러들어옴
MMSI	Maritime Mobile Service identity number	해상이동업무 식별부호
Moor (to) 계류	To secure a vessel in a particular place by means of wires or ropes made fast to the shore, to anchors, or to anchored mooring buoys, or to ride with both anchors down	선박을 육상, 닻, 계류용 부표 등에 고정된 와이어나 밧줄에 의하여 어떤 특정한 장소에 고정시킴, 또는 쌍묘박.
MRCC 해상구조조정본부	Maritime Rescue Co-ordination Centre : Land-based authority responsible for promoting efficient organization of maritime search and rescue and for co-ordinating the conduct of search and rescue operations within a search and rescue region	해상수색구조작업의 효율적인 조직화를 촉진하고 수색구조해역 내에서 수색 구조작업의 수행을 조정할 책임이 있는 육상의 당국자
Muster (to) 소집	To assemble crew, passengers or both in a special place for purposes of checking	점검을 하기 위하여 승무원, 여객 또는 모두를 특정의 장소에 소집시키는 것
Muster list 비상시 부서 배치표	List of crew, passengers and others on board and their functions in a distress or drill	조난 시 또는 훈련 시 선내의 승무원, 여객, 기타 인원의 명단과 그들의 직무표
Not under command 조종불능선	A vessel which through exceptional circumstances is unable to manoeuvre as required by the COLREGs (abbr. NUC)	예외적인 상황으로 인하여 COLREG에서 요구하는대로 조종을 할 수 없는 선박 (약어 : NUC)
Obstruction 장애물	An object such as a wreck, net, etc., which blocks a fairway, route, etc.	난파선, 그물 등과 같이 항로를 가로막는 물체

Off air 방송 중지	When the transmissions of a radio station etc., have broken down, been switched off or suspended	무선 방송국 등의 발신이 고장나거나 꺼졌거나 혹은 일시중지된 상태
Off station (of buoys) 위치이탈	Not in charted position	해도에 기재된 위치에 있지 않음
Oil clearance 유류 제거	Oil skimming from the surface of the water	수면의 유류를 제거하는 작업
Operational 작동 가능	Ready for immediate use	즉시 사용할 수 있음
Ordnance exercise 포격 훈련	Naval firing practice	해군의 사격 훈련
OSC 현장 조정관	On-Scene Co-ordinator : A person designated to coordinate search and rescue operations within a specified area	특정 해역에서 수색 구조 작업을 조정하도록 지정된 자
Overflow 넘침	Escape of oil or liquid from a tank because of a two-fold condition as a result of overflowing, thermal expansion, change in vessel trim or vessel movement	넘침, 열팽창, 선박의 트림 변화, 선체 운동에 따른 이중적인 조건에 의하여 유류나 액체가 탱크로부터 유출됨
Polluter 오염원 선박	A vessel emitting harmful substances into the air or spilling oil into the sea	유해물질을 대기 중에 방출하거나 해상에 유류를 유출하는 선박
Preventers 프리벤터	Ropes or wires attached to derricks to prevent them from swinging during cargo handling operations	화물 하역 작업 중에 데릭이 선회하는 것을 방지하기 위해 붙어있는 밧줄이나 와이어
Proceed (to) 항진	To sail or head for a certain position or to continue with the voyage	특정한 지점으로 항해하거나 향하는 것. 또는 항해를 계속함
PA-system PA장치	Public Address system : Loudspeakers in the vessel's cabins, mess rooms, etc., and on deck through which important information can be broadcast from a central point, mostly from the navigation bridge	확성방송장치 : 대개 항해 선교 등의 중앙 위치에서 중요한 통보 사항을 발송할 수 있도록 선박의 선실, 식당 등과 갑판에 있는 확성기
Recover (to) 인양	To pick up shipwrecked persons	난파된 사람을 인양함
Refloat (to) 재부양	To pull a vessel off after grounding; to set afloat again	좌초 후 선박을 끌어올리는 것; 다시 뜨게 만듦
Rendezvous 랑데뷰	An appointment between vessels normally made on radio to meet in a certain area or position	일반적으로 두 선박 사이에서 특정한 해역이나 위치에서 만나기로 무선으로 실시하는 약속
Reported 보고됨	in navigational warnings : Position of object unconfirmed	항해 경고에서 : 물체의 위치가 확인되지 않음

Restricted area 제한구역	A deck, space, area, etc., in vessels, where for safety reasons, entry is only permitted for authorized crew members	안전상의 이유로 선내에서 권한이 부여된 승무원에게만 진입이 허락된 갑판, 장소, 구역 등
Resume (to) 재개	To re-start a voyage, service or search	항해, 업무, 또는 수색을 다시 시작함
Retreat signal 철수신호	Sound, visual or other signal to a team ordering it to return to its base	작업조에게 원래의 기지로 돌아오라는 청각적, 시각적 또는 기타의 신호
Rig move 시추선 이동	The movement of an oil rig, drilling platform, etc., from one position to another	유류 시추선, 시추 플랫폼 등의 한 장소로부터 다른 장소로 이동
Roll call 인원점검	The act of checking whether the passengers and crew members are present, e.g. at assembly stations, by reading aloud a list of their names	집합 장소에서 명부를 크게 호명함으로써 승무원이나 승객들이 있는지를 확인하는 행위
Safe speed 안전속력	That speed of a vessel allowing the maximum possible time for effective action to be taken to avoid a collision and to be stopped within an appropriate distance	충돌을 피하기 위해 효율적인 행동을 취할 수 있는 최대한의 가능한 시간을 확보하고 적절한 거리 내에서 선박이 정지할 수 있는 속력
SWL	Safe Working Load : maximum working load of lifting equipment that should not be exceeded	안전 작업 하중 : 넘겨서는 안 되는 인양 장비의 최대 작업 하중
Safe working pressure 안전작업압력	The maximum permissible pressure in cargo hoses	화물 호스의 최대 허용 압력
SAR	Search and Rescue	수색과 구조
SART	Search and Rescue (Radar) Transponder	수색구조용 (레이더) 트랜스폰더
Scene 현장	The area or location where the event or an accident has happened	사고가 발생한 지역이나 위치
Search pattern 수색 방식	A pattern according to which vessels and/or aircraft may conduct a co-ordinated search (the IMOSAR offers seven search patterns)	선박 또는 항공기가 협조 수색을 수행할 수 있는 수색 방식 (IMOSAR에는 7가지의 수색 방식이 제시되어 있다)
Search speed 수색 속력	The speed of searching vessels directed by the OSC	OSC에 의하여 지시된 수색선의 속력
Seamark 해상 표지	A navaid placed to act as a beacon, or warning	비이콘이나 경고표지의 역할을 하도록 설치된 항행보조장치
Segregation (of goods) (화물의) 격리	Separation of goods which for different reasons must not be stowed together	서로 다른 이유로 인하여 같이 적재해서는 안 되는 화물의 격리
Shackle 샤클	Length of chain cable measuring 15 fathoms	15패덤의 닻줄 길이

Shifting cargo 화물 이동	Transverse movement of cargo, especially bulk, caused by rolling or a heavy list	선박의 횡동요나 큰 횡경사로 인하여 화물이 횡방향으로 이동하는 것 (특히나 산적 화물)
Slings 슬링	Ropes, nets and any other means for handling general cargoes	잡화를 취급할 때 사용하는 밧줄, 그물, 그리고 다른 도구들
Speed of advance 전진 속도	The speed at which a storm centre moves	폭풍 중심의 이동 속도
Spill (to) 누출	The accidental escape of oil, etc, from a vessel, container, etc., into the sea	선박, 컨테이너 등으로부터 유류 등이 사고로 해상에 빠져나감
Spill control gear 누출제어기구	Anti-pollution equipment for combating accidental spills of oils or chemicals	사고로 누출된 유류나 화학 물질을 제거하는 방제기구
Spreader 스프레더	Step of a pilot ladder which prevents the ladder from twisting	도선사용 사다리에서 사다리의 꼬임을 방지하도록 설치된 발판
Stand by (to) 스탠바이	To be in readiness or prepared to execute an order; to be readily available	명령을 실행할 대기 상태 혹은 준비 상태에 있음; 이용가능한 준비에 있음
Stand clear (to) 벗어나기	To keep a boat away from the vessel	보트를 선박으로부터 떨어진 곳에 둠
Standing orders 당직 복무 지침서	Orders of the master to the officer of the watch which s/he must comply with	선장이 당직 항해사에게 내리는 지시로서 당직사관이 지켜야 할 사항
Stand on (to) 유지	To maintain course and speed	선박의 침로와 속력을 유지함
Station 부서	The allotted place or the duties of each person on board	선내의 각 사람에게 할당된 장소나 임무
Stripping 스트리핑	Final pumping of tank's residues	탱크내의 잔류물을 최종적으로 퍼냄
Survivor 생존자	A person who continues to live in spite of being in an extremely dangerous situation, e.g. a shipping disaster.	극히 위험한 상황, 예를 들어 해난사고 중에도 계속 생명을 유지하고 있는 사람
Take off (to) 이륙	A helicopter lifts off from a vessel's deck	선체의 갑판으로부터 헬리콥터가 이륙함
Target 표적	The echo generated e.g. by a vessel on a radar screen	레이더 화면상에 나타난 영상 (예를 들어, 선박)
Tension winch 장력 윈치	A winch which applies tension to mooring lines to keep them tight	계류줄이 팽팽함을 유지하도록 장력을 주는 윈치
TEU	Twenty foot Equivalent Unit (standard container dimension)	20피트 기준 컨테이너 단위 (표준 컨테이너 규격)
Track 진로	The path followed, or to be followed, between one position and another	한 위치로부터 다른 위치까지 이동한 또는 이동할 경로
Transit 통과	The passage of a vessel through a canal, fairway, etc.	운하, 항로 등을 통한 선박의 통항
Transit speed 통과 속력	Speed of a vessel required for the passage through a canal, fairway, etc.	운하, 항로 등을 통과할 때 요구되는 선박의 속력

Transhipment (of cargo) (화물)이적	The transfer of goods from one vessel to another outside harbours	항구 바깥에서 화물을 한 선박에서 다른 선박으로 옮기는 것
Underway 항해 중	A vessel which is not at anchor, or made fast to the shore, or aground	선박이 묘박, 접안, 좌초 상태에 있지 않은 상태
Unlit 소등	When the light of a buoy or a lighthouse is inoperative	등대나 부표의 등화가 점등되어 있지 않은 것
UTC	Universal Time Co-ordinated	세계 협정시
Variable (of winds) 변풍	A wind that is constantly changing speed and direction	풍속과 풍향이 끊임없이 바뀌는 바람
veering (of winds) (풍향)순전	Clockwise change in the direction of the wind; opposite of backing	풍향이 시계방향으로 변함; 반전과 반대이다.
Veer out (to) (of anchors) (닻을) 풀어주기	To let out a greater length of cable	닻줄을 더 길게 풀어주는 것
VHF	Very High Frequency	초단파
Walk out (to) (of anchors)	To reverse the windlass to lower the anchor until it is clear of the hawse pipe and ready for dropping	호스 파이프에서 벗어날 때까지 닻을 풀어 내리기 위해 양묘기를 역전시키고 투묘 준비 상태로 하는 것
Walk back (to) (of anchors)	To reverse the windlass to ease the cable	닻줄을 늦춰주기 위하여 양묘기를 역전시키는 것
Way point 통과지점, 변침점	A position a vessel has to pass or at which she has to alter course according to her voyage plan	선박이 항해계획에 따라 통과해야 할 지점 또는 변침해야 할 지점
Windward 풍상측	The general direction from which the wind blows; opposite of leeward	바람이 불어오는 방향; 풍하측과 반대이다.
Wreck 난파선	A vessel which has been destroyed or sunk or abandoned at sea	파괴되었거나 침몰되었거나 바다에 버려진 선박

기출문제

14. 다음 지문과 가장 관계있는 용어는? `17년 1차`

To throw goods overboard in order to lighten the vessel or improves its stability in case of emergency.

① Abandon ship
② CPA
③ Jettison
④ Casualty

해설 Jettison : 비상시에 선박을 가볍게 하거나 복원성을 향상시키기 위하여 화물을 선외로 고의적으로 버리는 것

답 ❸

15. 다음 중 빈칸에 들어갈 말로 가장 옳은 것은? `17년 1차`

The term "( )" means a vessel which from the nature of her work is restricted in her ability to manoeuvre as required by these Rules and is therefore unable to keep out of the way of another vessel.

① vessel engaged in fishing
② vessel not under command
③ vessel restricted in her ability to manoeuvre
④ vessel constrained by her draught

해설 vessel restricted in her ability to manoeuvre : 작업의 성격상 조종성능이 제한받고 있는 선박

답 ❸

16. 다음 빈칸에 들어갈 말로 가장 적절한 것은? `15년 일반직 / 17년 2차`

Area which cannot be scanned by the radar of the vessel because they are shielded by parts of its superstructure, masts, etc. is called ( ).

① edge zone
② scanning zone
③ safe sector
④ blind sector

해설 맹목구간 : 선박의 상부 구조물, 마스트 등으로 인하여 차폐되어 선박의 레이더로 탐지 할 수 없는 구역

답 ❹

17. 다음 중 가장 옳지 않은 것은? `17년 1차`

① Air draft : The height from the waterline to the highest point of the vessel.
② Wreck : A vessel which has been destroyed or sunk or abandoned at sea.
③ Blind sector : An area which cannot be scanned by the ship's radar because it is shielded by parts of its superstructure, masts, etc.
④ Leeward : The general direction from which the wind blows.

해설 바람이 불어오는 방향, Windward에 대한 설명이다.

답 ❹

| 기출문제 |

18. 표준 해사 통신 용어(Standard Marine Communication Phrase)의 용어와 그에 대한 설명으로 바르게 연결된 것은 모두 몇 개인가? `14년 2차`

ⓐ Abandon Vessel : To evacuate crew and passengers from a vessel following a distress
ⓑ Adrift : Uncontrolled movement at sea under the influence of current, tide or wind
ⓒ Dragging : Moving of an anchor over the sea bottom to control the movement of the vessel.
ⓓ Underway : Navigable part of a waterway.

① 1개　　② 2개　　③ 3개　　④ 4개

해설 ⓒ Dredging에 대한 설명이다.
ⓓ fairway에 대한 설명이다.

답 ❷

19. 다음 설명 중 틀린 것은 모두 몇 개인가? `17년 2차`

ⓐ Dragging : A movement of an anchor over sea bottom to control the movement of the vessel
ⓑ Walk out(of anchor) : To reverse the action of a windlass to lower the anchor until it is clear of the hawse pipe and ready for dropping.
ⓒ Hogging : A stress which a ship's hull of keel experiences that the middle of the ship is pushed to bend upward.
ⓓ Backing : When the wind direction moves clockwise.
ⓔ A warm front : Where a cold air mass moves under warmer air mass.

① 1개　　② 2개　　③ 3개　　④ 4개

해설 ⓐ Dredging에 대한 설명이다.
ⓓ Veering에 대한 설명이다.
ⓔ A cold front에 대한 설명이다. 'A warm front(온난전선)'은 따뜻한 기단이 찬 기단 위로 올라오는 것이고, 'A cold front(한랭전선)'은 찬 기단이 따뜻한 기단 아래로 내려오는 것이다.

답 ❸

20. 다음 설명과 가장 관련이 깊은 것은? `18년 3차`

Moving of an anchor over sea bottom to control the movement of the vessel.

① Dredging (of anchor)　　② Dragging (of anchor)
③ Drifting　　　　　　　　④ Anchoring

해설 선박 조종을(to control) 목적으로 닻을 끄는 Dredging의 설명이다.

답 ❶

기출문제

21. 다음 용어 설명 중 잘못 된 것은? `13년 1차`

① Underway : A vessel which is not at anchor, or made fast to shore, or aground.
② Hampered vessel : A vessel restricted by her ability to manoeuvre by the nature of her work.
③ Dragging of anchor : Moving of an anchor over the sea bottom to control the movement of the vessel.
④ Standing orders : Orders of the Master to the officer of the watch which he must comply with.

해설 Dredging of anchor에 대한 설명이다.

답 ③

22. 「IMO SMCP(표준해사통신언어)」상 아래 문장이 의미하는 것은 무엇인가? `16년 일반직`

Place on deck, in mess rooms, etc., assigned to crew and passengers where they have to meet according to the muster list when the corresponding alarm is released or announcement made

① Assembly station ② List
③ Restricted area   ④ Segregation

해설 비상경보 나 비상방송이 들리면 비상배치표에 따라 모여야 하는 집합장소(Assembly station)에 대한 설명이다.

답 ①

23. 다음 설명과 가장 관련이 깊은 것은? `18년 3차`

On or towards the sheltered side of a ship.

① leeway   ② windway
③ leeward   ④ windward

해설 선박의 가려진 면 혹은 방향인 풍하측(leeward)에 대한 설명이다.

답 ③

24. 다음 중 빈칸에 들어갈 단어로 가장 옳은 것은? `18년 일반직`

(   ) is place on deck assigned to crew and passengers where they have to meet according to the muster list when the corresponding alarm is released or announcement made.

① Main deck   ② Assembly station
③ Accommodation   ④ Rescue Zone

해설 비상경보나 비상방송이 들리면 비상배치표에 따라 모여야 하는 집합장소(Assembly station)에 대한 설명이다.

답 ②

기출문제

25. 다음 중 용어와 그에 대한 설명으로 바르게 연결된 것은 모두 몇 개인가? `16년 2차`

> ⓐ OSC : A person designated to coordinate search and rescue operations within a specified area.
> ⓑ SWL : Maximum working load of lifting equipment that should not be exceeded.
> ⓒ COW : A system of cleaning the cargo tanks by washing them with the cargo of crude oil during discharge.
> ⓓ VTS : Services, designed to improve safety and efficiency of vessel traffic and to protect the environment.

① 4개　　　　　② 3개
③ 2개　　　　　④ 1개

해설 모두 옳음.

답 ❶

26. 다음 중 빈칸에 들어갈 말로 가장 옳은 것은? `18년 일반직`

> (　　　) : To increase the distance to the vessel ahead by reducing one's own speed.

① Drop back　　　　② Safe Distance
③ Backing　　　　　④ Crash-stop

해설 선박의 선속을 줄여 선수 방향의 선박과의 거리를 늘리는 Drop back에 대한 설명이다.

답 ❶

27. SMCP에 사용되는 용어에 대한 정의로 옳은 것은 모두 몇 개인가? `17년 2차`

> ⓐ Hampered vessel : A vessel restricted by her ability to manoeuvre by the nature of her work.
> ⓑ Muster : To disassemble crew, passengers or both in a special place for purposes of checking.
> ⓒ Ordance exercise : Naval firing practice.
> ⓓ Roll call : The act of checking who of the passengers and crew members are present, e.g. at assembly stations, by reading aloud a list of their names.

① 1개　　　　　② 2개
③ 3개　　　　　④ 4개

해설 ⓑ disassemble → assemble

답 ❸

I 기출문제

28. 다음 중 빈칸에 들어갈 말로 가장 적절한 것은? 〈16년 2차〉

(   ) means uncontrolled movement at sea under the influence of current, tide or wind.

① Adrift   ② Disabled   ③ Underway   ④ Beach

해설 조류, 조석, 바람의 영향으로 선박이 통제되지 않고 움직이는 것 표류(Adrift)에 대한 설명이다.

답 ❶

29. 표준해사통신용어(Standard Marine Communication Phrases) 상 가장 옳지 않은 것은? 〈19년 1차〉

① Abandon Vessel : To evacuate crew and passengers from a vessel following a distress
② Adrift : Uncontrolled movement at sea under the influence of current, tide or wind
③ Fairway : A vessel which is not at anchor, or made fast to the shore, or aground
④ Way Point : A position a vessel has to pass or at which she has to alter course according to her voyage plan

해설 Underway(항해중)에 대한 설명이다.

답 ❸

30. 표준해사통신용어(Standard Marine Communication Phrases) 상 다음 용어에 대한 설명 중 옳은 것은 모두 몇 개인가? 〈19년 1차〉

ⓐ Backing(of wind) : A wind that is constantly changing speed and direction
ⓑ Blast : A whistle signal made by the vessel
ⓒ Blind sector : An area which cannot be scanned by the ship's radar because it is shielded by parts of the superstructure, masts, etc.
ⓓ General emergency alarm : A sound signal of seven short blasts and one prolonged blast given with the vessel's sound system
ⓔ Destination : Port which a vessel is bound for
ⓕ Veering(of winds) : Shift of wind direction in an anticlockwise manner, for example from north to west
ⓖ EPIRB : Emergency Position Indicating Radio Beacon
ⓗ MMSI : Maritime Mobile Service Identity number

① 5개   ② 6개
③ 7개   ④ 모두 맞다

해설 ⓐ variable(변풍)에 대한 설명이다. ⓕ backing(반전)에 대한 설명이다.

답 ❷

I 기출문제

31. 다음 표준해사통신용어상 용어의 정의 중 가장 옳지 않은 것은? `20년 1차`

① Safe speed : That speed of a vessel allowing the maximum possible time for effective action to be taken to avoid a collision and to be stopped within an appropriate distance.
② Transit speed : The speed of a vessel adjusted to that of pilot boat at which the pilot can safely embark/disembark.
③ Fairway speed : Mandatory speed in a fairway.
④ Manoeuvring speed : A vessel's reduced rate of speed in restricted waters such as fairways or harbours.

해설 Boarding Speed(승선속력)에 대한 설명이다.

답 ❷

32. 〈Standard Marine Communication Phrases〉상 용어에 대한 설명 중 옳은 것은 모두 몇 개인가? `19년 3차`

ⓐ Dragging of anchor : An anchor moving over the sea bottom voluntarily because it is no longer preventing the movement of the vessel.
ⓑ Draught(Draft) : Height of highest point of vessel's structure above waterline.
ⓒ List : Inclination of the vessel to port side or starboard side.
ⓓ Fairway speed : Mandatory speed in a fairway.
ⓔ Disabled : A vessel damaged or impaired in such a manner as to be incapable of proceeding on its voyage.
ⓕ Close up (to) : To decrease the distance to the vessel ahead by increasing one's own speed.

① 3개 ② 4개
③ 5개 ④ 6개

해설 ⓐ voluntarily → involuntarily
     ⓑ Airdraft에 대한 설명이다.

답 ❷

I 기출문제

33. 다음은 표준해사통신영어〈Standard Marine Communication Phrases〉상 용어의 정의에 대한 설명이다. ㉠, ㉡, ㉢, ㉣에 해당하는 내용으로 가장 옳은 것은? [20년 3차]

㉠ Major uncontrolled flow of seawater into the vessel
㉡ Escape of liquids such as water, oil, etc., out of pipes, boilers, tanks, etc., or a minor inflow of seawater into the vessel due to damage to the hull
㉢ Seawater flowing into the vessel due to hull damage or hatches awash and not properly closed
㉣ The accidental escape of oil, etc. from a vessel, container, etc., into the sea

	Flooding	Leaking	Make water	Spill
①	㉠	㉡	㉢	㉣
②	㉠	㉣	㉢	㉡
③	㉢	㉡	㉠	㉣
④	㉢	㉣	㉠	㉡

해설
㉠ Flooding(침수)
㉡ Leaking(누출)
㉢ Make water(누수)
㉣ Spill(누출)

답 ❶

34. 다음은 표준해사통신영어(Standard Marine Communication Phrases)상 용어의 정의에 대한 설명이다. 가장 옳지 않은 것은? [20년 3차]

① List : Inclination of the vessel to port side or starboard side
② Muster : List of crew, passengers and others on board and their functions in a distress or drill
③ Unlit : When the light of a buoy or a lighthouse is inoperative
④ Beach to : To run a vessel up on a beach to prevent its sinking in deep water

해설 ② Muster list에 대한 설명이다.

답 ❷

기출문제

35. 다음 〈보기〉 중 표준해사통신용어(Standard Marine Communication Phrases)상 용어에 대한 설명으로 옳은 것은 모두 몇 개인가? `21년 상반기`

> ㉠ Bearing : The angle that the center line of a vessel, or the vessel's keel, makes with the meridian.
> ㉡ Manoeuvring speed : A vessel's reduced speed in circumstances where it may be required to use the engine at short notice.
> ㉢ Windward : On or towards the sheltered side of ship.
> ㉣ Precautionary area : A routing measure comprising an area within defined limits where ships must navigate with particular caution and within which the direction of traffic flow may be recommended.
> ㉤ INFORMATION : This indicates that the following message implies the intention of the sender to influence others by a regulation.

① 1개　　　　② 2개
③ 3개　　　　④ 4개

해설 ㉠ Course에 대한 설명이다.
　　　㉢ Leeward에 대한 설명이다.
　　　㉤ INSTRUCTION에 대한 설명이다.

답 ❷

36. 다음 〈보기〉 중 용어에 대한 설명으로 옳지 않은 것은 모두 몇 개인가? `22년 일반직`

> ㉠ Beach (to) : To run a vessel up on a beach to prevent its sinking in deep water
> ㉡ Located : In navigational warnings ; position of object confirmed
> ㉢ Half cardinal point : The four main points of the compass ; north, east, south and west
> ㉣ Muster : List of crew, passengers and others on board and their functions in a distress or drill
> ㉤ Derelict : A vessel which has been destroyed, sunk or abandoned at a sea

① 없음　　　　② 1개
③ 2개　　　　④ 3개

해설 ㉢ Cardinal point(방점)에 대한설명이다.
　　　㉣ Muster list에 대한 설명이다.
　　　㉤ Wreck에 대한 설명이다.

답 ❹

I 기출문제

37. 다음 〈보기〉 중 표준해사통신용어(Standard Marine Communication Phrases)상 용어에 대한 설명으로 옳지 않은 것은 모두 몇 개인가? `22년 일반직`

> ㉠ Adrift : Controlled movement at sea under the influence of current, tide or wind
> ㉡ Close up : To increase the distance to the vessel ahead by decreasing one's own speed
> ㉢ Walk back : To reverse the action of a windlass to ease the cable
> ㉣ Fairway : Navigable part of a waterway

① 1개　　　② 2개　　　③ 3개　　　④ 4개

해설　㉠ Controlled → Uncontrolled
　　　　㉡ Drop back에 대한 설명이다.

답 ❷

38. 다음 〈보기〉 중 용어의 정의가 옳은 것은 모두 몇 개인가? `22년 일반직`

> ㉠ Heading : The intended direction of movement of a vessel through the water
> ㉡ Embark : To go from a vessel
> ㉢ Leeway : The angle the ship's keel, or center line, makes with the wake of the vessel, or track through the water
> ㉣ Recover : To pick up shipwrecked persons
> ㉤ Give way : To keep in of the way of another vessel

① 2개　　　② 3개　　　③ 4개　　　④ 없음

해설　㉠ Course에 대한 설명이다.
　　　　㉡ Disembark에 대한 설명이다.
　　　　㉤ Give way : To keep out of the way of another vessel

답 ❶

39. 다음 빈칸에 들어갈 단어로 가장 옳은 것은? `22년 2차`

> "In SMCP (　　　) means a vessel damaged or impaired in such a manner as to be incapable of proceeding on its voyage"

① disabled　　　　② derelict
③ wrecked　　　　④ hampered

해설　SMCP상 손상되고(damaged), 성능이 저하(impaired)되어 항해를 진행하는 것이 불가능한 선박을 <u>disabled(손상선)</u>이라 한다.

답 ❶

04 약어 표현

A

ARPA : Automatic Radar Plotting Aids (자동 레이더 플로팅 장치)
A/CO : Alter Course (변침하다)
ACO : Aircraft Co-ordinator (항공기 조정관)
AMVER : Automated Mutual Assistance Vessel Rescue System (선박 자동 상호 구조 시스템)
Ah'd : Ahead (선수쪽으로, 앞쪽으로)
A.P.T. : After Peak Tank (선미탱크)
A/C : Aircraft (항공기)
AIS : Automatic Identification System (선박자동식별시스템)

B

BWE : Break Water Entrance (방파제 입구)
B.A. : Breathing Apparatus (호흡 보조기)
B.W.T : Ballast Water Tank (평형수 탱크)

C

COW : Crude Oil Washing (원유 세정법)
CPA : Closest Point of Approach (최근접점)
CES : Coast Earth Station (해안지구국)
COLREG : International Regulations for Preventing Collisions at Sea
CO. : Course (침로)
CSO : Company Security Officer (회사보안책임자)
CSR : Continuous Synopsis Record (선박이력기록부)

D

DSC : Digital Selective Calling (디지털 선택 호출 장치)
DGPS : Differential Global (satellite) Positioning System (위성항법 보정시스템)
D.R. : Dead Reckoning (추측위치)
D.W.T : Dead Weight Tonnage (재화중량톤수)
Dist : Distance (거리, 항정)

E

EPIRB : Emergency Position Indicating Radio Beacon (비상위치지시용 무선표지 설비)
ETA : Estimated Time of Arrival (도착예정시각)
ETD : Estimated Time of Departure (출발예정시각)
ELT : Emergency Locator Transmitter (비상 위치 탐사 발신기 : 경보 및 신호를 전송하기 위한 항공 무선 조난 표지)
E.P. : Estimated Position (추정위치)
E/R : Engine Room (기관실)

F

F.W.E. : Finished With Engines (기관 사용 종료)
F.P.T : Fore Peak Tank (선수탱크)
F.O.T : Fuel Oil Tank (연료유 탱크)
F.W.T : Fresh Water Tank (청수 탱크)
F/H : Full Ahead (기관 전속 전진)
F/S : Full Astern (기관 전속 후진)

G

GMDSS : Global Maritime Distress and Safety System (전 세계 해상 조난 및 안전 시스템)
GPS : Global Positioning System (전 세계적 위치항법장치)
GMT : Greenwich Mean Time (그리니치 평균시)
G.T : Gross Tonnage (총톤수)

H

H/H : Half Ahead (기관 반속 전진)
H.W. : Hight Water (고조)

I

IMO : International Maritime Organization (국제 해사 기구)
ILO : International Labour Organization (국제 노동 기구)
ITZ : Inshore Traffic Zone (연안 통항대)
IAMSAR : International Aeronautical and Maritime Search and Rescue
ISM : International Safety Management Code
ISPS : International Code for the Security of Ships and of Port Facilities
IHO : International Hydrographic Organization (국제 수로기구)
IALA : International Association of Light House Authority (국제항로표지협회)
ICS : International Chamber of shipping (국제해운회의소)

K

K.O. : Knock off (작업 종료)

L

L.H. : Light House (등대)
L.O.A : Length Over All (전장)
L.B.P : Length Between Perpendiculars (수선간장)
L.W.L : Length on Load Water Line (수선장)
L.O.P : Line Of Position (위치선)
L.M.T : Local Mean Time (지방 평균시)
Lat. : Latitude (위도)
Long. : Longitude (경도)
L.O. : Lubricating Oil (윤활유)
L.O.T : Lubricating Oil Tank (윤활유 탱크)
L.W. : Low Water (저조)
L.P.G. : Liquified Petroleum Gas (액화석유가스)
L.S.T. : Local Standard Time (지방표준시)
L.T : Local Time (지방시)
L.M.T. : Local Mean Time (지방평균시)

M

MMSI : Maritime Mobile Service Identity number (해상 이동통신 업무 식별번호)
M/V : Motor Vessel (동력선)
MARPOL : International Convention for the Prevention of Marine Pollution from Ships
MERSAR : Merchant Ship Search And Rescue (상선 수색 구조 지침서)
M.O.B. : Man Over Board (사람 선외 추락)
MID : Maritime Identification Digits (해상식별번호)

N

NUC : Not Under Command (조종불능선)
NBDP : Narrow Band Direct Printing (협대역인쇄전신)
N/R : Notice of Readiness (하역준비완료통지서)
N.T. : Net Tonnage (순톤수)

O

OSC : On Scene Co-ordinator (현장 조정관)
O/B : On Board (승선)

P

PA system : Public Address system (확성 방송장치)
P.O.B. : Pilot On Board (도선사 승선)
P/S : Port Side (좌현)
P/STN : Pilot Station (도선사 승선 지점)
PFSP : Port Facility Security Plan (항만시설보안계획서)
PFSO : Port Facility Security Officer (항만시설보안책임자)

Q

Q.M. : Quater Master (조타수)

R

RCC : Rescue Coordination Centre (구조 조정 본부)
RSC : Rescue Sub Centre (구조지부)
RB : Rescue Boat (구조정)
RV : Rescue Vessel (구조선)
R/up Eng. : Rung up Engine
RPM : Revolution Per Minutes (분당 회전수)
R.D.F : Radio Direction Finder (무선방향탐지기)
RSO : Recognized Security Organization (보안인증심사대행기관)

S

SWL : Safety Working Load (안전 사용 하중)
SART : Search And Rescue (Radar) Transponder (레이더 트랜스폰더)
SAR : Search and Rescue (수색 구조)
S/B : Stand By (준비)
S/H : Slow Ahead (기관 미속 전진)
S/Co : Set Course (정침하다)
S.O.S : Stop Other Service (구조요청신호)
S.S. : Steam Ship (증기선)
Stb'd : Starboard (우현)
S.B.E. : Stand By Engine (기관 사용 준비)
SMC : Search And Rescue Mission Coordinator (수색 구조 임무 조정관)
STCW : The International Convention on Standards of Training,
       Certification and Watchkeeping for Seafarers
SOLAS : International convention for the safety of life at sea
SSP : Ship Security Plan (선박보안계획서)

SSO : Ship Security Officer (선박보안책임자)
SIN : Ship Identification Number (선박식별번호)
SSAS : Ship Security Alert System (선박보안경보시스템)
SSA : Ship Security Assessment (선박보안평가서)

T

TCPA : Time to Closest Point of Approach (최근접점까지의 도달 시간)
TEU : Twenty foot Equivalent Unit (컨테이너 규격의 단위)
TSS : Traffic Separation Scheme (통항 분리 방식)
TMAS : Telemedical Assistance (원격의료 지원 서비스)

U

UTC : Universal Time Co-ordinated (세계시)
UKC : Under Keel Clearance (용골 하 여유 수심)
UNCLOS : United Nations Convention on the Law of the Sea
UHF : Ultra High Frequency (극초단파)

V

VHF : Very High Frequency (초단파)
VTS : Vessel Traffic Services (선박 통항 관제 업무)

W

W/H : Wheel House (조타실)
W.T : Water Tight (수밀)
WMO : World Meteorological Organization (세계기상기구)

Z

Z.D. : Zone Description (시간대명)
Z.T. : Zone Time (대시)

I 기출문제

40. 다음 약자 설명 중 틀린 것은 모두 몇 개 인가? `14년 2차`

㉠ M/V : 동력선
㉡ K.O. : 작업종료
㉢ L.H : 등대
㉣ CO. : 침로
㉤ ah'd : 선수 쪽
㉥ P/S : 좌현
㉦ B.W.E. : 방파제 입구
㉧ S.B.E : 기관 사용 준비
㉨ E/R : 기관실

① 없음　　　　　　② 1개
③ 2개　　　　　　④ 3개

해설　㉠ Motor Vessel
　　　㉡ Knocked off
　　　㉢ Light House
　　　㉣ Course
　　　㉤ ahead
　　　㉥ Port Side
　　　㉦ Break Water Entrance
　　　㉧ Stand By Engines
　　　㉨ Engine Room

답 ❶

41. 다음 영어 약어에 대한 설명 중 틀린 것은 모두 몇 개 인가? `16년 2차`

㉠ A/Co : Alter Course (변침하다)
㉡ B.W.E : Break Water Entrance (방파제 입구)
㉢ C.P.A : Closest Point of Approach (최근접거리)
㉣ E.T.D : Estimated Time of Dead line (출항예정시간)
㉤ Lat. : Latitude (경도)
㉥ S/B : Stand By (준비하다)

① 0개　　　② 1개　　　③ 2개　　　④ 3개

해설　㉣ E.T.D : Estimated Time of Departure (출항예정시간)
　　　㉤ Lat. : Latitude (위도)

답 ❸

기출문제

42. 「SMCP」상 다음 용어의 약어가 제대로 연결되지 않은 것은 모두 몇 개인가? `16년 2차`

㉠ VTS : Vessel Traffic Services
㉡ ETA : Estimated Time of Arrival
㉢ CPA : Closest Point of Approach
㉣ GPS : Global Positioning System
㉤ DSC : Digital Selective Calling
㉥ RCC : Radio Co-ordination Center

① 0개 ② 1개 ③ 2개 ④ 3개

해설 ㉥ RCC : Rescue Co-ordination Center

답 ❷

43. 다음 해사영어 약어에 대한 설명 중 틀린 것은 모두 몇 개인가? `18년 3차`

㉠ DSC : Digital Selective Calling
㉡ ETA : Estimated Time of Arrival
㉢ COW : Crude Oil Washing
㉣ GMDSS : Global Maritime Distress and Safety System
㉤ MMSI : Maritime Mobile Service Identity(number)
㉥ VTS : Vessel Traffic Service(s)

① 0개 ② 1개 ③ 2개 ④ 3개

해설 모두 옳음.

답 ❶

I 기출문제

44. 해사영어에서 사용되는 약어에 대한 설명 중 옳지 않은 것은 모두 몇 개인가? `19년 3차`

ⓐ A/Co. : 정침하다
ⓑ K.O. : 작업종료
ⓒ CPA : 최근접거리
ⓓ B.W.E : 방파제 입구
ⓔ D.W.T : 재화중량톤
ⓕ Lat. : 경도
ⓖ P/S : 좌현
ⓗ S.B.E. : 기관사용준비
ⓘ E.T.D. : 입항예정시간

① 1개　　② 2개　　③ 3개　　④ 없음

해설 틀린 항목
　ⓐ Alter Course : 변침하다.
　ⓕ Latitude : 위도
　ⓘ Estimated Time of Departue : 출항 예정시간
옳은 항목
　ⓑ Knocked off : 작업종료
　ⓒ Closest Point of Approach : 최근접거리(최근접점)
　ⓓ Break Water Entrane : 방파제 입구
　ⓔ Dead Weight Tonnage : 재화중량톤
　ⓖ Port Side : 좌현
　ⓗ Stand By Engine : 기관사용 준비

답 ❸

45. 다음 보기 중 약어에 대한 설명으로 옳지 않은 것은 모두 몇 개 인가? `21년 상반기`

㉠ LMT : 지방평균시
㉡ FWE : 기관사용 종료
㉢ ETA : 도착예정시간
㉣ OSC : 수색구조 임무 조정관
㉤ UHF : 초단파
㉥ MOB : 사람 선외 추락
㉦ CPA : 최근접점
㉧ Long. : 경도

① 1개　　② 2개　　③ 3개　　④ 4개

해설 틀린 항목
　㉣ On Scene Co-ordinator : 현장조정관
　㉤ Ultra High Frequency : 극초단파
옳은 항목
　㉠ Local Mean Time : 지방평균시
　㉡ Finish With Engine : 기관사용 종료
　㉢ Estimated Time of Arrival : 도착예정시각
　㉥ Man Over Board : 사람 선외 추락
　㉦ Closest Point of Approach : 최근접점
　㉧ Longitude : 경도

답 ❷

기출문제

46. 다음은 GMDSS(Global Maritime Distress and Safety System)에서 사용되는 약어이다. 가장 옳지 않은 것은? `21년 하반기`

① MMSI : Maritime mobile satellite identity number
② NBDP : Narrow-band direct printing
③ EPIRB : Emergency Position Indicating Radio Beacon
④ SART : Search and rescue radar transponder

해설 MMSI : Maritime mobile <u>service</u> identity number, 해상이동업무식별번호

답 ❶

47. 다음 중 해사영어의 약어의 설명으로 옳은 것은 모두 몇 개인가? `22년 2차`

㉠ M/V : Motor Vessel
㉡ W/H : Wheel House
㉢ C.O.W : Crude Oil Washing
㉣ Q.M : Qurantine Master
㉤ O/B : On Board
㉥ D.W.T : Dead Weight Tonnage
㉦ G.T : Great Tonnage
㉧ L.S.T : Local Separate Time
㉨ D.R. : Dead Reckoning
㉩ F/H : Full Ahead

① 5개 ② 6개
③ 7개 ④ 8개

해설 옳지 않은 것.
㉣ Q.M : <u>Quarter</u> Master
㉦ G.T : <u>Gross</u> Tonnage
㉧ L.S.T : Local <u>Standard</u> Time

답 ❸

chapter 05

Message Marker 통신부호

01 통신 부호의 적용

특별히 육상국과 선박간의 통신을 원활하게 하기 위해, 혹은 표준해사통신용어 중의 하나가 의도한 바와 의미전달이 일치 하지 않은 경우, 전달된 메시지가 잘 이해될 수 있는 가능성을 높이기 위해 다음의 여덟 가지 통신부호를 사용할 수 있다.

통신 부호 중의 어느 하나를 사용할 것인지의 여부는 육상 요원 또는 선박의 사관이 판단할 사항이며, 사용할 경우에 어떤 통보 부호를 사용할 것인지는 당시 상황에 대한 담당자의 적절한 평가에 따른다.
통신 부호가 사용된다면 통신 사항에 앞서서, 또는 통신 사항 중의 해당 부분에 앞서서 통신부호를 말해야 한다. IMO의 VTS 지침에 의하면 어떤 통보 사항이 선박에 통보될 때 그 전달 사항 내에 통보 권고, 경고, 지시 사항이 포함되어 있는지의 여부를 확실히 해야 하며, 실행 가능한 한 IMO표준해사 통신 용어를 사용해야한다.

표준화된 VTS교신에 관한 더 자세한 사항은 AI편의 다른 부분들을 참고해라. VTS의 표준 보고 절차에 관하여는 IMO 결의서 A.851(20), 위험 화물, 유해물질 및 또는 해양 오염 물질과 관련된 사건의 보고에 대한 지침이 포함된 선박 보고 제도 및 선박 보고 요구 사항에 관한 일반 원칙을 참고할 것.

01

Application of Message Marker

In order to especially facilitate shore-to-ship and ship-to-shore communication or when one of the Standard Marine Communication Phrases will not fit the meaning desired, one of the following eight message markers may be used to increase the probability of the purpose of the message being properly understood.

It is at the discretion of the shore personnel or the ship's officer whether to use one of the message markers and if so which of them to apply depending on the user's qualified assessment of the situation. If used the message marker is to be spoken preceding the message or the corresponding part of the message. The IMO VTS Guidelines recommend that in any message directed to a vessel it should be clear whether the message contains information, advice, warning, or instruction and IMO Standard Marine Communication Phrases should be used where practicable.

For further standardized VTS communications, also see other sections of PART AI. For VTS Standard Reporting Procedures see IMO Resolution A. 851 (20) on "General Principles for Ship Reporting Systems and Ship Reporting Requirements, including guidelines for reporting incidents involving dangerous goods, harmful substances and / or marine pollutants".

Note : All of the following phrases must come as the culmination (message content) of a radio message exchange between stations covered by the ITU Radio Regulations, and the relevant calling procedures have to be observed.

02
8 Massage Marker

① INSTRUCTION
This indicates that the following message implies the intention of the sender to influence others by a **Regulation.**

Comment : This means that the sender, e.g. a VTS - Station or a naval vessel, must have the full authority to send such a message. The recipient has to follow this legally binding message unless s/he has contradictory safety reasons which then have to be reported to the sender

Ex) "INSTRUCTION. Do not cross the fairway."

② ADVICE
This indicates that the following message implies the intention of the sender to influence others by a **Recommendation.**

Comment : The decision whether to follow the ADVICE still stays with the recipient. ADVICE does not necessarily have to be followed but should be considered very carefully.

Ex) "ADVICE. (Advise you) stand by on VHF Channel six nine."

③ WARNING
This indicates that the following message implies the intention of the sender to inform others about **danger.**

Comment : 이것은 의미한다. 경고의 수신자는 즉시 언급된 위험에 주의를 기울여야하고, 경고의 결과는 수신자의 책임이다.

Ex) "WARNING. 항로 내에 장애물이 존재함."

④ 정보
이는 뒤따르는 메세지가 관찰된 사실이나 상황 등에 국한됨을 나타낸다.

Comment : 이 통신부호는 가급적 항해, 교통 정보를 위해 사용된다. 정보에 따른 결과는 수신자의 책임이다.

Ex) "INFORMATION. 동력선 Noname 호가 귀선의 서쪽으로 추월할 것이다."

⑤ 질문
이는 뒤따르는 메세지가 의문형의 성격임을 나타낸다.

Comment : 이 통신부호를 사용하면 (특히 질문 시작 부분에 질문, 장소, 왜, 누구, 어떻게 와 같은 질문을 추가로 사용할 때) 질문 또는 진술이 이루어지고 있는지에 대한 의심을 제거할 수 있다. 해당 질문의 수신자는 답변을 해야 한다.

Ex) "QUESTION. 귀선의 흘수는 얼마인가?"

⑥ 응답
이는 뒤따르는 메세지가 앞의 질문에 대한 대답임을 나타낸다.

Comment : 답변에 다른 질문이 포함되어 있으면 안 됨을 인지하라.

Ex) "ANSWER. 본선의 현재 최대 흘수는 7미터이다."

Comment : This means that any recipient of a WARNING should pay immediate attention to the danger mentioned. Consequences of a WARNING will be up to the recipient.

Ex) "WARNING. Obstruction in the fairway."

④ INFORMATION
This indicates that the following message is restricted to **observed** facts, situations, etc.

Comment : This marker is preferably used for navigational and traffic information, etc.. Consequences of INFORMATION will be up to the recipient.

Ex) "INFORMATION. MV Noname will overtake to the West of you."

⑤ QUESTION
This indicates that the following message is of **interrogative** character.

Comment : The use of this marker removes any doubt on whether a question is being asked or statement being made, especially when interrogatives such as What, Where, Why, Who, How are additionally used at the beginning of the question. The recipient is expected to return an answer.

Ex) "QUESTION. (What is) your present maximum draft?"

⑥ ANSWER
This indicates that the following message is the **reply to** a previous question.

Comment : Note that an answer should not contain another question.

Ex) "ANSWER. My present maximum draft is zero seven metres."

⑦ REQUEST

This indicates that the following message is **asking for** action from others with respect to the vessel.

Comment : The use of this marker is to signal :
I want something to be arranged or provided, e.g. ship's stores requirements, tugs, permission, etc..

Note : REQUEST must not be used involving navigation, or to modify COLREGS.

Ex) "REQUEST. I require two tugs."

⑧ INTENTION

This indicates that the following message informs others about immediate navigational action **intended** to be taken.

Comment : The use of this message marker is logically restricted to messages announcing navigational actions by the vessel sending this message.

Ex) "INTENTION. I will reduce my speed."

---

⑦ 요구

이는 뒤따르는 메시지가 선박에 대한 다른 사람의 행동을 요구하고 있음을 나타낸다.

Comment : 이 통신부호의 사용은 다음의 의미의 신호를 보내는 것이다. : 예를 들어 선용품 수급이라던지 터그, 허가서 등을 수배하거나 제공받고 싶음을 의미.

Note : 이 부호는 항해에 영향을 주거나, COLREGS를 바꾸는 데에 사용돼선 안 된다.

Ex) "REQUEST. 본선은 예인선 두 척을 요청한다."

⑧ 의도

이는 뒤따르는 메시지가 취하고자 의도하는 즉각적인 항해 행동에 대해서 나타냄을 알려준다.

Comment : 이 통신부호의 사용은 방송된 메시지에 논리적으로 제한된다.

Ex) "INTENTION. 본선은 감속할 것이다."

기출문제

01. 다음 중 SMCP(Standard Marine Communication Phrase)상 용어와 그 정의에 대한 내용이다. 옳게 짝지어진 것을 모두 고르시오.　　　18년 1차

ⓐ INSTRUCTION : This indicates that the following message is of interrogative character.
ⓑ ANSWER : This indicates that the following message is the reply to previous question.
ⓒ ADVICE : This indicates that the following message implies the intention of the sender to inform others about danger.
ⓓ REQUEST : This indicates that the following message is asking for action from others with respect to the vessel.

① ⓐ, ⓑ　　　　　　　　　　② ⓑ, ⓓ
③ ⓑ, ⓒ, ⓓ　　　　　　　　④ ⓒ, ⓓ

해설 ⓐ QUESTION에 대한 설명이다.
　　　ⓒ WARNING에 대한 설명이다.

답 ❷

02. 다음 중 VTS Standard Phrases 상 Message Markers에 대한 설명 중 가장 옳지 않은 것은?　　　18년 일반직

① ADVICE : This indicates that the following message implies the intention of the sender to influence others by a Regulation
② WARNING : This indicates that the following message implies the intention of the sender to inform others about danger.
③ INFORMATION : This indicates that the following message is restricted to observed facts, situation, etc.
④ INTENTION : This indicates that the following message informs others about immediate navigational action intended to be taken.

해설 INSTRUCTION에 대한 설명이다.

답 ❶

03. 아래 문장에서 빈칸에 들어갈 IMO 표준해사통신영어로 가장 적절한 것은?　　　16년 일반직

In VTS standard phrases. (　　　) indicates that the following message is of interrogative character.

① QUESTION　　　　　　　② ANSWER
③ REQUEST　　　　　　　④ INTENTION

해설 QUESTION에 대한 설명이다.

답 ❶

기출문제

04. 다음은 VTS 센터에서 단계적으로 실시하는 정보제공의 실제교신내용이다. 빈칸에 들어갈 SMCP 용어로 가장 적절한 것은?

〔16년 일반직〕

> Information. Unknown vessel will overtake to the west of you.
> Advice. Stand-by on VHF CH.14.
> (   ), Do not alter your course to starboard side.

① Instruction   ② Command
③ Education   ④ Follow

해설 뒷 문장이 '변침하지 마시오'라고 명령하고 있고 있기 때문에 Instruction의 부호를 사용한다.

답 ①

05. 다음 중 표준해사통신용어(Standard Marine Communication Phrases)상 빈칸에 들어갈 말로 가장 옳은 것은?

〔19년 1차〕

> VTS : (   ), Obstruction in the fairway.

① INFORMATION   ② QUESTION
③ WARNING   ④ ADVICE

해설 뒷 문장이 '항로에 장애물이 있다'라고 되어 있기 때문에 경고하는 표현인 WARNING을 사용한다.

답 ③

06. 〈Standard Marine Communication Phrases〉상 빈칸에 들어갈 말로 가장 옳은 것은?

〔19년 3차〕

> "(   ), Unknown vessel will overtake to the west of you."

① Instruction   ② Intention
③ Information   ④ Request

해설 뒷 문장이 "잘 모르는 선박이 귀선의 서쪽으로 추월할 것이다." 라는 객관적인 사실을 알려주고 있기 때문에 Information을 사용한다.

답 ③

I 기출문제

07. 다음은 입항중인 선박과 VTS 센터와의 교신내용이다. IMO 표준해사통신용어로 빈칸에 가장 알맞은 말은?

`16년 일반직`

> M/V : VTS. This is KOREA. How do you (A) me over?
> VTS : KOREA. This is VTS. I (A) you good. What is your (B) to pilot station?
> M/V : VTS. My (B) to pilot station is 12:00 local time. Do you have any information?
> VTS : KOREA. No information. (C) Anchor in anchorage no.3. Stand-by on VHF CH.14.

① A : listen   B : ETD   C : Advice
② A : call   B : ETA   C : Advice
③ A : read   B : ETD   C : Advice
④ A : read   B : ETA   C : Advice

해설
How do you (A) read me? :
송수신 상태 좋습니까?
I (A) read you good. :
송수신 상태 좋습니다. (4단계)
What is your (B) ETA to pilot station? :
도선구역까지의 도착예정시간이 언제 입니까?
My (B) ETA to pilot station is 1200 local time :
본선 도착 예정시각은 지방시 1200입니다.
KOREA, No information (C) Advice. Anchor in anchorage no.3 :
KOREA호, 정보가 없습니다. 묘박지 3번에서 묘박하기를 권고합니다.

답 ④

08. 다음 〈보기〉는 일반영어에서 사용하는 애매한 어휘를 의미전달이 명확하게 해사영어로 변경한 것이다. 빈 칸에 들어갈 말로 가장 옳게 짝지어진 것은?

`21년 상반기`

> ㉠ I might enter the fairway.
> ➡ (ⓐ). I will enter the fairway.
> ㉡ You should anchor in anchorage B3.
> ➡ (ⓑ). Anchor in anchorage B3.

① ⓐ INFORMATION   ⓑ WARNING
② ⓐ INSTRUCTION   ⓑ ADVICE
③ ⓐ REQUEST   ⓑ WARNING
④ ⓐ INTENTION   ⓑ ADVICE

해설
㉠은 자선의 동작에 대해 말하기 때문에 INTENTION 통신 부호를 문장 앞에 사용한다.
㉡은 묘박지로의 정박을 권고 하고 있기 때문에 ADVICE 통신부호를 문장 앞에 사용한다.

답 ④

기출문제

09. 다음 중 육상과 선박 그리고 선박과 육상통신 또는 일반적인 무선통신에서, 표준해사통신영어(Standard Marine Communication Phrases) Part AI/6 "선박통항 서비스 표준절차"에 있는 8개 통보부호로 가장 옳지 않은 것은? <small>21년 하반기</small>

① Instruction
② Recommendation
③ Request
④ Warning

해설 권고의 경우 ADVICE통신 부호를 사용한다.

답 ❷

10. 다음 〈보기〉 중 표준해사통신용어(Standard Marine Communication Phrases)상 Message Marker에 대한 설명으로 옳지 않은 것은 모두 몇 개인가? <small>22년 일반직</small>

㉠ INFORMATION indicates that the following message is restricted to observed facts, situations, etc..
㉡ WARNING is preferably used for navigational and traffic information, etc..
㉢ The decision whether to follow the ADVICE still does not stay with the recipient.
㉣ REQUEST must be used involving navigation, or to modify COLREGS.
㉤ The use of INTENTION is logically restricted to messages announcing navigational actions by the vessel sending this message.

① 1개
② 2개
③ 3개
④ 4개

해설 ㉡ INFORMATION이 가급적 항해, 교통 정보로 사용된다.
 ㉢ The decision whether to follow the ADVICE still does ~~not~~ stay with the recipient.
  (ADVICE를 따를지 말지에 대한 결정은 수신자에게 달려 있다.)
 ㉣ REQUEST must not be used involving navigation or to modify COLREG
  (REQUEST는 항해에 관련해서 혹은 COLREG를 수정하는데 사용되어서는 안 된다.)

답 ❸

chapter 06

Standard Wheel Orders

01
기본 원칙

All wheel orders given should be repeated by the helmsman and the officer of the watch should ensure that they are carried out correctly and immediately. All wheel orders should be held until countermanded. The helmsman should report immediately if the vessel does not answer the wheel.

조타수는 주어진 모든 조타 명령을 복명복창해야 하며 당직사관은 조타 명령이 즉시 올바르게 수행되었는지의 여부를 확인해야 한다. 모든 조타 명령은 철회될 때까지 그대로 유지되어야 한다. 타효가 없는 경우 조타수는 즉시 보고하여야 한다.

When there is concern that the helmsman is inattentive s/he should be questioned:
"What is your heading?"

조타수가 태만할 염려가 있을 때에는 조타수에게 다음과 같이 질문해야 한다.
"선수방위는 몇 도인가?"

And s/he should respond:
"My heading is ... degrees."

그리고 조타수는 이렇게 응답해야 한다.
"선수방위는 …도입니다."

02 타각지시를 통한 조타 명령

Order	meaning	의미
Midships	Rudder to be held in the fore and aft position.	키를 선수미선상에 유지하시오.
Port/Starboard five	5° of port/starboard rudder to be held.	키를 좌현/우현 5도로 유지하라.
Port/Starboard ten	10° of port/starboard rudder to be held.	키를 좌현/우현 10도로 유지하라.
Port/Starboard fifteen	15° of port/starboard rudder to be held.	키를 좌현/우현 15도로 유지하라.
Port/Starboard twenty	20° of port/starboard rudder to be held.	키를 좌현/우현 20도로 유지하라.
Port/Starboard twenty-five	25° of port/starboard rudder to be held.	키를 좌현/우현 25도로 유지하라.
Hard-a-port/starboard	Rudder to be held fully over to port/starboard.	키를 좌현/우현 최대 전타 하라.
Nothing to port/starboard	Avoid allowing the vessel's head to go to port/starboard.	선수를 좌현/우현 쪽으로 가지 않게 하라.
Meet her	Check the swing of the vessel's head in a turn.	돌아가는 선수의 선회를 억제하라.
Steady	Reduce swing as rapidly as possible.	최대한 한 빨리 선회를 줄이시오.
Ease to five/ten/fifteen/twenty	Reduce amount of rudder to 5°/10°/15°/20° and hold.	타각을 5/10/15/20도로 줄여라.
Steady as she goes	Steer a steady course on the compass heading indicated at the time of the order.	명령이 내려진 순간에 컴퍼스가 지시한 선수 방위로 조타하라.

- Keep the buoy/mark/beacon/...on port side/starboard side.
- Report if she does not answer the wheel.
- Finished with wheel, no more steering

- 부표/물표/비이콘/…을 좌현/우현 측에 유지하라.
- 타효가 없으면 보고하라.
- 조타 종료.

03
침로 관련 조타명령

당직 항해사가 컴퍼스로 침로를 조타하고자 할 때에는, 조타기를 회전시키고자 하는 방향을 명령한 다음, 0을 포함한 각 숫자를 하나씩 구분하여 말해야 한다. 예를 들면, 다음과 같다.

When the officer of the watch requires a course to be steered by compass, the direction in which s/he wants the wheel turned should be stated followed by each numeral being said separately, including zero, for example:

Order	의미	Course to be steered
"Port, steer one eight two."	좌타를 사용하여 182도로 침로를 변경하라	182°
"starboard, steer zero eight two."	우타를 사용하여 082도로 침로를 변경하라	082°
"Port, steer three zero five."	좌타를 사용하여 305도로 침로를 변경하라	305°

조타명령을 받자마자(예를 들어 182도), 조타수는 그 명령을 복명복창하고 선박을 선회시켜 명령된 침로에 정침시켜야 한다. 선박이 명령된 침로로 정침되면 조타수는 다음과 같이 외쳐야 한다.
"182도에 정침되었습니다."

On receipt of an order to steer, for example, 182°, the helmsman should repeat it and bring the vessel round steadily to the course ordered. when the vessel is steady on the course ordered, the helmsman is to call out:
"steady on one eight two."

명령을 내린 사람은 조타수의 보고를 확인해야 한다.

The person giving the order should acknowledge the helmsman's reply.

선정된 물표를 향하여 조타하고자 할 경우에는 다음과 같이 조타수에게 지시한다.

If it is desired to steer on a selected mark the helmsman should be ordered to:

"…부표/…물표/…비이콘을 향해서 조타하시오."

"steer on…buoy/…mark/…beacon."

명령을 내린 사람은 조타수의 보고를 확인해야 한다.

The person giving the order should acknowledge the helmsman's reply.

기출문제

01. 다음 중 빈칸에 들어갈 표준 조타 명령으로 가장 옳은 것은 무엇인가? `18년 일반직`

( ) : Reduce swing as rapidly as possible.

① Midships
② Ease to five
③ Steady
④ Steady as she goes

해설 Steady에 대한 설명이다.

답 ❸

02. 다음 중 빈칸에 들어갈 표준 조타 명령(Standard Wheel Orders)으로 가장 옳은 것은? `19년 1차`

(ⓐ) : Rudder to be held in the fore and aft position.
(ⓑ) : Check the swing of the vessel's head in a turn.

	ⓐ	ⓑ
①	Midships	Meet her
②	Midships	Steady
③	Steady as she goes	Meet her
④	Steady as she goes	Midships

해설 ⓐ Midships에 대한 설명이다.
ⓑ Meet her에 대한 설명이다.

답 ❶

03. 아래 열거된 선내 표준 조타명령 중 의미가 가장 옳지 않은 것은? `19년 3차`

① Steady : Steer a steady course on the compass heading indicated at the time of the order.
② Hard-a-port : Rudder to be held fully over to port.
③ Meet her : Check the swing of the vessel's head in a turn.
④ Midships : Rudder to be held in the fore and aft position.

해설 'Steer a steady course on the compass heading indicated at the time of the order.'의 설명은 Steady as she goes에 대한 내용이다.

답 ❶

Chapter 6. Standard Wheel Orders **| 77**

Chapter 07 Standard Engine Order

선교의 텔레그래프를 작동하는 사람은 주어진 모든 기관 명령을 복명복창해야 하고, 당직사관은 그 명령이 올바르게 즉시 수행되는지 확인해야 한다.

Any engine order given should be repeated by the person operating the bridge telegraph(s) and the officer of the watch should ensure the order is carried out correctly and immediately.

Order	의미
(Port/starboard engines) Full ahead/astern	(좌측/우측 기관)전/후진 전속
(Port/starboard engines) Half ahead/astern	(좌측/우측 기관)전/후진 반속
(Port/starboard engines) Slow ahead/astern	(좌측/우측 기관)전/후진 미속
(Port/starboard engines) Dead slow ahead/astern	(좌측/우측 기관)전/후진 극미속
Stop (port/starboard engines) engines	(좌측/우측) 기관 정지
Emergency full ahead/astern	긴급 전/후진 전속
Stand by engine	기관사용 준비
Finished with engines - no more manoeuvring. (operation of engine no longer required.)	기관사용 종료 - 더 이상의 조종은 없음 (기관의 작동은 더 이상 필요하지 않음)

두 개의 프로펠러가 설치된 선박에서는 양 쪽 축을 다 돌리려면 "both"라는 말을 모든 명령에 추가해야한다. 예를 들어 "full ahead both" and "slow astern both" 단 예외적으로 기관 정지는 "Stop all engines"를 적절히 써야한다. 만약 두 프로펠러를 독립적으로 사용하고 싶을 때는, 예를 들어 "full ahead starboard" "half astern port"등이 지시되어야 한다.

In vessels fitted with twin propellers, the word "both" should be added to all orders affecting both shafts, e.g. "Full ahead both", and "Slow astern both", except that the words "Stop all engines" should be used, when appropriate. When required to manoeuvre twin propellers independently, this should be indicated, i.e. "Full ahead starboard", "Half astern port", etc.

Bow thruster가 사용될 경우 다음의 명령들이 사용된다.

Where bow thrusters are used, the following orders are used:

Truster	power	direction
Bow thruster	full	to starboard
Stern thruster	half	to port
	slow	

기출문제

01. An engine order to keep maximum revolution for ahead propulsion is (   ).

07년 2차

① full ahead   ② stop engine
③ full astern   ④ half ahead

해설 전직 출력을 위한 최대 회전수(분당)을 유지하는 명령은 full ahead 이다.

답 ❶

02. 아래에 열거된 선내 표준조타명령과 표준기관명령 중 의미가 일치하지 않는 것은?

14년 2차

① Steady   키를 선수미선상에 유지하라.
② Hard-a-starboard   타각을 우현 최대 전타하라.
③ Ease to five   타각을 5°로 줄이고 유지하라.
④ Dead slow astern   극미속 후진

해설 Steady는 'Reduce swing as rapidly as possible.' 즉, '가능한 한 빨리 선회를 줄이시오.'라는 뜻을 가지고 있다. '키를 선수미선상에 유지하라.'라는 명령은 'Midships'에 해당한다.

답 ❶

03. 다음 중 밑줄 친 단어에 대한 설명으로 가장 적절한 것은?

18년 3차

What are the advance and transfer distance in a crash stop?

① FULL SPEED에서 단계적으로 기관을 정지하는 것
② 전속전진 상태에서 기관을 전속후진 하는 것
③ 정지상태에서 기관을 전속후진 하는 것
④ 기관의 전진속도와 후진속도를 동일한 것으로 사용하여 전진에서 후진시키는 것

해설 Crash stop 명령은 긴급 시에 전속전진(Full Ahead) 상태에서 전속후진(Full Astern)하여 긴급 정지하는 명령이다.

답 ❷

chapter 08 VHF Standard GMDSS Message 표준 GMDSS 통신문

01 표준 조난 통신문

DSC 조난경보 수신 확인 통보를 수신하면, 조난선은 VHF 채널 16이나 2,182kHz(자동으로 전환되지 않는다면)와 같은 국제조난통화 주파수 중 하나로 다음과 같이 조난통화를 시작해야 한다.

01
Standard Distress Message

Upon receipt of a DSC Distress Alert acknowledgement the vessel in distress should commence the distress traffic on one of the international distress traffic frequencies such as **VHF Channel 16 or frequency 2,182kHz** (if not automatically controlled) as follows:

> MAYDAY (repeated three times)
> - THIS IS··· (the 9-digit Maritime Mobile Service Identity number (MMSI) plus name/call sign or other identification of the vessel calling)
> - the position of the vessel
> - the nature of distress
> - the assistance required
> - any other information which might facilitate rescue
>
> Example
> MAYDAY (repeated three times)
> - THIS IS TWO-ONE-ONE-TWO-THREE-NINE-SIX-EIGHT-ZERO MOTOR VESSEL "BIRTE" CALL SIGN DELTA ALPHA MIKE KILO
> - POSITION SIX TWO DEGREES ONE ONE DECIMAL EIGHT MINUTES NORTH, ZERO ZERO SEVEN DEGREES FOUR FOUR MINUTES EAST
> - I AM ON FIRE AFTER EXPLOSION
> - I REQUIRE FIRE FIGHTING ASSISTANCE
> - SMOKE NOT TOXIC, OVER

02 표준 긴급 통신문

DSC 긴급 호출을 발신한 후, 발신기를 VHF채널 16번이나 주파수 2,182kHz (자동으로 전환되지 않는다면)로 전환하고 다음과 같은 긴급 통화를 시작한다:

02
Standard Urgency Message

After the transmission of a DSC Urgency Call switch the transmitter to VHF Channel 16 or frequency 2,182kHz (if not automatically controlled) and commence the urgency traffic as follows:

PAN-PAN (repeated three times)
ALL STATIONS (repeated three times)
- THIS IS… (the 9-digit MMSI of the vessel plus name/call sign or other identification)
- the position of the vessel
- the text of the urgency message

Example
PAN-PAN PAN-PAN PAN-PAN
ALL STATIONS ALL STATIONS ALL STATIONS
- THIS IS TWO-ONE-ONE-TWO-THREE-NINE-SIX-EIGHT-ZERO MOTOR VESSEL "BIRTE" CALL SIGN DELTA ALPHA MIKE KILO
- POSITION SIX TWO DEGREES ONE ONE DECIMAL EIGHT MINUTES NORTH ZERO ZERO SEVEN DEGREES FOUR FOUR MINUTES EAST
- I HAVE PROBLEMS WITH ENGINES
- I REQUIRE TUG ASSISTANCE, OVER

03

Standard Safety Message

After the transmission of a DSC Safety Call switch the transmitter to VHF Channel 16 or frequency 2,182kHz (if not automatically controlled) and transmit the safety message as follows:

SECURITE (repeated three times)
ALL STATIONS (or all ships in a specific geographical area, or to a specific station) (repeated three times)
- THIS IS… (the 9-digit MMSI of the vessel plus name/call sign or other identification)
- the text of the safety message

Example
SECURITE SECURITE SECURITE
ALL SHIPS ALL SHIPS ALL SHIPS IN AREA PETER REEF
- THIS IS TWO-ONE-ONE-TWO-THREE-NINE-SIX-EIGHT-ZERO MOTOR VESSEL "BIRTE" CALL SIGN DELTA PLPHA MIKE KILO
- DANGEROUS WRECK LOCATED IN POSITION TWO NAUTICAL MILES SOUTH OF PETER REEF, OVER

03 표준 안전 통신문

DSC 안전 호출을 발신 후 다음, 발신기를 VHF 채널 16이나 주파수의 2,182kHz(자동으로 전환되지 않으면)로 전환하고 다음과 같은 안전 통신문을 전송한다.

기출문제

01. Select one which is not included in the factor of distress message.   10년 2차

① position of the vessel   ② safety requirement
③ 9-digit MMSI   ④ assistance required

해설 조난통신에서 송신해야할 내용에 안전 요청은(safety requirement) 포함되지 않는다.

답 ❷

chapter 09
Guide lines on the use of VHF at sea 해상에서의 VHF 사용 지침

01
Preparation

before transmitting, think about the subjects which have to be communicated and, if necessary, prepare written notes to avoid unnecessary interruptions and ensure that no valuable time is wasted on a busy channel

02
Listening

Listen **before commencing** to transmit to make certain that the channel is not already in use. This will avoid unnecessary and irritating interference.

03
Discipline

VHF equipment should be used correctly and in accordance with the Radio Regulations. The following in particular **should be avoided** :

① calling on channel 16 for purposes other than distress, urgency and very brief safety communications when another channel is available.

② communications not related to safety and navigation on port operation channels.

③ non-essential transmissions, e.g. needless and superfluous signals and correspondence.

④ transmitting without correct identification;

⑤ occupation of one particular channel under poor conditions; and

⑥ use of offensive language.

01 준비

송신을 하기 전 통신할 내용에 대해 생각하고, 불필요한 방해를 피하고 그리고 바쁜 채널에서 귀한 시간이 낭비되지 않도록 필요 하다면 노트를 따로 적어두라.

02 청취

채널이 이미 사용 중은 아닌지를 확인하기 위해 송신 전에 청취하라. 이것은 불필요하고 훼방되는 방해를 피하게 해준다.

03 규율

VHF장비는 올바르게 사용되어야 하고, 통신 규칙에 따라야 한다. 특히나 다음에 나오는 것들을 해서는 안 된다.

① 다른 채널이 사용 가능할 때, 조난이나 긴급, 그리고 안전과 관련한 매우 간략한 통신이 아닌 다른 목적으로 채널 16번에서 호출하는 것.

② 항만 작업 채널에서 안전과 항해와 관련이 없는 통신을 하는 것.

③ 중요하지 않은 통신. 예를 들어 필요 없는 신호나 그와 관련한 것.

④ 제대로 된 확인을 하지 않고 전송하는 것.

⑤ 좋지 않은 상태로 특정 한 채널을 차지하고 있는 것.

⑥ 불쾌한 언어의 사용

04
Repetition

Repetition of words and phrases **should be avoided** unless specifically requested by the **receiving station.**

05
Power reduction

When possible, the **lowest** transmitter power necessary for satisfactory communication should be used

06
AIS(Automatic Identification System)

AIS is used for the exchange of data in ship to ship communications and also in communication with shore-based facilities. The purpose of AIS is to help identify vessels; assist in target tracking; simplify information exchange (eg. reduce verbal reporting); and provide additional information to assist situation awareness.

AIS may be used together with VHF voice communications. AIS should be operated in accordance with resolution A.917(22), as amended by resolution use of shipborne automatic identification systems(AISs)

07
Communications with coast stations

① On VHF channels allocated to port operations service, the only messages permitted are restricted to those relating to the operational handling, the movement and the safety of ships and, in emergency, to the safety of persons; as the use of these channels for ship-to-ship communications may cause serious interference to communications related to the movement an safety of shipping in port arcas.

② Instructions given on communication matters by shore stations should be obeyed.

③ Communications should be carried out on the channel indicated by the coast station. When a change of channel is requested, this should be acknowledged by the ship.

④ On receiving instructions from a coast station to stop transmitting, no further communication should be made until otherwise notified (the coast station may be receiving distress or safety messages and any other transmissions could cause interference).

08
Communications with other ships

① VHF channel 13 is designated by the Radio Regulations for bridge-to-bridge communications. The ship called may indicate another working channel on which further transmissions should take place. The calling ship should acknowledge acceptance before changing channels.

② The listening procedure outlined in paragraph 1.2 should be followed before communications are commenced on the chosen channel.

09
Distress communications

① Distress calls/messages have absolute priority over all other communications. When receiving them all other transmissions should **cease and a listening** watch should be kept.

② Any distress call/message should be recorded in the ship's log and passed to the master.

③ On receipt of a distress message, if in the vicinity, immediately acknowledge receipt. If not in the vicinity, allow a short interval of time to elapse before acknowledging receipt of the message in order to permit ships nearer to the distress to do so.

③ 통신은 육상국에 의하여 지시 된 채널에서 이루어져야 한다. 채널 의 변경이 요청된 경우, 해당 변경 은 선박에 의해 확인돼야 한다.

④ 육상국으로 부터 송신 중단 명령 을 수신한 경우 더 이상의 통신은 따로 명시되기 전까지는 이루어져 서는 안 된다.(육상 국이 조난이나 안전 메시지를 수신하는 중일 수 있고, 또는 다른 어떠한 송신도 방 해를 야기할 수 있다.)

08 다른 선박과의 소통

① VHF 채널 13번이 선교간의 소통 을 위해 무선규정에서 지정이 되 어있다.
호출 받은 선박은 추가적인 전송 이 일어나게 될 다른 작업 채널을 지정할 수 있다. 호출하는 선박은 채널을 변경하기 전 수용하였음을 확인시켜야 한다.

② 1.2에서 명시된 청취절차는 선택 된 채널에서 통신이 시작되기 전 에 따라야 한다.

09 조난 통신

① 조난 호출/메시지는 모든 다른 통 신들 위에 완전한 우선순위를 갖 는다. 해당 내용을 수신한 경우 모 든 송신들은 중단되고 청수 당직 이 유지되어야 한다.

② 모든 조난 호출/메시지는 선박 로 그북에 기록 되어야하고 선장에게 보고돼야한다.

③ 조난 신호를 수신하면, 만약 근방 에 있다면, 즉시 수신을 확인하라. 만약 근방에 없다면 메시지 확인 전 조난 장소에 더 가까이의 선박 이 수신 확인을 가능하게 하게끔 잠시의 시간이 흐르게 허용하라.

10
Calling

① In accordance with the Radio Regulations channel 16 may only be used for distress, urgency and very brief safety communications and for calling to establish other communications which should then be conducted on a suitable working channel.

② Whenever possible, a working frequency should be used for calling.

If a working frequency is not available, VHF channel 16 may be used for calling, provided it is not occupied by a distress and urgency call/message.

③ In case of a difficulty in establishing contact with a ship or a coast station, allow adequate time before repeating the call. Do not occupy the channel unnecessarily and try another channel.

11
Changing channel

If communications on a channel are unsatisfactory, indicate change of channel and **await confirmation.**

12
Spelling

If spelling becomes necessary (e.g. descriptive names, call signs, words that could be misunderstood) use the spelling table contained in the International Code of Signals, the Radio Regulations and the IMO Standard Marine Communication Phrases (SMCP).

13
Addressing

The words "I" and "YOU" should be used prudently. Indicate to whom they refer.

Example:
"Seaship, this is Port Radar, Port Radar, do you have a pilot?"

"Port Radar, this is Seaship, I do have a pilot."

14
Watchkeeping

Every ship, while at sea, is required to maintain watches (Regulation on Watches in Chapter IV of SOLAS, 1974, as amended). Continuous watchkeeping is required on VHF DSC channel 70 and also when practicable, a continuous listening watch on VHF channel 16.

15
Exchange of message

① When it is necessary to indicate that the SMCP are to be used, the following message may be sent:

　A : "Please use Standard Marine Communication Phrases."
　B : "I will use Standard Marine Communication Phrases."

② During exchange of messages, a ship should invite a reply by saying **"OVER"**.

③ The end of a communication is indicated by the word **"OUT"**.

---

13 지명하기(상대국을)

단어 "I" 나 "YOU"는 신중하게 사용돼야 한다. 누구를 언급한 것인지도 나타내라.

14 당직

모든 선박은, 바다에 있는 동안 당직 유지가 요구된다. VHF채널 70번에서 지속적인 당직유지가 요구되고, 또한 가능한 한 VHF 채널 16번에서 지속적인 청수당직이 유지돼야 한다.

15 메시지 교환

표준해사통신용어를 사용하여 교신하고자 한다는 것을 나타낼 필요가 있는 경우에는 다음과 같은 통신문을 송신한다.

A : "표준해사통신용어를 사용하시오."
B : "표준해사통신용어를 사용하겠습니다."

메시지 교환 중 선박은 "OVER"을 말함으로서 응답을 요구해야 한다.

통신의 종료는 "OUT" 단어로 표현한다.

I 기출문제

01. Select a wrong explanation for proper use of VHF radio　　15년 2차

① When possible, the lowest transmitter power necessary for satisfactory communication should be used.
② Transmitting without correct identification should be avoided.
③ If communications on a channel are unsatisfactory indicate change of channel and do not await confirmation
④ Where the information isn't immediately available but soon will be, say "stand by"

해설 If communications on a channel are unsatisfactory indicate change of channel and await confirmation. : 채널에서의 소통이 불만족스럽다면, 채널의 변경을 지시하고 확인을 기다린다.

답 ❸

02. 다음은 VHF 통신기 운용 중 규율(Discipline)에 대한 내용이다. 옳은 것은 모두 몇 개인가?　　19년 3차

VHF equipment should be used correctly and in accordance with the Radio Regulations. The following in particular should be avoided :
Ⓐ calling on channel 16 for purposes other than distress, urgency and very brief safety communications when another channel is available.
Ⓑ communications related to safety and navigation on port operation channels.
Ⓒ non-essential transmissions, e.g. needless and superfluous signals and correspondence.
Ⓓ transmitting with correct identification;

① 4개　　　　　　　　② 3개
③ 2개　　　　　　　　④ 1개

해설 VHF장비는 올바르게 사용되어야 하고, 통신 규칙에 따라야 한다. 특히나 다음에 나오는 것들을 해서는 안 된다. (이 문제는 하지 말아야 할 행동을 골라야 한다.)
Ⓑ related → not related (관련이 없는 것)
Ⓓ with → without (올바른 확인 없는 전송)

답 ❸

기출문제

03. 다음 빈칸에 들어갈 말로 가장 적합한 것은? [18년 1차]

"Distress calls have absolute priority over all other communications. when hearing them, (   )."

① all other transmissions should cease and listen in
② a change of channel should be requested
③ further communications should be made
④ communications should be commenced on the chosen channel

해설 조난 통신은 다른 모든 통신에 앞선 우선권을 갖기 때문에 해당 통신을 들으면 모든 송신을 중단하고 청수를 유지해야한다.(all other transmissions should cease and listen in)

답 ①

04. 다음 밑줄 친 This가 설명하는 것으로 가장 옳은 것은? [22년 2차]

This is used for the exchange of data in ship to ship communications and also in communication with shore-based facilities. The purpose of This is to help identify vessels; assist in target tracking; simplify information exchange (eg. reduce verbal reporting); and provide additional information to assist situation awareness.

This may be used together with VHF voice communications.

① Maritime Safety Information (MSI)
② Digital Selective Calling (DSC)
③ Enhanced Group Calling (EGC)
④ Automatic Identification System (AIS)

해설 자동인식시스템(Automatic Identification System, AIS)에 대한 설명이다.

답 ④

05. 다음 중 VHF 통신에 있어 가장 옳지 않은 것은? [22년 일반직]

① Any distress call/message should be recorded in the ship's log and passed to the master.
② Distress calls/messages have absolute priority over all other communications. When receiving them all other transmissions should cease and a listening watch should be kept.
③ Instructions given on communication matters by shore station which authority was given should be obeyed.
④ When possible, the highest transmitter power necessary for satisfactory communication should be used.

해설 가능하면 만족스러운 통신을 위해 <u>최소한의(lowest)</u> 송신 출력이 사용되어야 한다.

답 ④

chapter 10 조난 통신의 예시

01 화재, 폭발

① 본선에/동력선 …호에 화재가 발생하였음.
② 갑판에/기관실에 화재가 발생하였음.
③ 위험화물에 화재가 발생하였나?
④ 폭발의 위험성이 있는가?
⑤ 본선은/동력선 …호는 조종불능 상태임.
⑥ 화재가 진압되고 있는가?
⑦ 네, 화재는 진압되고 있습니다.
⑧ 어떤 종류의 원조가 필요로 하는가?
⑨ 본선은/동력선 …호는 소화작업 원조/소화펌프/의료 원조/포말 소화기/이산화탄소 소화기/ 호흡보조기를 요구함.
⑩ 부상자에 대하여 보고하십시오.

02 침수

① 본선은/동력선 …은 수선 하부에서 물이 새고 있음.
② 어떤 종류의 원조가 필요한가?
③ 본선은/동력선 …은 펌프/잠수부/…를 요구함.
④ 본선은/동력선 …은 좌현/우현으로 위험한 횡경사가 되고 있음.
⑤ 침수는 진압되었음.
⑥ 본선은/동력선 …은 원조 없이 항진할 수 있음.
⑦ 본선은/동력선 …은 호송/예인선의 원조를 요구함.

01
Fire, Explosion

① I am/MV … **on fire.**
② Fire is **on** deck/in engine-room.
③ Are dangerous goods **on fire?**
④ Is there danger of explosion?
⑤ I am/MV … **not under command**.
⑥ Is the fire **under control**?
⑦ Yes, fire is **under control**.
⑧ What kind of assistance is required?
⑨ I require/MV … requires fire fighting assistance/fire pumps/medical assistance/foam extinguishers/CO_2 extinguishers/breathing apparatus.
⑩ Report injured persons.

02
Flooding

① I am/MV … is **flooding** below water line.
② What kind of assistance is required?
③ I require/MV … requires pumps/divers/….
④ I have/MV … has dangerous **list** to port/starboard.
⑤ Flooding is **under control**.
⑥ I/MV … can proceed without assistance.
⑦ I require/MV … requires escort/tug assistance/….

03
Collision

① I have/MV ⋯ has **collided with** MV ⋯/iceberg/unknown vessel/object/⋯.

② I have/MV ⋯ has **collided with** light vessel.

③ I have/MV ⋯ has damage above/below water line.

④ I/MV ⋯ can only **proceed at** slow speed.

⑤ What kind of assistance is required?

04
Grounding

① I am/MV ⋯ **aground**.
② What part of your vessel is **aground**?
③ **Aground** forward/amidships/aft/full length.
④ Warning. Uncharted rocks in position ⋯.
⑤ I/MV ⋯ will **jettison** cargo to refloat.
⑥ Warning! Do not **jettison** IMO-Class cargo!
⑦ When do you/does MV ⋯ expect to **refloat**?
⑧ I expect/MV ⋯ expects to refloat at 00 UTC.
⑨ I expect/MV ⋯ expects to **refloat** with tug assistance.
⑩ I expect/MV ⋯ expects to **refloat** when tide rises/when weather improves/when draft decreases.
⑪ Can you/Can MV ⋯ **beach**?
⑫ I/MV ⋯ can/will **beach** in position ⋯.

---

03 충돌

① 본선은/동력선 ⋯호는 동력선⋯와/빙산과/미상의 선박과/물체와/⋯와 충돌하였음.
② 본선은/동력선 ⋯호는 등선과 충돌하였음.
③ 본선은/동력선 ⋯호는 수선 상부/하부에 손상을 입었음.
④ 본선은/동력선 ⋯호는 오직 저속으로만 항진할 수 있음.
⑤ 어떤 종류의 원조가 필요한가?

04 좌초

① 본선은/동력선 ⋯호는 좌초됨.
② 귀선의 어느 부분이 좌초되었나?
③ 선수 부분/선체 중앙 부분/선미 부분/선체 전체가 좌초되었음.
④ 경고. 해도에 기재되어 있지 않은 암초가 ⋯위치에 있음.
⑤ 본선은/동력선 ⋯호는 재부양시키기 위해 화물을 투하할 것임.
⑥ 경고! IMO-class의 화물을 투하하지 마시오!
⑦ 언제 귀선이/동력선 ⋯호가 재부양할 것으로 예상되는가?
⑧ 본선은/동력선 ⋯호는 세계협정시 기준 00시에 재부양할 것으로 예상됨.
⑨ 본선은/동력선 ⋯호는 예인선의 원조와 함께 재부양할 것으로 예상됨.
⑩ 본선은/동력선 ⋯호는 조석이 상승할 때/날씨가 좋아질 때/흘수가 감소할 때 재부양할 것으로 예상됨.
⑪ 귀선은/동력선 ⋯호는 좌안할 수 있겠는가?
⑫ 본선은/동력선 ⋯호는 ⋯위치에서 좌안할 수 있음./좌안할 것임.

05 횡경사, 전복의 위험

① 본선은/동력선 …호는 좌현/우현으로 위험한 횡경사가 되었음.
② 본선은/동력선 …호는 횡경사를 막기 위하여 화물을/연료를 옮길 것임.
③ 본선은/동력선 …호는 횡경사를 막기 위하여 화물을 투하할 것임.
④ 본선은/동력선 …호는 전복의 위험이 있음.

06 침몰

① 본선은/동력선 …호는 충돌/좌초/침수/폭발/…한 이후에 침몰 중임.
② 본선은/동력선 …호는 귀선에게 원조를 제공하기 위해 항진 중임.
③ 조난 위치까지의 도착 예정 시간은 00시 이내/세계 협정시 기준 00시일 것임.

07 파손과 표류

① 본선은/동력선 …호는 조종이 불능함.
② 본선은/동력선 …호는 표류 중임. /…방향으로 00노트로 표류 중임.

08 무장 공격/해적

① 본선은/동력선 …호는 해적의 공격을 받고 있음.
② 어떤 종류의 원조가 필요한가?
③ 본선은/동력선 …호는 의료/항해상/군사적/예인선/… 의 원조를 요구한다.
④ 귀선은/동력선 …호는 항진할 수 있는가?
⑤ 예, 본선은/동력선 …호는 항진할 수 있습니다.

05
List, Danger of capsizing

① I have/MV … has dangerous **list** to port/starboard.

② I/MV … will transfer cargo/bunkers to stop **listing**.

③ I/MV … will jettison cargo to stop **listing**.

④ I am/MV … in danger of **capsizing**.

06
Sinking

① I am/MV … sinking after collision/grounding/flooding/explosion/….

② I am/MV … proceeding to your assistance.

③ ETA **at** distress position within 00 hours/at 00 UTC.

07
Disabled and Adrift

① I am/MV … **not under command**
② I am/MV **adrift/drifting** at 00knots to ….

08
Armed attack/Piracy

① I am/MV … **under attack** by pirates.

② What kind of assistance is required?
③ I require/MV … requires medical/navigational/military/tug/… assistance.

④ Can you/Can MV … proceed?

⑤ Yes, I/MV … can proceed.

09
Undesignated distress

① I have/MV ⋯ has problems with cargo/engine(s)/navigation/⋯.

② I require/MV ⋯ requires ⋯.

10
Abandoning vessel

① I/Crew of MV ⋯ must **abandon** vessel after explosion/collision/grounding/flooding/piracy/armed attack/⋯.

11
Person Overboard

① I have/MV ⋯ has lost persons **overboard** in position ⋯.

② Assist with search in vicinity of position ⋯.

③ All vessels in vicinity of position ⋯ **keep a sharp lookout** and report to ⋯.

④ I am/MV ⋯ is searching in vicinity of position ⋯.

⑤ Aircraft ETA at 00 UTC/within 0 hours to assist in search.

⑥ What is the result of search?
⑦ The result of search is negative.
⑧ I/MV ⋯ **located/picked up** person(s) in position ⋯.

⑨ Person **picked up** is crew member/passenger of MV ⋯.
⑩ What is condition of person(s)?

---

09 명시되지 않은 조난

① 본선은/동력선 ⋯호는 화물에/기관에/항해상에/ ⋯에 문제가 있음.
② 본선은/동력선 ⋯호는 ⋯을 요구한다.

10 퇴선

① 본선/동력선 ⋯의 승무원은 폭발/충돌/좌초/침수/해적/무장 공격/⋯ 이후 퇴선 해야 함.

11 사람의 선외 추락

① 본선은/동력선 ⋯호는 ⋯위치에서 사람이 선외로 실종되었음.
② ⋯위치 부근에서 수색을 원조하시오.
③ ⋯위치 부근의 모든 선박들은 엄중한 견시를 유지하고 ⋯에 보고하시오.
④ 본선은/동력선 ⋯호는 ⋯위치 부근에서 수색 중임.
⑤ 수색을 돕기 위한 항공기의 도착 예정시간은 세계 협정시 기준 00시/0시간 이내임.
⑥ 수색의 결과는 어떠한가?
⑦ 수색의 결과는 부정적임.
⑧ 본선은/동력선 ⋯호는 ⋯위치에서 사람들의 위치를 확인/사람들은 인양하였음.
⑨ 인양된 사람은 동력선 ⋯호의 승무원/여객임.
⑩ 사람들의 상태는 어떠한가?

기출문제

01. 아래 문장에서 빈칸에 들어갈 말로 가장 적절한 것은? `15년 일반직`

> "본선은 선박을 재부상 시키기 위해 화물을 투하할 것이다."
> I will (　　) cargo to refloat.

① overboard　　　　② let go
③ throw　　　　　　④ jettison

해설 본선의 조종을 용이하게 하기 위하여 또는 안정성을 확보하기 위해 화물을 고의적으로 투하하는 것을 jettison이라 한다. throw, let go, overboard 등도 투하의 의미를 지니지만 특정 목적을 위해 화물 투하를 하는 jettison과는 구별된다.

답 ④

02. 'Keep a sharp (　　) – 경계를 철저히 하라.' 빈칸에 알맞은 말은? `16년 일반직`

① steering　　　　　② course
③ lookout　　　　　 ④ order

해설 경계(견시)를 철저히 하다. : Keep a sharp lookout

답 ③

03. 다음 중 빈칸에 들어갈 단어로 가장 옳은 것은? `16년 2차`

> The last order that a captain has to give to his men in the perils of the sea is (　　　　).

① Abandon ship!　　　② All hands on deck!
③ All aboard!　　　　 ④ As you are!

해설 해상의 위험한 상황에서 선장이 그의 선원들에게 내리는 최후의 명령은 퇴선(abandon ship)이다.

답 ①

기출문제

04. VTS 관제구역내에서 KOREA호가 상선과 충돌한 상황이다. 다음 빈칸에 들어갈 말로 가장 적절한 것은?

_{15년 일반직}

> K : VTS. This is KOREA. I have (   ) a vessel.
> V : KOREA. This is VTS. What is the position of collision?
> K : The position of collision is 00 degrees and 00 miles from 00.
> V : How is damage of collision?
> K : I am investigating damage of collision.

① collide
② collided with
③ against
④ collocate with

해설 '~과 충돌하다'라는 표현은 collide 뒤에 with라는 전치사가 붙는다.

답 ❷

05. 다음 중 빈칸에 들어갈 단어로 가장 옳은 것은?

_{18년 2차}

> I have lost a man overboard, please help (   ).

① to emergency anchorage
② with search and rescue
③ I am sinking
④ medical assistance

해설 익수자가 발생했다. 수색구조(search and rescue)를 요청함.

답 ❷

chapter 11 On-Board Communication Phrases

01 조종

① 선회권의 직경은 얼마인가?
② 긴급 정지 시 종거와 횡거는 얼마인가?
③ 견시원을 대기시키시오.
④ 단음/장음 00회를 울리시오.
⑤ 프로펠러의 선회 효과는 아주 강합니까?
⑥ 침로를 따라 항해할 때, 키를 최대 전타한다. 최대 전타를 했을 때부터 침로가 90° 회두했을 때까지의 원침로에서 전진한 거리를 선회종거라 한다.
⑦ 침로를 따라 항해할 때, 키를 최대 전타한다. 최대 전타를 했을 때부터 침로가 90° 회두했을 때까지의 원침로에서 직각 방향으로 전진한 거리를 선회횡거라 한다.
⑧ 선박의 복원성이란, 약간 기울었을 때 다시 똑바로 되돌아오려고 하는 선박의 능력을 의미한다.

01 Manoeuvring

① What is the **diameter** of the **turning circle**?
② What is the **advance** and **transfer** distance in a crash-stop?
③ Stand by lookout
④ **Give** 00 short/prolonged blast(s) (on the whistle).
⑤ Is the turning effect of the propeller very strong?
⑥ When heading on a course, you put your rudder hard over. The distance traveled in the direction of the original course from when you put your rudder over until your heading differs by 90° is known as **advance**.
⑦ When heading on a course, you put your rudder hard over. The distance traveled in the right-angled direction of the original course from when you put your rudder over until your heading differs by 90° is known as **transfer**.
⑧ **Ship Stability** can be defined as the ability of the ship to return to the upright when slightly inclined.

기출문제

01. 다음 중 빈칸에 들어갈 단어로 가장 옳은 것은? 〔16년 2차〕

What is the (   ) of turning circle of your ship?

① diameter ② length
③ distance ④ height

해설 선회권(turning circle)의 기준은 직경(diameter)이다.

답 ❶

02. 다음 설명에 가장 적합한 것은 무엇인가? 〔17년 2차〕

This is the distance traveled in the direction of the original course by midship point of a ship from the position at which the rudder order is given to the position at which the heading has changed 90degrees from the original course.

① Pivot point ② Advance
③ Transfer ④ Kick

해설 선박이 전타 한 시점부터 선수 방위가 원침로 상에서 90도 만큼 이로한 위치에서 측정 했을 때, 선박이 원침로 방향(in the direction of the original course)으로 이동한 거리는 종거(Advance)이다.
원침로 방향에서 직각방향으로(in the right angle/perpendicular direction of the original course) 이동한 거리는 횡거(Transfer)이다.

답 ❷

03. 다음 보기의 괄호 안에 들어갈 순서로 가장 정확한 것은 무엇인가? 〔18년 3차〕

가. (   ) can be defined as the ability of the ship to return to the upright when slightly inclined.

나. When heading on a course, you put your rudder hard over. The distance traveled in the direction of the original course from when you put your rudder over until your heading differs by 90° is known as : (   )

① Ship capability - Transfer
② Ship capability - Advance
③ Ship stability - Transfer
④ Ship stability - Advance

해설 가. 선박이 약간 기울었을때 원래대로 돌아가려는 힘인 **복원력(Ship stability)**에 대한 설명이다.
나. **종거(Advance)**에 대한 설명이다.

답 ❹

기출문제

04. 다음 〈보기〉 중 빈 칸에 들어갈 용어로 가장 옳게 짝지어진 것은? `22년 일반직`

- (㉠) can be defined as the ability of the ship to return to the upright when slightly inclined.
- When heading on a course, you put your rudder hard over. (㉡) is the distance traveled by the ship's centre of gravity in a direction perpendicular to the ship's initial course. It is usually quoted for a 90° change of heading.

	㉠	㉡
①	Ship stability	Transfer
②	Ship stability	Advance
③	Ship capability	Transfer
④	Ship capability	Advance

해설 - ㉠ 선박 복원성(Ship stability)은 선박이 약간 기울었을 때 원래대로 돌아오려는 능력으로 정의 된다.
- 어느 침로로 항해하던 선박이 전타하였다. ㉡ 횡거(transfer)는 선박의 무게 중심점이 시작 침로(initial course)에서 직각 방향으로 이동한 거리이다. 이것은 보통 선수방위가 90도 바뀌었을 때 이용된다.

답 ①

02
Radar

① Is the radar **operational?**
② Does the radar have any **blind sectors?**
③ Change the radar to 00miles **range scale**
④ I have **located** you on my radar screen.

---

02 레이더

① 레이더는 작동 가능한가?
② 레이더에 맹목구간이 있는가?
③ 레이더를 00마일 레인지 스케일로 바꾸시오.
④ 본선의 레이더 스크린에 귀선을 탐지했다.

| 기출문제

05. 아래 문장에서 빈칸에 들어갈 IMO 표준해사통신영어로 가장 적절한 것은? [15년 일반직]

"본선 레이더 스크린에 귀선을 탐지했다."
I have (   ) you on my radar screen.

① contacting   ② touched
③ recognizing   ④ located

해설 locate은 물표나 선박을 발견(탐지)했다는 의미를 갖는다.

답 ❹

03 흘수

① 귀선의 현재 최대 흘수는 얼마인가?
② 귀선의 air draft는 얼마인가?
③ 건현이란 상갑판에서부터 선측에 새겨져 있는 원판의 중심(하기만 재 흘수선이 표시되어 있다.)까지의 수직 길이를 말한다.
④ 선체 중앙부 기준으로 측정하여 수선에서부터 상갑판까지를 잰 길이를 건현이라 한다.

03 Draft

① What is your present maximum **draft?**
② What is your **air draft?**
③ **Freeboard** is vertical distance from the uppermost deck to the center of the disc which is marked on the vessel's sides and which indicates the position of the **load water line in summer.**
④ The distance measured amidships from the water line to the main deck of the vessel is **freeboard.**

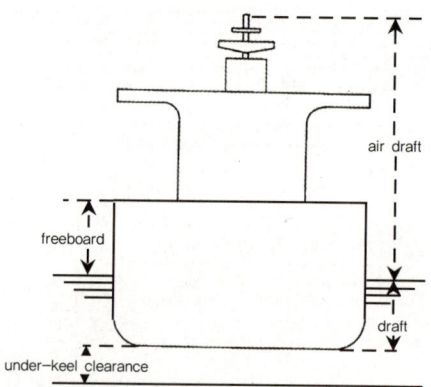

▌기출문제

06. 다음 빈칸에 들어갈 말로 가장 옳은 것은?　　　　　　　　　　　19년 3차

The distance measured amidships from the water line to the main deck of the vessel is (　　).

① draft　　② air draft　　③ gunwale　　④ freeboard

해설 선체 중앙부 기준으로 측정하여 수선에서부터 상갑판까지를 잰 길이를 건현(freeboard)이라 한다.

답 ④

07. 다음 중 순서에 맞게 빈칸에 들어갈 단어로 가장 옳은 것은?　　　　16년 2차

(　　) is vertical distance from the uppermost deck to the center of the disc which is marked on the vessel's sides and which indicates the position of the load water line in (　　).

① Draft - summer
② Freeboard - summer
③ Air draft - draft
④ Air draft - winter

해설 건현(Freeboard)이란 상갑판에서부터 선측 중심부에 기재되어 있는 하기만재흘수선(load water line in summer)까지의 수직 길이를 말한다.

답 ②

기출문제

08. SMCP (표준해사통신영어) "What is your <u>freeboard?</u>"에서 밑줄 친 부분의 의미는?

`15년 일반직`

① The height from load line mark to upper deck
② The height from water surface to the most high point of bulwark
③ The height from water surface to upper deck at a midship.
④ The height from water surface to the highest point of upper deck

[해설] 건현은 두 가지 뜻을 가지고 있다. 첫 번째, 상갑판에서부터 하기 만재흘수선까지, 두 번째, 상갑판에서 수면까지이다. ③의 내용은 선체 중앙에서 측정한 수면에서부터 상갑판까지의 수직 상 높이를 의미한다.

답 ③

09. Choose the correct one for the blank.

`18년 1차`

> In Standard Maritime Navigation Vocabulary, the height of a vessel is defined as the height of highest point of vessel's structure (   ).

① above waterline
② under masthead
③ over the keel
④ beyond deckline

[해설] 해사영어에서, 선박의 높이란 <u>수선위에서</u>(above waterline) 선박의 가장 윗부분까지 즉 Air draft를 의미한다.

답 ①

04
Anchoring 작업 시 질문 표현

① 체인이 어느 정도 풀려 나갔는가?
② 체인의 방향이 어떠한가?
③ 체인의 장력이 어떠한가?
④ 체인에 중량이 어느 정도 걸렸는가?
⑤ 닻에 파주력이 있는가?
⑥ 닻이 해저에 완전히 박혔는가?
⑦ 닻줄은 몇 샤클이나 남아 있는가?

① How much cable is **out?**
② How is the cable **leading?**
③ How is the cable **growing?**
④ How much weight is on the cable?
⑤ Is the anchor **holding?**
⑥ Is she **brought up?**
⑦ How many shackles are **left (=to come in)?**

기출문제

10. 아래 문장에서 표준해사통신용어(Standard Marine Communication Phrases) 상 빈 칸에 들어갈 말로 가장 옳은 것은? 〔19년 1차〕

> "닻줄의 장력은 어떠한가?"
> "How is the cable (   )?"

① leading   ② going
③ heaving   ④ growing

해설 장력을 표현 할 때는 growing을 사용한다.

답 ❹

11. 다음 중 빈칸에 공통으로 들어갈 단어로 가장 옳은 것은? 〔17년 1차〕

> Captain : How many shackles are (   )?
> Chief officer : Three shackles are (   ) in the water, sir

① heave to   ② turning
③ left   ④ inside

해설 선장 : 감아올릴 것이 몇 샤클 정도 남았는가(left)?
일항사 : 수면에 3샤클 정도 남았습니다(left).

답 ❸

기출문제

12. 표준해사통신영어(Standard Marine Communication Phrases)상 빈칸에 들어갈 단어로 가장 옳은 것은?　20년 1차

"How is the cable (　　)?"
"The cable is coming tight."

① weighing　　② growing
③ moving　　　④ leading

해설　"닻줄의 장력(growing)이 어떠한가?"
"닻줄은 팽팽해지고 있습니다."

답 ❷

05
투묘와 양묘의 과정

투묘
① 투묘를 위해 닻을 준비함.
② 닻을 Walk out 시킴
③ 닻을 투묘함
④ 닻이 완전히 박힘

양묘
① 닻을 양묘함
② Short stay
③ 닻이 묘쇄공에서 해저로 수직 상태가 됨
④ 닻이 해저를 벗어남
⑤ 닻을 적재함.

Let go anchor
① Stand by anchor for letting go
② Walk out the anchor
③ Let go anchor
④ Brought up anchor

Heave up anchor
① Heave up anchor
② Short stay
③ Up and down anchor
④ Anchor aweigh
⑤ The anchor is secured

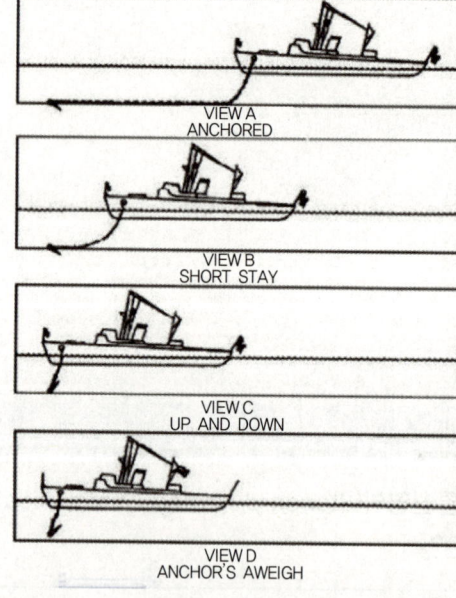

VIEW A ANCHORED
VIEW B SHORT STAY
VIEW C UP AND DOWN
VIEW D ANCHOR'S AWEIGH

MNV70193

기출문제

13. What is mean by the term "Anchor aweigh"? 　　15년 2차

① Anchor is clear of the bottom.
② Anchor is up anchor with short stay.
③ Brought up anchor with short stay.
④ Clearing the foul.

[해설] Anchor aweigh란, 닻이 해저에서 벗어난 상태를 의미한다.

답 ❶

14. 다음 보기 중 투묘부터 양묘까지의 작업 순서로 가장 알맞은 것은? 　　18년 3차

가. Heave up port anchor(cable).
나. Let go port anchor.
다. Walk out the port anchor.
라. The port anchor is secured.

① 라 - 가 - 나 - 다　　② 나 - 다 - 가 - 라
③ 가 - 나 - 다 - 라　　④ 다 - 나 - 가 - 라

[해설] 다. 좌현 묘쇄를 내려 투묘할 준비를 완료하시오.
　　 나. 좌현 묘쇄를 투묘하시오.
　　 가. 좌현 묘쇄를 감아올리시오.
　　 라. 좌현 묘쇄가 격납되었습니다.

답 ❹

06
Anchoring 용어

① Cock bill state : 묘쇄를 준비하고 투묘할 준비를 한 상태이다.
② Walk out : 호스 파이프에서 벗어 날 때까지 닻을 풀어 내리기 위해 양묘기를 역전시키고 투묘 준비 상태로 하는 것이다.
③ Walk back : 닻줄을 늦춰주기 위하여 양묘기를 역전시키는 것이다.
④ Dragging(주묘) : 닻이 선체의 이동을 더 이상 저지하지 못하여 어쩔 수 없이 해저를 따라 끌리고 있는 상태
⑤ Dredging : 선체의 운동을 제어하기 위하여 해저를 따라서 닻을 이동시키는 것

① A cock bill state : **The situation** standing by anchor and **about to let go anchor**.
② Walk out : **To reverse** the action of a windlass to lower the anchor until it is clear of the hawse pipe and **ready for dropping.**
③ Walk back : To reverse the windlass **to ease** the cable.
④ Dragging : Moving of an anchor over the sea bottom **involuntarily** because it is no longer preventing the movement of the vessel.
⑤ Dredging : Moving of an anchor over the sea bottom **to control** the movement of the vessel.

▌기출문제

15. 다음 빈칸에 들어갈 말로 가장 적절한 것은? `16년 일반직`

A movement of an anchor over sea bottom to control the movement of the vessel is called (　　　).

① dragging of anchor　　② dredging of anchor
③ sliding of anchor　　④ movement of anchor

해설 선체의 운동을 제어하기 위하여(to control the movement of the vessel) 해저를 따라서 닻을 이동시키는 것을 Dredging이라 한다.

답 ❷

16. 다음 「IMO SMCP(표준해사통신언어)」의 표현 중 옳지 않은 것은? `18년 일반직`

① 귀선의 위치에서의 기상 상태는 어떠한가? : What is the weather situation in your position?
② 귀선은 항해중인가? : Are you underway?
③ 귀선은 주묘중인가? : Are you dredging anchor?
④ 귀선은 항로를 가로막고 있다. : You are obstructing the fairway.

해설 주묘는 dredging이 아니라 <u>dragging</u>이다.

07
투묘 작업 예문

① **Stand by** port/starboard/both anchor(s) for letting go.

② **Walk out** the anchor(s).

③ We are going to anchorage.

④ We will **let go** port/starboard/both anchor(s).

⑤ **Put** 00shackles in the water/in the pipe/on deck.

⑥ **Walk back** port/starboard/both anchor(s) one/one and a half shackle(s).

⑦ We will **let go** port/starboard/both anchor(s) 00shackle(s) and **dredge** it/them.

⑧ Let go port/starboard/both anchor(s).

⑨ **Slack out** the cable(s).

⑩ **Check** the cable(s).

⑪ **Hold on** the port/the starboard/both cable(s).

⑫ How is the cable **leading?**
 - The cable is leading ahead/astern.
 - The cable is leading to port/to starboard.
 - The cable is leading round the bow.
 - The cable is leading up and down.

⑬ How is the cable **growing?**
 - The cable is slack.
 - The cable is tight.
 - The cable is coming tight.

⑭ Is/are the anchor(s) **holding?**
 - Yes, the anchor(s) is/are holding.
 - No, the anchor(s) is/are not holding.

⑮ Is she **brought up?**

⑯ **Switch on** the anchor light.

⑰ **Hoist** the anchor ball.

⑱ **Check** the anchor position by bearing

① 좌현/우현/양현 묘를 투묘할 준비를 하시오.
② 닻을 풀어서 투묘 준비 상태로 하시오.
③ 본선은 투묘지로 가고 있습니다.
④ 본선은 좌현/우현/양현 묘를 투묘할 것입니다.
⑤ 닻줄을 00샤클만큼 수면/묘쇄공/갑판 상까지 풀어 주시오.
⑥ 좌현/우현/양현 닻줄을 1/1.5샤클까지 양묘기를 역전시켜 풀어 주시오.
⑦ 본선은 좌현/우현/양현 닻을 00절로 투묘하고 그것(들)을 끌겠습니다.
⑧ 좌현/우현/양현 닻을 투묘하시오.
⑨ 닻줄을 늦추어 주시오.
⑩ 닻줄을 억제하시오.
⑪ 좌현/우현/양현 닻줄을 멈춘 채로 있으시오.
⑫ 닻줄의 방향은 어떠한가?
 - 닻줄의 방향은 정선수/정선미 입니다.
 - 닻줄의 방향은 좌현/우현입니다.
 - 닻줄의 방향은 선수를 감아 돌았습니다.
 - 닻줄의 방향은 수직입니다.
⑬ 닻줄의 장력은 어떠한가?
 - 닻줄은 느슨합니다.
 - 닻줄은 팽팽합니다.
 - 닻줄은 팽팽해지고 있습니다.
⑭ 닻/양현 닻은 파주력이 있는가?
 - 예, 파주력이 있습니다.
 - 아니오, 파주력이 없습니다.
⑮ 닻이 해저에 완전히 박혔는가?
⑯ 정박등을 켜시오.
⑰ 흑구를 게양하시오.
⑱ 방위를 측정하여 투묘 위치를 점검하시오.

⑲ 투묘 위치는 …를 향하여 방위 00도, 거리 00킬로미터/해리입니다.

⑳ 매 00분마다 묘박 위치를 점검하시오.

⑲ The anchor position is bearing 00 degrees, distance 00 kilometers/nautical miles to….

⑳ **Check** the anchor position every 00 minutes.

08
양묘 작업 예문

① 닻줄은 몇 샤클 풀려나가 있는가?
  - 00 샤클 풀려나가 있습니다.
② 닻을 감아올릴 준비를 하십시오.
③ 양묘기의 기어를 연결하시오.
  - 양묘기의 기어가 연결되어 있습니다.
④ 좌현/우현/양현 닻줄을 감아올리시오.
⑤ 닻줄에 중량이 얼마나 걸려 있는가?
  - 닻줄에 중량이 많이/매우 많이 걸려 있습니다.
  - 닻줄에 중량이 걸려 있지 않습니다.
⑥ 감아들이기를 멈추시오.
⑦ 더 감아 들여야 할 닻줄은 몇 샤클이나 남았는가?
  - 00샤클 정도 남아 있습니다.
⑧ 주의! 닻줄이 꼬였습니다.
⑨ 닻줄은 엉켜 있지 않습니다.
⑩ 닻은 수면 위로 떠올랐습니다./묘쇄공 안으로 들어왔습니다./엉켜 있습니다./완전히 격납되었습니다.

① How much cable is **out?**
  - 00shackles are out.
② Stand by for **heaving up.**
③ **Put the windlass in gear.**
  - The **windlass is in gear.**
④ **Heave up** port/starboard/both cable(s).
⑤ How much weight is on the cable?
  - Much/Too much weight is on the cable.
  - No weight is on the cable.
⑥ Stop heaving.
⑦ How many shackles are **left(to come in)?**
  - 00shackles are left(to come in).
⑧ Attention! Turn **in** cable(s).
⑨ The cables are **clear.**
⑩ The anchor(s) is/are clear of the water/home/fouled/secured.

기출문제

17. 다음 중 빈칸에 들어갈 단어를 가장 옳게 나열한 것은?   22년 2차

How much cable is (㉠)?
닻줄은 몇 절 풀려나가 있는가?
The windlass is (㉡) gear.
양묘기의 기어가 연결되었음.
Attention! Turn (㉢) cable.
주의하시오! 닻줄이 꼬였음.
How much weight is (㉣) the cable?
닻줄에 중량이 얼마나 걸려있는가?

	㉠	㉡	㉢	㉣
①	in	on	in	of
②	in	in	out	on
③	out	on	on	of
④	out	in	in	on

해설
㉠ How much cable is <u>out</u>?
㉡ The windlass is <u>in</u> gear.
㉢ Attention! Turn <u>in</u> cable.
㉣ How much weight is <u>on</u> the cable?

답 ④

09
접안/이안 표현

① 부두에 접근했을 때, 굵은 밧줄을 보내기 위해 부두에 먼저 heaving line을 던진다.

② 부두에서 떠날 준비를 하기 위해 중요한 줄만 남겨두고, 모든 줄을 선내로 감아들이는 행위를 single up이라 한다.

③ fairleader란, 선박이 접안할 때 줄을 인도해주는 역할을 하는 선박의 장치이다.

① Approaching a dock, you will throw **heaving line** first to pier to send a hawser.

② The instruction to haul or pull on board all but essential lines mentioned, so that the ship is ready to leave the quay or berth is **single up.**

③ **Fair leader** is the fitting on the deck of a ship which guides the ropes when the ship is being moored.

기출문제

18. Choose the best one for the blank. [14년 2차]

Approaching a dock, you will throw (　　) first to pier to send a hawser.

① heaving line　　② towing line
③ mooring line　　④ spring line

해설　heaving line은 무거운 계선줄을 부두에 연결하기 전에 던져주는 가벼운 줄이다.

답 ❶

19. 다음 밑줄에 들어갈 말은? [13년 2차]

The instruction to haul or pull on board all but essential lines mentioned, so that the ship is ready to leave the quay or berth is _____.

① make fast　　② let go
③ single up　　④ heave away

해설　선박이 부두를 떠날 준비를 하도록 언급 되는 핵심 줄만을 남기고 모두 선내로 줄을 끌어 올리라는 명령은 single up이다.

답 ❸

기출문제

20. 다음 괄호 안에 들어갈 알맞은 말의 순서로 가장 옳게 연결된 것은 무엇인가? `18년 3차`

> 가. The instruction to haul or pull on board all but essential lines mentioned, so that the ship is ready to leave the quay or berth is (　　　).
> 나. In Standard Marine Navigational Vocabulary, the height of a vessel is defined as the height of highest point of vessel's structure (　　　).

① single up - over the keel
② let go - over the keel
③ make fast - above waterline
④ single up - above waterline

해설　가. singe up
　　　　나. above waterline

답 ❹

21. 다음 박스의 질문에 가장 적절한 것은? `16년 2차`

> What is the fitting on the deck of a ship which guides the ropes when the ship is being moored?

① Fairway　　　　　② Bitt
③ Fair leader　　　　④ Bollard

해설 선박이 계류될 때 로프가 잘 빠져나가도록(guide) 해주는 갑판의 설비(fitting)는 <u>Fair leader</u>이다.

답 ❸

10
Berthing(접안) 작업 예문

① 선수에, 선미에 방현재를 준비하십시오.
② 본선은 좌현/우현을 안벽에 대고 접안할 것입니다.
③ 본선은 접안할 것입니다.
④ 선수줄/선미줄/옆줄을 내어주시오.
⑤ 선수, 선미의 스프링라인 00줄을 내어주시오.
⑥ 히빙 라인을 육상으로 보내시오.
⑦ 중앙부 도삭기를 사용하시오.
⑧ 좌현 선미/우현 선미 도삭기를 사용하시오.
⑨ …줄을 계속 감으시오.
⑩ …줄을 팽팽하게 유지하시오.
⑪ … 줄의 늘어짐을 팽팽하게 하시오.
⑫ … 줄을 계속 늦추어 주시오.
⑬ … 줄을 억제하시오.
⑭ … 줄을 계속 잡고 있으시오.
⑮ 계속 감아들이시오.
⑯ 감아들이기를 멈추시오.
⑰ 천천히 감아들이시오.
⑱ 안벽 쪽으로 끌어당기시오.
⑲ 선수와 선미를 잡아매시오.
⑳ 조종부서를 종료합니다.

① Have **fenders** ready fore and aft.
② We will **berth** port/starboard side **alongside.**
③ We will moor **alongside.**
④ **Send out** the head/stern/breast line.
⑤ **Send out** the 00 spring(s) forward/aft.
⑥ Send the heaving line ashore.
⑦ Use the centre lead/panama lead/bow lead.
⑧ Use the port quarter/starboard quarter lead.
⑨ **Heave on** the … line.
⑩ Keep the … line tight.
⑪ **Pick up the slack** on the … line.
⑫ **Slack** away … line.
⑬ **Check** the … line.
⑭ **Hold on** the … line.
⑮ Heave away.
⑯ Stop heaving.
⑰ Heave **in easy.**
⑱ Heave alongside.
⑲ **Make fast** fore and aft.
⑳ Finished with manoeuvring stations.

11
Unberthing(이안) 작업 예문

① 기관 사용 준비 하십시오.
② 귀선은 항해를 할 준비가 되었는가?
③ (계류줄을) 풀어줄 준비를 하시오.
④ … 줄을 싱글업 하시오.
⑤ 선수/선미 스프링을 풀어주시오.
⑥ 조종부시를 종료함.

① Stand by Engine(s).
② Are you ready to get underway?
③ Stand by for letting go.
④ Single up the … lines.
⑤ Let go the fore/aft spring.
⑥ Finished with manoeuvring stations.

chapter 12 / Log Book 항해일지

01
항해일지의 종류(Kinds of Log Book)

Log Book은 선박이 항해 중 선박의 위치나 상태 및 모든 사항을 기록하는 선내 기록물을 말한다. 선박에서 통상 언급하는 Log Book이란 Deck Log Book을 말한다. 항해일지의 종류는 다음과 같다.

① Deck Log Book : 항해 및 정박 당직 중에 일어난 모든 사항을 기록한다.
② Engine Log Book : 기관 당직 중에 일어난 모든 사항을 기록한다.
③ Ship's Log Book : 일등항해사가 Deck Log Book의 주요 내용을 정리 기록하는 일지였으나 번거로움으로 Deck Log Book과 통합하여 작성한다.
④ Abstract Log Book : 항차별 중요 사항(running hour, average speed, average RPM, consumption quantity of F.O, D.O etc.)을 요약한다.
⑤ Official Log Book : 선박등록국의 법령에 의해 규정된 기재사항을 기록한다.

02
항해일지 작성 시 주의 사항

① 볼펜이나 잉크로 기록
② 지우지 말 것, 잘못 적은 경우 잘못된 부분을 **한 줄로 긋고 옆에 다시 적고 서명한다.**
③ 간결하고 명료하게 기록
④ 주의를 가지고 기록
⑤ 과거형으로 기록
⑥ 중요기록의 누락이 없도록 기록

기출문제

01. 다음 중 항해일지 작성 시 오기가 발생한 경우에 수정하는 방법으로 가장 옳은 것은?

20년 1차

① Remove this page of the log book and rewrite all entries on a clean page.
② Blot out the error completely and rewrite the entry correctly.
③ Cross out the error with a single line and rewrite the entries correctly.
④ Carefully and neatly erase the entry and rewrite it correctly.

해설 항해일지 작성 시 오기가 발생한 경우, 해당 부분을 지우면(Remove, Blot out, erase 등) 안 된다. 해당 오기 부분 중앙을 한 줄로 긋고 수정내용을 옆에 기록해야 한다.

답 ③

03
출, 입항 기사

① All crew returned aboard from shore leave and all shore people **left her**.
② Finished lashing, all **longshoremen disembarked**.
③ **Inspected** all deck lashing & hull opening.
④ **Secured** all derrick booms & other fittings.
⑤ **Filled up** all ballast tanks with seawater.
⑥ Tested steering gear, whistle, means of communications. All in good order. Synchronized bridge & E/R clocks.
⑦ **Singled up** fore & aft, prepared for sea.
⑧ **Inspected** all parts of the ship in search of any **contraband** & **stowaway** and found none.
⑨ Stand by for leaving port.
⑩ **Stationed** for entering port, called master to bridge.
⑪ Harbour Pilot, Capt, Kim **on board**.
⑫ Last line to pier **let go/cast off**.
⑬ **Took** a tug.
⑭ **Commenced** unmooring from buoy.
⑮ Used engine var'ly as per master's order.
⑯ Anchor up/up anchor and **stowed** it.
⑰ Passed B.W.E on her port bow.
⑱ Pilot away. Master conning vessel.
⑲ Clear of harbour, **R/up Eng**. S/CO on 160°.
⑳ Approaching Busan, S.B.E and slowed down.
㉑ **Brought up** anchor with 3 shackles of port cable in water.

① 전 승무원이 상륙에서 귀선하였고 육상인원이 하선하였습니다.
② 고박작업을 마치고, 모든 하역인부가 하선하였습니다.
③ 갑판 고박상태와 선체 개구부를 모두 점검하였습니다.
④ 모든 데릭 붐과 기타 속구를 고박하였습니다.
⑤ 밸러스트 탱크를 해수로 채웠습니다.
⑥ 조타장치, 기적신호 장치, 통신수단을 모두 시험하였습니다. 모두 양호합니다. 선교와 기관실의 시계를 일치시켰습니다.
⑦ 선수미에 계류줄을 하나씩만 남기고 거두어 들였으며 출항 준비를 하였습니다.
⑧ 밀수품과 밀항자를 수색하였으나, 아무것도 발견하지 못했습니다.
⑨ 출항부서 배치하였습니다.
⑩ 입항부서 배치하였습니다. 선교로 선장을 호출하였습니다.
⑪ 도선사 김 선장님 승선하였습니다.
⑫ 부두의 마지막 계류줄을 풀어 회수하였습니다.
⑬ 예인선 착선하였습니다.
⑭ 부표에서 계류줄을 풀기 시작하였습니다.
⑮ 선장의 지시에 따라 엔진을 수시로 사용하였습니다.
⑯ 닻이 수면상으로 올라왔고 격납하였습니다.
⑰ 방파제 입구를 좌현 선수로 지났습니다.
⑱ 도선사가 하선하였습니다. 선장이 조선합니다.
⑲ 항구를 완전히 벗어나서, 전속항진을 하고, 160°에 정침하였습니다.
⑳ 부산항에 접근중입니다. 기관 사용 준비하고 감속하였습니다.
㉑ 좌현 묘쇄 3샤클로 수면속에서 묘박하였습니다.

㉒ 점검을 마치고 항만 관리인들이 하선하였습니다.	㉒ Finished inspection and port officials left her.
㉓ 검역증을 발급받았습니다. 닻을 감아 올리고 정박지로 항진하였습니다.	㉓ Pratique granted, weighed anchor and proceeded to her berth.
㉔ 부두에 도착하여, 수시로 기관을 사용하여, 예인선의 도움을 받아 선회시키기 시작하였습니다.	㉔ Arrived off pier and started to swing her round assisted by tug, using Eng. var'ly.
㉕ 부두에 계류줄 첫 줄이 나갔습니다.	㉕ First line to pier.
㉖ 2번 부두에 계류 완료하였고, 기관 사용을 종료하였습니다.	㉖ Made fast all lines to No.2 wharf, F.W.E.
㉗ 실습선 한바다호의 현측에 계류시켰습니다.	㉗ Made her fast alongside T/S HANBADA.
㉘ 선수미의 정 위치에 계류하였습니다. 부서 배치를 해제하였습니다.	㉘ In position fore & aft. **Dismissed** all station.
㉙ 계류 완료하였고, 기관 사용을 종료하였습니다. 도선사와 예인선이 떠났습니다.	㉙ Vessel secured. F.W.E. Pilot & tug away.

기출문제

02. 다음 중 빈칸에 들어갈 단어로 가장 옳은 것은? `16년 2차`

(   ) up No.2 ballast tank with fresh water.

① Finished ② Filled
③ Replaced ④ Tested

해설   2번 발라스트 탱크에 청수를 채웠습니다(Filled).

답 ❷

03. 다음 중 의미가 다른 하나를 고르시오. `20년 1차`

① Picked up pilot.
② Pilot left her.
③ Dropped pilot.
④ Disembarked pilot.

해설   disembark, left her, drop은 '하선하다'라는 뜻을 가지고 있고, pick up은 '태우다'라는 뜻을 가지고 있다.

답 ❶

기출문제

04. 다음 밑줄 친 단어에 대한 설명으로 가장 적절한 것은? `18년도 3차/14년도 2차`

> The Coast guard seized the shipment of **contraband** that had been smuggled into the country.

① manufactured articles
② edible goods
③ stowaway
④ goods imported or exported illegally

해설 contraband은 '밀수품'이라는 뜻을 가지고 있다. 다시 말해서 불법적으로 수입되거나 수출된 물품을 의미한다.

답 ④

Chapter 12. Log Book 항해일지 | **117**

04
항해 중 기사

① 3마일 떨어진 곳에서 영도 등대를 180°로 보며 통과하고 258°에서 정침하였습니다.
② 2마일 떨어진 곳에서 제주 등대를 우현 정횡 방향으로 통과하였고, 180°로 변침하였습니다.
③ 홍도 등대를 30마일 떨어진 곳에서 290°방향으로 초인하였습니다.
④ 수에즈 운하를 통과하기 위해 부서 배치하였습니다.
⑤ 해협을 빠져 나왔고, 전속항진 하였으며 부서 배치를 해제하였습니다.

① Passed Yeongdo L.H. on 180°, 3' off and **S/Co**, on 258°.
② Jeju L.H. ab'm on stb'd side 2' off, **A/Co.** to 180°.
③ **Made out** Hongdo L.H. on 290°, 30' off.
④ **Stationed** for passing Suez Canal.
⑤ Cleared out of strait, R/up Engine and dismissed the station.

▌기출문제

05. 다음 중 선박 출항 시 시간의 순서에 따라 배열한 것 중 가장 옳은 것은?   20년 1차

㉠ S.B.E Stationed all hands for leaving Mokpo.
㉡ Cast off last line to pier.
㉢ Clear out B.W. R/up engine.
㉣ Single up for & aft.

① ㉠ → ㉢ → ㉣ → ㉡
② ㉣ → ㉠ → ㉢ → ㉡
③ ㉠ → ㉣ → ㉡ → ㉢
④ ㉣ → ㉠ → ㉡ → ㉢

해설 ㉠ 기관 사용 준비를 하였고, 목포항에서 출항하기 위하여 부서 배치를 하였습니다.
㉣ 선수와 선미의 한 개의 계류줄들을 두고 나머진 모두 거두어 들였습니다.
㉡ 마지막 계류줄을 풀었습니다.
㉢ 방파제를 빠져 나왔고, 전속 항주를 시작하였습니다.

답 ❸

06. 다음 중 접안부터 이안까지의 작업 순서를 가장 옳게 나열한 것은?   22년 2차

㉠ Made fast fore and aft   ㉡ R/up Eng.
㉢ Single up.   ㉣ First Line to pier

① ㉣ → ㉠ → ㉢ → ㉡
② ㉡ → ㉢ → ㉠ → ㉣
③ ㉠ → ㉡ → ㉢ → ㉣
④ ㉢ → ㉡ → ㉠ → ㉣

해설 ㉣ 첫줄을 부두에 연결하였습니다.
㉠ 선수미 줄을 모두 부두에 연결하였습니다.
㉢ 한 개의 계류줄을 두고 나머진 모두 거두어 들였습니다.
㉡ 전속 항주를 시작 하였습니다.

답 ❶

05
기상상태

① **Vis**. good. Sky overcast. Traffic heavy.

② Squall passed frequently throughout watch.

③ Vessel **pitching** easily in rough sea & low confused swell.

④ Reduced speed to 100rpm to ease vessel in rough sea.

⑤ **Laboured** heavily, shipping seas on deck frequently.

⑥ Tidal stream set ship NW. 3'

⑦ Tidal against, 14 knots.

⑧ Vessel setting too far off her course by strong current.

① 시정이 양호하다. 구름이 껴 있다. 교통량이 많다.
② 당직 중에 스콜이 빈번히 지나간다.
③ 선박이 거친 파도와 낮고 방향이 일정치 않은 너울로 인해 쉽게 피칭을 하였다.
④ 거친 파도에서 선박이 덜 흔들리도록 100rpm까지 속력을 감소시켰다.
⑤ 심하게 동요하고, 해수가 갑판에 자주 올라옵니다.
⑥ 조류가 북서쪽으로 3해리만큼 흐르고 있습니다.
⑦ 14노트의 역조가 일고 있습니다.
⑧ 강한 조류로 인해 선박이 침로에서 많이 멀어졌습니다.

06
시정의 불량

① Dense fog **set in**, S.B.E. proceeded at safe speed.

② Visibility reduced.

③ Fog **lifted/got cleared/clear/all clear.**

④ Visibility improved.

⑤ Sounded **Fog signal** and **kept a sharp lookout.**

⑥ All fog regulation strictly complied with.

① 짙은 안개가 끼어 기관 사용 준비를 하였고, 안전 속력으로 항진합니다.
② 시정이 감소되었습니다.
③ 안개가 걷혔습니다.
④ 시정이 양호해졌습니다.
⑤ 무중 신호를 울리고, 경계를 철저히 하였습니다.
⑥ 모든 무중 항해 규정을 엄격하게 준수하였습니다.

07
선위, 이로

① **Fixed her position** by star sighting.

② Got her position by cross bearing.

③ Checked gyro error by transit and obtained the error 1°W.

① 천측을 통해 선위를 구하였습니다.
② 교차방위법을 통해 선위를 구하였습니다.
③ 중시선을 가지고 자이로 오차를 확인하였고, 1°W의 오차를 알아냈습니다.

④ 갑판부 선원 박씨가 맹장염을 겪었습니다. 그를 병원에 보내기 위해 가장 가까운 항구인 부산항에 입항하였습니다.

④ Deck crew, Mr. Park suffered from appendicitis seriously. Dropped in the nearest port, Busan, to hospitalize him ashore.

08
선내 시계, 날짜 변경선

① 선내시계를 ZD-9에 맞추기 위해 1시간 전진하였고, 기관실에 통보하였습니다.

① **Advance** all ship's clock 1 hour to ZD-9, Notified E/R.

② 부산항의 지방평균시각에 맞추기 위해 30분을 후진시켰습니다.

② **Retarded** clocks 30 minutes for Local Mean Time at Busan.

③ 북위 38° 지점에서 서경으로 넘어갔으므로 5월 6일이 반복되었습니다.

③ Crossed 180° meridian into **west longitude** at Lat. 38°N, Friday May 6 was **repeated**.

④ 날짜 변경선을 통과하여 금요일인 5월 6일이 생략되었습니다.

④ Due to crossing International Date Line, Friday May 6 was **skipped/omitted**.

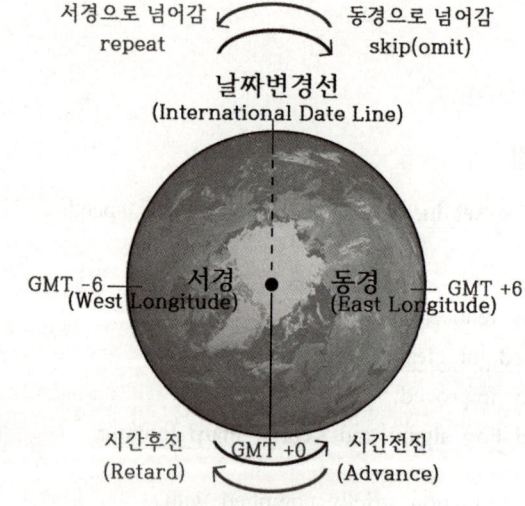

09
고장, 사고

① 계류줄이 프로펠러에 감겼습니다.

① Mooring line **fouled** propeller.

② 등화를 켜지 않은 어선과 충돌하였습니다.

② **Collided with** a fishing boat which carried out no lights.

③ 동력선 Star호가 본선 우현 선수와 충돌하였습니다.

③ MV Star came into collision with our stb'd bow.

④ 기관실에 화재가 발생하였습니다.

④ Fire **broke out** in E/R.

10
정박 중의 기사

① Vessel idle. Frequent rounds made for lines, lights and gangway. **All in good order**.

② Started to pick up anchor to shift her berth.

③ Let go shore lines and **commenced** shifting her berth.

④ **Turn to**

⑤ **Resumed** work.

⑥ **Commenced** taking in ship's store/bunker.

⑦ **Loaded** 100 tons of fuel oil in No.1 F.O.T.

⑧ **Filled up** No.3 F.W.T.

⑨ Finished receiving bunker.

⑩ Ex-master. Capt. Kim **relieved** by newly appointed master. Capt. Lee.

⑪ Finished preparation for **fumigation**. All crews except duty left ships.

⑫ Started **fumigation** for the destruction of vermin.

⑬ Finished **fumigation** and opened all openings and ventilators of living quarters.

⑭ USCG officer checked marine pollution protection certificate.

⑮ Longshore gangs **knocked off** for duty.

⑯ Vessel idle awaiting longshore man.

⑰ Commenced/Started loading cargo in No.3 hold.

⑱ Completed all cargo work and closed all hatches.

① 선박이 대기 중입니다. 계류줄, 등화, 갱웨이의 점검을 수시로 진행하였고 이상 없습니다.

② 정박지를 이동하기 위해서 닻을 감아들이기 시작하였습니다.

③ 계류줄을 풀고 정박지의 이동을 시작하였습니다.

④ 작업 시작

⑤ 작업 재개

⑥ 선용품/벙커유의 적재를 시작하였습니다.

⑦ 1번 연료탱크에 연료유를 100톤 적재하였습니다.

⑧ 3번 청수 탱크를 채웠습니다.

⑨ 벙커유 수급을 마무리했습니다.

⑩ 전임 김 선장이 새롭게 지정된 이 선장과 교대하였습니다.

⑪ 소독 준비를 완료하였습니다. 당직 승무원을 제외한 모든 승무원이 하선하였습니다.

⑫ 해충의 박멸을 위한 소독을 시작하였습니다.

⑬ 소독을 마무리하고 거주구역의 개구와 통풍구를 모두 열었습니다.

⑭ 미국 연안 경비대가 오염방제증서를 점검하였습니다.

⑮ 하역 인부가 작업을 마무리하였습니다.

⑯ 하역 인부를 기다리며 선박 대기 중입니다.

⑰ 3번 화물창에 화물을 적재하기 시작하였습니다.

⑱ 모든 화물 작업을 마무리하고 모든 화물창을 닫았습니다.

I 기출문제

07. 다음 중 표준해사통신용어 표현으로 잘못된 것은? `18년 1차 / 19년 3차`

① 좌현묘쇄 4샤클로 묘박함 : Brought up anchor with 4shackles of port cable on the water.
② 1번 연료유 탱크에 연료유 50톤을 적재하였다. : Commenced 50ton of F.O in NO.1 F.O.T.
③ 거친 파도와 낮고 방향이 일정치 않은 너울을 받아 쉽사리 피칭을 함 : Vessel pitching easily in rough sea and low confused swells.
④ 북쪽방향의 어선군을 보았다. : Sighted a number of fishing boats to northward.

해설 Commence는 '착수하다, 시작하다'라는 뜻을 가지고 있다. '적재하다'라는 뜻을 가진 단어는 Load가 있다.

답 ❷

08. 다음 Ship's log book 기사 중 빈 칸에 들어갈 말로 가장 적절한 것은? `14년 1차`

Crossed the (　　) of 180° into west longitude at Lat. 43°N. July 12 was (　　).

① meridian, repeated　　　② equator, repeated
③ meridian, skipped　　　④ equator, skipped

해설 경도(meridian) 180°의 날짜 변경선을 지나 서경으로 가게 되면 날짜는 반복(repeated)된다.

답 ❶

09. 다음 중 항해일지의 기사를 바르게 해석한 것은 모두 몇 개인가? `20년 1차`

㉠ Secured all derrick booms & other fittings.
　: 데릭 붐 및 기타 속구를 모두 점검함.
㉡ Singled up fore & aft, prepared for sea.
　: 선수미에 계류삭을 하나씩만 남기고 거두어 들였으며 출항준비를 함.
㉢ Laboured heavily, shipping seas on deck frequently.
　: 선체가 심하게 흔들리고 해수가 갑판으로 자주 올라옴.
㉣ Last line to pier let go.
　: 부두의 마지막 계류삭을 벗김.
㉤ Started to heave up port anchor.
　: 좌현묘를 내리기 시작함.

① 2개　　　　　　　　② 3개
③ 4개　　　　　　　　④ 5개

해설 옳지 않은 것
　㉠ Secure : 고박하다. *Inspect, Check : 점검하다.*
　㉤ heave up : 닻을 감아올리다.

답 ❷

chapter 13 Safety on board 선내 안전

01
출입금지 구역, 갑판, 장소에 대한 설명

Safety regulations do not permit passengers to enter the following spaces :

① navigating bridge
② engine room
③ manoeuvring areas at the front and back end of the vessel
④ cargo rooms and compartment
⑤ service rooms
⑥ all areas and spaces marked "Crew Only"
⑦ all closed, sealed or roped off areas, spaces and rooms
⑧ car deck when the vessel is at sea.

안정규정에 의거하여 여객들은 다음의 장소에 들어가서는 안 된다.
① 항해 선교
② 기관실
③ 선박의 선수, 선미에 있는 조종 구역
④ 화물실과 구획
⑤ 운항실
⑥ "승무원에게만"이라는 표시가 되어 있는 구역과 장소
⑦ 모든 밀폐, 봉인 또는 로프로 격리된 구역, 장소 그리고 방
⑧ 선박이 해상에 있을 때의 차량 갑판

02
여객에 관한 사항

① In the unlikely event of an emergency, please obey the orders given on the public address system.

② International regulations require all passengers to be assembled in a drill which has to take place within 24 hours of departure.

③ A drill will be held to familiarize passengers with board assembly stations, with their life-saving equipment and with emergency procedures.

④ All passengers must attend this drill.

⑤ General Emergency Alarm : In case of emergency seven short blasts and one prolonged blast will be given with the ship's whistle and the alarm system.

① 비상상황이 발생할 경우, PA시스템에서 주어진 명령에 따라주십시오.
② 국제 규정에 따라 모든 여객은 출항 이후 24시간 이내에 실시되는 훈련에 참가해야 합니다.
③ 훈련은 여객이 집합장소, 구명설비, 비상절차에 친숙화되도록 실시될 것이다.
④ 모든 여객은 이 훈련에 참가해야 합니다.
⑤ 일반 비상 경보 : 비상 사태 발생 시 선박의 기적신호 장치와 알람 장치로 7회의 단음과 1회의 장음이 울릴 것입니다.

⑥ 안전상의 이유로, 모든 승객들은 집합장소로 가시기 바랍니다.
⑦ 각자의 구명정 부서로 가십시오.
⑧ 안내된 탈출 통로를 따라가십시오.

⑥ For safety reasons we request all passengers to go to their assembly station.
⑦ Go to your lifeboat stations.
⑧ Follow the escape routes shown.

기출문제

01. 〈Standard Marine Communication Phrases〉의 일반 용어 중 General emergency alarm에 대한 설명이다. 각각의 빈칸에 들어갈 말로 가장 옳은 것은? `19년 3차`

> A sound signal of (ⓐ) blast and (ⓑ) blast given with the vessel's sound system.

① ⓐ one short　　　　　ⓑ seven prolonged
② ⓐ one prolonged　　　ⓑ seven short
③ ⓐ seven short　　　　ⓑ one prolonged
④ ⓐ seven prolonged　　ⓑ one short

해설 일반비상경보는 7회의 단음과 1회의 장음으로 이루어져 있다.

답 ❸

03
화재 발생시 행동

If you detect a fire, smell, fumes or smoke, act immediately as follows :

- **Call out** "Fire!"
- **Operate** the nearest fire alarm.
- **Inform** a member of the crew.
- **Telephone** the navigating bridge.

만약 불, 냄새, 유해가스 또는 연기를 감지했을 때에는 즉시 다음과 같이 행동해야 합니다.
- "불이야!"라고 외칠 것
- 가장 가까운 화재 알람 장치를 작동시킬 것
- 승무원에게 알릴 것
- 항해 선교에 전화할 것

기출문제

02. 다음 중 빈칸에 들어갈 단어로 가장 옳은 것은? 〔17년 1차〕

If you detect a fire, smell, fume or smoke, act immediately as follows :
(A) "Fire!"
(B) the nearest fire alarm.
(C) a member of the crew.
(D) the navigation bridge.

	A	B	C	D
①	Call out	Operate	Inform	Telephone
②	Shout	Break	Search	Assembly
③	Call out	Operate	Search	Go to
④	Shout	Cancel	Tell	Contact

해설 "불이야!"라고 외칠 것(Call out). 가장 가까운 화재 알람 장치를 작동시킬 것(Operate). 승무원에게 알릴 것(Inform). 항해 선교에 전화할 것(Telephone).

답 ①

04
사람의 선외 추락시 행동

사람이 선외로 떨어진 것을 보았을 때, 다음과 같이 행동해야 한다.
- "사람이 선외로 추락했다!"라고 외칠 것
- 구명부환을 선외로 던질 것
- 물에 빠진 사람에게 시선을 고정시킬 것
- 물에 빠진 사람의 위치를 사관/승무원에게 보여줄 것/말할 것. 또는 즉시 선교에 전화할 것.

If you see anybody fall overboard, act as follows:

- Call out "Man overboard!"
- Throw life buoys overboard.
- Keep your eyes on the person in the water.
- Show/Tell an officer/crew the person's position in the water, or Telephone the bridge immediately.

05
사람의 선외 추락시 항해사가 해야 할 3가지 행동

① 사람이 물에 빠진 쪽으로 최대 전타한다.
② 기관을 정지한다.
③ 자기 점화등을 가진 구명부환을 밖에 던진다.

① **To order the helm hard over towards the side from which the man fell.**
② To **stop engine.**
③ To **release a life buoy to which a self-igniting.**

기출문제

03. Your vessel is proceeding at sea when a man falls overboard on the starboard side. As the mate on watch you should first :   15년 2차

① notify the master.
② turn the wheel hard right.
③ put the engine full astern.
④ call the standby of the watch.

해설 사람이 물에 빠진 것을 발견했을 때, 사관이 가장 먼저 할 일은 사람이 물에 빠진 쪽으로 최대 전타하는 것이다. 사람이 오른쪽으로 물에 빠졌기 때문에 우현 최대 전타를 한다.
mate : 사관

답 ❷

기출문제

04. In an emergency of "man overboard", the watch officer should carry out three simultaneous actions. Which of the following is not one of them? `18년 1차`

① To transmit a general urgency signal to all ships in the vicinity
② To stop engine
③ To release a life buoy to which a self-igniting
④ To order the helm hard over towards the side from which the man fell

해설 사람이 물에 빠졌을 경우 IAMSAR에서 규정하고 있는 당직 항해사가 해야 할 세 가지 행동을 기억하도록 한다.

답 ❶

05. 다음 중 빈칸에 들어갈 말로 가장 옳은 것은? `17년 1차`

> Your vessel is proceeding at sea when a man falls overboard on the starboard side. As the mate on watch you should first (　　).

① turn the wheel hard left.
② turn the wheel hard right.
③ put the engine full astern.
④ call the standby of the watch.

해설 사람이 물에 빠진 것을 발견했을 때, 사관이 가장 먼저 할 일은 사람이 물에 빠진 쪽으로 최대 전타하는 것이다. 사람이 오른쪽으로 물에 빠졌기 때문에 우현 최대 전타를 한다.

답 ❷

06
집합 장소에 대한 설명

① 7회의 단음과 1회의 장음으로 구성된 일반 비상경보가 울리면, 모든 여객은 각자의 집합장소로 가야한다.
② 모든 여객은 다음을 착용해야 합니다.
　- 보온용 의복
　- 긴 바지, 긴 소매의 셔츠/재킷
　- 단단한 신발과 머리 보호구
③ 모든 여객들은 안내된 탈출 통로를 따라가야 합니다.
④ 모든 승객은 사관/승무원에게 받은 지시에 철저하게 따라야 합니다.
⑤ 1회의 장음과 1회의 단음을 계속적으로 반복하는 퇴선 경보를 들으면, 일반 비상경보의 상황과 같이 행동을 해야 합니다.

① When the general emergency alarm is sounded which consists of **seven short blasts and one prolonged blast**, all passengers have to go to their **assembly station.**

② All passengers must put on :
　- warm clothing
　- long trousers, long-sleeved shirts/jacket
　- strong shoes and head covering

③ All passengers are requested to follow the escape routes shown.

④ All passengers are requested to strictly obey the instructions given by the officers or crew.

⑤ When you hear the abandon ship alarm which consists of one prolonged and one short blast repeated continuously, please act in the same manner as under the general emergency alarm.

07
인원점검(Roll call) 실시

① 집합 장소에서 사관/승무원 중 한 명이 인원 점검을 수행할 것입니다.
② 사관/승무원이 "이것은 인원 점검입니다."라고 외치고, 승객의 이름을 개별적으로 부를 것입니다.
③ 이름이 불렸을 때, "네"라고 크게 대답합니다.
④ 만약 같은 선실의 승객이 인원 점검에 참여할 수 없다면, 즉시 사관/승무원에게 알리세요

① At your assembly station one of the officers/crew will perform a **roll call.**

② The officer/crew will say "This is a **roll call**." and s/he will call out the passengers individually by their names.

③ When your name is called out, please answer loudly "HERE."

④ If one of your cabinmates is not able to attend the roll call, please inform the officer/crew immediately.

chapter 14 자주 나오는 SMCP 표현

① Keep a sharp **look out**.
② **Keep clear** of me.
③ Are you **dragging** anchor?
④ You are **obstructing** the fairway.
⑤ What is the weather situation in your position?
⑥ Which side should I **rig** the pilot ladder?
⑦ We **call at** Busan a week ago.
⑧ As weather getting threatening, **put off** sailing.
⑨ What is **visibility** in your position?
⑩ **Brought up** anchor with 4shackles of port cable on the water.
⑪ I will **make a lee** for you.
⑫ Please, **make a lee** for my boat
⑬ We will **dredge** it.
⑭ I will **carry out** radar search.
⑮ You are **running into** danger.
⑯ The master of ship on receiving a wireless distress signal from any other ships is bound to proceed with all speed to the **assistance** of the persons in distress.
⑰ Correct the **list** of the vessel.
⑱ **Disembarkation** is not possible.
⑲ What is your **MMSI**?
⑳ From what direction are you **approaching**?
㉑ What was your last **port of call**?
㉒ Person **picked up** is crew member.
㉓ What are the maximum revolution ahead?

① 경계를 철저히 하라.
② 본선을 피하여 가시오.
③ 귀선은 주묘중인가?
④ 귀선은 항로를 가로 막고 있다.
⑤ 귀선의 위치에서의 기상 상태는 어떠한가?
⑥ 어느 현쪽의 도선용 사다리를 설치해야 할까요?
⑦ 일주일 전에 부산에 기항하였습니다.
⑧ 날씨가 악화되어 출항을 연기하였습니다.
⑨ 귀선의 위치에서의 시정은 얼마인가?
⑩ 좌현묘쇄 4샤클로 묘박 완료함.
⑪ 귀선을 본선의 풍하측으로 막아드리겠습니다.
⑫ 내 보트가 귀선의 풍하측이 되도록 해주세요.
⑬ 본선은 묘쇄를 끌겠습니다.
⑭ 본선은 레이더 수색을 수행할 것입니다.
⑮ 귀선은 위험물을 향해 가고 있습니다.
⑯ 다른 선박으로부터 무선 조난 신호를 받은 선박의 선장은 조난에 빠진 사람을 원조하기 위해 전속력으로 항진할 의무가 있습니다.
⑰ 선박의 경사를 수정하십시오.
⑱ 하선이 불가능하다.
⑲ 귀선의 식별번호는 무엇입니까?
⑳ 귀선은 어느 방향에서 접근 중입니까?
㉑ 귀선의 최후 기항지는 어디인가?
㉒ 인양된 사람은 승무원이다.
㉓ 전진 최대 회전수는 얼마인가?

㉔ 조난 호출은 다른 통신보다 절대적인 우선권을 갖는다. 그것을 들었을 때, 다른 통신을 중지하고 청취해야 한다.
㉕ 좌현묘를 올리기 시작하였음.
㉖ Bitt에 예인삭의 eye를 넣지 말아라.
㉗ Center fairleader를 통해 예인삭을 잡아라.
㉘ 그 선박은 타효 속력을 잃고, 타효가 없음.
㉙ 본선은 감속하여 진입중이다.
㉚ 본선은 항로를 항진 중이다.
㉛ 입항 부서 배치함.
㉜ No.2 부두에 계류하였음.
㉝ 부서 배치를 해제함.
㉞ 계류줄에 대한 점검을 자주 하였으며 이상이 없음.
㉟ 우현으로 변침하는 것은 위험함.
㊱ 화물이 해충에 감염되었다.
㊲ 주의하여 항행하시오.
㊳ 최근의 보안순찰은 17시였음.
㊴ 어구가 본선 추진기에 감겼음.
㊵ 로켓을 발사해도 귀선은 안전합니까?
㊶ 본선은 대수속력이 있습니다.
㊷ 귀선의 침로를 145도로 맞추길 권고합니다.
㊸ 출항 및 입항할 때 마약, 밀항자, 밀수품을 모두 수색하였습니다.
㊹ 본선은 조타 가능한 최소의 속력을 유지하고 있다.
㊺ 화물창은 적하 전에 검사관에 의해 검사되어야 함.
㊻ 일시 중단하다, 유예하다, 연기하다.
㊼ 의무적인
㊽ ~과 친숙화하다.

㉔ Distress calls have absolute priority over all other communications. When hearing them, **all other transmissions should cease and listen in**.
㉕ Started to **heave up** port anchor.
㉖ Do not **put** the eye of tug's line **on** the bitt.
㉗ **Take** tug's line **through** center fairlead.
㉘ She is lost of **steerageway**, she does not answer the wheel.
㉙ I am proceeding **at** reduced speed.
㉚ I am proceeding **by** fairway.
㉛ Stationed for entering port.
㉜ Made fast all lines to No.2 wharf.
㉝ **Dismissed** all station.
㉞ Frequent rounds made for lines. All in good order.
㉟ It is dangerous to **alter course** to starboard.
㊱ The cargo is infect with vermin.
㊲ Navigate **with** caution.
㊳ The latest **security patrol** was at 1700 hours UTC.
㊴ Fishing gear has **fouled** my propeller.
㊵ It is safe **to** fire a rocket?
㊶ I am **making way speed through the water**.
㊷ Advise you **make course** 145.
㊸ **Narcotics, stowaway, contraband goods** are **searched** for when entering or leaving port.
㊹ I have **steerageway**
㊺ The hold must be inspected by the surveyors before loading.
㊻ suspend
㊼ compulsory, mandatory, obligatory
㊽ familiar with

I 기출문제

01. Choose the correct one for the blank.　　　　　　　　　　　　　18년 1차

> Attention all vessels. This is Yeosu Vessel Traffic Service(VTS) Center. There has been a collision with a submerged wreck in position 240 degrees 4 cables from Jindo Bank buoy. (　　　　　).

① Do you require tug boats?
② What is your position?
③ Keep clear
④ Please single up.

해설 충돌이 일어난 상황이기 때문에, '피하라'라는 뜻을 가진 'keep clear'가 답이 된다.

답 ❸

02. 입항 중인 선박과 도선사와의 대화이다. IMO 표준해사영어로 빈 칸에 가장 알맞은 말은?

14년 1차 / 15년 일반직

> A : This is M/V KCG. Korea pilot, do you read me?
> B : Good mornig KCG. This is Korea Pilot. What is your (　A　)?
> A : My (　A　) is 09:00, Over.
> B : Roger that. Please approach the (　B　) with dead slow ahead.
> A : Roger that. Which side should I (　C　) the pilot ladder?
> B : Lee-side please.

	A	B	C
①	ETA	breakwater	hang
②	ETA	pilot station	rig
③	ETD	breakwater	rig
④	ETD	pilot station	hang

해설 A는 도착예정시각이 언제인지를 묻는 표현이다.
　　 B는 도선사와 대화 중이기 때문에 도선구역을 의미하는 pilot station이 와야 한다.
　　 C는 '사다리를 설치하다.'라는 뜻을 가진 rig가 답으로 와야 한다.

답 ❷

기출문제

03. 다음 보기의 괄호 안에 들어갈 순서로 가장 정확한 것은 무엇인가? [18년 3차]

> Ⓐ We (   ) Busan a week ago.
> - 일주일 전에 부산에 기항하였습니다.
> Ⓑ As weather getting threatening, put (   ) sailing.
> - 날씨가 악화되어 출항을 연기함.

① called at - out
② called at - off
③ called in - off
④ called in - out

해설 기항하다 : call at,
연기하다 : put off

답 ❷

04. 아래 문장에서 빈칸에 들어갈 IMO 표준해사통신영어로 가장 적절한 말은? [16년 일반직]

> "귀선 위치에서의 시정은 얼마인가?"
> "What is (   ) in your position."

① maximum winds
② sea state
③ swell
④ visibility

해설 시정은 visibility 이다.

답 ❹

05. 다음 빈칸에 들어갈 말로 가장 적절한 것은? [18년 1차]

> "Distress calls have absolute priority over all other communications. When hearing them, (   )."

① all other transmissions should cease and listen in
② a change of channel should be requested
③ further communications should be made
④ communications should be commenced on the chosen channel

해설 조난 호출은 다른 통신보다 절대적인 우선권을 갖는다. 그것을 들었을 때, 다른 통신을 중지(cease)하고 청취(listen in)해야 한다.

답 ❶

기출문제

06. Choose the suitable one to fill the blank `17년 2차`

> When the general emergency alarm is sounded with seven short blasts and one prolonged blast, all passengers have to go to their (　　　).

① store
② galley
③ assembly station
④ lounge

[해설] 단음 7회와 장음 1회로 구성된 일반 비상경보를 들었을 때, 모든 승객들은 집합장소(assembly station)로 가야 한다.

답 ❸

07. Rewrite the following sentence into Standard Marine Navigational Vocabulary `15년 2차`

> I will bring the vessel beam on to the wind and sea, to protect the vessel in distress from the wind.

① I will protect you from the wind.
② I am going to make a wind for you.
③ I am coming to rescue you in distress.
④ I will make a lee for you.

[해설] I will make a lee for you : 귀선을 본선의 풍하측으로 막아드리겠습니다.

답 ❹

08. 다음 중 밑줄 친 부분을 해석한 것으로 가장 옳은 것은? `15년 2차`

> Captain : I have rigged pilot ladder on my starboard side.
> Pilot : Roger. Please, **make a lee for my boat.**

① 귀선이 내 보트의 풍하측이 되도록 하여라.
② 내 보트가 귀선의 풍하측이 되도록 하여라.
③ 귀선이 배를 돌려서 내 보트가 갈 수 있는 길을 열어라.
④ 귀선은 내 보트의 선미로 접근하라.

[해설] 자신의 보트가 상대선박의 풍하측 되도록 해달라는 말이다.

답 ❷

I 기출문제

09. 다음 〈보기〉 중 빈 칸에 들어갈 단어로 가장 옳게 짝지어진 것은? `21년 상반기`

> ㉠ : Which side should I (ⓐ) the pilot ladder?
>   (도선사용 사다리를 어느 쪽에 설치 할까요?)
> ㉡ : Advise you change (ⓑ) VHF channel. 13.
>   (VHF채널을 13번으로 변경하기를 권고합니다.)
> ㉢ : We will let go port anchor 1shackle and (ⓒ) it.
>   (본선은 좌현 닻을 1절로 투묘하고, 그것을 끌겠습니다.)

	ⓐ	ⓑ	ⓒ
①	hang	on	drag
②	rig	to	drag
③	hang	on	dredge
④	rig	to	dredge

해설 ㉠ 도선사 사다리 설치는 동사 Rig를 사용한다.
㉡ 채널 변경 시 Change to라 말한다.
㉢ 닻을 의도적으로 끄는 것은 Dredge이다.

답 ④

10. 다음 괄호 안에 들어갈 단어가 가장 적절한 것으로 짝지어진 것은? `19년 3차`

> - I am in danger of (A)
>   : 본선은 전복의 위험이 있습니다.
> - What is your (B)?
>   : 귀선의 식별번호는 무엇입니까?
> - From what direction are you (C)?
>   : 귀선은 어느 방향에서 접근중인가?
> - What was your (D)?
>   : 귀선의 최후 기항지는 어디인가?

① sinking, MMSI, approaching, port of destination
② capsizing, MMSI, approaching, last port of call
③ sinking, call sign, proceeding, port of destination
④ capsizing, call sign, approaching, last port of call

해설 (A) 전복 : capsizing,
(B) 식별번호 : MMSI *호출부호 : call sign*
(C) 접근 : approaching,
(D) 최후 기항지 : last port of call

답 ②

I 기출문제

11. 다음 표준해사통신용어(Standard Marine Communication Phrases) 표현 중 가장 옳지 않은 것은? `19년 1차`

① 엔진 후진하라 : Put engine(s) astern.
② 귀선의 좌현 쪽으로 바람을 막아 달라 : Make a lee on your port side.
③ 선박의 경사를 수정하라 : Correct the list of the vessel.
④ 하선이 불가능하다. : Embarkation is not possible.

해설 embarkation : 승선, disembarkation : 하선

답 ❹

12. 아래 문장에서 빈칸에 들어갈 SMCP (Standard Marine Communication Phrases) 용어로 가장 적절한 것은? `16년 일반직`

> WARNING. You are (　　　　) danger.
> "경고. 귀선은 위험물 쪽으로 향하고 있다."

① moving to　　② meeting　　③ running into　　④ having to

해설 위험물을 향하여 가다 : running into danger

답 ❸

13. 다음 중 밑줄 친 부분의 가장 가까운 의미는? `16년 2차`

> Large vessel is leaving.
> **Keep clear** of approach channel.

① Avoid　　　　　　　② Close
③ Pass　　　　　　　 ④ Go by

해설 keep clear : ~을 피하다.

답 ❶

14. Choose the best one for the blank. `15년 2차`

> The master of ship on receiving a wireless distress signal from any other ships is bound to proceed with all speed to the (　　　　) of the persons in distress.

① avoidance　　② attendance　　③ assistance　　④ agreement

해설 다른 선박으로부터 무선 조난 신호를 받은 선박의 선장은 조난에 빠진 사람을 원조(assistance) 하기 위해 전속력으로 항진할 의무가 있습니다.

답 ❸

chapter 15 다양한 SMCP 심화형 문제

I 기출문제

01. VTS 관제구역내에서 VTS 센터와 선박국간 SMCP을 이용한 통화내용이다. 다음 빈 칸에 들어갈 말로 가장 적절한 것은?
  `15년 일반직`

V : M/V korea, you are (　　　) from the traffic lane and reversing. Confirm your position.
K : I estimate I (　　　) from the traffic lane slightly.
V : I advise you to alter course immediately to return the correct traffic lane.
K : I will return to the correct traffic lane immediately.

① not correct, correct
② wrong, correct
③ deviating, deviated
④ deviated, deviating

해설
V : 동력선 Korea호, 귀선은 통항로에서 이로 중이며(deviating *현재진행형*) 반대 방향으로 항행하고 있습니다. 위치를 확인하세요.
K : 본선은 본선이 통항로에서 약간 벗어났다고(deviated *과거형*) 추정 중입니다.
V : 지금 즉시 변침하여 올바른 통항로로 되돌아가기를 권고합니다.
K : 본선은 지금 즉시 올바른 통항로로 돌아가겠습니다.

답 ③

02. The following sentences are some entries in the remark column of Deck log book. Select the most appropriate one for the remark at sea. (at sea ; not at anchor, or made fast to the shore, or aground) `14년 2차`

① Single up fore & aft and prepared for sea.
② S.B.E. & prepared unmooring.
③ F.W.E Pilot & tug away and dismissed the station.
④ Cleared out of Canal, R/up eng. and dismissed the station.

해설 다음 문장들은 항해일지에 remark란에 들어갈 내용들이다. 항해중일 때 remark란에 들어갈 가장 알맞은 말을 고르시오.
① single up 상태는, 중요한 줄만 남겨두고 출항 준비를 하는 과정이다. 또한 항해를 하기 전 준비 중인 상태이다. 그러므로 항해 전인 상태라고 할 수 있다.
② S.B.E.은 기관사용 준비상태이고 이안을 준비하고 있다는 것으로 보아 항해 전인 상태라고 할 수 있다.
③ F.W.E.은 기관 종료상태이고, 도선사와 예인선이 떠났으며 부서 배치 해제를 한 것으로 보아 입항 완료 후 정박 중인 상태라고 할 수 있다.
④ 운하를 지났고, R/up engine을 했으며 부서배치 해제를 했으므로, 출항 후 항해중인 상태라고 할 수 있다.

답 ④

| 기출문제

03. 다음 중 빈칸에 들어갈 단어로 가장 옳은 것은? `16년 2차`

> You estimate that you will arrive at your port of destination at 2330 hours. 2330 hours is your (　　).

① ETA　　　　② ETD
③ TCPA　　　④ CPA

[해설] 귀선은 23시 30분에 귀선의 목적 항에 도착할 것이다. 23시 30분은 귀선의 ETA이다.
　ETA (Estimated Time of Arrival) : 도착 예정 시각
　ETD (Estimated Time of Departure) : 출발 예정 시각
　TCPA (Time to Closest Point of Approach) : 최근접점까지의 시간
　CPA (Closest Point of Approach) : 최근접점(거리)

답 ❶

04. IMO 표준 해사 통신 용어상 아래 문장이 의미하는 것은 무엇인가? `16년 일반직`

> Services, designed to improve safety and efficiency of vessel traffic and to protect the environment.

① TSS　　　　② VTS
③ ITZ　　　　④ SAR

[해설] 선박 통항의 안전(safety), 효율(efficiency)을 향상시키고 환경을 보호(protect the environment)하기 위하여 설정된 업무 : VTS(Vessel Traffic Service)

답 ❷

05. 다음 괄호 안에 들어가기에 적절치 않은 것은? `18년 2차`

> Salvage operation includes (　　) a vessel which is in danger of running aground, (　　) a vessel which is aground, (　　) a submerged wreck.

① clearing　　　② towing
③ foundering　　④ raising

[해설] 인양 작업은 좌초의 위험에 빠지고 있는 선박을 (　)하는 것, 좌초된 선박을 (　)하는 것, 수중 난파선을 (　)하는 것을 포함한다. clearing은 (인양) 작업을 완벽하게 마무리하는 것, towing은 (예인)하는 것, raising은 (인양)하는 것으로 빈 칸에 들어갈 수 있으나 foundering은 침몰을 뜻하기 때문에 옳지 않다.

답 ❸

기출문제

06. "귀선은 어업금지구역에 접근하고 있다." 적절한 표현은? `18년 2차`

> You are (①) a (②) fishing area.

① approached, prohibited
② approached, prohibiting
③ approaching, prohibiting
④ approaching, prohibited

해설 문법상 "귀선은 어업이 금지된(prohibited) 구역에 접근하고 있다(approaching)."가 적절하다.

답 ④

07. 다음 중 빈칸에 들어갈 말로 가장 옳은 것은? `18년 일반직`

> The distress traffic controlling station/other station may impose radio (A) on any interfering stations by using the term : "(B) Mayday/Distress" unless the latter have messages about the distress.

① A : silence   B : Seelonce
② A : silence   B : Warning
③ A : switch off   B : Seelonce
④ A : switch off   B : All stations

해설 조난 통신 통제국에서는 조난통신 외에 다른 통신으로 조난통신을 방해할 때에 "Seelonce Mayday"를 사용하여 무선 통신 사용 금지 요구를 할 수 있다.

답 ①

기출문제

08. 다음 대화 중 문맥상 밑줄 친 부분에 들어갈 말로 가장 알맞은 것은? `18년 2차`

> A : In this voyage, we have 2,000 tons of steel H beam bound for Singapore. Chief officer, have any plans for loading?
> B : _____
> A : No, it's not possible. We have 4,000 tons of scrap there. So we have to load it on deck.
> B : On deck loading in winter season? What if the lashing wire breaks and the load is scattered?
> A : I also worry about that, but I think we can do it by holding up stanchions at both sides and tighten it hard with wire rope using the turnbuckles.

① How about hatching #6 which has the least wave strike?
② If the sharp beam strikes the shell plate, even steel plate can't bear it.
③ It's for under deck transportation, isn't it?
④ We have to make a temporary locker on the upper twin deck for storage.

해설
A : 이번 항차 싱가폴로 가는 H빔 2000톤이 있습니다. 일항사님 적화계획이 있으신가요?
B : _____
A : 아니요. 그건 불가능합니다. 그곳에는 4000톤의 고철이 있습니다. 그래서 갑판적해야 합니다.
B : 겨울철에 갑판적 화물이라뇨? 만일 고박 와이어가 끊어져 적화물이 흩어지면 어떡하죠?
A : 저도 그 점이 걱정입니다만, 양현에 stanchion을 세우고 턴버클을 사용하여 와이어를 조여주면 될 것 같습니다.
빈 칸에 들어갈 말은 "그것은 선창에 들어갈 화물입니다. 그렇지 않습니까?"가 문맥상 맞다.

답 ❸

09. 다음 문장을 읽고 각각의 빈칸에 들어갈 말로 가장 옳은 것은? `19년 3차`

> Haenuri : Badaro, this is Haenuri. Change to channel 6, Over.
> Badaro : Haenuri, this is Badaro. Changing to channel 6, Over.
>   I (   ) to overtake you on your port side. Over.
> Haenuri : Badaro, this is Haenuri. Do not overtake me. Repeat not overtake me. A vessel is about to pass my port side. Over.
> Badaro : Haenuri, this is Badaro. I will not overtake you. I am (   ) speed with caution. Over.

① take, increasing　　② wish, increasing
③ take, reducing　　　④ wish, reducing

해설 해누리호 : 바다로호, 여기는 해누리호입니다. 채널을 6번으로 바꾸어주십시오.
바다로호 : 해누리호, 여기는 바다로호입니다. 채널을 6번으로 바꾸었습니다.
　　　　　본선은 귀선의 좌현쪽으로 귀선을 추월하길 바랍니다(wish).
해누리호 : 바다로호, 여기는 해누리호입니다. 본선을 추월하지 마십시오. 다시 한번, 본선을 추월하지 마십시오. 본선 좌현 쪽으로 통과하는 선박이 있습니다.
바다로호 : 해누리호, 여기는 바다로호입니다. 본선은 귀선을 추월하지 않겠습니다. 본선은 주의하여 감속(reducing)하도록 하겠습니다.

답

기출문제

10. VTS에서 제공하는 서비스 중에서 다음 빈 칸에 들어갈 말로 가장 적절한 것은? [15년 일반직]

( ) is especially important in difficult navigational or meteorological circumstances or in case of defects or deficiencies. This service is normally rendered at the request of a vessel or by the VTS when deemed necessary.

① Navigational assistance service
② Information service
③ Traffic organization service
④ General information service

해설 항행원조업무(Navigational assistance service)는 항행 상 혹은 기상상태가 어려울 때 혹은 장애와 결함이 있을 때 특별히 중요하다. 이 업무는 통상 선박의 요청 혹은 VTS에 의해 필요하다고 간주될 때 제공된다.

답 ❶

11. 다음 문장 중 틀린 것은? [13년]

① Is it safe on fire a rocket?
② Stand by on channel one-two.
③ Change to channel one-two.
④ Advise try channel two-six.

해설 로켓을 발사하다는 'to fire a rocket'으로 표현한다.

답 ❶

12. 선박의 상태를 [ ] 안에 잘못 표시한 것은? [11년]

① Arrived at pier and started to make her fast. [안벽계류 시작]
② Made fast port side to pier F.W.E. [기관사용 종료]
③ Made her fast alongside M/S Korea. [코리아호 현측에 계류]
④ Made her stern fast to pier. [부두에 선수 계류함]

해설 'stern'이기 때문에 '부두에 <u>선미</u> 계류함'으로 되어야 한다.

답 ❹

기출문제

13. 다음 빈칸에 들어갈 가장 적절한 것은? `11년`

> You are a chief officer on a tanker and have loaded a wing tank with ballast to assist tank cleaning. Your vessel inclines 5° to port. This inclination is called (   ).

① a port list of 5°
② a rolling of 5°
③ even keel
④ a pitching of 5°

해설 당신은 유조선의 일등항해사이고, 탱크 세척을 돕기 위해 윙 탱크에 밸러스트를 적재하였다. 귀선이 좌현으로 5° 기울었을 때, 이 기울음을 좌현 5° 횡경사라 한다.

답 ❶

14. 선내에서 일반적으로 사용되는 약자와 원어가 잘못 연결된 것은? `11년 3차`

① F.W.T. : fresh water temperature
② F.W.E. : finished with engine
③ S.B.E. : stand by engine
④ B.W.E : breakwater entrance

해설 F.W.T : Fresh Water Tank (청수탱크)

답 ❶

15. VHF 교신 중 숫자를 잘못 송신한 것은? `11년`

① 200 : two-zero-zero
② 122 : one-two-two
③ 3.2 : three decimal two
④ 300 : three-ten

해설 SMCP상 타각지시 시의 경우를 제외한 모든 숫자는 분리 해야 한다.
   300 : three-zero-zero

답 ❹

해사영어 기본이론 임하람

PART 02 UNCLOS (United Nations Convention on the Law of the Sea)

Chapter 1	Preamble 서문
Chapter 2	Use of terms and scope 용어의 사용과 적용 범위
Chapter 3	Baseline 영해기선
Chapter 4	Internal Water 내수
Chapter 5	Territorial Sea 영해
Chapter 6	Contiguous zone 접속수역
Chapter 7	Exclusive Economic Zone 배타적 경제 수역
Chapter 8	High Seas 공해
Chapter 9	Right of innocent passage 무해통항권
Chapter 10	Right of Visit 임검권
Chapter 11	Right of Hot Pursuit 추적권
Chapter 12	Archipelagic State 군도국가
Chapter 13	Nationality and Status of ships 선박의 국적과 지위
Chapter 14	Criminal Jurisdiction 형사적관할권
Chapter 15	Transit Passage 해협에서의 통과 통항
Chapter 16	Continental Shelf 대륙붕
Chapter 17	UNCLOS의 다양한 규정

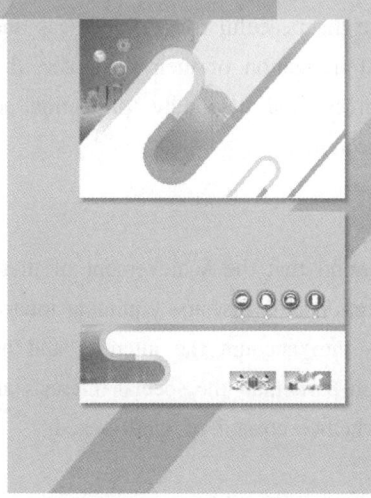

chapter 01 Preamble 서문

이 협약의 당사국은,	The States Parties to this Convention,
해양법과 관련된 모든 문제를 상호이해와 협력의 정신으로 해결하고자 하는 희망에 따라, 또한 세계 모든 사람들을 위한 평화·정의 및 진보의 유지에 대한 중대한 공헌의 하나로서 이 협약이 가지는 역사적 의의를 인식하고,	Prompted by the desire to settle, in a spirit of mutual understanding and co-operation, all issues relating to the law of the sea and aware of the historic significance of this Convention as an important contribution to the maintenance of peace, justice and progress for all peoples of the world,
1958년과 1960년에 제네바에서 개최된 국제연합해양법회의 이래의 발전에 따라 새롭고도 일반적으로 수락될 수 있는 해양법협약의 필요성이 강조되고 있음에 유의하고,	Noting that developments since the United Nations Conferences on the Law of the Sea held at Geneva in 1958 and 1960 have accentuated the need for a new and generally acceptable Convention on the law of the sea,
해양의 여러 문제가 서로 밀접하게 관련되어 있으며 전체로서 고려되어야 할 필요성이 있음을 인식하고,	Conscious that the problems of ocean space are closely interrelated and need to be considered as a whole,
이 협약을 통하여 모든 국가의 주권을 적절히 고려하면서, 국제교통의 촉진, 해양의 평화적 이용, 해양 자원의 공평하고도 효율적인 활용, 해양 생물자원의 보존, 그리고 해양환경의 연구, 보호 및 보전을 촉진하기 위하여 해양에 대한 법질서를 확립하는 것이 바람직함을 인식하고,	Recognizing the desirability of establishing through this Convention, with due regard for the sovereignty of all States, a legal order for the seas and oceans which will facilitate international communication, and will promote the peaceful uses of the seas and oceans, the equitable and efficient utilization of their resources, the conservation of their living resources, and the study, protection and preservation of the marine environment,
이러한 목적의 달성이 인류 전체의 이익과 필요, 특히 연안국이거나 내륙국이거나 관계없이 개발도상국의 특별한 이익과 필요를 고려한 공정하고도 공평한 국제경제질서의 실현에 기여할 것이라는 점을 유념하고,	Bearing in mind that the achievement of these goals will contribute to the realization of a just and equitable international economic order which takes into account the interests and needs of mankind as a whole and, in particular, the special interests and needs of developing countries, whether coastal or land-locked,

Desiring by this Convention to develop the principles embodied in resolution 2749 (XXV) of 17 December 1970 in which the General Assembly of the United Nations solemnly declared inter alia that the area of the sea-bed and ocean floor and the subsoil thereof, beyond the limits of national jurisdiction, as well as its resources, are the common heritage of mankind, the exploration and exploitation of which shall be carried out for the benefit of mankind as a whole, irrespective of the geographical location of States,

Believing that the codification and progressive development of the law of the sea achieved in this Convention will contribute to the strengthening of peace, security, co-operation and friendly relations among all nations in conformity with the principles of justice and equal rights and will promote the economic and social advancement of all peoples of the world, in accordance with the Purposes and Principles of the United Nations as set forth in the Charter,

Affirming that matters not regulated by this Convention continue to be governed by the rules and principles of general international law,

Have agreed as follows:

국제연합총회가 국가관할권 한계 밖의 해저·해상 및 그 하층토 지역은 그 자원과 함께 인류공동유산이며, 이에 대한 탐사와 개발은 국가의 지리적 위치에 관계없이 인류전체의 이익을 위하여 수행되어야 한다고 특별히 엄숙하게 선언한 1970년 12월 17일자 결의 제2749(XXV)호에 구현된 여러 원칙을 이 협약에 의하여 발전시킬 것을 희망하고,

이 협약이 이룩한 해양법의 법전화와 점진적 발달이 정의와 평등권의 원칙에 따라 모든 국가간에 평화·안전·협력 및 우호관계의 강화에 기여하고 국제연합헌장에 규정된 국제연합의 목적과 원칙에 따라 세계 모든 사람들의 경제적·사회적 진보를 증진할 것임을 믿으며,

이 협약에 의하여 규율되지 아니한 사항은 일반국제법의 규칙과 원칙에 의하여 계속 규율될 것임을 확인하며,

다음과 같이 합의하였다.

chapter 02 / Use of terms and scope 용어의 사용과 적용 범위

이 협약에서

① "심해저"라 함은 국가관할권 한계 밖의 해저해상 및 그 하층토를 말한다.

② "해저기구"라 함은 국제해저기구를 말한다.

③ "심해저활동"이라 함은 심해저자원을 탐사하고 개발하는 모든 활동을 말한다.

④ "해양환경오염"이라 함은 생물자원과 해양생물에 대한 손상, 인간의 건강에 대한 위험, 어업과 그 밖의 적법한 해양이용을 포함한 해양활동에 대한 장애, 해수이용에 의한 수질악화 및 쾌적도 감소 등과 같은 해로운 결과를 가져오거나 가져올 가능성이 있는 물질이나 에너지를 인간이 직접적으로 또는 간접적으로 강어귀를 포함한 해양환경에 들여오는 것을 말한다.

⑤ ⓐ "투기"라 함은 다음을 말한다.
 (ⅰ) 선박·항공기·플랫폼 또는 그 밖의 인공해양 구조물로부터 폐기물이나 그 밖의 물질을 고의로 버리는 행위
 (ⅱ) 선박·항공기·플랫폼 또는 그 밖의 인공해양 구조물을 고의로 버리는 행위

For the purposes of this Convention:

① "Area" means the sea-bed and ocean floor and subsoil thereof beyond the limits of national jurisdiction;

② "Authority" means the International Sea-Bed Authority;

③ "activities in the Area" means all activities of exploration for, and exploitation of, the resources of the Area;

④ "pollution of the marine environment" means the introduction by man, directly or indirectly, of substances or energy into the marine environment, including estuaries, which results or is likely to result in such deleterious effects as harm to living resources and marine life, hazards to human health, hindrance to marine activities, including fishing and other legitimate uses of the sea, impairment of quality for use of sea water and reduction of amenities;

⑤ ⓐ "dumping" means:
 (ⅰ) any deliberate disposal of wastes or other matter from vessels, aircraft, platforms or other man-made structures at sea;

 (ⅱ) any deliberate disposal of vessels, aircraft, platforms or other man-made structures at sea

ⓑ "dumping" does not include:
  (i) the disposal of wastes or other matter incidental to, or derived from the normal operations of vessels, aircraft, platforms or other man-made structures at sea and their equipment, other than wastes or other matter transported by or to vessels, aircraft, platforms or other man-made structures at sea, operating for the purpose of disposal of such matter or derived from the treatment of such wastes or other matter on such vessels, aircraft, platforms or structures;

  (ii) placement of matter for a purpose other than the mere disposal thereof, provided that such placement is not contrary to the aims of this Convention.

⑥ "States Parties" means States which have consented to be bound by this Convention and for which this Convention is in force.

⑦ This Convention applies mutatis mutandis to the entities referred to in article 305, paragraph 1(b), (c), (d), (e) and ⓕ, which become Parties to this Convention in accordance with the conditions relevant to each, and to that extent "States Parties" refers to those entities.

ⓑ "투기"에는 다음이 포함되지 아니한다.
  (i) 선박·항공기·플랫폼 또는 그 밖의 인공해양구조물 및 이들 장비의 통상적인 운용에 따라 발생되는 폐기물이나 그 밖의 물질의 폐기. 단, 폐기물이나 그 밖의 물질을 버릴 목적으로 운용되는 선박·항공기·플랫폼 또는 그 밖의 인공해양 구조물에 의하여 운송되거나 이들에게 운송된 폐기물이나 그 밖의 물질, 이러한 선박·항공기·플랫폼 또는 그 밖의 인공해양구조물에서 이러한 폐기물 또는 그 밖의 물질을 처리함에 따라 발생되는 폐기물이나 그 밖의 물질은 제외
  (ii) 이 협약의 목적에 어긋나지 아니하는 단순한 폐기를 목적으로 하지 아니하는 물질의 유치

⑥ "당사국"이라 함은 이 협약에 기속받기로 동의하고 이 협약이 발효하고 있는 국가를 말한다.

⑦ 이 협약은 제305조 제1항 (b), (c), (d), (e) 및 ⓕ에 해당하는 주체로서 각기 관련되는 조건에 따라 이 협약의 당사자가 된 주체에 대하여 준용되며, 그러한 경우 "당사국"이라 함은 이러한 주체를 포함한다.

chapter 03 Baseline 영해기선

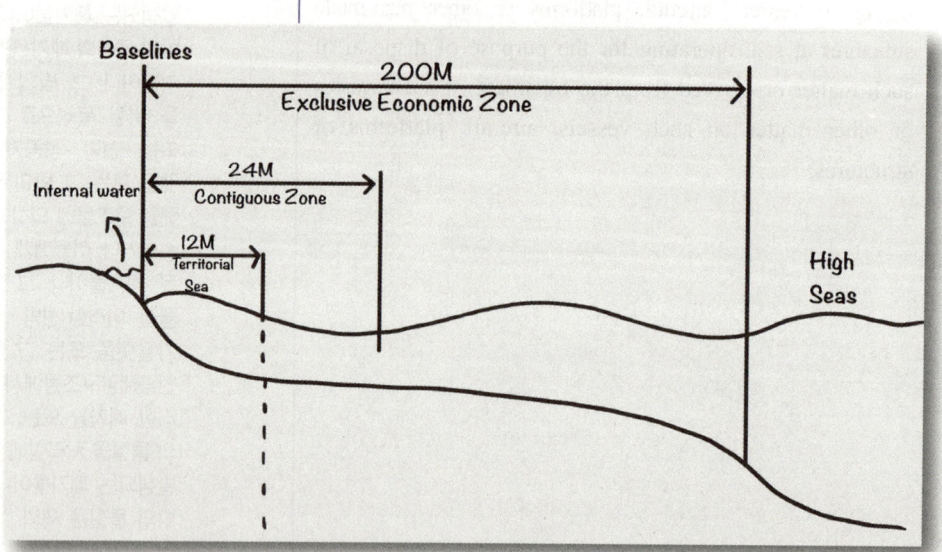

제 5조 통상기선

영해의 폭을 측정하기 위한 통상기선은 이 협약에 달리 규정된 경우를 제외하고는 연안국이 공인한 대축적해도에 표시된 해안의 저조선으로 한다.

제 7조 직선기선

① 해안선이 깊게 굴곡이 지거나 잘려 들어간 지역 또는 해안을 따라 아주 가까이 섬이 흩어져 있는 지역에서는 영해기선을 설정함에 있어서 적절한 지점을 연결하는 직선기선의 방법이 사용될 수 있다.

② 삼각주가 있거나 그 밖의 자연조건으로 인하여 해안선이 매우 불안정한 곳에는, 바다쪽 가장 바깥 저조선을 따라 적절한 지점을 선택할 수 있으며, 그 후 저조선이 후퇴하더라도 직선기선은 이 협약에 따라 연안국에 의하여 수정될 때까지 유효하다.

Article 5 Normal baseline

Except where otherwise provided in this Convention, the **normal baseline** for measuring the breadth of the territorial sea is the **low water line** along the coast as marked on large-scale charts officially recognized by the coastal state.

Article 7 Straight baselines

① In localities where the coastline is deeply **indented** and **cut into**, or if there is a **fringe of islands** along the coast in its immediate vicinity, the method of **straight baselines** joining appropriate points may be employed in drawing the baseline from which the breadth of the territorial sea is measured.

② Where because of the presence of a delta and other natural conditions the coastline is highly unstable, the appropriate points may be selected along the furthest seaward extent of the low-water line and, notwithstanding subsequent regression of the low-water line, the straight baselines shall remain effective until changed by the coastal state in accordance with this convention.

③ The drawing of straight baselines must not depart to any appreciable extent from the general direction of the coast, and the sea areas lying within the lines must be sufficiently closely linked to the land domain to be subject to the regime of internal waters.

④ Straight baselines shall not be drawn to and from low-tide elevations, unless lighthouses or similar installations which are permanently above sea level have been built on them or except in instances where the drawing of baselines to and from such elevations has received general international recognition.

⑤ Where the method of straight baselines is applicable under paragraph 1, account may be taken, in determining particular baselines, of economic interests peculiar to the region concerned, the reality and the importance of which are clearly evidenced by long usage.

⑥ The system of straight baselines may not be applied by a state in such a manner as to cut off the territorial sea of another state from the high seas or an exclusive economic zone

③ 직선기선은 해안의 일반적 방향으로부터 현저히 벗어나게 설정할 수 없으며, 직선기선안에 있는 해역은 내수제도의 의하여 규율될 수 있을 만큼 육지와 충분히 밀접하게 관련되어야 한다.

④ 직선기선은 간조노출까지 또는 간조노출지로부터 설정할 수 없다. 다만, 영구적으로 해면 위에 있는 등대나 이와 유사한 시설이 간조노출지에 세워진 경우 또는 간조노출지 사이의 기선설정이 일반적으로 국제적인 승인을 받은 경우에는 그러하지 아니하다.

⑤ 제1항의 직선기선의 방법을 적용하는 경우, 특정한 기선을 결정함에 있어서 그 지역에 특유한 경제적 이익이 있다는 사실과 그 중요성이 오랜 관행에 의하여 명백히 증명된 경우 그 경제적 이익을 고려할 수 있다.

⑥ 어떠한 국가도 다른 국가의 영해를 공해나 배타적 경제수역으로부터 격리시키는 방식으로 직선기선 제도를 적용할 수 없다.

chapter 04 Internal Water 내수

제 8조 내수

① 제4부에 규정된 경우를 제외하고는 영해기선의 육지 쪽 수역은 그 국가의 내수의 일부를 구성한다.
② 제7조에 규정된 방법에 따라 직선기선을 설정함으로써 종전에 내수가 아니었던 수역이 내수에 포함되는 경우, 이 협약에 규정된 무해통항권이 그 수역에서 계속 인정된다.

Article 8 Internal waters

① Except as provided in Part VI, waters on the landward side of the baseline of the territorial sea form part of the **internal waters** of the State.
② Where the establishment of a straight baseline in accordance with the method set forth in article 7 has the effect of enclosing as internal waters areas which had not previously been considered as such, a right of innocent passage as provided in this Convention shall exist in those waters.

Chapter 05 Territorial Sea 영해

Article 3 Breadth of the territorial sea

Every state has the right to establish the breadth of its territorial sea up to a limit not exceeding **12 nautical miles**, measured from **baselines** determined in accordance with this Convention.

Article 2 Legal status of the territorial sea, of the air space over the territorial sea and of its bed and subsoil

① The **sovereignty** of a coastal state extends, beyond its land territory and internal waters and, in the case of an archipelagic state, its archipelagic waters, to an adjacent belt of sea, described as the **territorial sea**.
② This sovereignty extends to the **air space** over the **territorial sea** as well as to its **bed** and **subsoil**.
③ The sovereignty over the **territorial sea** is exercised subject to this Convention and to other rules of **international law**.

Article 4 Outer limit of the territorial sea

The outer limit of the territorial sea is the line every point of which is at a distance from the nearest point of the baseline equal to the breadth of the territorial sea.

Article 6 Reefs

In the case of islands situated on atolls or of islands having fringing reefs, the baseline for measuring the breadth of the territorial sea is the **seaward low-water line** of the reef, as shown by the appropriate symbol on charts officially recognized by the coastal state.

제 3조 영해의 폭

모든 국가는 이 협약에 따라 결정된 기선으로부터 12해리를 넘지 아니하는 범위에서 영해의 폭을 설정할 권리를 가진다.

제 2조 영해, 영해의 상공, 해저 및 하층토의 법적지위

① 연안국의 주권은 영토와 내수 밖의 영해라고 하는 인접해역, 군도국가의 경우에는 군도 수역 밖의 영해라고 하는 인접해역에까지 미친다.
② 이러한 주권은 영해의 상공·해저 및 하층토에까지 미친다.
③ 영해에 대한 주권은 이 협약과 그 밖의 국제법 규칙에 따라 행사된다.

제 4조 영해의 바깥 경계

영해의 바깥한계는 기선상의 가장 가까운 점으로부터 영해의 폭과 같은 거리에 있는 모든 점을 연결한 선으로 한다.

제 6조 암초

환초상에 위치한 섬 또는 가장자리에 암초를 가진 섬의 경우, 영해의 폭을 측정하기 위한 기선(이하 "영해기선"이라 한다)은 연안국이 공인한 해도상에 적절한 기호로 표시된 암초의 바다쪽 저조선으로 한다.

제 9조 강의 하구

강이 직접 바다로 유입하는 경우, 기선은 양쪽 강둑의 저조선상의 지점을 하구를 가로 질러 연결한 직선으로 한다.

제 10조 만

① 이 조는 그 해안이 한 국가에 속하는 만에 한하여 적용한다.

② 이 협약에서 만이라 함은 그 들어간 정도가 입구의 폭에 비하여 현저하여 육지로 둘러싸인 수역을 형성하고, 해안의 단순한 굴곡 이상인 뚜렷한 만입을 말한다. 그러나 만입 면적이 만입의 입구를 가로 질러 연결한 선을 지름으로 하는 반원의 넓이에 미치지 못하는 경우, 그러한 만입은 만으로 보지 아니한다.

③ 측량의 목적상 만입면적이라 함은 만입해안의 저조선과 만입의 자연적 입구의 양쪽 저조지점을 연결하는 선 사이에 위치한 수역의 넓이를 말한다. 섬이 있어서 만이 둘 이상의 입구를 가지는 경우에는 각각의 입구를 가로질러 연결하는 선의 길이의 합계와 같은 길이인 선상에 반원을 그려야 한다. 만입의 안에 있는 섬은 만입수역의 일부로 본다.

④ 만의 자연적 입구 양쪽의 저조지점간의 거리가 24해리를 넘지 아니하는 경우, 폐쇄선을 두 저조지점간에 그을 수 있으며, 이 안에 포함된 수역은 내수로 본다.

⑤ 만의 자연적 입구 양쪽의 저조지전간의 거리가 24해리를 넘는 경우, 24해리의 직선으로서 가능한 한 최대의 수역을 둘러싸는 방식으로 만안에 24해리 직선기선을 그어야 한다.

Article 9 Mouths of rivers

If a river flows directly into the sea, the baseline shall be a straight line across the mouth of the river between points on the low-water line of its banks.

Article 10 Bays

① This article relates only to bays the coasts of which belong to a single State.

② For the purposes of this Convention, a bay is a well-marked indentation whose penetration is in such proportion to the width of its mouth as to contain land-locked waters and constitute more than a mere curvature of the coast. An indentation shall not, however, be regarded as a bay unless its area is as large as, or larger than, that of the semi-circle whose diameter is a line drawn across the mouth of that indentation.

③ For the purpose of measurement, the area of an indentation is that lying between the low-water mark around the shore of the indentation and a line joining the low-water mark of its natural entrance points. Where, because of the presence of islands, an indentation has more than one mouth, the semicircle shall be drawn on a line as long as the sum total of the lengths of the lines across the different mouths. Islands within an indentation shall be included as if they were part of the water area of the indentation.

④ If the distance between the low-water marks of the natural entrance points of a bay does not exceed 24 nautical miles, a closing line may be drawn between these two low-water marks, and the waters enclosed thereby shall be considered as internal waters.

⑤ Where the distance between the low-water marks of the natural entrance points of a bay exceeds 24 nautical miles, a straight baseline of 24 nautical miles shall be drawn within the bay in such a manner as to enclose the maximum area of water that is possible with a line of that length.

⑥ The foregoing provisions do not apply to so-called "historic" bays, or in any case where the system of straight baselines provided for in article 7 is applied.

Article 11 Ports

For the purpose of delimiting the territorial sea, the outermost permanent harbour works which form an integral part of the harbour system are regarded as forming part of the coast. Off-shore installations and artificial islands shall not be considered as permanent harbour works.

Article 12 Roadsteads

Roadsteads which are normally used for the loading, unloading and anchoring of ships, and which would otherwise be situated wholly or partly outside the outer limit of the territorial sea, are included in the territorial sea.

Article 13 Low-tide elevations

① A low-tide elevation is a naturally formed area of land which is surrounded by and above water at low tide but submerged at high tide. Where a low-tide elevation is situated wholly or partly at a distance not exceeding the breadth of the territorial sea from the mainland or an island, the low-water line on that elevation may be used as the baseline for measuring the breadth of the territorial sea.

② Where a low-tide elevation is wholly situated at a distance exceeding the breadth of the territorial sea from the mainland or an island, it has no territorial sea of its own.

Article 14 Combination of methods for determining baselines

The coastal State may determine baselines in turn by any of the methods provided for in the foregoing articles to suit different conditions.

⑥ 전항의 규정들은 이른바 "역사적" 만에 대하여 또는 제7조에 규정된 직선기선제도가 적용되는 경우에는 적용하지 아니한다.

제 11조 항구

영해의 경계를 획정함에 있어서, 항만체계의 불가분의 일부를 구성하는 가장 바깥의 영구적인 항만시설은 해안의 일부를 구성하는 것으로 본다. 근해시설과 인공섬은 영구적인 항만시설로 보지 아니한다.

제 12조 정박지

선박이 화물을 싣고, 내리고, 닻을 내리기 위하여 통상적으로 사용되는 정박지는 전부 또는 일부가 영해의 바깥한계 밖에 있는 경우에도 영해에 포함된다.

제 13조 간조노출지

① 간조노출지는 썰물일 때에는 물로 둘러싸여 물위에 노출되나 밀물일 때에는 물에 잠기는 자연적으로 형성된 육지지역을 말한다. 간조노출지의 전부 또는 일부가 본토나 섬으로부터 영해의 폭을 넘지 아니하는 거리에 위치하는 경우, 그 간조노출지의 저조선을 영해기선으로 사용할 수 있다.

② 간조노출지 전부가 본토나 섬으로부터 영해의 폭을 넘는 거리에 위치하는 경우, 그 간조노출지는 자체의 영해를 가지지 아니한다.

제 14조 기선결정 방법의 혼합

연안국은 서로 다른 조건에 적합하도록 앞의 각 조에 규정된 방법을 교대로 사용하여 기선을 결정할 수 있다.

제 15조 대향국간 또는 인접국간의 영해의 경계획정

두 국가의 해안이 서로 마주보고 있거나 인접하고 있는 경우, 양국 간 달리 합의하지 않는 한 양국의 각각의 영해 기선상의 가장 가까운 점으로부터 같은 거리에 있는 모든 점을 연결한 중간선 밖으로 영해를 확장할 수 없다. 다만, 위의 규정은 역사적 권원이나 그 밖의 특별한 사정에 의하여 이와 다른 방법으로 양국의 영해의 경계를 획정할 필요가 있는 경우에는 적용하지 아니한다.

제 16조 해도와 지리적 좌표목록

① 제7조, 제9조 및 제10조에 따라 결정되는 영해기선 또는 그로부터 도출된 한계, 그리고 제12조 및 제15조에 따라 그어진 경계선은 그 위치를 확인하기에 적합한 축척의 해도에 표시되어야 한다. 또는 측지자료를 명기한 각 지점의 지리적 좌표목록으로 이를 대체할 수 있다.

② 연안국은 이러한 해도나 지리적 좌표목록을 적절히 공표하고, 그 사본을 국제연합 사무총장에게 기탁한다.

Article 15 Delimitation of the territorial sea between States with opposite or adjacent coasts

Where the coasts of two States are opposite or adjacent to each other, neither of the two States is entitled, failing agreement between them to the contrary, to extend its territorial sea beyond the median line every point of which is equidistant from the nearest points on the baselines from which the breadth of the territorial seas of each of the two States is measured. The above provision does not apply, however, where it is necessary by reason of historic title or other special circumstances to delimit the territorial seas of the two States in a way which is at variance therewith.

Article 16 Charts and lists of geographical co-ordinates

① The baselines for measuring the breadth of the territorial sea determined in accordance with articles 7, 9 and 10, or the limits derived therefrom, and the lines of delimitation drawn in accordance with articles 12 and 15 shall be shown on charts of a scale or scales adequate for ascertaining their position. Alternatively, a list of geographical co-ordinates of points, specifying the geodetic datum, may be substituted.

② The coastal State shall give due publicity to such charts or lists of geographical co-ordinates and shall deposit a copy of each such chart or list with the Secretary-General of the United Nations.

기출문제

01. '해양법에 관한 국제연합 협약(UNCLOS)'상에서 다음 빈칸에 들어갈 말로 가장 적절한 것은?

> 14년 1차

> The (   ) of a coastal State extends, beyond its land territory and internal water and, in the case of an archipelagic State, its archipelagic waters, to an adjacent belt of sea, described as the territorial sea.

① right
② force
③ power
④ sovereignty

해설 연안국의 주권(sovereignty)은 영토와 내수 밖의 영해라고 하는 인접해역, 군도국가의 경우에는 군도수역 밖의 영해라고 하는 인접해역까지 미친다.

답 ❹

02. 다음은 UNCLOS(United Nations Convention on the Law of the Sea)의 내용이다. 빈칸에 공통으로 들어갈 단어로 가장 옳은 것은?

> 19년 1차

> ⓐ The sovereignty of a coastal State extends, beyond its land territory and internal waters and, in the case of an archipelagic State, its archipelagic waters, to an adjacent belt of sea, described as the (   ).
> ⓑ This sovereignty extends to the air space over the (   ) as well as to its bed and subsoil.
> ⓒ The sovereignty over the (   ) is exercised subject to this Convention and to other rules of international law.

① territorial sea
② normal baseline
③ straight baselines
④ contiguous zone

해설 주권(sovereignty)은 영해(territorial sea), 영해의 상공(air space)과 해저(bed)와 하층토(subsoil)까지 미친다.

답 ❶

기출문제

03. 다음은 UNCLOS상 Territorial sea에 대한 설명이다. 옳지 않은 것은 모두 몇 개인가? `20년 3차`

> The sovereignty of a coastal State extends, beyond its land territory and ㉠ **international waters** and, in the case of an archipelagic State, its archipelagic waters, to an adjacent belt of sea, described as the territorial sea. This sovereignty extends to the ㉡ **air space** over the territorial sea as well as to its ㉢ **bed and subsoil**. The sovereignty over the territorial sea is exercised subject to this Convention and to other rules of ㉣ **internal law**.

① 없음　　　　　　　　　② 1개
③ 2개　　　　　　　　　④ 3개

[해설] The sovereignty of a coastal State extends, beyond its land territory and ㉠ internal waters(내수) and, in the case of an archipelagic State, its archipelagic waters, to an adjacent belt of sea, described as the territorial sea.
This sovereignty extends to the air space over the territorial sea as well as to its bed and subsoil.
The sovereignty over the territorial sea is exercised subject to this Convention and to other rules of ㉣ international law(국제 법).
옳지 않은 것 : ㉠, ㉣

[답] ❸

04. 다음은 UNCLOS상 Territorial sea에 대한 설명이다. 옳지 않은 것은 모두 몇 개인가?
`22년 일반직`

> The sovereignty of a coastal State extends, beyond its land territory and ㉠ **international waters** and, in the case of an archipelagic State, its archipelagic waters, to an adjacent belt of sea, described as the territorial sea. This sovereignty extends to the ㉡ **air space** over the territorial sea as well as to its ㉢ **sea and subsoil**. The sovereignty over the territorial sea is exercised subject to this Convention and to other rules of ㉣ **internal law**.

① 1개　　　　　　　　　② 2개
③ 3개　　　　　　　　　④ 없음

[해설] The sovereignty of a coastal State extends, beyond its land territory and ㉠ internal waters(내수) and, in the case of an archipelagic State, its archipelagic waters, to an adjacent belt of sea, described as the territorial sea.
This sovereignty extends to the air space over the territorial sea as well as to its ㉢ bed and subsoil.
The sovereignty over the territorial sea is exercised subject to this Convention and to other rules of ㉣ international law(국제 법).
옳지 않은 것 : ㉠, ㉢, ㉣

[답] ❸

Chapter 06 Contiguous zone 접속수역

Article 33 Contiguous zone

① The **contiguous zone** may not extend beyond **24 nautical miles** from the **baselines** from which the breadth of the territorial sea is measured.

② In a zone contiguous to its territorial sea, described as the **contiguous zone**, the coastal State may exercise the control necessary to:

ⓐ prevent infringement of its **customs, fiscal, immigration or sanitary** laws and regulations within its territory or territorial sea;

ⓑ punish infringement of the above laws and regulation committed within its territory or territorial sea.

제 33조 접속수역

① 접속수역은 영해기선으로부터 24해리 밖으로 확장할 수 없다.

② 연안국은 영해에 접속해 있는 수역으로서 접속수역이라고 불리는 수역에서 다음을 위하여 필요한 통제를 할 수 있다.

ⓐ 연안국의 영토나 영해에서의 관세·재정·출입국관리 또는 위생에 관한 법령의 위반 방지

ⓑ 연안국의 영토나 영해에서 발생한 위의 법령 위반에 대한 처벌

기출문제

01. The sentence below is a part of an article from the UNCLOS. Choose the correct one for the blank.　　　14년 2차

In ( ) the Coastal state may exercise the control necessary to prevent infringement of its customs, fiscal, immigration or sanitary laws and regulations within its territory or territorial sea.

① the territorial sea　　② the contiguous zone
③ the exclusive economic zone　　④ the high seas

해설 접속수역(the contiguous zone)에서, 연안국은 연안국의 영토나 영해에서의 관세·재정·출입국관리 또는 위생에 관한 법령의 위반 방지를 위한 제한을 둘 수 있다.

답 ❷

chapter 07 Exclusive Economic Zone 배타적 경제 수역

제 57조 배타적 경제수역의 폭

배타적 경제수역은 영해기선으로부터 200해리를 넘을 수 없다.

Article 57 Breadth of the exclusive economic zone

The exclusive economic zone shall not extend beyond **200 nautical miles** from the **baselines** from which the breadth of the territorial sea is measured.

제 56조 배타적 경제수역에서의 연안국의 권리, 관할권 및 의무

배타적 경제수역에서 연안국은 다음의 권리와 의무를 갖는다.

ⓐ 해저의 상부수역, 해저 및 그 하층토의 생물이나 무생물 등 천연자원의 탐사, 개발, 보존 및 관리를 목적으로 하는 주권적 권리와, 해수·해류 및 해풍을 이용한 에너지 생산과 같은 이 수역의 경제적 개발과 탐사를 위한 그 밖의 활동에 관한 주권적 권리

ⓑ 이 협약의 관련규정에 규정된 다음 사항에 관한 관할권
- 인공섬, 시설 및 구조물의 설치와 사용
- 해양과학조사
- 해양환경의 보호와 보존

ⓒ 이 협약에 규정된 그 밖의 권리와 의무

Article 56 Rights, jurisdiction and duties of the coastal state in the exclusive economic zone

In the **exclusive economic zone**, the coastal State has:

ⓐ **sovereign rights** for the purpose of exploring and exploiting, conserving and managing the natural resources, whether living or non-living, of the waters superjacent to the seabed and of the seabed and its subsoil, and with regard to other activities for the economic exploitation and exploration of the zone, such as the production of energy from the water, currents and winds;

ⓑ **jurisdiction** as provided for in the relevant provisions of this Convention with regard to:
- the establishment and use of artificial islands, installations and structures;
- marine scientific research;
- the protection and preservation of the marine environment;

ⓒ other rights and duties provided for in this convention.

기출문제

01. 다음은 'UNCLOS(United Nations Convention On The Law of the Sea)'에 나오는 정의 중 일부를 발췌한 것이다. 다음 빈칸에 공통적으로 들어갈 말로 가장 적절한 것은? `17년 2차`

> 가. Every State has the right to establish the breadth of its territorial sea up to a limit not exceeding 12 nautical miles, measured from (　　)s determined in accordance with this Convention.
>
> 나. The contiguous zone may not extend beyond 24 nautical miles from the (　　)s from which the breadth of the territorial sea is measured.
>
> 다. The exclusive economic zone shall not extend beyond 200 nautical miles from the (　　)s from which the breadth of the territorial sea is measured.

① baseline　　　　② horizontal line
③ straight line　　④ vertical line

해설 영해와 접속수역, 배타적 경제수역은 '영해기선'(baseline)을 기점으로 정한다.

답 ❶

02. 다음은 UNCLOS(United Nations Convention on the Law of the Sea)의 내용이다. 빈칸에 들어갈 단어로 가장 옳은 것은? `21년 하반기`

> 1. In the exclusive economic zone, the coastal State has:
> (a) ...
> (b) (　　) as provided for in the relevant provisions of this Convention with regard to:
> • the establishment and use of artificial islands, installations and structures;
> • marine scientific research;
> • the protection and preservation of the marine environment;

① Right　　　　　② Duties
③ Jurisdiction　　④ Sovereignty

해설 연안국은 배타적 경제수역에서(exclusive economic zone) 인공 섬, 설치물, 구조물의 사용과 설정, 해양과학조사 그리고 해양환경의 보존과 보호에 대한 관할권(Jurisdiction)을 갖는다.

답 ❸

chapter 08 High Seas 공해

제 86조

이 부의 규정은 어느 한 국가의 배타적경제수역, 영해, 내수 또는 군도국가의 군도수역에 속하지 아니하는 바다의 모든 부분에 적용한다.

Article 86 Application of the provisions of this Part

The provisions of this Part apply to all parts of the sea that are not included in the exclusive economic zone, in the territorial sea or in the internal waters of a State, or in the archipelagic waters of an archipelagic State.

제 87조 공해의 자유

공해는 연안국이거나 내륙국이거나 관계없이 모든 국가에 개방된다. 공해의 자유는 이 협약과 그 밖의 국제법규칙이 정하는 조건에 따라 행사된다. 연안국과 내륙국이 향유하는 공해의 자유는 특히 다음의 자유를 포함한다.

ⓐ 항행의 자유
ⓑ 상공비행의 자유
ⓒ 제6부에 따른 해저전선과 관련 부설의 자유
ⓓ 제6부에 따라 국제법상 허용되는 인공섬과 그 밖의 시설 건설의 자유
ⓔ 제2절에 정하여진 조건에 따른 어로의 자유
ⓕ 제6부와 제13부에 따른 과학조사의 자유

Article 87 Freedom of the high seas

The **high seas** are open to all states, whether coastal or land-locked. **Freedom** of the high seas is exercised under the conditions laid down by this Convention and by other rules of international law, it comprises, inter alia, both for coastal and land-locked states:

ⓐ freedom of navigation;
ⓑ freedom of overflight;
ⓒ freedom to lay submarine cables and pipelines, subject to part Ⅵ;
ⓓ freedom to construct artificial islands and other installations permitted under international law, subject to part Ⅵ;
ⓔ freedom of fishing, subject to the conditions laid down in section 2;
ⓕ freedom of scientific research, subject to Parts Ⅳ and Ⅷ.

제 88조 평화적 목적을 위한 공해의 보존

공해는 평화적 목적을 위하여 보존된다.

Article 88 Reservation of the high seas for peaceful purposes

The **high seas** shall be reserved for peaceful purposes.

Article 89 Invalidity of claims of sovereignty over the high seas

No State may validly purport to subject any part of the **high seas** to its sovereignty.

제89조 공해에 대한 주권 주장의 무효
어떠한 국가라도 공해의 어느 부분을 유효하게 자국의 주권하에 둘 수 없다.

Article 90 Right of navigation

Every State, whether coastal or land-locked, has the right to sail ships flying its flag on the **high seas**.

제 90조 항행의 권리

연안국이든 내륙국이든 모든 국가는 공해 상에 자국의 기를 게양한 선박을 항행시킬 권리를 갖는다.

Right of innocent passage
무해통항권

제 17조 무해통항권

연안국이거나 내륙국이거나 관계없이 모든 국가의 선박은 이 협약에 따라, 영해에서 무해통항권을 향유한다.

Article 17 Right of innocent passage

Subject to this Convention, ships of all States, whether coastal or land-locked, enjoy the **right of innocent passage** through the **territorial sea**.

제 18조 통항의 의미

① 통항이라 함은 다음의 목적을 위하여 영해를 지나서 항행함을 말한다.

ⓐ 내수에 들어가지 아니하거나 내수 밖의 정박지나 항구시설에 기항하지 아니하고 영해를 횡단하는 것 또는

ⓑ 내수를 향하여 또는 내수로부터 항진하거나 또는 이러한 정박지나 항구시설에 기항하는 것

② 통항은 계속적이고 신속하여야 한다. 다만, 정선이나 닻을 내리는 행위가 통상적인 항해에 부수되는 경우, 불가항력이나 조난으로 인하여 필요한 경우 또는 위험하거나 조난 상태에 있는 인명·선박 또는 항공기를 구조하기 위한 경우에는 통항에 포함된다.

Article 18 Meaning of passage

① Passage means navigation through the territorial sea for the purpose of:

ⓐ traversing that sea without entering internal waters or calling at a roadstead or port facility outside internal waters ; or

ⓑ proceeding to or from internal waters or a call at such roadstead or port facility.

② Passage shall be **continuous** and **expeditious**. However, passage includes stopping and anchoring, but only in so far as the same are **incidental to ordinary navigation** or are rendered necessary by **force majeure or distress** or for the purpose of rendering assistance to persons, ships or aircraft in danger or distress.

Article 19 Meaning of innocent passage

① Passage is **innocent** so long as it is not prejudicial to the peace, good order or security of the coastal state. Such passage shall take place in conformity with this convention and with other rules of international law.

② Passage of a foreign ship shall be considered to be prejudicial to the peace, good order or security of the coastal state if in the territorial sea it engages in any of the following activities:

ⓐ **any threat or use of force** against the sovereignty, territorial integrity or political independence of the coastal State, or in any other manner in violation of the principles of international law embodies in the charter of the United Nations;

ⓑ any **exercise or practice with weapons** of any kind;

ⓒ any act aimed at **collecting information** to the prejudice of the defence or security of the coastal state;

ⓓ any act of **propaganda** aimed at affecting the defence or security of the coastal State;

ⓔ the **launching, landing or taking on board** of any aircraft;

ⓕ the **launching, landing or taking on board** of any military device;

ⓖ the **loading or unloading of any commodity, currency or person** contrary to the customs, fiscal, immigration or sanitary laws and regulations of the coastal State;

ⓗ any act of **wilful and serious pollution** contrary to this Convention;

ⓘ any **fishing activities**;

ⓙ the carrying out of **research or survey activities**;

ⓚ any act aimed at **interfering** with any systems of communication or any other facilities or installations of the coastal State;

제 19조 무해통항의 의미

① 통항은 연안국의 평화, 공공질서 또는 안전을 해치지 아니하는 한 무해하다. 이러한 통항은 이 협약과 그 밖의 국제법 규칙에 따라 이루어진다.

② 외국선박이 영해에서 다음의 어느 활동에 종사하는 경우, 외국선박의 통항은 연안국의 평화, 공공질서 또는 안전을 해치는 것으로 본다.

ⓐ 연안국의 주권, 영토보전 또는 정치적 독립에 반하거나 또는 국제연합헌장에 구현된 국제법의 원칙에 위반되는 그 밖의 방식에 의한 무력의 위협이나 행사

ⓑ 무기를 사용하는 훈련이나 연습

ⓒ 연안국의 국방이나 안전에 해가 되는 정보수집을 목적으로 하는 행위

ⓓ 연안국의 국방이나 안전에 해로운 영향을 미칠 것을 목적으로 하는 선전행위

ⓔ 항공기의 선상 발진·착륙 또는 탑재

ⓕ 군사기기의 선상 발진·착륙 또는 탑재

ⓖ 연안국의 관세·재정·출입국관리 또는 위생에 관한 법령에 위반되는 물품이나 통화를 싣고 내리는 행위 또는 사람의 승선이나 하선

ⓗ 이 협약에 위배되는 고의적이고도 중대한 오염행위

ⓘ 어로활동

ⓙ 조사활동이나 측량활동의 수행

ⓚ 연안국이 통신체계 또는 그 밖의 설비·시설물에 대한 방해를 목적으로 하는 행위

ⓛ 통항과 직접 관련이 없는 그 밖의 활동	ⓛ any other activity not having a direct bearing on passage.
제 20조 잠수함과 그 밖의 잠수항행기기 잠수함과 그 밖의 잠수항행기기는 영해에서 해면 위로 국기를 게양하고 항행한다.	Article 20 Submarines and other underwater vehicles In the **territorial sea**, submarines and other underwater vehicles are required to navigate **on the surface** and to show their **flag**.

I 기출문제

01. Which is a not suitable word at blank? [11년 2차]

Passage is innocent so long as it is not prejudicial to the (   ), (   ) or (   ) of the coastal state. Such passage shall take place in conformity with this convention and with other rules of international law.

① peace
② good order
③ force
④ security

해설 통항은 연안국의 평화(peace), 공공질서(good order), 또는 안전(security)을 해치지 않는 한 무해(innocent)하다. force는 무력 혹은 힘을 의미한다.

답 ③

02. 다음 중 밑줄 친 단어의 의미와 가장 비슷한 것은? [18년 일반직]

Subject to this Convention, ships of all States, whether coastal or land-locked, enjoy the right of **innocent** passage through the territorial sea.

① emergency
② safe
③ promptly
④ harmless

해설 right of innocent passage은 무해통항권으로, innocent는 '무해한'이라는 뜻을 가지고 있다. harmless 역시 '해가 없는'의 의미를 지니므로 가장 비슷한 단어라고 볼 수 있다.

답 ④

기출문제

03. 다음 '해양법에 관한 국제연합 협약(UNCLOS)' 중 무해통항(Innocent passage) 조항에서 외국 선박이 연안국의 평화, 공공질서 또는 안전을 해치는 활동으로 규정한 것은 모두 몇 개인가?

14년 1차

가. any exercise or practice with weapons of any kind
나. the launching, landing or taking on board of any aircraft
다. any fishing activities
라. any act of propaganda aimed at affecting the defence or security of the coastal State
마. the carrying out of research or survey activities

① 2개 ② 3개
③ 4개 ④ 5개

해설 모든 항목이 무해통항 조항에서의 연안국의 평화, 공공질서 또는 안전을 해치는 활동으로 규정한 것이다.

답 ❹

04. 다음 보기는 UNCLOS상 무해통항 조항에서 외국 선박이 연안국의 평화, 공공질서 또는 안전을 해치는 활동으로 규정한 내용이다. 빈 칸에 들어갈 단어로 가장 옳은 것은?

21년 상반기

㉠ any act of (ⓐ) pollution contrary to this Convention
㉡ any (ⓑ) activities

① ⓐ : wilful and serious   ⓑ : fishery
② ⓐ : wilful or negligent   ⓑ : fishing
③ ⓐ : wilful and serious   ⓑ : fishing
④ ⓐ : wilful or negligent   ⓑ : fisher

해설 ㉠ any act of willful and serious(고의적이고 심각한) pollution contrary to this Convention
㉡ any fishing(어로) activities

답 ❸

Chapter 9. Right of innocent passage 무해통항권 | **165**

기출문제

05. 다음 중 UNCLOS상 무해 통항(Innocent passage)조항에서 외국선박이 연안국의 평화, 공공질서 또는 안전을 해치는 활동으로 규정한 것이 아닌 것은 모두 몇 개 인가? `22년 2차`

ⓐ any threat or use of force against the sovereignty, territorial integrity or political independence of the coastal State, or in any other manner in violation of the principles of international law embodies in the charter of the United Nations;
ⓑ any exercise or practice with weapons of any kind;
ⓒ any act aimed at collecting information to the prejudice of the defence or security of the coastal state;
ⓓ any act of propaganda aimed at affecting the defence or security of the coastal State;
ⓔ any act of negligent pollution contrary to this Convention;
ⓕ the carrying out of research or survey activities;

① 없다. ② 1개
③ 2개   ④ 3개

해설 ⓔ any act of <u>wilful and serious pollution</u> contrary to this Convention;
negligent는 느긋한, 태만한 등의 의미를 갖는다.

답 ②

Article 21 Laws and regulations of the coastal State relating to innocent passage

① The coastal State may adopt laws and regulations, in conformity with the provisions of this Convention and other rules of international law, relating to innocent passage through the territorial sea, in respect of all or any of the following:

ⓐ the safety of navigation and the regulation of maritime traffic;
ⓑ the protection of navigational aids and facilities and other facilities or installations;
ⓒ the protection of cables and pipelines;
ⓓ the conservation of the living resources of the sea;
ⓔ the prevention of infringement of the fisheries laws and regulations of the coastal State;
ⓕ the preservation of the environment of the coastal State and the prevention, reduction and control of pollution thereof;
ⓖ marine scientific research and hydrographic surveys;
ⓗ the prevention of infringement of the customs, fiscal, immigration or sanitary laws and regulations of the coastal State.

② Such laws and regulations shall not apply to the design, construction, manning or equipment of foreign ships unless they are giving effect to generally accepted international rules or standards.

③ The coastal State shall give due publicity to all such laws and regulations.

④ Foreign ships exercising the right of innocent passage through the territorial sea shall comply with all such laws and regulations and all generally accepted international regulations relating to the prevention of collisions at sea.

제 21조 무해통항에 관한 연안국의 법령

① 연안국은 이 협약의 규정과 그 밖의 국제법규칙에 따라 다음 각호의 전부 또는 일부에 대하여 영해에서의 무해통항에 관한 법령을 제정할 수 있다.

ⓐ 항행의 안전과 해상교통의 규제
ⓑ 항행보조수단과 설비 및 그 밖의 설비나 시설의 보호
ⓒ 해저전선과 관선의 보호
ⓓ 해양생물자원의 보존
ⓔ 연안국의 어업법령 위반방지
ⓕ 연안국의 환경보전과 연안국 환경오염의 방지, 경감 및 통제
ⓖ 해양과학조사와 수로측량
ⓗ 연안국의 관세, 재정, 출입국관리 또는 위생에 관한 법령의 위반방지

② 이러한 법령이 일반적으로 수락된 국제규칙이나 기준을 시행하는 것이 아닌 한 외국선박의 설계, 구조, 인원배치 또는 장비에 대하여 적용하지 아니한다.

③ 연안국은 이러한 모든 법령을 적절히 공표하여야 한다.

④ 외국선박이 영해에서 무해통항권을 행사하는 경우, 이러한 모든 법령과 해상충돌방지에 관하여 일반적으로 수락된 모든 국제규칙을 준수하여야 한다.

제22조 영해내의 항로대와 통항분리방식

① 연안국은 항행의 안전을 위하여 필요한 경우 자국의 영해에서 무해통항권을 행사하는 외국선박에 대하여 선박통항을 규제하기 위하여 지정된 항로대와 규정된 통항분리방식을 이용하도록 요구할 수 있다.

② 특히 유조선, 핵추진선박 및 핵물질 또는 본래 위험하거나 유독한 그 밖의 물질이나 재료를 운반중인 선박에 대하여서는 이러한 항로대만을 통항하도록 요구할 수 있다.

③ 연안국은 이 조에 따라 항로대를 지정하고 통항분리방식을 규정함에 있어서 다음 사항을 고려한다.

ⓐ 권한 있는 국제기구의 권고
ⓑ 국제항행에 관습적으로 이용되고 있는 수로
ⓒ 특정한 선박과 수로의 특성
ⓓ 선박교통량

④ 연안국은 이러한 항로대와 통항분리방식을 해도에 명시하고 이를 적절히 공표한다.

제23조 외국의 핵추진선박과 핵물질 또는 본래 위험하거나 유독한 그 밖의 물질을 운반하는 선박

외국의 핵추진선박과 핵물질 또는 본래 위험하거나 유독한 그 밖의 물질을 운반중인 선박은 영해에서 무해통항권을 행사하는 경우, 이러한 선박에 대하여 국제협정이 정한 서류를 휴대하고 또한 국제협정에 의하여 확립된 특별예방조치를 준수한다.

Article 22 Sea lanes and traffic separation schemes in the territorial sea

① The coastal State may, where necessary having regard to the safety of navigation, require foreign ships exercising the right of innocent passage through its territorial sea to use such sea lanes and traffic separation schemes as it may designate or prescribe for the regulation of the passage of ships.

② In particular, tankers, nuclear-powered ships and ships carrying nuclear or other inherently dangerous or noxious substances or materials may be required to confine their passage to such sea lanes.

③ In the designation of sea lanes and the prescription of traffic separation schemes under this article, the coastal State shall take into account:

ⓐ the recommendations of the competent international organization;
ⓑ any channels customarily used for international navigation;
ⓒ the special characteristics of particular ships and channels; and
ⓓ the density of traffic.

④ The coastal State shall clearly indicate such sea lanes and traffic separation schemes on charts to which due publicity shall be given.

Article 23 Foreign nuclear-powered ships and ships carrying nuclear or other inherently dangerous or noxious substances

Foreign nuclear-powered ships and ships carrying nuclear or other inherently dangerous or noxious substances shall, when exercising the right of innocent passage through the territorial sea, carry documents and observe special precautionary measures established for such ships by international agreements.

Article 24 Duties of the coastal State

① The coastal State shall not hamper the innocent passage of foreign ships through the territorial sea except in accordance with this Convention. In particular, in the application of this Convention or of any laws or regulations adopted in conformity with this Convention, the coastal State shall not:

ⓐ impose requirements on foreign ships which have the practical effect of denying or impairing the right of innocent passage; or

ⓑ discriminate in form or in fact against the ships of any State or against ships carrying cargoes to, from or on behalf of any State.

② The coastal State shall give appropriate publicity to any danger to navigation, of which it has knowledge, within its territorial sea.

Article 25 Rights of protection of the coastal State

① The coastal State may take the necessary steps in its territorial sea to prevent passage which is not innocent.

② In the case of ships proceeding to internal waters or a call at a port facility outside internal waters, the coastal State also has the right to take the necessary steps to prevent any breach of the conditions to which admission of those ships to internal waters or such a call is subject.

③ The coastal State may, without discrimination in form or in fact among foreign ships, suspend temporarily in specified areas of its territorial sea the innocent passage of foreign ships if such suspension is essential for the protection of its security, including weapons exercises. Such suspension shall take effect only after having been duly published.

제 24조 연안국의 의무

① 연안국은 이 협약에 의하지 아니하고는 영해에서 외국선박의 무해통항을 방해하지 아니한다. 특히, 연안국은 이 협약이나 이 협약에 따라 제정된 법령을 적용함에 있어 다음 사항을 행하지 아니한다.

ⓐ 외국선박에 대하여 실질적으로 무해통항권을 부인하거나 침해하는 효과를 가져 오는 요건의 부과

ⓑ 특정국의 선박, 또는 특정국으로 화물을 반입반출하거나 특정국을 위하여 화물을 운반하는 선박에 대한 형식상 또는 실질상의 차별

② 연안국은 자국이 인지하고 있는 자국 영해에서의 통항에 관한 위험을 적절히 공표한다.

제 25조 연안국의 보호권

① 연안국은 무해하지 아니한 통항을 방지하기 위하여 필요한 조치를 자국 영해에서 취할 수 있다.

② 연안국은 선박이 내수를 향하여 항행하거나 내수 밖의 항구시설에 기항하고자 하는 경우, 그 선박이 내수로 들어가기 위하여 또는 그러한 항구시설에 기항하기 위하여 따라야 할 허가조건을 위반하는 것을 방지하기 위하여 필요한 조치를 취할 권리를 가진다.

③ 연안국은 무기를 사용하는 훈련을 포함하여 자국의 안전보호상 긴요한 경우에는 영해의 지정된 수역에서 외국선박을 형식상 또는 실질상 차별하지 아니하고 무해통항을 일시적으로 정지시킬 수 있다. 이러한 정지조치는 적절히 공표한 후에만 효력을 가진다.

제 26조 외국선박에 부과할 수 있는 수수료

① 외국선박에 대하여 영해의 통항만을 이유로 어떠한 수수료도 부과할 수 없다.

② 수수료는 영해를 통항하는 외국선박에 제공된 특별한 용역에 대한 대가로서만 그 선박에 대하여 부과할 수 있다. 이러한 수수료는 차별 없이 부과된다.

Article 26 Charges which may be levied upon foreign ships

① No charge may be levied upon foreign ships by reason only of their passage through the territorial sea.

② Charges may be levied upon a foreign ship passing through the territorial sea as payment only for specific services rendered to the ship.

These charges shall be levied without discrimination.

Chapter 10 Right of Visit 임검권

Article 110 Right of visit

① Except where acts of interference derive from powers conferred by treaty, a warship which encounters on the high seas a foreign ship, other than a ship entitled to complete immunity in accordance with articles 95 and 96, is not justified in boarding it unless there is reasonable ground for suspecting that:

ⓐ the ship is engaged in **piracy;**
ⓑ the ship is engaged in the **slave trade;**
ⓒ the ship is engaged in **unauthorized broadcasting** and the flag state of the warship has jurisdiction under article 109;
ⓓ the ship is **without nationality;** or
ⓔ though **flying a foreign flag** or **refusing to show its flag**, the ship is, in reality, of the same nationality as the warship.

② In the cases provided for in paragraph1, the warship may proceed to verify the ship's right to fly its flag. To this end, it may send a boat under the command of an officer to the suspected ship. If suspicion remains after the documents have been checked, it may proceed to a further examination on board the ship, which must be carried out with all possible consideration.

③ If the suspicions prove to be unfounded, and provided that the ship boarded has not committed any act justifying them, **it shall be compensated** for any loss or damage that may have been sustained.

제 110조 임검권

① 제95조와 제96조에 따라 완전한 면책을 가지는 선박을 제외한 외국선박을 공해에서 만난 군함은 다음과 같은 혐의를 가지고 있다는 합리적 근거가 없는 한 그 선박을 임검하는 것은 정당화되지 아니한다. 다만, 간섭행위가 조약에 따라 부여된 권한에 의한 경우는 제외한다.
ⓐ 그 선박의 해적행위에의 종사
ⓑ 그 선박의 노예거래에의 종사
ⓒ 그 선박의 무허가 방송에의 종사 및 군함 기국이 제109조에 따른 관할권 보유
ⓓ 무국적선
ⓔ 선박이 외국기를 게양하고 있거나 국기 제시를 거절하였음에도 불구하고 실질적으로 군함과 같은 국적보유

② 위 조항에 규정된 경우에 있어서 군함은 그 선박이 그 국기를 게양할 권리를 가지는가를 확인할 수 있다. 이러한 목적을 위하여 군함은 혐의선박에 대하여 장교의 지휘하 보조선을 파견할 수 있다. 서류를 검열한 후에도 혐의가 남아 있는 경우, 가능한 한 신중하게 그 선박 내에서 계속하여 검사를 진행할 수 있다.

③ 혐의가 없는 것으로 밝혀지고 임검을 받은 선박이 그 혐의를 입증할 어떠한 행위도 행하지 아니한 경우에는 그 선박이 입은 모든 손실이나 피해에 대하여 보상을 받는다.

④ 이러한 규정은 군용항공기에 준용한다.

④ These provisions apply mutatis mutandis to military aircraft.

⑤ 이러한 규정은 또한 정부 업무에 사용 중인 것으로 명백히 표시되어 식별이 가능하며 정당하게 권한이 부여된 그 밖의 모든 선박이나 항공기에도 적용한다.

⑤ These provisions also apply to any other duly authorized ships or aircraft clearly marked and identifiable as being on **government service**.

기출문제

01. "임검권"의 올바른 영어 표기로 가장 옳은 것은? 〔17년 1차〕

① Right of hot pursuit
② Right of navigation
③ Right of visit
④ Status of ships

해설 ① 추적권 ② 항행의 권리 ③ 임검권 ④ 선박의 지위

답 ③

Chapter 11 Right of Hot Pursuit 추적권

Article 111 Right of hot pursuit

① The hot pursuit of a foreign ship may be undertaken when the competent authorities of the coastal State have good reason to believe that the ship has violated the laws and regulations of that State.

② Such pursuit must be commenced when the foreign ship or one of its boats is within the **internal waters, the archipelagic waters, the territorial sea or the contiguous zone** of the pursuing state, and may only be continued outside the territorial sea or the contiguous zone if the pursuit has not been interrupted.

③ It is **not necessary** that, at the time when the foreign ship within the territorial sea or the contiguous zone receives the order to stop, the ship giving the order should likewise be within the territorial sea or the contiguous zone.
If the foreign ship is within a contiguous zone, as defined in article 33, the pursuit may only be undertaken if there has been a violation of the rights for the protection of which the zone was established.

④ The right of hot pursuit **ceases** as soon as the ship pursued enters the **territorial sea** of its own states or of a third State.

⑤ The pursuit may only be commenced after a visual or auditory signal to stop has been given at a distance which enables it to be seen or heard by the foreign ship.

제 111조 추적권

① 외국선박에 대한 추적은 연안국의 권한 있는 당국이 그 선박이 자국의 법령을 위반한 것으로 믿을 만한 충분한 이유가 있을 때 행사할 수 있다.

② 이러한 추적은 외국선박이나 그 선박의 보조선이 추적국의 내수·군도수역·영해 또는 접속수역에 있을 때 시작되고 또한 추적이 중단되지 아니한 경우에 한하여 영해나 접속수역 밖으로 계속될 수 있다.

③ 영해나 접속수역에 있는 외국선박이 정선명령을 받았을 때 정선명령을 한 선박은 반드시 영해나 접속수역에 있어야 할 필요는 없다. 외국 선박이 제33조에 정의된 접속수역에 있을 경우 추적은 그 수역을 설정함으로써 보호하려는 권리가 침해되는 경우에 한하여 행할 수 있다.

④ 추적권은 추적당하는 선박이 그 국적국 또는 제3국의 영해에 들어감과 동시에 소멸한다.

⑤ 추적은 외국선박이 보거나 들을 수 있는 거리에서 시각이나 음향 정선신호가 발신된 후 비로소 이를 시작할 수 있다.

⑥ 추적권은 군함·군용항공기 또는 정부업무에 사용 중인 것으로 명백히 표시되어 식별이 가능하며 그러한 권한이 부여된 그 밖의 선박이나 항공기에 의하여서만 행사될 수 있다.

⑥ The right of hot pursuit may be exercised only by **warships or military aircraft**, or other ships or aircraft clearly marked and identifiable as being on **government service** and authorized to that effect.

⑦ 어느 국가의 관할권 내에서 나포되어 권한 있는 당국의 심리를 받기 위하여 그 국가의 항구에 호송된 선박은 부득이한 사정에 의하여 그 항행 도중에 배타적 경제수역의 어느 한 부분이나 공해의 어느 한 부분을 통하여 호송되었다는 이유만으로 그 석방을 주장할 수 없다.

⑦ The release of a ship arrested within the jurisdiction of a State and escorted to a port of that State for the purposes of an inquiry before the competent authorities **may not be claimed** solely on the ground that the ship, in the course of its voyage, was escorted across a portion of the exclusive economic zone or the high seas, if the circumstances rendered this necessary.

⑧ 추적권의 행사가 정당화되지 아니하는 상황에서 선박이 영해 밖에서 정지되거나 나포된 경우, 그 선박은 이로 인하여 받은 모든 손실이나 피해를 보상받는다.

⑧ Where a ship has been stopped or arrested outside the territorial sea in circumstances which do not justify the exercise of the right of hot pursuit, it **shall be compensated** for any loss or damage that may have been thereby sustained.

⑨ 추적이 항공기에 의하여 행하여지는 경우 : 정선명령을 한 항공기는 선박을 직접 나포할 수 있는 경우를 제외하고는 그 항공기가 요청한 연안국의 선박이나 다른 항공기가 도착하여 추적을 인수할 때까지 그 선박을 스스로 적극적으로 추적해야 한다.

⑨ Where hot pursuit is effected by an aircraft : the aircraft giving the order to stop must itself actively pursue the ship until a ship or another aircraft of the coastal state, summoned by the aircraft, arrives to take over the pursuit, unless the aircraft is itself able to arrest the ship.

기출문제

01. '추적권'의 올바른 영어표기로 가장 적절한 것은?　　　　　　　18년 1차

① Right of innocent passage
② Right of hot pursuit
③ Right of visit
④ Right of navigation

해설　① 무해통항권 ② 추적권 ③ 임검권 ④ 항행의 권리

답 ❷

기출문제

02. 다음 중 외국선박에 대한 '추적권(Right of hot pursuit)'에 대한 설명 중 가장 옳지 않은 것은?

14년 1차

① The right of hot pursuit may be exercised only by warships or military aircraft, or other ships or aircraft clearly marked and identifiable as being on government service and authorized to that effect.

② The release of a ship arrested within the jurisdiction of a State and escorted to a port of that State for the purposes of an inquiry before the competent authorities may not be claimed solely on the ground that the ship, in the course of its voyage, was escorted across a portion of the exclusive economic zone or the high seas, if the circumstances rendered this necessary.

③ The right of hot pursuit ceases as soon as the ship pursued enters the territorial sea of its own State or of a third State.

④ Where a ship has been stopped or arrested outside the territorial sea in circumstances which do not justify the exercise of the right of hot pursuit, it shall not be compensated for any loss or damage that may have been thereby sustained.

해설 'not'이 빠져야한다. : it shall not(×) be compensated

답 ④

03. 다음 밑줄 친 빈칸에 들어갈 말로 가장 옳지 않은 것은?

17년 1차 / 19년 3차

> The hot pursuit of a foreign ship may be undertaken when the competent authorities of the coastal State have good reason to believe that the ship has violated the laws and regulations of that State. Such pursuit must be commenced when the foreign ship or one of its boats is within (　　　　) of pursuing State.

① the internal waters　　② the archipelagic waters
③ the high seas　　　　④ the territorial sea

해설 추적권은 추적국의 내수, 영해, 접속수역, 군도국가의 경우 군도수역 내에 있을 때 행할 수 있다. 공해(high seas)는 제외된다.

답 ③

I 기출문제

04. According to 'UNCLOS(United Nations Convention On The Law of the Sea)', What's wrong explanation of the "Right of hot pursuit"?   `17년 2차`

① The hot pursuit of a foreign ship undertaken when the competent authorities of the coastal State have good reason to believe that the ship has violated the laws and regulations of that State.
② It is necessary that, at the time when the foreign ship within the territorial sea or the contiguous zone receives the order to stop, the ship giving the order should likewise be within the territorial sea or the contiguous zone.
③ The right of hot pursuit ceases as soon as the ship pursued enters the territorial sea of its own State or of a third State.
④ The right of hot pursuit may be exercised only by warships or military aircraft, or other ships or aircraft clearly marked and identifiable as being on government service and authorized to that effect.

해설 It is 뒤에 not이 붙어야한다.

05. 다음은 UNCLOS(United Nations Convention on the Law of the Sea)상 Right of hot pursuit에 대한 내용이다. 옳은 것은 모두 몇 개 인가?   `19년 1차`

ⓐ The hot pursuit of a foreign ship may be undertaken when the competent authorities of the coastal State have good reason to believe that the ship has violated the laws and regulations of the State.
ⓑ It is necessary that, at the time when the foreign ship within the territorial sea or the contiguous zone receives the order to stop, the ship giving the order should likewise be within the territorial sea or the contiguous zone.
ⓒ The right of hot pursuit ceases as soon as the ship pursued enters the contiguous zone of its own State or of a third State.
ⓓ Where a ship has been stopped or arrested outside the territorial sea in circumstances which do not justify the exercise of the right of hot pursuit, it shall be compensated for any loss or damage that may have been thereby sustained.

① 1개　　　② 2개
③ 3개　　　④ 모두 맞다

해설 ⓑ It is 뒤에 not이 붙어야 한다.
　　　ⓒ contiguous zone → territorial sea

chapter 12 Archipelagic State 군도국가

Article 46 Use of terms in archipelagic State

For the purposes of this Convention:

ⓐ "archipelagic State" means a state constituted wholly by one or more archipelago and may include other islands;

ⓑ "archipelago" means a group of islands, including parts of islands, interconnecting waters and other natural features which are so closely interrelated that such islands, waters and other natural features form an intrinsic geographical, economic and political entity, or which historically have been regarded as such.

Article 49 Legal status of archipelagic waters, of the air space over archipelagic waters and of their bed and subsoil

① The **sovereignty** of an archipelagic state extends to the waters enclosed by the archipelagic baselines drawn in accordance with article 47, described as **archipelagic waters**, regardless of their depth or distance from the coast.

② This sovereignty extends to the air space over the archipelagic waters, as well as to their bed and subsoil, and the resources contained therein.

제 46조 군도국가의 용어의 사용

이 협약에서

ⓐ "군도국가"라 함은 전체적으로 하나 또는 둘 이상의 군도로 구성된 국가를 말하며, 그 밖의 섬을 포함할 수 있다.

ⓑ "군도"라 함은 섬의 무리(섬들의 일부를 포함한다), 연결된 수역 및 그 밖의 자연지형으로서, 이들이 서로 밀접하게 관련되어 있어 그러한 섬, 수역 및 그 밖의 자연지형이 고유한 지리적·경제적 또는 정치적 단일체를 이루고 있거나 또는 역사적으로 그러한 단일체로 인정되어 온 것을 말한다.

제 49조 군도수역과 그 상공·해저 및 하층토의 법적지위

① 군도국가의 주권은 군도수역의 깊이나 해안으로부터의 거리에 관계없이 제47조에 따라 그은 군도기선에 의하여 둘러싸인 군도수역이라고 불리는 수역에 미친다.

② 이러한 주권은 군도수역의 상공·해저와 하층토 및 이에 포함된 자원에까지 미친다.

제 47조 군도기선

① 군도국가는 군도의 가장 바깥쪽 섬의 가장 바깥 점과 드러난 암초의 가장 바깥 점을 연결한 직선군도기선을 그을 수 있다. 다만, 이러한 기선 안에는 주요 섬을 포함하며 수역의 면적과 육지면적(환초 포함)의 비율이 1대1에서 9대1 사이이어야 한다.

② 이러한 기선의 길이는 100해리를 넘을 수 없다. 다만, 군도를 둘러싼 기선 총수의 3퍼센트까지는 그 길이가 100해리를 넘어 최장 125해리까지 될 수 있다.

③ 이러한 기선은 군도의 일반적 윤곽으로부터 현저히 벗어날 수 없다.

④ 군도국가는 다른 국가의 영해를 공해나 배타적 경제수역으로부터 격리시키는 방식으로 이러한 기선제도를 적용할 수 없다.

⑤ 군도국가의 군도수역의 어느 일부가 바로 이웃한 국가의 두 부분 사이에 있는 경우, 이웃한 국가가 이러한 수역에서 전통적으로 행사하여 온 기존의 권리와 그 밖의 모든 합법적인 이익 및 관련국 간의 합의에 의하여 규정되는 모든 권리는 계속하여 존중된다.

Article 47 Archipelagic baselines

① An archipelagic State may draw straight **archipelagic baselines** joining the outer most points of the outermost islands and drying reefs of the archipelago provided that within such baselines are included the main islands and an area in which the ratio of the area of the water to the area of the land, including atolls, is between <u>1to1 and 9to1</u>.

② The length of such baselines shall not exceed <u>100</u> nautical miles, except that up to <u>3</u> percent of the total number of baselines enclosing any archipelago may exceed that length, up to a maximum length of <u>125</u> nautical miles.

③ The drawing of such baselines shall not depart to any appreciable extent from the general configuration of the archipelago.

④ The system of such baselines shall not be applied by an archipelagic State in such a manner as to cut off from the high seas or the exclusive economic zone the territorial sea of another State.

⑤ If a part of the archipelagic waters of an archipelagic State lies between two parts of an immediately adjacent neighbouring State, existing rights and all other legitimate interests which the latter state has traditionally exercised in such waters and all rights stipulated by agreement between those states shall continue and be respected.

Chapter 13. Nationality and Status of ships 선박의 국적과 지위

Article 91 Nationality of ships

Every State shall fix the conditions for the grant of its nationality to ships, for the registration of ships in its territory, and for the right to fly its flag. Ships have the nationality of the State whose flag they are entitled to fly. There must exist a genuine like between the State and the ship.

Article 92 Status of ships

① Ships shall sail under the flag of the state only and, save in exceptional cases expressly provided for in international treaties or in this convention, shall be subject to its exclusive jurisdiction on the high seas. A ship may not change its flag during a voyage or while in a port of call, save in the case of a real transfer of ownership or change of registry.

② A ship which sails under the flags of two or more states, using them according to convenience, may not claim any of the nationalities in question with respect to any other state, and may be assimilated to a ship without nationality.

제 91조 선박의 국적

모든 국가는 선박에 대한 자국 국적의 부여, 자국 영토에서의 선박의 등록 및 자국기를 게양할 권리에 관한 조건을 정해야 한다. 어느 국기를 게양할 자격이 있는 선박은 그 국가의 국적을 가진다. 그 국가와 선박 간에는 진정한 관련이 있어야 한다.

제 92조 선박의 지위

① 국제조약이나 이 협약에 명시적으로 규정된 예외적인 경우를 제외하고는 선박은 어느 한 국가의 국기만을 게양하고 항행하며 공해에서 그 국가의 배타적인 관할권에 속한다. 선박은 진정한 소유권 이전 또는 등록변경의 경우를 제외하고는 항행 중이나 기항 중에 그 국기를 바꿀 수 없다.

② 2개국 이상의 국기를 편의에 따라 게양하고 항행하는 선박은 다른 국가에 대하여 그 어느 국적도 주장할 수 없으며 무국적선으로 취급될 수 있다.

Chapter 14: Criminal Jurisdiction 형사적관할권

제 27조 외국선박의 선내 형사관할권

연안국의 형사관할권은 오직 다음의 각 호의 경우를 제외하고는 영해를 통항하고 있는 외국선박의 선박 내에서 통항 중에 발생한 어떠한 범죄와 관련하여 사람을 체포하거나 수사를 행할 수 없다.

ⓐ 범죄의 결과가 연안국에 미치는 경우
ⓑ 범죄가 연안국의 평화나 영해의 공공질서를 어지럽히는 경우
ⓒ 선박의 선장이나 기국의 외교관 또는 영사에 의해 현지 당국에 지원이 요구되는 경우
ⓓ 마약이나 향정신성물질의 불법거래를 진압하기 위해 필요한 경우

Article 27 Criminal jurisdiction on board a foreign ship

The criminal jurisdiction of the coastal State should not be exercise on board a foreign ship passing through the territorial sea to arrest any person or to conduct any investigation in connection with any crime committed on board the ship during its passage, save only in the following cases;

ⓐ if the consequences of the crime extend to the **coastal State**;
ⓑ if the crime is of a kind to disturb the peace of **the country** or the good order of the territorial sea;
ⓒ if the assistance of the local authorities has been requested by the master of the ship or by a diplomatic agent or consular officer of **the flag state**; or
ⓓ if such measures are necessary for the suppression of illicit traffic in narcotic drugs or psychotropic substances.

기출문제

01. 다음은 UNCLOS(United Nations Convention on the Law of the Sea)상 외국선박의 선내 형사관할권에 관한 내용이다. 밑줄 친 부분에 해당하는 경우로 가장 옳지 않은 것은? `21년 하반기`

The criminal jurisdiction of the coastal State should not be exercise on board a foreign ship passing through the territorial sea to arrest any person or to conduct any investigation in connection with any crime committed on board the ship during its passage, save only in the <u>following cases;</u>

① if the consequences of the crime extend to the coastal state
② if the crime is of a kind to disturb the peace of the country or the good order of the territorial sea
③ if the assistance of the local authorities has been requested by the master of the ship or by a diplomatic agent or consular officer of the Port State; or
④ if such measures are necessary for the suppression of illicit traffic in narcotic drugs or psychotropic substances

해설 형사적관할권은 선박의 선장이나 기국(flag state)의 외교관(diplomatic agent) 또는 영사(consular officer)에 의해 현지 당국에 지원이 요구되는 경우 행사될 수 있다.
the Port state는 항만국이다.

답 ③

chapter 15

Transit Passage 해협에서의 통과 통항

Article 37 Scope of this section

This section applies to **straits** which are used for international navigation between one part of the high seas or an exclusive economic zone and another part of the high seas or an exclusive economic zone.

Article 38 Right of transit passage

① In straits referred to in article 37, all ships and aircraft enjoy the **right of transit passage**, which shall not be impeded; except that, if the strait is formed by an island of a State bordering the strait and its mainland, transit passage shall not apply if there exists seaward of the island a route through the high seas or through an exclusive economic zone of similar convenience with respect to navigational and hydrographical characteristics.

② Transit passage means the exercise in accordance with this Part of the freedom of navigation and overflight solely for the purpose of continuous and expeditious transit of the strait between one part of the high seas or an exclusive economic zone and another part of the high seas or an exclusive economic zone. However, the requirement of continuous and expeditious transit does not preclude passage through the strait for the purpose of entering, leaving or returning from a State bordering the strait, subject to the conditions of entry to that State.

③ Any activity which is not an exercise of the right of transit passage through a strait remains subject to the other applicable provisions of this Convention.

제 37조 이 절의 적용범위

이 절은 공해나 배타적경제수역의 일부와 공해나 배타적경제수역의 다른 부분간의 국제항행에 이용되는 해협에 적용한다.

제 38조 통과통항권

① 제37조에 언급된 해협 내에서, 모든 선박과 항공기는 방해받지 아니하는 통과통항권을 향유한다. 다만, 해협이 해협연안국의 섬과 본토에 의하여 형성되어 있는 경우, 항행상 및 수로상 특성에서 유사한 편의가 있는 공해 통과항로나 배타적경제수역 통과항로가 그 섬의 바다쪽에 있으면 통과통항을 적용하지 아니한다.

② 통과통항이라 함은 공해 또는 배타적경제수역의 일부와 공해 또는 배타적 경제수역의 다른 부분간의 해협을 오직 계속적으로 신속히 통과할 목적으로 이 부에 따라 항행과 상공비행의 자유를 행사함을 말한다. 다만, 계속적이고 신속한 통과의 요건은 해협연안국의 입국조건에 따라서 그 국가에 들어가거나 그 국가로부터 나오거나 되돌아가는 것을 목적으로 하는 해협통항을 배제하지 아니한다.

③ 해협의 통과통항권의 행사가 아닌 활동은 이 협약의 다른 적용 가능한 규정에 따른다.

제 39조 통과통항중인 선박과 항공기의 의무

① 선박과 항공기는 통과통항권을 행사함에 있어서 다음과 같이 하여야 한다.

ⓐ 해협 또는 그 상공의 지체 없는 항진

ⓑ 해협연안국의 주권, 영토보전 또는 정치적 독립에 반하거나, 또는 국제연합헌장에 구현된 국제법의 원칙에 위반되는 그 밖의 방식에 의한 무력의 위협이나 무력의 행사의 자제

ⓒ 불가항력 또는 조난으로 인하여 필요한 경우를 제외하고는 계속적이고 신속한 통과의 통상적인 방식에 따르지 아니하는 활동의 자제

ⓓ 이 부의 그 밖의 관련규정 준수

② 통과통항중인 선박은 다음과 같이 하여야 한다.

ⓐ 해상충돌방지를 위한 국제규칙을 포함하여 해상안전을 위하여 일반적으로 수락된 국제규칙, 절차 및 관행의 준수

ⓑ 선박에 의한 오염의 방지, 경감 및 통제를 위하여 일반적으로 수락된 국제규칙, 절차 및 관행의 준수

③ 통과통항중인 항공기는 다음과 같이 하여야 한다.

ⓐ 국제민간항공기구가 제정한 민간항공기에 적용되는 항공규칙 준수. 국가 항공기도 통상적으로 이러한 안전조치를 준수하고 항상 비행의 안전을 적절히 고려하여 운항

Article 39 Duties of ships and aircraft during transit passage

① Ships and aircraft, while exercising the right of transit passage, shall:

ⓐ proceed without delay through or over the strait;

ⓑ **refrain** from any **threat or use of force** against the sovereignty, territorial integrity or political independence of States bordering the strait, or in any other manner in violation of the principles of international law embodied in the Charter of the United Nations;

ⓒ **refrain** from any activities other than those incident to their normal modes of continuous and expeditious transit unless rendered necessary **by force majeure or by distress;**

ⓓ comply with other relevant provisions of this Part.

② Ships in transit passage shall:

ⓐ **comply with generally accepted international regulations**, procedures and practices for safety at sea, including the **International Regulations for Preventing Collisions at Sea;**

ⓑ **comply with generally accepted international regulations,** procedures and practices for the prevention, reduction and control of **pollution from ships.**

③ Aircraft in transit passage shall:

ⓐ observe the Rules of the Air established by the International Civil Aviation Organization as they apply to civil aircraft; state aircraft will normally comply with such safety measures and will at all times operate with due regard for the safety of navigation;

ⓑ at all times monitor the radio frequency assigned by the competent internationally designated air traffic control authority or the appropriate international distress radio frequency.

ⓑ 국제적으로 지정된 권한 있는 항공교통통제기구가 배정한 무선주파수나 적절한 국제조난 무선주파수의 상시 청취

Article 40 Research and survey activities

During transit passage, foreign ships, including marine scientific research and hydrographic survey ships, **may not carry out any research or survey activities** without the prior authorization of the States bordering straits.

제 40조 조사 및 측량활동

해양과학조사선과 수로측량선을 포함한 외국선박은 통과통항 중 해협연안국의 사전허가 없이 어떠한 조사활동이나 측량활동도 수행할 수 없다.

Article 41 Sea lanes and traffic separation schemes in straits used for international navigation

① In conformity with this Part, States bordering straits may designate sea lanes and prescribe traffic separation schemes for navigation in straits where necessary to promote the safe passage of ships.

② Such States may, when circumstances require, and after giving due publicity thereto, substitute other sea lanes or traffic separation schemes for any sea lanes or traffic separation schemes previously designated or prescribed by them.

③ Such sea lanes and traffic separation schemes shall conform to generally accepted international regulations.

④ Before designating or substituting sea lanes or prescribing or substituting traffic separation schemes, States bordering straits shall refer proposals to the competent international organization with a view to their adoption. The organization may adopt only such sea lanes and traffic separation schemes as may be agreed with the States bordering the straits, after which the States may designate, prescribe or substitute them.

⑤ In reaspect of a strait where sea lanes or traffic separation schemes through the waters of two or more States bordering the strait are being proposed, the States concerned shall co-operate in formulating proposals in consultation with the competent international organization.

제 41조 국제항행에 이용 되는 해협의 항로대와 통항분리방식

① 해협연안국은 선박의 안전통항을 촉진하기 위하여 필요한 경우, 이 부에 따라 해협내 항행을 위하여 항로대를 지정하고 통항분리방식을 설정할 수 있다.

② 해협연안국은 필요한 경우, 적절히 공표한 후, 이미 지정되거나 설정되어 있는 항로대나 통항분리방식을 다른 항로대나 통항분리방식으로 대체할 수 있다.

③ 이러한 항로대와 통항분리방식은 일반적으로 수락된 국제규칙에 따른다.

④ 해협연안국은 항로대를 지정대체하거나 통항분리방식을 설정대체하기에 앞서 권한 있는 국제기구가 이를 채택하도록 제안한다. 국제기구는 해협연안국과 합의된 항로대와 통항분리방식만을 채택할 수 있으며, 그 후 해협연안국은 이를 지정, 설정 또는 대체할 수 있다.

⑤ 2개국 이상의 해협연안국의 수역을 통과하는 항로대나 통항분리방식이 제안된 해협에 대하여는, 관계국은 권한 있는 국제기구와의 협의 하에 제안을 작성하기 위하여 협력한다.

⑥ 해협연안국은 자국이 지정하거나 설정한 모든 항로대와 통항분리방식을 해도에 명시하고 이 해도를 적절히 공표한다.

⑦ 통과통항중인 선박은 이 조에 따라 설정되어 적용되는 항로대와 통항분리방식을 준수한다.

제 42조 통과통항에 관한 해협연안국의 법령

① 이 절의 규정에 따라 해협연안국은 다음의 전부 또는 일부에 관하여 해협의 통과통항에 관한 법령을 제정할 수 있다.

ⓐ 제41조에 규정된 항행의 안전과 해상교통의 규제

ⓑ 해협에서의 유류, 유류폐기물 및 그 밖의 유독성물질의 배출에 관하여 적용하는 국제규칙을 시행함으로써 오염의 방지경감 및 통제

ⓒ 어선에 관하여서는 어로의 금지 (어구의 적재에 관한 규제 포함)

ⓓ 해협연안국의 관세·재정·출입국관리 또는 위생에 관한 법령에 위반되는 상품이나 화폐를 싣고 내리는 행위 또는 사람의 승선과 하선

② 이러한 법령은 외국선박을 형식상 또는 실질상으로 차별하지 아니하며, 그 적용에 있어서 이 절에 규정된 통과통항권을 부정, 방해 또는 침해하는 실질적인 효과를 가져오지 아니한다.

③ 해협연안국은 이러한 모든 법령을 적절히 공표한다.

④ 통과통항권을 행사하는 외국선박은 이러한 법령을 준수한다.

⑥ States bordering straits shall clearly indicate all sea lanes and traffic separation schemes designated or prescribed by them on charts to which due publicity shall be given.

⑦ Ships in transit passage shall respect applicable sea lanes and traffic separation schemes established in accordance with this article.

Article 42 Laws and regulations of States bordering straits relating to transit passage

① Subject to the provisions of this section, States bordering straits may adopt laws and regulations relating to transit passage through straits, in respect of all or any of the following:

ⓐ the safety of navigation and the regulation of maritime traffic, as provided in article 41;

ⓑ the prevention, reduction and control of pollution, by giving effect to applicable international regulations regarding the discharge of oil, oily wastes and other noxious substances in the strait;

ⓒ with respect to fishing vessels, the prevention of fishing, including the stowage of fishing gear;

ⓓ the loading or unloading of any commodity, currency or person in contravention of the customs, fiscal, immigration or sanitary laws and regulations of States bordering straits.

② Such laws and regulations shall not discriminate in form or in fact among foreign ships or in their application have the practical effect of denying, hampering or impairing the right of transit passage as defined in this section.

③ States bordering straits shall give due publicity to all such laws and regulations.

④ Foreign ships exercising the right of transit passage shall comply with such laws and regulations.

⑤ The flag State of a ship or the State of registry of an aircraft entitled to sovereign immunity which acts in a manner contrary to such laws and regulations or other provisions of this Part shall bear international responsibility for any loss or damage which results to States bordering straits.

⑤ 주권면제를 향유하는 선박의 기국 또는 항공기의 등록국은 그 선박이나 항공기가 이러한 법령이나 이 부의 다른 규정에 위배되는 방식으로 행동한 경우 그로 인하여 해협연안국이 입은 손실 또는 손해에 대하여 국제책임을 진다.

Article 43 Navigational and safety aids and other improvements and the prevention, reduction and control of pollution

User States and States bordering a strait should by agreement co-operate:

ⓐ in the establishment and maintenance in a strait of necessary navigational and safety aids or other improvements in aid of international navigation; and

ⓑ for the prevention, reduction and control of pollution from ships.

제43조 항행 및 안전보조시설, 그 밖의 개선시설과 오염의 방지·경감 및 통제

해협이용국과 해협연안국은 합의에 의하여 다음을 위하여 서로 협력한다.

ⓐ 항행 및 안전보조시설 또는 국제항행에 유용한 그 밖의 개선시설의 해협내 설치와 유지

ⓑ 선박에 의한 오염의 방지·경감 및 통제

Article 44 Duties of States bordering straits

States bordering straits shall not hamper transit passage and shall give appropriate publicity to any danger to navigation or overflight within or over the strait of which they have knowledge. There shall be no suspension of transit passage.

제44조 해협연안국의 의무

해협연안국은 통과통항권을 방해할 수 없으며 자국이 인지하고 있는 해협내 또는 해협 상공에 있어서의 항행이나 비행에 관한 위험을 적절히 공표한다. 통과통항은 정지될 수 없다.

I 기출문제

01. 다음 보기는 UNCLOS상의 일부이다. 밑줄 친 부분에 해당되는 것으로 가장 옳은 것은?

`21년 상반기`

> Article 37
> This section applies to straits which are used for international navigation between one part of the high seas or an exclusive economic zone and another part of the high seas or an exclusive economic zone.
> Article 38
> In straits referred to in article 37, all ships and aircraft enjoy the _____ which shall not be impeded.

① right of innocent passage   ② right of hot pursuit
③ right of transit passage   ④ right of criminal jurisdiction

해설 모든 선박과 항공기는 해협(Strait)을 통항하는 권리인 통과통항권리(right of transit passage)을 향유한다.

답 ❸

02. 다음 UNCLOS에서 통과통항(transit passage)중인 선박의 의무로 가장 옳지 않은 것은?

`22년 2차`

① Foreign ships, including marine scientific research and hydrographic survey ships, shall be carry out any research or survey activities without the prior authorization of the States bordering straits.
② refrain from any activities other than those incident to their normal modes of continuous and expeditious transit unless rendered necessary by force majeure or by distress;
③ comply with generally accepted international regulations, procedures and practices for safety at sea, including the International Regulations for Preventing Collisions at Sea;
④ comply with generally accepted international regulations, procedures and practices for the prevention, reduction and control of pollution from ships.

해설 과학조사, 수로측량 등을 하는 외국 선박들은 해협을 끼고 있는 국가들의 우선적 허가 없이 조사활동이나 측량 활동을 <u>수행할 수 없다</u>(may not carry out...).

답 ❶

chapter 16 Continental Shelf 대륙붕

Article 76 Definition of the continental shelf

① The continental shelf of a coastal State comprises the **sea-bed and subsoil** of the submarine areas that extend beyond its territorial sea throughout the **natural prolongation of its land territory** to the **outer edge of the continental margin**, or to a distance of **200 nautical miles** from the baselines from which the breadth of the territorial sea is measured where the outer edge of the continental margin does not extend up to that distance.

② The continental shelf of a coastal State shall not extend beyond the limits provided for in paragraphs 4 to 6.

③ The continental margin comprises the submerged prolongation of the land mass of the coastal State, and consists of the **sea-bed and subsoil of the shelf the slope and the rise**. It does not include the deep ocean floor with its oceanic ridges or the subsoil thereof.

제76조 대륙붕의 정의

① 연안국의 대륙붕은 영해 밖으로 영토의 자연적 연장에 따라 대륙변계의 바깥 끝 까지, 또는 대륙변계의 바깥 끝이 200해리에 미치지 아니하는 경우, 영해기선으로부터 200해리까지의 해저지역의 해저와 하층토로 이루어진다.

② 연안국의 대륙붕은 제4항부터 제6항까지 규정한 한계 밖으로 확장될 수 없다.

③ 대륙변계는 연안국 육지의 해면 아래쪽 연장으로서, 대륙붕·대륙사면·대륙융기의 해저와 하층토로 이루어진다. 대륙변계는 해양산맥을 포함한 심해대양저나 그 하층토를 포함하지 아니한다.

chapter 17　UNCLOS의 다양한 규정

편의치적선

편의치적선이란 세금을 줄이고 값싼 외국인 선원을 승선시키기 위해 선주가 소유한 선박을 자국에 등록시키지 않고 다른 나라에 가입시키는 것을 말한다.

제 221조 해난사고에 의한 오염을 방지하기 위한 조치

① 이 부의 어떠한 규정도, 각국이 관습국제법이나 성문국제법에 따라, 중대한 해로운 결과를 초래할 것이 합리적으로 예측되는 해난사고나 이러한 사고에 관련된 행위로 인한 오염, 또는 오염의 위험으로부터 자국의 해안이나 어로를 포함한 관계이익을 보호하기 위하여, 실제상의 피해 또는 발생할 위험이 있는 피해에 상응하는 조치를 영해 밖까지 취하고 집행할 권리를 침해하지 아니한다.

② UNCLOS에 따르면, 해난이란 선박의 충돌, 좌초 혹은 기타의 항행상 사고 혹은 선내에서나 선외에서 물질적 손상을 발생시키는 것을 의미한다.

제 100조 해적행위 진압을 위한 협력의무

모든 국가는 공해나 국가 관할권 밖의 어떠한 곳에서라도 해적행위를 진압하는데 최대한 협력한다.

Flag of convenience

If a shipowner registers his ships in a country other than his own to **escape paying some home taxations**, to **employ labour cheaper** than that at home, or to **benefit financially** in any similar way, his ships are said to fly a **flag of convenience.**

Article 221 Measures to avoid pollution arising from maritime casualties

① Nothing in this Part shall prejudice the right of States, pursuant to international law, both customary and conventional, to take and enforce measures beyond the territorial sea proportionate to the actual or threatened damage to protect their coastline or related interests, including fishing, from pollution or threat of pollution following upon a maritime casualty or acts relating to such a casualty, which may reasonably be expected to result in major harmful consequences.

② According to UNCLOS, **maritime casualty** means a collision of vessels, stranding or other incident of navigation, or other occurrence on board a vessel or external to it resulting in material damage or imminent threat of material damage to a vessel or cargo.

Article 100 Duty to cooperate in the repression of piracy

All States shall cooperate to the fullest possible extent in the **repression of piracy** on the high seas or in any other place outside the jurisdiction of any State

Article 108 Illicit traffic in narcotic drugs or psychotropic substances

① All States shall co-operate in the **suppression of illicit traffic** in narcotic drugs and psychotropic substances engaged in by ships on the high seas contrary to international conventions.

② Any State which has reasonable grounds for believing that a ship flying its flag is engaged in illicit traffic in narcotic drugs or psychotropic substances may request the co-operation of other States to suppress such traffic.

제 108조 마약 및 향정신 물질의 불법 운송

① 모든 국가는 공해에서 선박에 의하여 국제협약을 위하반하여 행하여지는 마약과 항정신성물질의 불법거래를 진압하기 위하여 협력한다.

② 자국기를 게양한 선박이 미약이나 향정신성물질의 불법거래에 종사하고 있다고 믿을 만한 합리적인 근거를 가지고 있는 국가는 다른 국가에 대하여 이러한 거래의 진압을 위한 협력을 요청할 수 있다.

기출문제

01. 다음 빈칸에 들어갈 말로 가장 적합한 것은? [18년 1차]

If a shipowner registers his ships in a country other than his own to escape paying some home taxations, to employ labour cheaper than that at home, or to benefit financially in any similar way, his ships are said to fly a (   ).

① flag of discrimination
② courtesy flag
③ flag of destination
④ flag of convenience

해설 편의치적(flag of convenience) 선박에 대한 설명이다.

답 ④

02. Choose the correct one for the blank. [15년 2차 / 18년 1차]

According to UNCLOS, "(   )" means a collision of vessels, stranding or other incident of navigation, or other occurrence on board a vessel or external to it resulting in material damage or cargo.

① aeronautical
② maritime casualty
③ maritime insurance
④ maritime pollution

해설 해난사고(maritime casualty)에 대한 설명이다.

답 ②

기출문제

03. Choose the correct one for the blank.　　12년

UNCLOS 1982 shall prevail, as between State Parties, (　　) the Geneva Conventions on the Law of the Sea on 29 April 1958.

① over
② of
③ on
④ from

해설　1982 UNCLOS는 1958년 4월 29일 발효된 제네바 해양법협약에 비준한 협약국들에게 우선한다.
　　　prevail over : 우위를 차지하다.

답 ❶

PART 03 IAMSAR(International Aeronautical and Marine Search and Rescue manual)

Chapter 1	Glossary 용어
Chapter 2	구명용품 용기의 색깔
Chapter 3	Distress 조난
Chapter 4	Search Pattern
Chapter 5	인명구조법
Chapter 6	Rescue or assistance by aircraft
Chapter 7	On- Scene Co -ordination 현장 조정
Chapter 8	Man Overboard

chapter 01 Glossary 용어

조난의 단계	meaning	의미
Alert Phase 경계 단계	A situation wherein apprehension exists as to the safety of a vessel and of the persons on board.	선박과 선내 승선 인원의 안전이 우려되는 상태
Uncertainty Phase 불확실 단계	A situation wherein uncertainty exists as to the safety of a vessel and the persons of board.	선박과 선내 승선 인원의 안전이 불확실한 상태
Distress Phase 조난 단계	A situation wherein there is a reasonable certainty that a vessel or a person is threatened by grave and imminent danger and requires immediate assistance.	선박이나 사람이 중대하고 급박한 위험에 위협받고 있고 즉각적인 도움이 필요하다는 합리적 확실성이 있는 상태
Emergency Phase 긴급 단계	A generic term meaning, as the case may be, uncertainty phase, alert phase or distress phase.	불확실 단계, 경계 단계 또는 조난 단계를 모두 말하는 통상적인 뜻

수색 구조 설비 및 제도	meaning	의미
EPIRB	Emergency Position-indicating Radio Beacon, A device, usually carried aboard maritime craft, that transmits a signal that alert search and rescue authorities and enables rescue units to locate the scene of the distress.	비상위치표시 무선표지, 통상 선박에 비치하는 장치로, 수색 구조 당국에 경보를 보내고, 조난 현장에 구조대를 위치시키도록 신호를 전송시키는 장비이다.
SART	Search and Rescue Transponder, A survival craft transponder that, when activated, sends out a signal automatically when a pulse from a nearby radar reaches it. The signal appears on the interrogating radar screen and gives the bearing and distance of the transponder from the interrogating radar for search and rescue purposes.	생존정 트랜스폰더로, 작동시키면 근처의 레이더로부터 펄스파가 도달했을 때 자동적으로 신호를 전송해주는 장치이다. 그 신호는 레이더 스크린에 나타나고 수색 구조의 목적으로 레이더 스크린에 SART의 방위와 거리가 나타난다.
NAVTEX	Telegraphy system for transmission of maritime safety information, navigation and meteorological warnings, and urgent information to ships.	NAVTEX : 해사 안전정보, 항해경보, 기상경보, 긴급정보를 선박에게 전송해주기 위한 전신시스템
GMDSS	Global Maritime Distress and Safety System, A global communications service based upon automated systems, both satellite-based and terrestrial, to provide distress alerting and promulgation of maritime safety information to mariners	선원들에게 조난 경보를 제공하고 해사 안전정보를 알리기 위하여 만들어졌고, 위성과 지상에 기반을 둔 자동화 시스템 기반 전 세계 통신 서비스

Cospas-Sarsat System 수색구조용 위성 지원 추적 시스템	A satellite system designed to detect distress beacons transmitting on the frequencies 121.6㎒ and 406㎒.	주파수121.6㎒ 와 406㎒에서 송신하는 조난 표지를 탐지하도록 설계된 위성
INMARSAT 국제 해상 위성 기구	An organization which operates a system of geostationary satellites for world-wide mobile communications services, and which supports the GMDSS and other emergency communications systems.	전 세계 이동 통신 업무를 위한 정지궤도 위성 시스템을 작동시키는 기구이다. 이는 GMDSS와 기타 비상 통신 시스템을 지원한다.
DSC 디지털 선택호출	A technique using digital codes which enables a radio station to establish contact with, and transfer information to, another station or group of stations.	한 무선국을 다른 무선국 또는 무선국 집단과 접속하고 정보를 전송할 수 있게 해주는 디지털 코드를 사용하는 기술
ELT 비상위치탐사 발신기	Emergency locator transmitter : Aeronautical radio distress beacon for alerting and transmitting homing signals.	경보 및 호밍 신호 전송을 취한 항공 무선 조난표지
NBDP 협대역 직접 인쇄 전신	Narrow-band direct printing: Automated telegraphy, as used by the NAVTEX system and telex-over radio	NAVTEX 장치 및 무선텔렉스에 사용되는 자동 전신
NAVAREA	One of 16 areas into which the world's oceans are divided by the International Maritime Organization for dissemination of navigation and meteorological warnings.	항해 및 기상경보를 전파하기 위하여 국제해사기구가 세계의 대양을 16개로 분할한 구역중의 하나
NAVTEX	The system for the broadcast and automatic reception of maritime safety information by means of narrow-band direct-printing telegraphy	협대역 직접인쇄전신 수단에 의한 해사안전정보의 방송 및 자동 수신을 위한 시스템
SafetyNET	A service of Inmarsat enhanced group call (EGC) system specifically designed for promulgation of maritime safety information (MSI) as a part of the Global Maritime Distress and Safety System (GMDSS).	GMDSS의 일부로서 MSI(해사안전정보)의 공포를 위해 특별하게 선정된 INMARSAT 집단호출체제(EGC) 서비스
MSI 해사안전정보	Maritime Safety Information, Navigational and meteorological warnings and forecasts and other urgent safety-related messages broadcast to ships, as defined in regulation IV/2 of the 1974 SOLAS Convention.	항해, 기상 경보와 예보 그리고 선박으로 방송되는 기타 안전 관련 긴급 정보이다.
LRIT 선박장거리위치추적 시스템	Long-range identification and tracking, A system which requires certain vessels to automatically transmit their identity, position and date/time at six-hour intervals in accordance with SOLAS regulation V/19-1.	6시간 간격으로 선박의 식별, 위치, 그리고 날짜/시간 정보를 특정 선박에게 자동으로 송신하는 시스템이다.

수색 구조의 직책 및 직위	meaning	의미
Captain 선장	Master of a ship or pilot-in-command of an aircraft, commanding officer of a warship, or an operator of any other vessel.	선박의 선장 또는 항공기의 조종사, 군함의 지휘관 혹은 기타 선박의 운항사
ACO 항공기 조정관	Aircraft Coordinator, A person who co-ordinates the involvement of multiple aircraft in SAR operations.	수색구조 작업 도중 다수의 항공기의 개입을 조정하는 사람
OSC 현장 조정관	On-scene Co-ordinator, A person designated to co-ordinate search and rescue operations within a specified area.	특정 구역에서 수색과 구조 작업을 조정하도록 지정된 사람
SMC 수색구조 임무 조정관	Search and rescue Mission Coordinator, The officer temporarily assigned to co-ordinate response to an actual or apparent distress situation.	실질적인 또는 명백한 조난 상황의 대응을 조정하기 위하여 임시적으로 임명된 관리
RCC 구조조정본부	Rescue Co-ordination Centre, A unit responsible for promoting efficient organization of search and rescue services and for co-ordinating the conduct of search and rescue operations within a search and rescue region.	수색 및 구조 해역 내에서의 수색 및 구조 업무의 효율적인 조직화를 촉진할 책임과 이 구역 내에서 수색 및 구조 활동의 수행을 조정할 책임을 지는 기관
RSC 구조지부	Rescue Sub-centre, A unit subordinate to a rescue co-ordination centre established to complement the latter within a specified area within a search and rescue region.	수색 및 구조 해역 내의 특정구역 안에서 구조조정본부를 보조하기 위하여 설치된 구조조정본부에 종속된 기관
SRU 수색 구조대	Search and Rescue Unit, A unit composed of trained personnel and provided with equipment suitable for the expeditious conduct of search and rescue operations.	훈련된 요원으로 구성되고, 수색 구조 작업의 신속한 수행을 위해 적합한 장비들을 갖춘 부대
Search and Rescue facility 수색 구조 시설	Any mobile resource, including designated search and rescue units, used to conduct search and rescue operations.	수색 및 구조 작업을 하는데 사용되는 지정된 수색구조대를 포함한 이동식 자원이다.
CSS 해상 수색 조정선	Co-ordinator Surface Search, A vessel, other than a rescue unit, designated to co-ordinate surface search and rescue operations within a specified search area.	구조대 이외의 선박으로 특정 수색 구역 내에서 해상 수색 및 구조 활동을 조정하기 위하여 지정된 선박
수색 구조 용어	meaning	의미
Rescue 구조	An operation to retrieve persons in distress, provide for their initial medical or other needs, and deliver them to a place of safety.	조난에 빠진 사람들을 다시 되찾이오고 그들에게 초기의 의학적인 대응과 기타 대응을 제공하며, 그들을 안전한 공간으로 이송시키는 작업

Search 수색	An operation, normally co-ordinated by a rescue co-ordination centre or rescue sub-centre, using available personnel and facilities to locate persons in distress.	구조조정본부나 구조지부에 의해 조정되는 작업으로, 가능한 인적 요소와 시설물을 사용하여 조난에 빠진 사람들을 찾는 작업
Rescue Action Plan 구조 활동 계획	A plan for rescue operations normally prepared by the SMC for implementation by the OSC and facilities on-scene.	현장의 OSC와 현장 시설물들의 수행을 위해 SMC가 통상적으로 준비하는 구조 작업의 계획
SRR 수색 구조 해역	Search and Rescue Region, An area of defined dimensions within which search and rescue services are provided	수색 및 구조 업무가 제공되는 일정한 범위의 구역
AMVER 선박자동 상호구조 시스템	A world-wide vessel reporting system for SAR for maintaining estimated position and other data of merchant vessels that voluntarily participate.	수색 구조를 위한 전 세계적 선박 위치보고 시스템으로, 자진하여 참여하여 평상시 상선의 추정위치와 기타 정보를 보유하고 있도록 한다.
CES 해안지구국	Coast Earth Station, Maritime name for an Inmarsat shore-based station linking ship earth stations with terrestrial communicational networks.	해사위성에 기반을 둔 연안국으로서 선박국과 지상국을 연결하는 국
CSP 수색 착수지점	Commence search Point, Point, normally specified by the SMC, where a SAR facility is to begin its search pattern.	SMC에 의해 구체화 되어지는, SAR 구조대의 수색 패턴이 시작되는 지점
Craft	Any air or sea-surface vehicle, or submersible of any kind or size.	모든 종류 및 크기의 항공기, 수상비행기, 잠수함
Datum 기준점	A geographic point, line, or area used as a reference in search planning.	수색 계획에 참조로 사용되는 지리적인 지점, 선 또는 구역
On-scene 현장	The search area or the actual distress site.	수색 구역 혹은 실제적인 조난 장소.
Distress Alert 조난 경보	Notification by any means that a distress situation exists and assistance is needed.	조난 상황이 존재하고 원조가 필요하다는 뜻의 알림
False alarm 오발신 경보	Distress alert initiated for other than an appropriate test, by communications equipment intended for alerting, when no distress situation actually exists.	실제 조난 상황이 존재하지 않는 경우, 경보를 발할 의도를 가지고 통신장비에 의해 적절한 시험이 아닌 것으로 발송된 조난 경보
False alert 오수신 경보	Distress alert received from any source, including communications equipment intended for alerting, when no distress situation actually exists, and a notification of distress should not have resulted.	실제 조난 상황이 존재하지 않는 경우에 경보용 통신장비를 포함한 모든 장치로부터 수신된 조난경보 (조난 통보가 없었을 경우)
Hypothermia 저체온증	Abnormal lowering of internal body temperature(heat loss) from exposure to cold air, wind, or water.	찬 공기, 바람, 물에 노출되어 신체 내부의 온도가 비정상적으로 낮아지는 것

Term	Definition (EN)	Definition (KR)
TMAS 원격의료지원서비스	Telemedical Assistance, A medical service permanently staffed by doctors qualified in conducing remote consultations and well versed in the particular nature of treatment on shipboard ship.	원격진료경험이 있고 선상 치료의 특수상황에 정통한, 상시로 근무하는 의사에 의해 제공되는 의료서비스
MEDEVAC 의료수송	Evacuation of a person for medical reasons	의료적 목적으로 인원을 이송시키는 것.
MEDICO 무선 의료 조언	Medical advice. Exchange of medical information and recommended treatment for sick or injured persons where treatment cannot be administered directly by prescribing medical personnel.	의료 조언. 전문적인 의료인에 의해서 직접 치료를 받을 수 없는 경우, 환자나 부상자를 위해 의료정보를 교환하거나 권고되는 처방을 교환 하는 것이다.
To Ditch 불시착수	In the case of an aircraft, to make a forced landing on water.	항공기가 수면 상에 불시착한 경우
Leeway 풍압차	The movement of a search object through water caused by winds blowing against exposed surfaces.	불어오는 바람에 의해 수면에서 수색 목표물의 움직임
Course 침로	Intended horizontal direction of travel of a craft	선박이나 항공기 이동의 예정된 수평의 방향
Heading	The horizontal direction in which a craft is pointed	선박이 가리키는 수평 방향
Coverage factor 탐색범위 계수	The ratio of the search effort (Z) to the area searched (A). C = Z/A. For parallel track searches, it may be computed as the ratio of sweep width (W) to track spacing (S). C = W/S.	수색지역(A)에 대한 수색 시도(노력)(Z) 비율. C=Z/A. 평행선항적 수색에서는 수색간격(S)에 대한 수색범위 너비(W)의 비로 계산할 수 있다. C=W/S
Sweep width (W) 수색 너비	A measure of the effectiveness with which a particular sensor can detect a particular object under specific environmental conditions.	특정 환경조건에서 어떤 센서가 특정한 물표를 탐지할 수 있는 효율적인 치수
Track spacing (S) 항적간 거리	The distance between adjacent parallel search tracks	인접한 수평의 수색항적 간의 거리.
Sea 해상	Condition of the surface resulting from waves and swells	파도 및 너울로부터의 수면의 상태
Direction of waves, swell, or seas 파도, 너울, 해수의 방향	Direction from which the waves, swells or seas are moving.	파도, 너울, 해수가 움직인 방향
Wave (or chop)	The condition of the surface caused by local wind and characterized by irregularity, short distance between crests, whitecaps and breaking motion.	지역적인 바람에 의해 만들어지고, 물미루, 흰 물결과 부서지는 움직임간의 불규칙이고 짧은 거리의 특징을 갖는 수면의 상태

Swell 너울	Condition of the surface caused by a distant wind system. The individual swell appears to be regular and smooth with considerable distance between rounded crests.	원거리 바람으로 야기된 수면의 상태. 각 너울은 연속된 물마루 사이가 상당한 거리를 규칙적이고 완만히 나타난다.
Swell face 너울 전면	The side of the swell toward the observer. The back side is the side away from the observer. These definitions apply regardless of the direction of swell movement.	관측자 쪽으로의 너울의 면이다. 후면은 관측자로부터 멀어지는 면이다. 이 정의는 너울의 움직임 방향과는 관계없이 적용한다.
Swell direction 너울 방향	The direction from which a swell is moving. The direction toward which the swell is moving is called the down swell direction.	너울이 이동해 오는 방향. 너울이 이동해 가는 방향은 down swell direction이라 불린다.
Swell velocity 너울 속도	Velocity with which the swells advance with relation to a fixed point, measured in knots.	고정된 지점에 관련해 너울이 이동하는 속도를 의미한다. 노트로 측정된다.
Primary Swell 주 너울	The swell system having the greatest height from trough to crest.	골에서 마루까지의 가장 높은 높이를 가진 너울체계
Direction of wind 풍향	Direction from which the wind is blowing.	바람이 불어오는 방향
True air speed (TAS) 진 풍속	The speed an aircraft is travelling through the air mass. TAS corrected for wind equals ground speed.	대기를 통과하여 이동하는 항공기의 속도. 바람에 의해 수정된 TAS는 대지속력과 같다.
Wind current 취송류	The water current generated by wind acting upon the surface of water over a period of time.	일정기간 동안 물의 표면에 부는 바람에 의해 생기는 물의 흐름
Drift 표류	Movement of a search object caused by environmental force	환경적인 힘에 의한 수색대상의 움직임
Fetch 대안 거리	The distance the wave have been driven by a wind blowing in a constant direction, without obstruction.	일정한 방향에서 불어오는 바람에 의해 파도가 다른 방해 없이 밀려난 거리
MRO 대규모 구조작업	Search and rescue services characterized by the need for immediate response to large numbers of persons in distress, such that the capabilities normally available to search and rescue authorities are inadequate.	다수의 조난자들에 대한 즉각적인 대응의 필요성에 따라 특성화된 수색구조업무. 수색구조 당국이 통상적으로 이용 가능한 능력으로는 불충분한 경우다.
MAYDAY	The international radio telephony distress signal.	국제 무선 조난 신호
PAN-PAN	The international radio telephony urgency signal.	국제 무선 긴급 신호

기출문제

01. 다음은 1979년 해상수색 및 구조에 관한 국제협약 내용 중 용어 정의이다. 다음에 해당하는 것은?
〔18년 1차〕

> A situation wherein there is a reasonable certainty that a vessel or a person is threatened by grave and imminent danger and requires immediate assistance.

① Emergency phase ② Uncertainty phase
③ Alert phase ④ Distress phase

해설 Distress phase : 선박이나 사람이 중대하고 급박한 위험에 위협받고 있고 즉각적인 도움이 필요하다는 합리적 확실성이 있는 상태

답 ④

02. "1979년 해상수색 및 구조에 관한 국제협약"에 따를 때 다음에 해당하는 상황은 무엇인가?
〔17년 2차〕

> A situation wherein apprehension exists as to the safety of a vessel and of the persons on board.

① Emergency phase ② Uncertainty phase
③ Alert phase ④ Distress phase

해설 Alert phase : 선박과 선내 승선 인원의 안전이 우려되는 상태

답 ③

03. 다음 IAMSAR Manual상 용어에 대한 설명으로 가장 옳은 것은?
〔14년 1차 / 18년 1차〕

> A survival craft transponder that, when activated, sends out a signal automatically when a pulse from a nearby radar reaches it. The signal appears on the interrogating radar screen and gives the bearing and distance of the transponder from the interrogating radar for search and rescue purposes.

① EPIRB ② SART ③ SafetyNET ④ Inmarsat

해설 SART에 대한 설명이다.

답 ②

04. 다음 설명이 의미하는 것은?
〔18년 1차〕

> A device, usually carried aboard maritime craft, that transmits a signal that alerts search and rescue authorities and enables rescue units to locate the scene of the distress.

① PLB ② NAVTEX
③ SART ④ EPIRB

해설 EPIRB에 대한 설명이다.

답 ④

기출문제

05. 다음 내용은 IAMSAR Manual상 용어에 대한 설명이다. 다음 중 아래에서 설명하고 있는 것은? `15년 일반직`

> A survival craft transponder that, when activated, sends out a signal automatically when a pulse from a nearby radar reaches it. The signal appears on the interrogating radar screen and gives the bearing and distance of the transponder from the interrogating radar for search and rescue purposes.

① SART
② EPIR
③ Inmarsat
④ VHF-DSC

해설 SART에 대한 설명이다.

답 ❶

06. 〈IAMSAR manual〉상의 용어 중 다음에서 설명하는 것으로 가장 옳은 것은? `19년 3차`

> A global communications service based upon automated systems, both satellite-based and terrestrial, to provide distress alerting and promulgation of maritime safety information for mariners.

① INMARSAT
② NAVTEX
③ TMASS
④ GMDSS

해설 GMDSS에 대한 설명이다.

답 ❹

07. 다음 IAMSAR(International Aeronautical and Maritime Search and Rescue) Manual 상 영문 표기에 대한 설명 중 가장 옳지 않은 것은? `20년 1차`

① RCC : Rescue co-ordination centre (구조 조정 본부)
② SRU : Search and Rescue Unit (수색 구조대)
③ OSC : On-scene commander (현장 지휘관)
④ SMC : Search and rescue mission co-ordinator (수색구조 임무 조정관)

해설 OSC : On-Scene Co-ordinator (현장 조정관)

답 ❸

I 기출문제

08. 다음 용어에 대한 설명 중 옳지 않은 것은 모두 몇 개인가?   17년 1차

ⓐ Rescue : An operation to retrieve persons in distress, provide for their initial medical or other needs, and deliver them to a place of safety.
ⓑ Alert phase : A situation wherein apprehension exists as to the safety of a vessel and the persons on board.
ⓒ Uncertainty phase : A situation wherein uncertainty exists as to the safety of a vessel and the persons on board.
ⓓ Distress phase : A situation wherein there is a reasonable certainty that a vessel or a person is threatened by grave and imminent danger and requires immediate assistance.

① 1개   ② 2개
③ 3개   ④ 없음

해설 모두 옳다.

답 ④

09. 다음 IAMSAR manual상용어의 정의가 옳지 않은 것은 모두 몇 개인가?   18년 1차

ⓐ Emergency phase : A situation wherein there is a reasonable certainty that a vessel or a person is threatened by grave and imminent danger and requires immediate assistance.
ⓑ Alert phase : A situation wherein uncertainty exists as to the safety of a vessel and the persons on board.
ⓒ On-scene co-ordinator : The commander of a rescue unit designated to co-ordinate search and rescue operations within a specified search area.
ⓓ Search : An operation to retrieve persons in distress, provide for their initial medical or other needs, and deliver them to a place of safety.

① 1개   ② 2개
③ 3개   ④ 4개

해설 옳지 않은 것:
  ⓐ Distress Phase
  ⓑ Uncertainty Phase
  ⓓ Rescue

답 ③

기출문제

10. "Rescue co-ordination centre" is ; `15년 2차`

① A unit subordinate to a rescue co-ordination centre established to complement within a specified area within a search and rescue region.
② A land unit, stationary or mobile, designated to maintain a watch on the safety of vessels in coastal area.
③ A unit composed of trained personnel and provided with equipment suitable for the expeditious conduct of search and rescue operations.
④ A unit responsible for promoting efficient organization of search and rescue services and for co-ordinating the conduct of search and rescue operations within a search and rescue region.

해설 구조조정본부(Rescue co-ordination centre) : 수색 및 구조 해역 내에서의 수색 및 구조업무의 효율적인 조직화를 촉진할 책임과 이 구역 내에서 수색 및 구조 활동의 수행을 조정할 책임을 지는 기관

답 ④

11. 아래는 IAMSAR 협약에 대한 용어이다. 다음 중 틀린 것은? `18년 2차`

① NAVTEX - Telegraphy system for transmission of maritime safety information, navigation and meteorological warnings, and urgent information to ships.
② Leeway - The movement of a search object through water caused by winds blowing against exposed surfaces.
③ MAYDAY - Spoken international distress signal, repeated three times.
④ Rescue action plan - An operation to retrieve persons in distress, provide for their initial medical or other needs, and deliver them to a place of safety.

해설 'Rescue'에 대한 설명이다.

답 ④

12. 다음 중 IAMSAR Manual Volume III 상 용어와 정의가 가장 옳은 것은? `18년 일반직`

① 'Emergency Position Indicating Radio Beacon' is a survival craft transponder that, when activated, sends out a signal automatically when a pulse from a nearby radar reaches it.
② 'Rescue' is An operation, normally co-ordinated by a rescue co-ordination centre or rescue sub-centre, using available personnel and facilities to locate persons in distress.
③ 'Datum' is the intended horizontal direction of travel of a craft.
④ 'PAN-PAN' is the international radiotelephony urgency signal. When repeated three times, indicates uncertainty or alert, followed by nature of urgency.

해설 ① SART ② Search ③ Course

답 ④

기출문제

13. '1979년 해상수색 및 구조에 관한 협약'에 대한 용어 설명 중 옳은 것은 모두 몇 개인가?

`14년 1차`

ⓐ Search and rescue area : An area of defined dimensions within which search and rescue services are provided.
ⓑ Rescue unit : A unit composed of trained personnel and provided with equipment suitable for the expeditious conduct of search and rescue operations.
ⓒ Uncertainty phase : A situation wherein apprehension exists as to the safety of a vessel and the persons on board.
ⓓ To ditch : in the case of an aircraft, to make a forced landing on water.
ⓔ Rescue sub-centre : A unit responsible for promoting efficient organization of search and rescue services and for co-ordinating the conduct of search and rescue operations within a search and rescue region.

① 2개　　　　　　② 3개
③ 4개　　　　　　④ 5개

 옳지 않은 것:
ⓐ Search and Rescue Region에 대한 설명이다.
ⓒ Alert phase에 대한 설명이다.
ⓔ Rescue Co-ordination Centre에 대한 설명이다.

답

14. 다음 국제항공 및 해상수색구조 편람의 용어설명 중 틀린 것은 모두 몇 개인가?

`14년 2차`

ⓐ Amver : A world-wide ship reporting system for search and rescue.
ⓑ Craft : Any air or sea-surface vehicle, or submersible of any kind or size.
ⓒ Datum : A geographic point, line, or area used as a reference in search planning.
ⓓ Fetch : The distance the waves have been driven by a wind blowing in a constant direction, without obstruction.

① 1개　　　　　　② 2개
③ 3개　　　　　　④ 없음

 모두 옳음

답

기출문제

15. IAMSAR Manual Volume Ⅲ 에서 아래 문장이 의미하는 것은 무엇인가? `16년 일반직`

> An operation to retrieve persons in distress, provide for their initial medical or other needs, and deliver them to a place of safety.

① MEDICO ② Search
③ Rescue ④ Hypothermia

해설 구조(Rescue)에 대한 설명이다.

답 ③

16. 〈IAMSAR manual〉 상의 용어에 대한 설명으로 옳은 것은 모두 몇 개인가? `19년 3차`

ⓐ Craft : Any air or sea-surface vehicle, or submersible of any kind or size.
ⓑ Datum : Point, normally specified by the SMC, where a SAR facility is to begin its search pattern.
ⓒ Hypothermia : Abnormal lowering of internal body temperature from exposure to cold air, wind, or water.
ⓓ Rescue Unit : An operation to retrieve persons in distress.
ⓔ Fetch : The distance the wave have been driven by a wind blowing in a constant direction, without obstruction.

① 2개 ② 3개
③ 4개 ④ 5개

해설 옳지 않은 것:
ⓑ Commence Search Point
ⓓ Rescue

답 ②

17. 다음은 79 해상수색 및 구조에 관한 국제협약에서 말하는 영문 표기 설명이다. 가장 적절하지 않은 것은? `18년 3차`

① CES : Coast Earth Station (해안지구국)
② IMO : International Maritime Organization (국제해사기구)
③ MDRC : Marine Development Rescue Centre (해상발전구조본부)
④ MERSAR : Merchant Ship Search And Rescue Manual (상선수색구조지침서)

해설 MDRC : Marine Disaster Response Committee (해난대응위원회)

답 ③

기출문제

18. '79 해상 수색 및 구조에 관한 국제협약'에서 말하는 영문 표기 설명 중 틀린 것은 모두 몇 개인가?

[18년 2차]

가. A/C 항공기	나. ILS 국제인명구조연합
다. MID 해양식별숫자	라. IMO 국제해사기구
마. OSC 현장조정관	바. RB 구조정
사. RV 구조선박	아. WMO 세계기상기구

① 없음   ② 1개
③ 2개   ④ 3개

해설 옳은 것:
가. A/C : Aircraft 항공기
나. ILS : International Life Saving Federation 국제 인명구조 연합
 (ILF : International Life Boat Federation 국제 구명정 연합)
다. MID : Maritime Identification Digits 해양 식별 숫자
라. IMO : International Maritime Organization 국제 해사기구
마. OSC : On-Scene Co-ordinator 현장 조정관
바. RB : Rescue Boat 구조정
사. RV : Rescue Vessel 구조선
아. WMO : World Meteorological Organization 세계 기상기구

답 ❶

19. 다음 〈보기〉 중 IAMSAR Manual상 용어의 정의가 옳지 않은 것은 모두 몇 개인가?

[21년 상반기]

㉠ Search and rescue radar transponder : Aeronautical radio distress beacon for alerting and transmitting homing signals.
㉡ MAYDAY : The international radiotelephony urgency signal. When repeated three times, indicates uncertainty or alert, followed by nature of urgency.
㉢ Leeway : The movement of a search object through water caused by winds blowing against exposed surface.
㉣ Heading : The intended horizontal direction of travel of a craft.

① 1개   ② 2개
③ 3개   ④ 4개

해설 옳지 않은 것:
㉠ Emergency Locator Transmitter
㉡ PAN-PAN
㉣ Course

답 ❸

chapter 02 구명용품 용기의 색깔

Supply dropping

The contents of each container or package should:

① be clearly indicated in print, in English and one or more other languages
② have self-explanatory symbol
③ have streamers colored according to the following code :

Red 빨강	medical supplies and first aid equipment	의약품, 응급 처치장비
Blue 파랑	food and water	식량, 물
Yellow 노랑	blankets and protective clothing	담요, 방호복
Black 검정	miscellaneous equipment such as stoves, axes, compasses and cooking utensils	기타 장비로서 스토브, 도끼, 나침반, 조리기구 등

보급품 투하

각 용기 혹은 상자의 내용물은 다음과 같아야 한다.

① 영어 혹은 하나 이상의 다른 언어로 명확히 표기되어 있어야 한다.
② 자체설명이 가능한 심볼이 있어야 한다.
③ 다음의 코드에 따라서 색깔이 입혀진 꼬리표등이 있어야한다. :

I 기출문제

01. According to SAR 1979, the colour of the contents of droppable containers and packages containing miscellaneous equipment such as stoves, axes, compasses and cooking utensils is :

① red　　　　② blue　　　　③ yellow　　　　④ black

답 ❹

02. According to SAR 1979, the colour of the contents of droppable containers and packages containing medical supplies and first aid equipment is :

① blue　　　　② black　　　　③ red　　　　④ yellow

답 ❸

03. 다음 빈칸에 들어갈 말로 가장 옳은 것은?

> According to SAR 1979, the colour identification of the contents of droppable containers and packages containing (A) is yellow

① medical supplies and first aid equipment
② food and water
③ blankets and protective clothing
④ Miscellaneous equipment such as stoves, axes, compasses and cooking utensils.

답 ❸

04. 다음 중 빈칸에 들어갈 단어가 가장 적절한 것으로 짝지어진 것은?

> Survival Equipment
> The colour identification of the contents of droppable containers and packages containing survival equipment should take the form of streamers coloured according to the following code :

가. Food and water
나. Blankets and protective clothing
다. Miscellaneous equipment such as stoves, axes, compasses and cooking utensils
라. Medical supplies and first aid equipment

① 가. blue　　나. black　　다. yellow　　라. red
② 가. blue　　나. yellow　　다. black　　라. red
③ 가. black　　나. blue　　다. yellow　　라. red
④ 가. yellow　　나. blue　　다. black　　라. red

답 ❷

Chapter 03 — Distress 조난

01
Methods of distress notification

① A distress call or signal or other emergency information from another vessel at sea, either directly or by relay.

② A distress call or message from aircraft. This will normally occur by relay from CRS(Coast Radio Station).

③ Alert sent from a vessel's alerting equipment and then relayed shore to ship.

④ Visual signals or sound signals from a nearby distress craft

Visual international distress signals are shown below

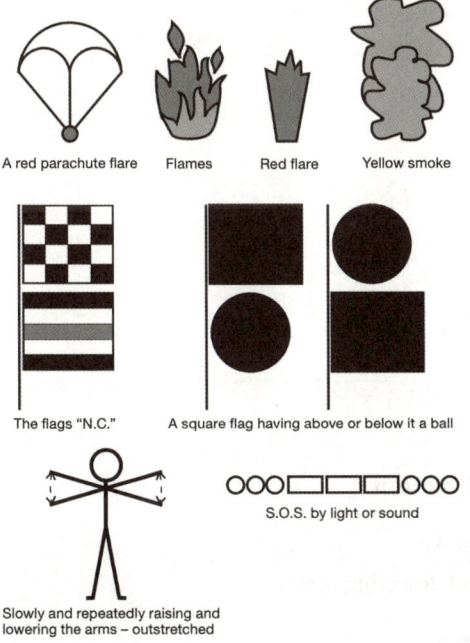

01 조난의 인지

① 해상의 다른 선박으로부터의 경보 신호 또는 조난 호출을 직접 혹은 경유하여 받는 경우

② 항공기로부터 조난 호출 또는 통보, 보통 연안무선국(CRS)을 경유하여 전달 받는다.

③ 선박의 경보 장비로부터 송신되어 지구국-선박으로 중계되는 경보

④ 인근의 조난선으로부터의 시각 또는 음향신호

시각적인 국제 조난 신호는 아래에서 볼 수 있다.

① 적색 낙하산 화염신호
② 불꽃 신호
③ 적색 화염신호
④ 오렌지색 발연신호
⑤ 국제기류신호 "N.C."기
⑥ 상부 또는 하부에 구 모양을 붙인 사각기
⑦ 천천히 그리고 반복적으로 팔을 올렸다 내렸다 하는 것. - 팔을 쭉 뻗고
⑧ 빛 또는 소리에 의한 S.O.S 신호

기출문제

01. All of the following are distress signal except :

① red flare
② orange smoke
③ international code AA
④ raising and lowering arms

14년 2차

답 ③

02
Immediate action

The following immediate action should be taken by any ship receiving a distress message:

① acknowledge receipt of message (for DSC acknowledgement see flow charts)
② gather the following information from the craft in distress if possible:

- position of distressed craft
- distressed craft's identity, call sign, and name
- number of persons on board
- nature of the distress or casualty
- type of assistance required
- number of victims, if any
- distressed craft's course and speed
- type of craft, and cargo carried
- any other pertinent information that might facilitate the rescue

③ maintain a continuous watch on the following international frequencies, if equipped to do so:

- 500 kHz (radiotelegraphy)
- 2,182 kHz (radiotelephony)
- 156.8 MHz FM (channel 16, radiotelephony) for vessel distress
- 121.5 MHz AM (radiotelephony) for aircraft distress or beacon distress signals.

④ Vessels subject to the SOLAS Convention must comply with applicable equipment carriage and monitoring requirements

⑤ SOLAS communications equipment is referred to as Global Maritime Distress and Safety System (GMDSS) equipment and includes:
- Inmarsat ship earth stations
- VHF, MF, and HF digital selective calling (DSC) radios
- maritime safety information receivers like NAVTEX and SafetyNET

02 즉각적인 행동

조난 통보를 수신한 선박은 다음과 같이 즉각적인 행동을 해야 한다.

① 통보의 수신을 인지한다.

② 기능하면 조난선박으로부터 다음 정보를 수집한다.

- 조난선박의 위치
- 조난선박의 식별, 호출부호, 선박명
- 승선인원 숫자
- 조난 또는 사고의 종류
- 요구되는 지원의 타입
- 발생한 경우 희생자의 수
- 조난선박의 침로와 속도
- 선종과 운송되는 화물
- 구조를 촉진할 수 있는 기타관련정보

③ 장비가 설치되어 있는 경우, 다음의 국제 주파수에서 지속적인 청수당직을 유지하라.

- 500 kHz (무선전신)
- 2,182 kHz (무선전화)
- 조난선박 전용 156.8 MHz FM (채널 16, 무선전화)
- 조난 항공기용 혹은, 조난용 비콘 신호용 121.5 MHz AM (무선전화)

④ SOLAS 협약의 적용을 받는 선박은 해당 장비 운반 및 검사 요구사항을 준수해야한다.

⑤ SOLAS 통신 장비는 GMDSS라고 말하며 다음의 것들을 포함한다.

- INMARSAT 선박 지구국
- VHF, MF, 그리고 HF 디지털 선택호출(DSC) 무선장비
- NAVTEX와 SafetyNET과 같은 해사 안전정보 수신기

- 휴대용 VHF 장비
- 비상위치지시 무선 비콘설비 (EPIRBs)
- 수색구조 레이더 트렌스폰더 (SARTs)
- AIS 수색구조 송신기 (AIS-SARTs)

⑥ 다음의 정보를 조난당한 선박에게 알려야 한다.
- 자선의 식별, 호출부호, 그리고 선명
- 자선의 위치
- 자선의 선속, 조난선박이 있는 장소까지의 도착예정시각(ETA)
- 조난선박의 진방위와 본선으로 부터의 거리

- hand-held VHF equipment
- emergency position-indicating radio beacons (EPIRBs)
- search and rescue radar transponders (SARTs)
- AIS search and rescue transmitters (AIS-SARTs)

⑥ The following information should be communicated to the distressed craft:
- own vessel's identity, call sign, and name
- own vessel's position
- own vessel's speed and estimated time of arrival (ETA) to distressed craft site
- distressed craft's true bearing and distance from ship

chapter 04 Search Pattern

01
Expanding Square Search (SS)

① Most effective when the location of the search object is known within **relatively close limits.**

② The **commence search point** is always the **datum(start) position.**

③ Often appropriate for vessels or small boats to use when searching for persons in the water or other search objects **with little or no leeway**.

④ Due to the small area involved, this procedure **must not be used simultaneously** by **multiple aircraft** at similar altitudes or by **multiple vessels**.

⑤ **Accurate navigation is required**; the first leg is usually oriented directly **into the wind** to **minimize** navigational errors.

⑥ It is difficult for fixed-wing aircraft to fly legs close to datum if S is less than 2NM.

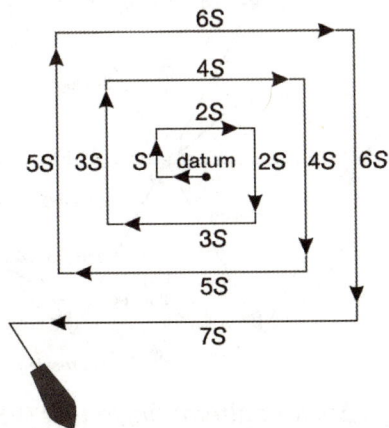

Expanding square search (SS)

01 확대 사각 수색법

① 수색 목표물의 위치가 상대적으로 가까운 한계 내에 있는 것으로 알려졌을 때 가장 효과적이다.

② 수색 개시지점은 항상 기준위치이다.

③ 풍압차가 거의 없거나 전혀 없는 바닷속에 있는 사람 또는 다른 수색 목표물을 수색할 때, 선박이나 소형 보트에 자주 사용된다.

④ 수색구역이 좁으므로, 비슷한 고도에서 다수의 항공기 또는 다수의 선박이 동시에 절차를 사용해서는 안된다.

⑤ 정확한 항해가 요구된다. 첫 번째 구간은 항해 오차를 최소화시키기 위해서 바람이 불어오는 쪽으로 방향을 맞춘다.

⑥ 1S의 길이가 2해리보다 적다면, 고정 윙 항공기가 기준점에 근접한 구간을 비행하는 것은 어렵다.

02

부채꼴 수색법

① 수색 목표물의 위치를 정확하게 알고 수색 구역이 좁을 때 효과적이다.

② 기준점을 중심으로 한 원형구역을 수색하기 위하여 사용된다.

③ 수색구역이 좁으므로, 비슷한 고도에서 다수의 항공기 또는 다수의 선박이 동시에 절차를 사용해서는 안된다.

④ 항공기와 선박은 동일한 구역에서 독립된 부채꼴 수색을 수행할 수 있다.

⑤ 적절한 표지(예를 들면, 연기 부표나 무선 비이콘)를 기준점 위치에 투하하여 수색 패턴의 중심점을 표시하는 기준점 또는 항로표지로 사용되어질 수 있다.

⑥ 항공기의 경우, 수색패턴 반경은 일반적으로 5해리에서 20해리 사이이다.

⑦ 선박의 경우, 수색패턴 반경은 2해리에서 5해리 사이이며, 각 회전은 120도이고, 통상적으로 우현쪽으로 선회한다.

02

Sector Search (VS)

① Most effective when the position of the search object is **accurately known** and the **search area is small**.

② Used to search a circular area centered on a **datum point**.

③ Due to the **small** area involved, this procedure must **not be used simultaneously** by **multiple** aircraft at similar altitudes or by **multiple** vessels.

④ An aircraft and a vessel **may be used together** to perform independent sector searches of the same area.

⑤ A **suitable marker** (for example, a smoke float or a radio beacon) may be dropped at the **datum position** and used as a reference or navigational aid marking the center of the pattern

⑥ For **aircraft**, the search pattern radius is usually between **5NM and 20NM.**

⑦ For **vessels**, the search pattern radius is usually between **2NM and 5NM**, and each unit is **120°**, normally turned to **starboard**.

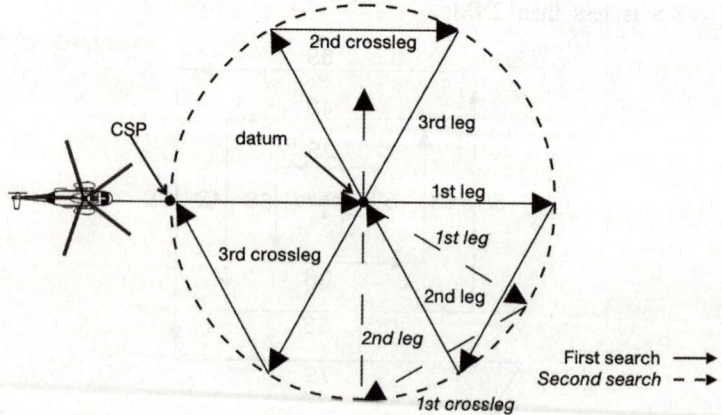

Sector pattern: single-unit (VS)

03
Parallel Sweep Search (parallel track search) (PS)

① Used to search a **large area** when survivor location is **uncertain**.

② Most effective over **water or flat terrain**.

③ Usually used when a **large** search area must be **divided into sub-areas** for assignment to individual search facilities on-scene at the same time.

④ The commence search point is in one corner of the sub-area, one-half track space inside the rectangle from each of the two sides forming the corner.

⑤ Search legs are **parallel** to each other and to the long sides of the sub-area.

⑥ **Multiple vessels may be used**

⑦ Searching speed is the **maximum** speed of the **slowest searching vessel**

03 평행선 항적 수색법

① 생존자의 위치가 불확실할 때 광범위한 지역을 수색할 때 사용된다.

② 수상이나 평지에서 가장 효과적이다.

③ 현장에 있는 각 수색 시설물에게 동시에 넓은 구역을 소구획으로 분할하여 할당할 때 일반적으로 사용한다.

④ 수색 개시지점은 소구획의 한 가장자리에 있으며 이곳은 사각형을 이루는 모서리에서 수색 간격의 1/2만큼 안에 위치해 있다.

⑤ 수색 진행 구간은 서로 평행이고 소구획의 긴 측면도 서로 평행이다.

⑥ 다수의 선박이 사용될 수 있다.

⑦ 수색속력은 가장 느린 선박의 최고 속력이다.

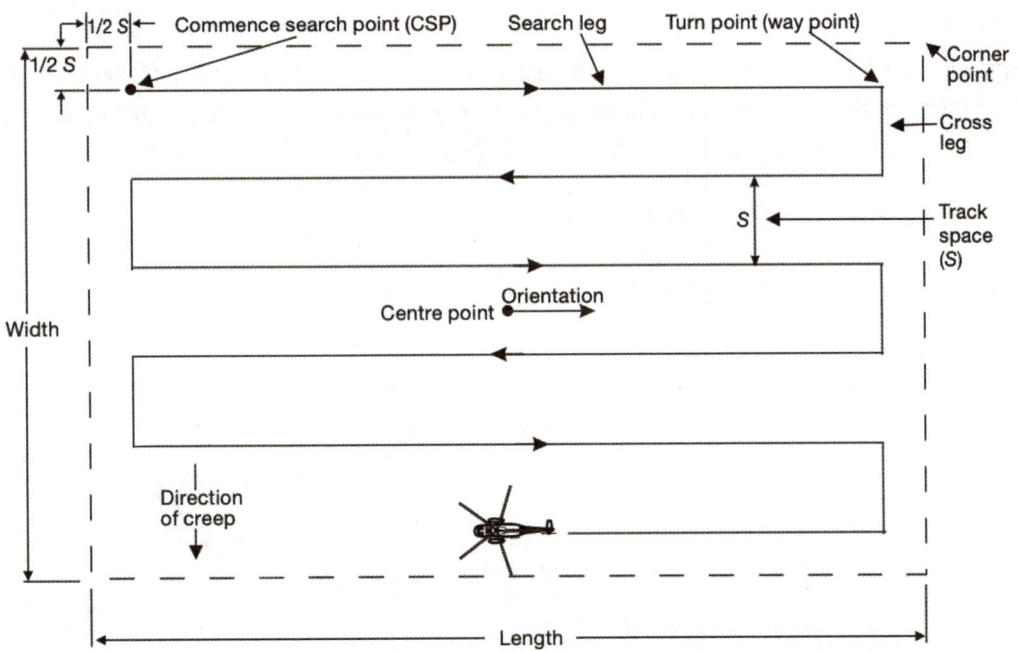

Parallel track search (PS)

04 항정선 수색법

① 알려진 경로를 따라가지 않고 항공기나 선박이 사라졌을 때 일반적으로 사용된다.
② 계획 수립과 시행이 쉽기 때문에 초기의 수색 노력으로 종종 사용된다.
③ 조난에 빠진 선박이나 항공기의 의도된 항로를 따라서 빠르고 합리적으로 구성된다.
④ 수색은 항정선의 한 쪽을 따라서 이루어지고, 반대쪽으로 되돌아오면서 다른 쪽을 수색한다. (TSR, Track Line Search Return)
⑤ 수색은 의도된 항로를 따라가고 한번에 양쪽을 같이 수색한다. 그리고 난 후 수색 시설물은 자신의 길을 가고 되돌아오지 않는다. (TSN, Track Line Search Non-Return)
⑥ 항공기는 빠른 속도 때문에 주로 TS를 사용한다.
⑦ 항공기의 수색 고도는 주간에 300~600m, 야간에 600~900m 이다.

04 Track Line Search (TS)

① Normally used when an aircraft or vessel has disappeared without a trace along a known route.

② Often used as **initial** search effort due to **ease** of planning and implementation.

③ Consists of a **rapid and reasonably** thorough search along intended route of the distressed craft.

④ Search may be along one side of the track line and return in the opposite direction on the other side(TSR)

⑤ Search may be along the intended track and once on each side, then search facility continues on its way and does not return(TSN).

⑥ Aircraft are frequently used for TS due to their high speed.

⑦ Aircraft search height usually 300m to 600m(1,000ft to 3,000ft) during daylight or 600m to 900m(2,000ft to 3,000ft) at night.

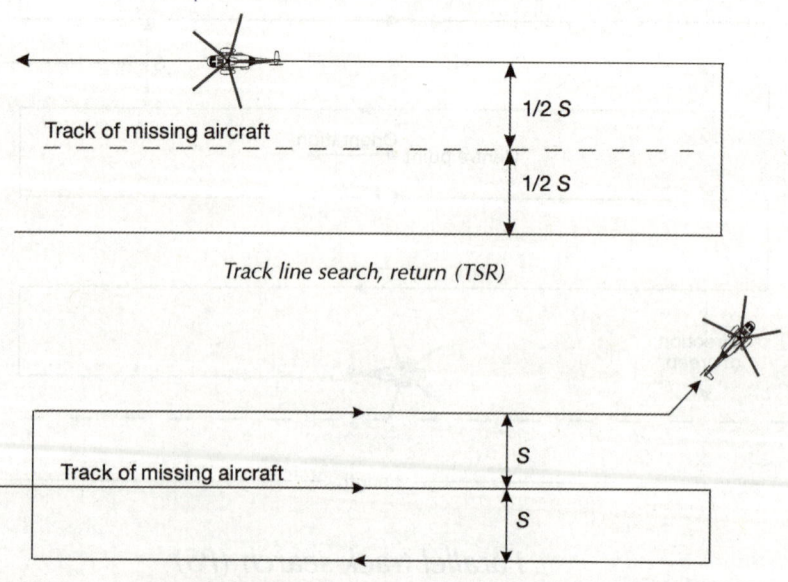

Track line search, return (TSR)

Track line search, non-return (TSN)

05

Contour Search (OS)

① It is used around mountains and in valleys when sharp changes in elevation make other patterns not practical.

② Search is started from highest peak and goes from top to bottom with new search altitude for each circuit

05 등고선 수색
① 이 수색 법은 산주변이나 계곡에서 급격한 고도의 변화로 다른 수색방식들이 불가능한 경우 사용된다.
② 수색은 가장 높은 산 정상에서부터 시작해 각 선회시마다 새로운 수색 고도로 정상에서 바닥까지 수색한다.

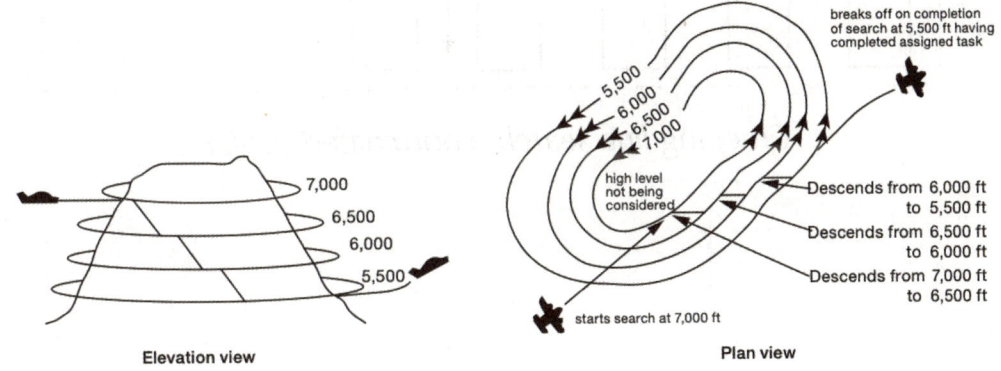

Contour search (OS)

06

Co-ordinated Vessel-Aircraft Search Pattern

① Normally used only if there is an **OSC** present to give direction to and provide communications with the participating craft.

② **Creeping line search, Coordinated(CSC)** is often used.

③ **The aircraft does most of the searching**, while the ship steam along a course at **a speed as directed by the OSC** so that the aircraft can use it as a navigational checkpoint.

④ The aircraft, as it passes over the ship, can easily make corrections to stay on the track of its search pattern.

⑤ Give a **higher probability** of detection than can normally be attained by an aircraft searching alone.

06 항공기, 선박 합동 수색
① 참가하는 선박에게 지침을 제공하고 그 선박과 통신을 하기 위하여 일반적으로 OSC가 현장에 있는 경우에만 사용된다.
② 종종 지정된 탐해 법 선 수색(CSC)을 사용한다.
③ 항공기가 항해 확인지점으로 사용할 수 있도록 선박이 OSC가 지시한 속도로 침로를 따라 움직이는 동안에 항공기는 수색의 대부분을 수행한다.
④ 항공기가 선박 위로 지나치기 때문에, 항공기는 수색 패턴의 항적에 머무르기 위해 위치 수정을 쉽게 할 수 있다.
⑤ 통상 항공기만의 수색으로 얻어질 수 있는 것보다 더 높은 탐지 가능성을 가능케 한다.

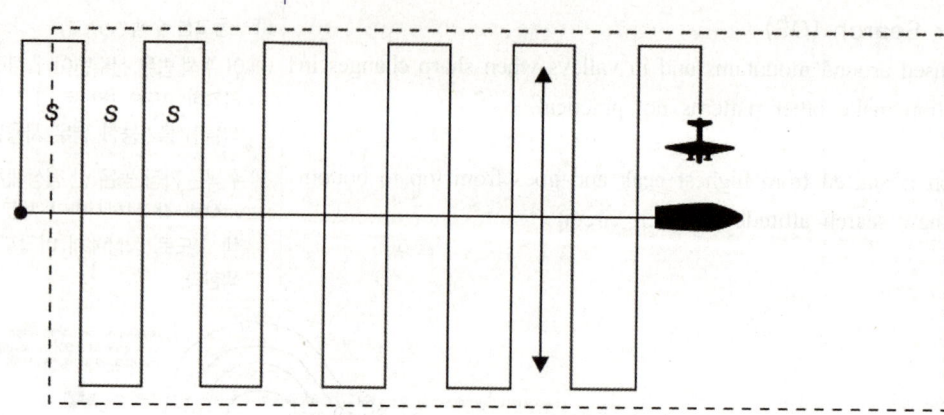

Creeping line search, coordinated (CSC)

기출문제

01. 다음은 IAMSAR Manual에 나오는 수색 방식 중 하나이다. 가장 적합한 수색 방식은?

14년 1차

- Used to search a large area when survivor location is uncertain.
- Usually used when a large search area must be divided into sub-areas for assignment to individual search facilities on-scene at the same time.
- The commence search point is in one corner of the sub-area, one-half track space inside the rectangle from each of the two sides forming the corner.

① Track Line Search
② Parallel Sweep Search
③ Expanding Square Search
④ Sector Search

해설 평행항적수색법(Parallel Sweep Search)에 대한 내용이다.

답 ②

기출문제

02. IAMSAR Manual상 수색 패턴(Search pattern) 중 아래 내용이 설명하는 것은? `17년 1차`

- Most effective when the position of the search object is accurately known and the search area is small.
- Used to search a circular area centred on a datum point.
- For vessels, the search pattern radius is usually between 2 NM and 5 NM, and each turn is 120°, normally turned to starboard.

① Track Line Search ② Expanding Square Search
③ Sector Search ④ Parallel Track Search

해설 부채꼴수색법(Sector Search)에 대한 설명이다.

 ❸

03. IAMSAR Manual Volume III의 부채꼴 수색(Sector Search)에 대한 설명 중 틀린 것은? `18년 1차`

① Most effective when the position of the search object is accurately unknown and the search area is large.
② Used to search a circular area centred on a datum point.
③ Due to the small area involved, this procedure must not be used simultaneously by multiple aircraft at similar altitudes or by multiple vessels.
④ For aircraft, the search pattern radius is usually between 5 NM and 20 NM.

해설 unknown → known
large → small

❶

04. IAMSAR(International Aeronautical and Maritime Search And Rescue) Manual상의 Sector Search에 대한 설명으로 가장 옳지 않은 것은? `20년 1차`

① Most effective when the position of the search object is accurately known and the search area is small. Used to search a circular area centred on a datum point.
② Due to the small area involved, this procedure must not be used simultaneously by multiple aircraft at similar altitude or by multiple vessels.
③ Search legs are parallel to each other and to the long sides of the sub-area.
④ A suitable marker (for example, a smoke float or a radio beacon) may be dropped at the datum position and used as a reference or navigational aid marking the centre of the pattern.

해설 평행항적수색법(Parallel Sweep Search)에 대한 설명이다.

 ❸

기출문제

05. IAMSAR manual 상 Expanding Square Search에 대한 아래 설명 중 옳은 것은 모두 몇 개인가? `19년 1차`

ⓐ Most effective when the location of the search object is known within relatively close limits.
ⓑ The commence search point is always the datum position.
ⓒ Due to the small area involved, this procedure must not be used simultaneously by multiple aircraft at similar altitudes or by multiple vessels.
ⓓ Used around mountains and in valleys when sharp changes in elevation make other patterns not practical.
ⓔ Accurate navigation is required; the first leg is usually oriented directly into the wind to minimize navigational errors.

① 2개　　② 3개
③ 4개　　④ 모두 맞다

해설 옳지 않은 것:
　ⓓ 등고선 수색법(Contour Search)에 대한 설명이다.

답 ❸

06. 다음은「IAMSAR(The International Aeronautical and Maritime Search and Rescue) Manual」상 수색패턴에 대한 설명이다. 옳은 것은 모두 몇 개인가? `20년 3차`

㉠ Expanding Square Search(SS) : Most effective when the location of the search object is known within relatively close limits.
㉡ Sector Search(VS) : Most effective when the position of the search object is accurately known and the search area is small.
㉢ Parallel Track Search(PS) : Used to search a large area when survivor location is certain.
㉣ Track Line Search(TS) : The aircraft does most of the searching, while the ship steams along a course at a speed as directed by the OSC so that the aircraft can use it as a navigational checkpoint.
㉤ Co-ordinated Vessel-Aircraft Search Pattern : Normally used when an aircraft or vessel has disappeared without a trace along a known route.

① 2개　　② 3개
③ 4개　　④ 5개

해설 옳지 않은 것:
　㉢ certain → uncertain
　㉣ Co-ordinated Vessel-Aircraft Search Pattern에 대한 설명이다.
　㉤ Track Line Search(TS)에 대한 설명이다.

답 ❶

기출문제

07. 다음 〈보기〉는 IAMSAR Manual상 수색패턴(Search pattern)의 하나이다. 아래 내용이 설명하는 것은? `21년 상반기`

> ㉠ Often appropriate for vessels or small boats to use when searching for persons in the water or other search objects with little or no leeway.
> ㉡ Due to the small area involved, this procedure must not be used simultaneously by multiple aircraft at similar altitudes or by multiple vessels.
> ㉢ Accurate navigation is required; the first leg is usually oriented directly into the wind to minimize navigational errors.

① Sector search ② Expanding square search
③ Parallel track search ④ Track line search

해설 확대사각수색법(Expanding square search)에 대한 설명이다.

답 ❷

08. 다음 〈보기〉는 「IAMSAR Manual」상 수색패턴(Search pattern)에 대한 설명이다. 이 중 Track Line Search(TS)에 대한 것으로 가장 올바르게 짝지어진 것은? `22년 일반직`

> ㉠ Used to search a large area when survivor location is uncertain.
> ㉡ Often used as initial search effort due to ease of planning and implementation.
> ㉢ Most effective over water of flat terrain.
> ㉣ The commence search point is always the datum position.
> ㉤ Aircraft are frequently used for TS due to their high speed.

① ㉠, ㉢ ② ㉡, ㉤ ③ ㉢, ㉣ ④ ㉣, ㉤

해설 ㉡ 항적선 수색법(TS)는 계획과 실행이 쉽기 때문에 보통 수색 초기에 많이 시도된다.
㉤ 빠른 속력 때문에 항공기가 항적선 수색법(TS)에 자주 사용된다.

답 ❷

09. 다음 IAMSAR MANUAL 상 Parallel Track(Sweep) Search에 대한 설명 중 가장 옳지 않은 것은? `22년 2차`

① Used to search a large area when survivor location is certain.
② Usually used when a large search area must be divided into sub-areas for assignment to individual search facilities on-scene at the same time.
③ Search legs are parallel to each other and to the long sides of the sub-area.
④ Searching speed is the maximum speed of the slowest searching vessel.

해설 certain → uncertain

답 ❶

chapter 05 인명구조법

01
Williamson's Turn
① 절차

ⓐ 최대 전타한다. ("즉각적인 행동"을 하는 상황에서 사용된다. 사고 지점의 현측으로 사용한다.)
ⓑ 원 침로의 60°로 전타가 된 후, 반대 현측으로 최대 전타한다.
ⓒ 원 침로의 반대 침로에 선수 20° 정도 남았을 때, midships 하여 선박을 원 침로의 반대 침로로 맞춘다.

ⓐ **Rudder hard over** (in an "immediate action" situation, only to the side of the casualty).
ⓑ After deviation from the original course by **60°**, rudder **hard over to the opposite side**.
ⓒ When heading **20° short of opposite course**, rudder to **midship position** and ship to be turned to opposite course.

② 특징

ⓐ 원래의 항적선으로 양호하게 돌아간다.
ⓑ 제한 시계에서 효과적이다.
ⓒ 간단하다.
ⓓ 사고 현장에서 멀리 떨어진다.
ⓔ 절차가 느리다.

ⓐ makes good original track line
ⓑ good in reduced visibility
ⓒ simple
ⓓ takes the ship farther away from the scene of the incident
ⓔ slow procedure

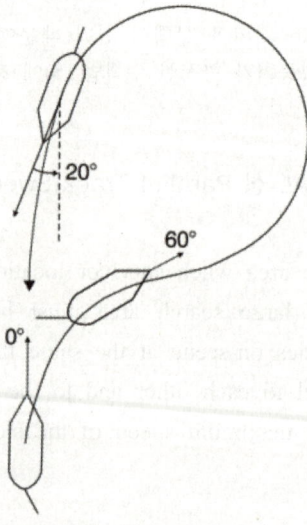

02
Scharnov Turn

① 절차

ⓐ **Rudder hard over.**
ⓑ After deviation from the original course by **240°**, rudder **hard over to the opposite side**.
ⓒ When heading **20° short of opposite course**, rudder to **midship position** so that ship will turn to opposite course.

② 특징

ⓐ will take vessel back into her wake

ⓑ less distance is covered, saving time

ⓒ cannot be carried out effectively unless the time elapsed between occurrence of the incident and the commencement of the manoeuvre is known

ⓓ Not to be used in an "immediate action" situation.

ⓐ 최대 전타한다.
ⓑ 원 침로의 240°로 전타가 된 후, 반대 현측으로 최대 전타한다.
ⓒ 원 침로의 반대 침로에 선수 20° 정도 남았을 때, midships하여 선박을 원 침로의 반대 침로로 맞춘다.

ⓐ 그 선박의 원래 항적으로 되돌아가게 한다.
ⓑ 항정이 짧아, 시간을 절약한다.
ⓒ 사고가 일어난 시점과 조종의 착수 시점 사이에 흐른 시간을 모른다면, 효율적으로 수행될 수 없다.
ⓓ "즉각적인 행동"을 하는 상황에서 사용되지 않는다.

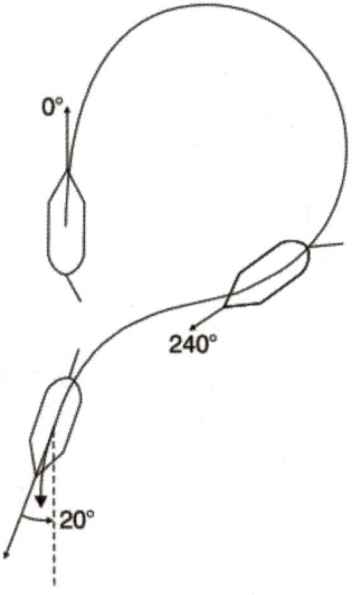

03
One Turn (Single turn, Anderson turn)

① 절차

ⓐ **Rudder hard over** (in an "immediate action" situation, only to the side of the casualty).

ⓑ After deviation from the original course by **250°**, rudder to **midship position** and stopping manoeuvre to be initiated.

② 특징

ⓐ fastest recovery method
ⓑ good for ships with tight turning characteristics
ⓒ used most by ships with considerable power
ⓓ very difficult for a single-screw vessel
ⓔ difficult because approach to person is not straight

ⓐ 사람이 물에 빠진 현측으로 최대 전타한다. ("즉각적인 행동"을 하는 상황에서 사용된다. 사고 지점의 현측으로 사용한다.)
ⓑ 원 침로에서 250도 선회하면 midship하여 멈추게 한다.

ⓐ 가장 빠른 구조법이다.
ⓑ 선회 성능이 좋은 선박에게 유리하다.
ⓒ 상당한 출력을 지닌 선박에 흔히 사용된다.
ⓓ 단추진기 선박에게 사용하기 어렵다.
ⓔ 사람에 대한 접근이 직선이 아니기 때문에 구출하기 어렵다.

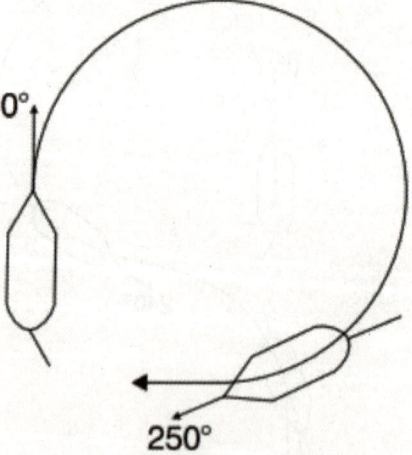

기출문제

01. The following sentence is about a kind of standard methods of recovery in the IAMSAR manual when a person overboard is noticed. What is the name of it?

_{14년 2차}

> It makes good original track line and is good in reduced visibility.
> It is simple but takes the ship farther away from the scene of the incident.

① Single turn ② One turn
③ Williamson turn ④ Scharnov turn

해설 Williamson turn에 대한 설명이다.

답

02. IAMSAR MANUAL상 아래의 절차에 따라 행하는 구조 방법은 무엇인가?

_{17년 2차}

> (Not to be used in an "immediate action" situation.)
> 1. Rudder hard over.
> 2. After deviation from the original course by 240°, rudder hard over to the opposite side.
> 3. When heading 20° short of opposite course, rudder to midship position so that ship will turn to opposite course.

① Williamson turn ② Anderson turn
③ Single turn ④ Scharnov turn

해설 Scharnov turn에 대한 설명이다.

답 ④

03. 다음 중 IAMSAR Manual Volume III 상 "man overboard" 상황에서의 조선 방법에 대한 설명으로 가장 옳지 않은 것은?

_{18년 일반직}

① "Scharnov turn" cannot be carried out effectively unless the time elapsed between occurrence of the incident and the commencement of the manoeuvre is known.
② "Scharnov turn" is proper in an 'immediate action' situation.
③ "Williamson turn" makes good original track line.
④ "Williamson turn" is good in reduced visibility.

해설 Scharnov turn은 즉각적인 행동을 해야 하는 상황에서 사용되지 않는다.

답

기출문제

04. IAMSAR manual 상 Single turn 구조방법의 특징에 대한 설명으로 가장 옳지 않은 것은?

19년 1차

① fastest recovery
② good for ships with tight turning characteristics
③ used most by ships with considerable power
④ easy because approach to person is straight

해설 difficult because approach to person is not straight

답 ④

chapter 06 Rescue or assistance by aircraft

01
Rescue sling

① The **most widely used** means for evacuating persons is the rescue sling, if possible together with a helicopter crew member

② Slings are suited for quickly picking up **uninjured** persons, but are unsuitable for persons with **injuries**.

01 구조 밧줄

① 사람을 인양 구조 할 때 가장 널리 사용되는 장치로, 가능한 헬기의 승무원이 함께한다.
② 이 슬링은 부상당하지 않은 사람을 위한 구조에는 적합하나, 부상을 입은 사람을 구조하기에는 적합하지 않다.

Rescue sling

02
Rescue basket

① Use of the rescue basket does not require any special measures. To use the basket, the person merely climbs in, remains seated and holds on.

02 구조용 바스켓

① 구조용 바스켓의 사용은 특별한 사용법을 필요로 하지는 않는다. 사용을 위해서는 그저 탈것에 사람이 올라가 앉은 채 고정되면 된다.

Rescue basket

03
Rescue seat

① The rescue seat looks like a three-pronged anchor with two flat flukes or seats.

② Persons to be hoisted merely sit astride on one or two of the seats and wrap their arms around the shank.

③ this device can be used to which two persons at once.

Rescue seat

04
Rescue net

① The rescue net has a conical "bird cage" appearance and is open on one side.

② To use the net the person merely enters the opening, sits in the net, and holds on.

Rescue net

05
Rescue litter

① Patients will in most cases be disembarked by means of a rescue stretcher.
② The evacuation of patients can be done in a special stretcher provided by the helicopter or in a litter provided at the site (if approved by the helicopter crew).
③ Bridles are fitted to this litter and can quickly and safely be hooked on and off.
④ The litter provided by helicopter should be unhooked from the winch cable while the patient is being loaded

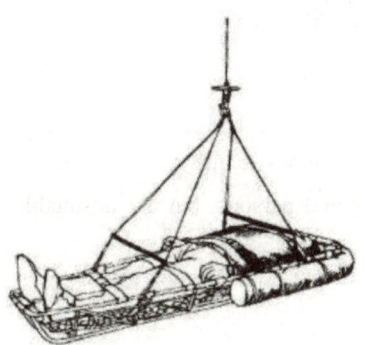

05 구조용 들것

① 환자는 대개 구조 들것에 의해 구조가 된다.
② 환자의 구조는 헬기나 구조현장에서 제공되는 특수 들것에 의해서 구조될 수 있다.(만약 헬리콥터 크루에게 승인을 받는다면)
③ 이 들것에는 묶는 밧줄이 설치되어 신속하고 안전하게 후크를 채우고 풀 수 있다.
④ 환자가 실리는 중에는 헬기에서 제공된 이 들것이 윈치로부터 풀려 있어야 한다.

기출문제

01. Choose an answer in the blank　　　　　　　　　　　　　　　　　　　　11년 2차

ⓐ The most widely used means for evacuating persons is the (　　　).

ⓑ (　　) are suited for quickly picking up uninjured persons, but are unsuitable for persons with injuries.

① hoist　　　　　　　　　　② stretcher
③ rescue net　　　　　　　　④ rescue sling

해설 ⓐ 인명 구조를 위해 가장 보편적으로 사용되는 것은 <u>구조용 밧줄(rescue sling)</u>이다.
　　　ⓑ <u>구조용 밧줄(rescue sling)</u>은 부상당하지 않은 사람을 빠르게 인양하는데 적합하나 부상자를 위해서는 부적합하다.

답 ❹

02. 다음 〈보기〉의 IAMSAR 상 아래에서 설명하는 This device로 가장 옳은 것은?　　21년 상반기

㉠ This device looks like a three-pronged anchor with two flat flukes or seats.
㉡ Persons to be hoisted merely sit astride on one or two of the seats and wrap their arms around the shank.
㉢ this device can be used to which two persons at once.

① Rescue Seat　　　　　　② Rescue Basket
③ Rescue Net　　　　　　　④ Rescue Litter

해설 구조용 시트(Rescue Seat)에 대한 설명이다.

답 ❶

chapter 07
On- Scene Co -ordination 현장 조정

01
Designation of On-Scene Co-ordinator (OSC)

① When two or more SAR facilities conduct operations together, the SMC should designate an OSC.

② If this is not practicable, facilities involved should designate, by mutual agreement, an OSC.

③ This should be done as early as practicable and preferably before arrival within the search area.

④ **Until an OSC has been designated**, the first facility arriving at the scene should assume the duties of an OSC.

⑤ When deciding how much responsibility to delegate to the OSC, the SMC normally considers the communications and personnel capabilities of the facilities involved.

⑥ The poorer the communications, the more authority the OSC will need to initiate actions.

01 현장조정관의 임명

① 두 개 이상의 SAR 시설물이 같이 작업을 수행할 때, SMC는 OSC를 임명해야 한다.

② 이것이 실행 가능하지 않다면, 포함되어 있는 시설물들은 상호 합의에 의해 OSC를 임명해야 한다.

③ 이것은 실행 가능한 한 빨리 되어야 하고 가급적이면 수색구역에 도착하기 전에 시행되어야 한다.

④ OSC가 임명될 때 까지는, 처음으로 현장에 도착한 SAR시설물이 OSC의 임무를 맡아야 한다.

⑤ OSC에게 얼마나 많이 권한을 부여할지를 정할 때, SMC는 일반적으로 포함된 시설물의 소통 능력과 개인적인 역량을 고려해야 한다.

⑥ 소통이 원활하지 않을수록 OSC는 더 많은 권한을 가지고 행동을 개시해야 할 것이다.

기출문제

01. IAMSAR manual 상 Designation of On-Scene Co-ordinator(OSC)에 대한 설명으로 가장 옳지 않은 것은?　19년 1차

① When two or more SAR facilities conduct operations together, the SMC should designate an OSC.
② This should be done as early as practicable and preferably before arrival within the search area.
③ Until SAR is over, the first facility arriving at the scene should assume the duties of an OSC.
④ When deciding how much responsibility to delegate to the OSC the SMC normally considers the communications and personnel capabilities of the facilities involved.

해설 Until an OSC has been designated, the first facility arriving at the scene should assume the duties of an OSC. : OSC가 임명될 때 까지는, 처음으로 현장에 도착한 SAR시설물이 OSC의 임무를 맡아야 한다.

답 ③

chapter 08 Man Overboard

01
Three situations

① Immediate action
   The person overboard is noticed from the bridge and action is taken immediately.
② Delayed action
   The person is reported to the bridge by an eyewitness and action is initiated with some delay.
③ Person-missing action
   The person is reported to the bridge as missing.

01 세 가지 상황

① 즉각적인 행동
   익수자가 선교로부터 발견되고 조치가 즉각적으로 이루어짐
② 지연된 행동
   익수자가 목격자에 의해서 선교로 보고되고, 조치는 약간의 지연이 있고나서 이루어짐
③ 실종자 발생 행동
   사람이 실종되었음이 선교로 보고됨

02
Ship manoeuvres

① When the possibility exists that a person has fallen overboard, the crew must attempt to recover the individual as soon as possible.

② Some factors that will affect the speed of recovery include:

☐ ship's manoeuvring characteristics
☐ wind direction and sea state
☐ crew's experience and level of training
☐ capability of the engine plant
☐ location of the incident
☐ visibility level
☐ recovery technique
☐ possibility of having other vessels assist.

02 선박의 조종

① 사람이 물에 빠졌을 가능성이 존재 할 때 선원은 가능한한 빠르게 사람을 구하기 위한 조치를 반드시 취해야한다.
② 구조속도에 영향을 주는 요소들은 다음의 것들을 포함한다.
☐ 선박의 조종 성능(특성)
☐ 풍향과 해면의 상태
☐ 선원의 경험과 훈련수준
☐ 기관의 성능
☐ 사고 위치
☐ 시정의 정도
☐ 구조기술
☐ 다른 선박들의 지원가능성

03 초기 동작

① GNSS로부터의 위치 그리고 시간을 노트하고 표시하라
② 가능한 익수자와 가까운 현 쪽으로 구명부환을 던져라
③ 3회의 장음을 선박 휘슬로 울리고, "익수자발생" 이라고 외쳐라
④ 아래 나타나 있는 구조를 위한 조선을 시작하라(chapter5의 인명구조법들)
⑤ 위치, 바람의 속도와 방향 및 시간을 기록하라
⑥ 선장과 기관실에 알려라
⑦ 익수자를 주시하기위해 견시원을 배치하라
⑧ 색을 내는 표지나, 발연 화염신호를 발생시켜라.
⑨ 청수당직자에게 알리고 해당 위치에서 업데이트를 유지해라
⑩ 기관을 준비를 하라
⑪ 구조 설비를 준비하라.
⑫ 선교, 갑판, 구명보트 간의 통신을 위하여 이동식 VHF 라디오를 배분하라.

03 Initial action

① Mark and note position and time from GNSS(Global Navigation Satellite system).
② Throw a life-ring over the side as close to the person as possible.
③ Sound three prolonged blasts of ship's whistle; hail "man overboard".
④ Commence recovery manoeuvre as indicated below.
⑤ Note wind speed and direction.
⑥ Inform master of vessel and engine-room.
⑦ Post look-outs to keep the person in sight.
⑧ Set off dye marker or smoke flare.
⑨ Inform radio operator; keep updated on position.
⑩ Stand by the engines.
⑪ Prepare recovery equipment – see section 2, Recovery of survivors by assisting vessels.
⑫ Distribute portable VHF radios for communication between bridge, deck, and lifeboat.

PART 04 COLREG(International Regulations for preventing Collision at Sea.)

Part A − General

Rule1 Application
Rule2 Responsibility
Rule3 General definitions

Part B − Steering and sailing rules

Section I - Conduct of vessels in any condition of visibility
Rule4 Application
Rule5 Look-out
Rule6 Safe speed
Rule7 Risk of collision
Rule8 Action to avoid a collision
Rule9 Narrow channels
Rule10 Traffic separation schemes

Section II - Conduct of vessels in sight of one another
Rule 11 Application
Rule 12 Sailing vessels
Rule 13 Overtaking
Rule 14 Head-on situation
Rule 15 Crossing situation
Rule 16 Action by give-way vessel
Rule 17 Action by stand-on vessel
Rule 18 Responsibilities

Section III - Conduct of vessels in restricted visibility
Rule 19 Conduct of vessels in restricted visibility

Part C − Light and shapes

Rule 20 Application
Rule 21 Definitions
Rule 22 Visibility of lights
Rule 23 Power-driven vessels underway
Rule 24 Towing and pushing
Rule 25 Sailing vessels underway and vessels under oars
Rule 26 Fishing vessels
Rule 27 Vessels not under command or restricted in their ability to manoeuvre
Rule 28 Vessels constrained by their draught
Rule 29 Pilot vessels

Rule 30 Anchored vessels and vessels aground
Rule 31 Seaplanes

Part D – Sound and light signals
Rule 32 Definitions
Rule 33 Equipment for sound signals
Rule 34 Manoeuvring and wearing signals
Rule 35 Sound signals in restricted visibility
Rule 36 Signals to attract attention
Rule 37 Distress signals

Part E – Exemptions
Rule 38 Exemptions

PART A – General

Rule 1

Application

ⓐ These Rules shall apply to all vessels upon the **high seas** and in all waters connected therewith navigable by seagoing vessels.

ⓑ Nothing in these Rules shall interfere with the operation of special rules made by an appropriate authority for roadsteads, harbours, rivers, lakes or inland waterways connected with the high seas and navigable by seagoing vessels. Such special rules shall conform as closely as possible to these Rules.

ⓒ Nothing in these Rules shall interfere with the operation of any special rules made by the Government of any State with respect to additional station or signal lights, shapes or whistle signals for ships of war and vessels proceeding under convoy, or with respect to additional station or signal lights or shapes for fishing vessels engaged in fishing as a fleet. These additional station or signal lights, shapes or whistle signals shall, so far as possible, be such that they cannot be mistaken for any light, shapes or signal authorized elsewhere under these Rules.

ⓓ Traffic separation schemes may be adopted by the Organization for the purpose of these Rules.

ⓔ Whenever the Government concerned shall have determined that a vessel of special construction or purpose cannot comply fully with the provisions of any of these Rules with respect to the number, position, range or arc of visibility of lights or shapes, as well as to the disposition and characteristics of sound-signalling appliances, such vessel shall comply with such other provisions in regard to the number, position, range or arc of visibility of lights or shapes, as well as to the disposition and characteristics of sound-signalling appliances, as her Government shall have determined to be the closest possible compliance with these Rules in respect to that vessel.

제 1 조

적용

ⓐ 이 규칙은, 외양항행선이 항행할 수 있는 해양과 이와 접속한 모든 수역의 수상에 있는 모든 선박에 적용한다.

ⓑ 이 규칙의 어떤 규정도, 해양과 접속되어 있고 외양항행선이 항행할 수 있는 묘박지, 항내, 하천, 호수 및 내수로에 관하여 관할관청이 제정한 특별규칙의 시행을 배제하는 것은 아니다. 그러나 특별규칙은 될 수 있는 한 이 규칙에 일치되어야 한다.

ⓒ 이 규칙의 규정은, 군함이나 호송되어 항행하고 있는 선단이 부가하여 다는 위치등, 신호등, 형상물이나 기적신호, 또는 선단을 지어, 어로에 종사하는 어선이 부가하여 다는 위치등, 신호등 또는 형상물에 관하여 각국 정부가 제정한 특별규칙의 시행을 막는 것은 아니다. 이들 부가 위치등, 신호등, 형상물 또는 기적신호 등은, 가능한 한 이 규칙에서 규정한 등화, 형상물 또는 신호와 오인되지 아니하는 것이라야 한다.

ⓓ 이 규칙의 목적을 위하여, 정부간 해사자문기구(IMO)는 통항분리방식을 채택할 수 있다.

ⓔ 특수한 구조나 목적을 가진 선박이 이 규칙에서 규정하는 등화나 형상물의 수, 위치, 시인 거리, 사광권 및 음향신호기구의 배치 및 특성을 따를 수 없을 때에는 그 정부는 그 선박에 관하여 가능하면 이 규칙에 가깝게 그러한 규정을 만들고, 그러한 선박은 등화나 형상물의 수, 위치, 시인거리, 사광권 및 신호기구의 배치와 특성에 관하여, 그 정부가 제정한 규정을 따라야 한다.

기출문제

01. 다음 밑줄에 공통으로 들어갈 용어와 가장 거리가 먼 것은?   `15년 2차`

(1) COLREG Rule 1 - Application

These Rules shall apply to all vessels upon the _____(s) and in all waters connected therewith navigable by seagoing vessels.

(2) UNCLOS Article 110- Right of visit

Except where acts of interference derive from powers conferred by treaty, a warship which encounters on the _____(s) a foreign ship, other accordance with articles 95 and 96, is not justified in boarding it unless there is reasonable ground for suspecting that;

① open sea   ② high sea
③ international water   ④ marine sea

해설 밑줄에 들어갈 해역은 공해(high sea)이다. 공해는 열린 바다(open sea), 국제해역(international sea) 등으로 불릴 수 있다. 해양(marine sea)는 그 범주가 너무 넓다.

답 ❹

제 2 조
책임

ⓐ 이 규칙의 어느 규정도 이 규칙의 이행을 태만히 한 결과 또는 선원의 통상적인 업무수행 상이나 특수한 사정에 의하여 필요로 하는 주의를 태만히 함으로써 생긴 결과에 대하여 어떠한 선박, 선박소유자, 선장 또는 해원의 책임을 면제하여 주지 아니한다.

ⓑ 이 규칙을 해석하고 실행에 옮기는데 있어서는 항해 및 충돌상의 모든 위험과 그리고 관계 선박의 성능의 한계에서 오는 사정도 포함하여 모든 특수한 사정에 대하여 합당한 주의를 하여야 하고, 그러한 위험이나 특수한 사정이 있을 때에는 절박한 위험을 피하기 위하여 이 규칙에 따르지 아니할 수도 있다.

제 3 조
일반정의

이 규칙의 적용상 사용하는 용어의 정의는 문맥상 다른 의미로 해석하여야 할 필요가 있을 경우를 제외하고는 다음과 같다.

ⓐ '선박'이라 함은, 배수량을 갖지 아니하는 선박, WIG 및 수상항공기를 포함한 수상의 운송수단으로 사용되거나 또는 사용될 수 있는 모든 배 종류를 말한다.

ⓑ '동력선'이라 함은, 기계를 사용하여 추진하는 모든 선박을 말한다.

Rule 2
Responsibility

ⓐ Nothing in these Rules shall exonerate **any vessel, or the owner, master or crew** thereof, from the consequences of any **neglect** to comply with these Rules or of the **neglect** of any precaution which may be required by the ordinary practice of seamen, or by the special circumstances of the case.

ⓑ In construing and complying with these Rules due regard shall be had to all dangers of navigation and collision and to any special circumstances, including the limitations of the vessels involved, which may make a departure from these Rules necessary to avoid immediate danger.

Rule 3
General Definitions

For the purpose of these Rules, except where the context otherwise requires:

ⓐ The word **'vessel'** includes every description of water craft, including non-displacement craft, WIG craft and seaplanes, used or capable of being used as a means of transportation on water.

ⓑ The term **'power-driven vessel'** means any vessel propelled by machinery.

ⓒ The term **'sailing vessel'** means any vessel under sail provided that propelling machinery, if fitted, is not being used.

ⓓ The term **'vessel engaged in fishing'** means any vessel fishing with nets, lines, trawls or other fishing apparatus which restrict manoeuvrability, but does not include a vessel fishing with trolling lines or other fishing apparatus which do not restrict manoeuvrability.

ⓔ The word **'seaplane'** includes any aircraft designed to manoeuvre on the water.

ⓕ The term **'vessel not under command'** means a vessel which through some exceptional circumstance is unable to manoeuvre as required by these Rules and is therefore unable to keep out of the way of another vessel.

ⓖ The term **'vessel restricted in her ability to manoeuvre'** means a vessel which from the nature of her work is restricted in her ability to manoeuvre as required by these Rules and therefore is unable to keep out of the way of another vessel.
The term 'vessels restricted in their ability to manoeuvre' shall include but not be limited to;

(i) a vessel engaged in laying, servicing or picking up a navigation mark, submarine cable or pipeline;

(ii) a vessel engaged in dredging, surveying or underwater operations;

(iii) a vessel engaged in replenishment or transferring persons, provisions or cargo while underway;

(iv) a vessel engaged in the launching or recovery of aircraft;

(v) a vessel engaged in mineclearance operations;

ⓒ '범선'이라 함은, 추진기계를 장비하였다 할지라도 이를 사용하고 있지 않고서, 돛을 사용하고 있는 일체의 선박을 말한다.

ⓓ '어로에 종사하고 있는 선박'이라 함은, 어망, 밧줄, 트로올망 또는 기타 조종성능을 제한하는 어구를 사용하여 어로하고 있는 선박을 말하며, 조종성능을 제한하지 아니하는 인승 또는 기타 어구를 사용하여 어로하고 있는 선박을 포함하지 아니한다.

ⓔ '수상항공기'라 함은 수상에서 조종할 수 있도록 설계된 비행기를 말한다.

ⓕ '운전부자유선'이라 함은 어떤 예외적인 사정으로 인하여 이 규칙이 요구하는 대로 조종될 수 없고, 따라서 타선의 진로를 피할 수 없는 선박을 말한다.

ⓖ '조종성능이 제한된 선박'이라 함은 종사하고 있는 작업의 성질상 이 규칙이 요구하는 대로 조종될 수 없고, 따라서 타선의 진로를 피할 수 없는 선박을 말한다. 다음은 '조종 성능이 제한되어 있는 선박'에 포함되나 이에 한정되지 아니한다.

(ⅰ) 항로표지, 수저전선, 또는 도관의 부설보수, 또는 인양에 종사하고 있는 선박 ;

(ⅱ) 준설, 측량, 또는 수중작업에 종사하고 있는 선박 ;

(ⅲ) 항해하면서 해상보급 또는 인원, 식량 또는 화물의 이송에 종사 중인 선박 ;

(ⅳ) 비행기의 발착에 종사하고 있는 선박 ;

(ⅴ) 기뢰제거 작업에 종사하고 있는 선박 ;

(vi) 예선이나 피예선이 자기의 침로에서 벗어날 수 없도록 심히 행동을 제약하는 성질의 예인작업에 종사하고 있는 선박.

(h) '흘수에 의하여 제약을 받는 선박'이라 함은 흘수로 인하여 가항수역의 수심과 폭에 여유가 적어서 현재 취하고 있는 침로를 이탈할 능력이 극히 제한된 동력선을 말한다.

(i) '항해중'이라 함은, 선박이 묘박하거나, 또는 육안에 계류하거나, 또는 좌초되어 있지 아니하는 상태를 말한다.

(j) '선박의 길이 및 폭'이라 함은, 그 선박의 전장 및 최대의 폭을 말한다.

(k) 선박이 서로 다른 선박을 육안으로 볼 수 있는 경우만을 상호 시계 내에 있는 것으로 한다.

(l) '제한시계'라 함은 안개, 강설, 폭풍우, 모래폭풍 또는 기타 유사한 원인으로 인하여 시계가 제한된 모든 상태를 말한다.

(m) '표면효과작용(WIG) 선박'이란 표면효과작용을 이용하여 표면에 근접하여 주로 비행하는 다용도 선박을 의미한다.

(vi) a vessel engaged in a towing operation such as severely restricts the towing vessel and her tow in their ability to deviate from their course.

(h) The term **'vessel constrained by her draught'** means a power-driven vessel which because of her draught in relation to the available depth and width of navigable water, is severely restricted in her ability to deviate from the course she is following.

(i) The word **'underway'** means that a vessel is not at anchor, or made fast to the shore, or aground.

(j) The words **'length' and 'breadth'** of a vessel mean her length overall and greatest breadth.

(k) Vessels shall be deemed to be **in sight of one another** only when one can be observed visually from the other.

(l) The term **'restricted visibility'** means any condition in which visibility is restricted by fog, mist, falling snow, heavy rainstorms, sandstorms or any other similar causes.

(m) The term **'Wing-In-Ground (WIG) craft'** means a multimodal craft which, in its main operational mode, flies in close proximity to the surface by utilizing surface-effect action.

ⓒ The term **'sailing vessel'** means any vessel under sail provided that propelling machinery, if fitted, is not being used.

ⓓ The term **'vessel engaged in fishing'** means any vessel fishing with nets, lines, trawls or other fishing apparatus which restrict manoeuvrability, but does not include a vessel fishing with trolling lines or other fishing apparatus which do not restrict manoeuvrability.

ⓔ The word **'seaplane'** includes any aircraft designed to manoeuvre on the water.

ⓕ The term **'vessel not under command'** means a vessel which through some exceptional circumstance is unable to manoeuvre as required by these Rules and is therefore unable to keep out of the way of another vessel.

ⓖ The term **'vessel restricted in her ability to manoeuvre'** means a vessel which from the nature of her work is restricted in her ability to manoeuvre as required by these Rules and therefore is unable to keep out of the way of another vessel.
The term 'vessels restricted in their ability to manoeuvre' shall include but not be limited to;

(i) a vessel engaged in laying, servicing or picking up a navigation mark, submarine cable or pipeline;

(ii) a vessel engaged in dredging, surveying or underwater operations;

(iii) a vessel engaged in replenishment or transferring persons, provisions or cargo while underway;

(iv) a vessel engaged in the launching or recovery of aircraft;

(v) a vessel engaged in mineclearance operations;

ⓒ '범선'이라 함은, 추진기계를 장비하였다 할지라도 이를 사용하고 있지 않고서, 돛을 사용하고 있는 일체의 선박을 말한다.

ⓓ '어로에 종사하고 있는 선박'이라 함은, 어망, 밧줄, 트로올망 또는 기타 조종성능을 제한하는 어구를 사용하여 어로하고 있는 선박을 말하며, 조종성능을 제한하지 아니하는 인승 또는 기타 어구를 사용하여 어로하고 있는 선박을 포함하지 아니한다.

ⓔ '수상항공기'라 함은 수상에서 조종할 수 있도록 설계된 비행기를 말한다.

ⓕ '운전부자유선'이라 함은 어떤 예외적인 사정으로 인하여 이 규칙이 요구하는 대로 조종될 수 없고, 따라서 타선의 진로를 피할 수 없는 선박을 말한다.

ⓖ '조종성능이 제한된 선박'이라 함은 종사하고 있는 작업의 성질상 이 규칙이 요구하는 대로 조종될 수 없고, 따라서 타선의 진로를 피할 수 없는 선박을 말한다. 다음은 '조종 성능이 제한되어 있는 선박'에 포함되나 이에 한정되지 아니한다.

(ⅰ) 항로표지, 수저전선, 또는 도관의 부설보수, 또는 인양에 종사하고 있는 선박 ;

(ⅱ) 준설, 측량, 또는 수중작업에 종사하고 있는 선박 ;

(ⅲ) 항해하면서 해상보급 또는 인원, 식량 또는 화물의 이송에 종사 중인 선박 ;

(ⅳ) 비행기의 발착에 종사하고 있는 선박 ;

(ⅴ) 기뢰제거 작업에 종사하고 있는 선박 ;

(vi) 예선이나 피예선이 자기의 침로에서 벗어날 수 없도록 심히 행동을 제약하는 성질의 예인작업에 종사하고 있는 선박.	(vi) a vessel engaged in a towing operation such as severely restricts the towing vessel and her tow in their ability to deviate from their course.
ⓗ '흘수에 의하여 제약을 받는 선박'이라 함은 흘수로 인하여 가항수역의 수심과 폭에 여유가 적어서 현재 취하고 있는 침로를 이탈할 능력이 극히 제한된 동력선을 말한다.	ⓗ The term **'vessel constrained by her draught'** means a power-driven vessel which because of her draught in relation to the available depth and width of navigable water, is severely restricted in her ability to deviate from the course she is following.
ⓘ '항해중'이라 함은, 선박이 묘박하거나, 또는 육안에 계류하거나, 또는 좌초되어 있지 아니하는 상태를 말한다.	ⓘ The word **'underway'** means that a vessel is not at anchor, or made fast to the shore, or aground.
ⓙ '선박의 길이 및 폭'이라 함은, 그 선박의 전장 및 최대의 폭을 말한다.	ⓙ The words **'length' and 'breadth'** of a vessel mean her length overall and greatest breadth.
ⓚ 선박이 서로 다른 선박을 육안으로 볼 수 있는 경우만을 상호 시계 내에 있는 것으로 한다.	ⓚ Vessels shall be deemed to be **in sight of one another** only when one can be observed visually from the other.
ⓛ '제한시계'라 함은 안개, 강설, 폭풍우, 모래폭풍 또는 기타 유사한 원인으로 인하여 시계가 제한된 모든 상태를 말한다.	ⓛ The term **'restricted visibility'** means any condition in which visibility is restricted by fog, mist, falling snow, heavy rainstorms, sandstorms or any other similar causes.
ⓜ '표면효과작용(WIG) 선박'이란 표면효과작용을 이용하여 표면에 근접하여 주로 비행하는 다용도 선박을 의미한다.	ⓜ The term **'Wing-In-Ground (WIG) craft'** means a multimodal craft which, in its main operational mode, flies in close proximity to the surface by utilizing surface-effect action.

기출문제

02. 다음 빈 칸에 들어갈 말로 가장 적절한 것은? `14년 1차`

> The term (   ) means a multimodal craft which, in its main operational mode, flies in close proximity to the surface by utilizing surface-effect action

① seaplane
② hovercraft
③ Wing-In-Ground craft
④ hydrofoil

해설 WIG(Wing In Ground) craft 에 대한 설명이다.

답 ❸

03. According to the COLREG which is the correct definition of the term 'vessel not under command'? `14년 2차`

① A vessel under sail provided that propelling machinery, if fitted, is not being used.
② A vessel which through some exceptional circumstances is unable to manoeuvre as required by COLREG and is therefore unable to keep out of the way of another vessel.
③ A vessel which from the nature of her work is restricted in her ability to manoeuvre as required by COLREG and is therefore unable to keep out of the way of another vessel.
④ A power-driven vessel which, because of her draught in relation to the available depth and width of navigable water, is severly restricted in her ability to deviate from the course she is following

해설 ① Sailing vessel
③ A vessel restricted in her ability to manoeuvre
④ A vessel constrained by her draught

답 ❷

04. COLREG(국제해상충돌예방규칙)상 아래 문장이 의미하는 것은 무엇인가? `16년 일반직`

> A vessel which through some exceptional circumstance is unable to manoeuvre as required by these Rules and is therefore unable to keep out of the way of another vessel.

① vessel engaged in fishing
② vessel restricted in her ability to manoeuvre
③ vessel constrained by her draught
④ vessel not under command

해설 조종불능선(vessel not under command)에 대한 설명이다.

답 ❹

기출문제

05. 다음 중 빈칸에 들어갈 말로 가장 옳은 것은? 〔17년 1차〕

The term "(   )" means a vessel which from the nature of her work is restricted in her ability to manoeuvre as required by these Rules and therefore is unable to keep out of the way of another vessel.

① vessel engaged in fishing
② vessel not under command
③ vessel restricted in her ability to manoeuvre
④ vessel constrained by her draught

해설 조종제한선(vessel restricted in her ability to manoeuvre)에 대한 설명이다.

답 ❸

06. 준설작업에 종사하는 선박은 다음 중 어디에 해당하는가? 〔04년 2차〕

① vessel not under command
② vessel restricted in her ability to manoeuvre
③ vessel constrained by her draught
④ vessel engaged in fishing

해설 준설 작업에 종사하는 선박(vessel engaged in dredging)은 조종제한선(vessel restricted in her ability to manoeuvre)으로 분류된다.

답 ❷

07. 〈국제해상충돌방지규칙〉에서 다음 빈칸에 들어갈 말을 우리말로 가장 잘 바꾼 것은? 〔15년 일반직〕

The word (   ) means that a vessel is not at anchor, or made fast the shore, or aground.

① 접안 중   ② 항행 중
③ 정박 중   ④ 투묘 중

해설 해당 빈칸에 들어갈 말은 항해 중(underway)이다.

답 ❷

기출문제

08. 다음 중 COLREG(국제해상충돌예방규칙)상 용어의 정의에 대한 설명으로 가장 옳지 않은 것은? `18년 일반직`

① The word 'underway' means that a vessel is not at anchor, or made fast the shore, or aground.
② The word 'length of a vessel' means her length overall
③ The term 'restricted visibility' means any condition in which visibility is restricted by fog, mist or any other similar causes.
④ The term 'prolonged blast' means a blast of from two to three seconds duration.

해설 The term 'prolonged blast' means a blast of from four to six seconds duration.
　＊The term 'short blast' means a blast of about one second duration.＊

답 ❹

09. 다음은 「COLREG(International Regulations for Preventing Collisions at Sea)」상 용어의 정의에 대한 설명이다 옳지 않은 것은 모두 몇 개인가? `20년 3차`

㉠ Power-driven vessel : Any vessel propelled by machinery.
㉡ Vessel : Includes every description of water craft, including non-displacement craft and seaplanes, used or capable of being used as a means of transportation on water.
㉢ Sailing vessel : Any vessel under sail provided that propelling machinery, if fitted, is not being used.
㉣ WIG craft : Includes any aircraft designed to manoeuvre on the water.

① 없음　　　　　　　② 1개
③ 2개　　　　　　　④ 3개

해설 옳지 않은 것:
　㉣ 수상항공기(Seaplane)에 대한 설명이다.

답 ❷

PART B - Steering and sailing rules

제 1 절 모든 상태의 시계 내에서의 선박의 운항

SECTION I—CONDUCT OF VESSELS IN ANY CONDITION OF VISIBILITY

제 4 조

적용

이 절의 규칙은 모든 상태의 시계에 대하여 적용한다.

Rule 4

Application

Rules in this Section apply in any condition of visibility.

제 5 조

견 시

모든 선박은 시각 및 청각은 물론 그 당시의 사정과 상태에 적절한 모든 유효한 수단을 동원하여, 처하여 있는 상황 및 충돌의 위험을 충분히 평가할 수 있도록 항상 적절한 견시를 유지하여야 한다.

Rule 5

Look-out

Every vessel shall at all times maintain a proper **look-out** by sight and hearing as well as by all available means appropriate in the prevailing circumstances and conditions so as to make a full appraisal of the situation and of the risk of collision.

제 6 조

안전속력

모든 선박은, 충돌을 피하기 위하여 적절하고 유효한 동작을 취할 수 있고 그 당시의 사정과 상태에 알맞은 거리에서 정선할 수 있도록 항상 안전한 속력으로 항행하여야 한다.
안전한 속력을 결정함에 있어서 다음의 요소를 고려하여야 한다.

Rule 6

Safe Speed

Every vessel shall at all times proceed **at a safe speed** so that she can take proper and effective action to avoid collision and be stopped within a distance appropriate to the prevailing circumstances and conditions. In determining a safe speed the following factors shall be among those taken into account:

ⓐ 모든 선박에 대하여 :

ⓐ By all vessels:

(i) 시정의 상태 ;

(i) the state of visibility;

(ii) 어선 혹은 기타 선박들의 집결을 포함한 교통량의 밀도 ;

(ii) the traffic density including concentrations of fishing vessels or any other vessels;

(iii) the manoeuvrability of the vessel with special reference to stopping distance and turning ability in the prevailing conditions;	(iii) 그 당시의 상태하에서, 특히 정지거리와 선회능력을 참작한 선박의 조종성능 ;
(iv) at night the presence of background light such as from shore lights or from back scatter of her own lights;	(iv) 야간에 육상 등화 또는 자선의 등화의 역산광으로부터 오는 것과 같은 배경 광선의 존재 여부 ;
(v) the state of wind, sea and current, and the proximity of navigational hazards;	(ⅴ) 바람, 해면 및 조류의 상태, 그리고 항해 장애물의 근접상태 ;
(vi) the draught in relation to the available depth of water.	(vi) 항행가능한 수심과 흘수 ;
ⓑ Additionally, by vessels with operational radar:	ⓑ Radar 사용가능선박이 추가하여 고려할 사항 :
(i) the characteristics, efficiency and limitations of the radar equipment;	(ⅰ) Radar 장비의 특성, 능력 및 한계 ;
(ii) any constraints imposed by the radar range scale in use;	(ⅱ) 활용되는 Radar 거리 눈금에서 오는 제약 ;
(iii) the effect on radar detection of the sea state, weather and other sources of interference;	(iii) 해면상태, 기상 및 기타의 장애 요인이 Radar 탐색에 미치는 영향 ;
(iv) the possibility that small vessels, ice and other floating objects may not be detected by radar at an adequate range;	(iv) 소형선, 유빙, 기타의 부유물은 적당한 거리 내에서 Radar에 의하여 탐지되지 아니할 수도 있다는 사실 ;
(v) the number, location and movement of vessels detected by radar;	(ⅴ) Radar에 의하여 탐지된 선박의 척수, 위치 및 이동상태 ;
(vi) the more exact assessment of the visibility that may be possible when radar is used to determine the range of vessels or other objects in the vicinity.	(vi) 부근의 선박이나 기타의 목표물의 거리를 측정하기 위하여 Radar을 사용할 때 할 수 있는 보다 정확한 시정의 추정.

I 기출문제

10. Choose best answer in the blank   [10년 3차]

> Every vessel shall at all times proceed at a (   ) so that she can take proper and effective action to avoid collision and be stopped within a distance appropriate to the prevailing circumstances and conditions.

① slow speed   ② minimum speed
③ safe speed   ④ fairway speed

해설 안전속력(safe speed)에 대한 설명이다.

답 ③

11. According to COLREG'72, every vessel should be all times proceed at a "safe speed". "safe speed" is defined as that speed which :   [15년 2차 / 16년 일반직 / 18년 일반직]

① you can stop within your visibility range.
② you can take proper and effective action to avoid collision.
③ you are travelling at a slower speed than surrounding vessels.
④ no wake comes from your vessel.

해설 안전속력이란, 충돌을 피하기 위한 '적절'하고 '효율'적인 행동을 취할 수 있는 속력이다.

답 ②

12. 다음 중 「COLREG(International Regulations for Preventing Collisions at Sea)」상 Safe Speed를 결정함에 있어 고려해야 할 사항은 모두 몇 개인가?   [20년 3차]

> ㉠ the state of visibility
> ㉡ the traffic density including concentrations of fishing vessels or any other vessels
> ㉢ the manoeuvrability of the vessel with special reference to stopping distance and turning ability in the prevailing conditions
> ㉣ at night the presence of background light such as from shore lights or from back scatter of her own lights
> ㉤ the draught in relation to the available depth of water

① 2개   ② 3개
③ 4개   ④ 5개

해설 모두 안전속력(Safe Speed)을 결정함에 있어 고려해야하는 사항이다.

답 ④

Rule 7

Risk of Collision

ⓐ Every vessel shall use all available means appropriate to the prevailing circumstances and conditions to determine if risk of collision exists. **If there is any doubt such risk shall be deemed to exist.**

ⓑ Proper use shall be made of radar equipment if fitted and operational, including **long-range scanning** to obtain **early warning** of risk of collision and radar plotting or equivalent systematic observation of detected objects.

ⓒ Assumptions shall **not** be made on the basis of **scanty** information, especially **scanty** radar information.

ⓓ In determining if risk of collision exists the following considerations shall be among those taken into account:

(i) Such risk shall be deemed to exist if the **compass bearing** of an approaching vessel **does not appreciably change;**

(ii) such risk may sometimes exist even when an appreciable bearing change is evident, particularly when approaching a **very large vessel** or a **tow** or when approaching a vessel **at close range.**

제 7 조
충돌의 위험

ⓐ 모든 선박은 충돌 위험의 유무를 판단하기 위하여 당시의 사정과 상태에 적절한 모든 유용한 수단을 이용하여야 한다. 만일 의심스러우면 그와 같은 위험이 존재한다고 보아야 한다.

ⓑ Radar를 장비하고 작동 가능하면, 충돌의 위험에 대한 조기경보를 얻기 위한 장거리주사, Radar 작도, 또는 같은 효과를 얻을 수 있는 탐지된 물체의 체계적인 관측 등을 포함하여 Radar 장비를 올바르게 사용하여야 한다.

ⓒ 불확실한 정보, 특히 Radar에 의한 불확실한 정보에 근거를 두고 억측을 하여서는 아니된다.

ⓓ 충돌의 위험 유무를 결정함에 있어서는 다음의 상황을 고려하여야 한다.

(ⅰ) 만일 접근 중인 선박의 나침의 방위가 현저히 변화하지 않을 때에는 충돌의 위험이 존재한다고 보아야 한다.

(ⅱ) 그와 같은 위험은 때에 따라서는 방위의 변화가 충분한 경우에도 있을 수 있으며, 특히 거대형선이나 예인선열에 접근하거나 근거리에서 다른 선박에 접근하는 경우는 그러하다.

기출문제

13. 다음 밑줄 친 빈칸에 가장 알맞은 것은?　　　11년 3차

> Risk of collision can be ascertained by carefully watching _____ of an approaching vessel.

① compass bearing　　② true course
③ ship's motion　　　④ track

해설 충돌의 위험은 접근하는 선박의 컴퍼스 방위(compass bearing)를 주의 깊게 관찰하면서 확인할 수 있다.

답 ①

14. 다음 중 빈칸에 들어갈 단어로 가장 옳은 것은?　　　20년 1차

> Risk of collision can be ascertained by carefully watching (　　) of an approaching vessel.

① track　　　　　② true course
③ ship's motion　④ compass bearing

해설 위 문제와 동일

답 ④

Rule 8

Action to avoid Collision

ⓐ Any action to avoid collision shall be taken in accordance with the Rules of this Part and shall, if the circumstances of the case admit, be **positive**, made in **ample time** and with due regard to the observance of **good seamanship.**

ⓑ Any alteration of course and/or speed to avoid collision, shall, if the circumstances of the case admit, be **large** enough to be readily apparent to another vessel observing visually or by radar ; a succession of **small alterations of course and/or speed should be avoided.**

ⓒ If there is **sufficient sea room**, **alteration of course** alone may be the most effective action to avoid a close-quarters situation provided that it is made in good time, is substantial and does not result in another close-quarters situation.

ⓓ Action taken to avoid collision with another vessel shall be such as to result in passing at a **safe distance**. The effectiveness of the action shall be carefully checked until the other vessel is finally past and clear.

ⓔ If necessary to avoid collision or allow more to assess the situation, a vessel shall **slacken her speed** or **take all way off** by stopping or reversing her means of propulsion.

제 8 조
충돌을 피하기 위한 동작

ⓐ 충돌을 피하기 위한 모든 동작은 이편의 규칙에 따라서 취하여져야 하며, 사정이 허락하는 한 적극적이고, 충분한 시간을 두고 그리고 적절한 선박운용술에 따라 행하여야 한다.

ⓑ 충돌을 피하기 위한 침로와 속력의 동시변경, 침로 또는 속력만의 변경은, 사정이 허락하는 한, 육안이나 또는 레이더에 의하여 관찰하고 있는 타선에게 즉시 명백하도록 충분히 하여야 한다; 연속적인 작은 침로와 속력의 변경, 침로 또는 속력만의 변경은 피하여야 한다.

ⓒ 만일 충분한 해면이 있고 적시에 충분하게 행하고 다른 또 하나의 근접상태가 형성되지 아니한다면, 침로만의 변경도 근접 상황을 피하는 가장 유효한 동작이 될 수 있다.

ⓓ 타선과의 충돌을 피하기 위하여 취하는 동작은 안전한 거리를 두고 항과하도록 하여야 한다. 취한 동작의 효과는 타선이 완전히 항과할 때까지 주의 깊게 확인하여야 한다.

ⓔ 충돌을 피하기 위하여 또는, 상황을 판단하는 데 더 많은 시간을 얻기 위하여 필요하다면 선박은 감속을 하거나 또는 모든 타력을 없애기 위하여 기관을 정지하거나 역전하여야 한다.

ⓕ

(i) 이 규칙의 어느 규정에 의하여 다른 선박의 통항 또는 안전 통항을 방해하지 아니하도록 요구된 선박은, 그 당시의 사정이 요구할 때는, 다른 선박의 안전통항을 위한 충분한 수역이 부여될 수 있도록 조기에 동작을 취하여야 한다.

(ii) 다른 선박의 통항 또는 안전통항을 방해하지 아니하도록 요구된 선박이 충돌의 위험이 내포되도록 다른 선박에 접근하면 그 책임을 면할 수 없다. 따라서, 동작을 취할 때는, 이 장의 규정이 요구하는 동작에 대하여 충분한 고려를 하여야 한다.

(iii) 통항의 방해를 받지 아니하도록 되어 있는 선박은, 두 선박이 충돌의 위험을 안고 접근할 때는 이 장의 규정을 충실하게 이행할 의무가 있다.

ⓕ

(i) A vessel which, by any of these Rules, is required not to impede the passage or safe passage of another vessel shall, when required by the circumstances of the case, take early action to allow sufficient sea room for the safe passage of the other vessel.

(ii) A vessel required not to impede the passage or safe passage of another vessel is not relieved of this **obligation** if approaching the other vessel so as to involve risk of collision and shall, when taking action, have full regard to the action which may be required by the Rules of this part.

(iii) A vessel the passage of which is not to be impeded remains fully **obliged to comply with the rules** of this part when the two vessels are approaching one another so as to involve risk of collision.

기출문제

15. 다음은 COLREG(International Regulations for Preventing Collisions at Sea) RULE 8 "Action to avoid collision"에 대한 내용이다. 빈칸에 들어갈 가장 적절한 단어는 무엇인가?

18년 1차

Any action to avoid collision shall be taken in accordance with the Rules of this Part and shall, if the circumstances of the case admit, be (   ), made in ample time and with due regard to the observance of good seamanship.

① careful　　　　　　② safe
③ enough　　　　　　④ positive

해설 충돌을 피하기 위한 모든 동작은 사정이 허락하는 한 적극적(positive)으로 또 충분한 시간을 두고 적절한 선박운용술에 따라 행하여야 한다.

답 ④

기출문제

16. 다음 중 〈COLREG(국제해상충돌예방규칙)〉상 "Action to avoid collision"에 대한 설명으로 가장 옳지 않은 것은? `11년 3차 / 18년 일반직`

① Action to avoid collision shall be positive.
② Action to avoid collision shall be made in ample time.
③ Action to avoid collision shall be a succession of small alterations of course.
④ Action to avoid collision shall be taken with due regard to the observance of good seamanship.

해설 소각도로 변침을 연속적으로 하는 것은 피해야 한다.

답 ❸

17. Choose suitable answer in the blank `09년 3차`

> Any action to avoid collision shall be taken in accordance with the Rules of this Part and shall, if the circumstances of the case admit, be positive, made in (　) time and with due regard to the observance of good seamanship

① urgent　　② respective　　③ negative　　④ ample

해설 충돌을 피하기 위한 동작은 적극적(positive)이어야 하고 충분한(ample) 시간을 갖고 이루어져야 하고 적절한 항해 운용술(good seamanship)의 준수를 고려하여 이루어져야 한다.

답 ❹

18. 다음 〈보기〉 중 「COLREG(International Regulations for Preventing Collisions at Sea)」 Rule 8. "Action to avoid Collision"에 대한 내용으로 옳은 것은 모두 몇 개인가? `22년 일반직`

> ㉠ Any action to avoid collision shall be taken in accordance with the Rules of this Part and shall, if the circumstances of the case admit, be positive, made in ample time and with due regard to the observance of good seamanship.
> ㉡ Any alteration of course and/or speed to avoid collision shall, if the circumstances of the case admit, be large enough to be readily apparent to another vessel observing visually or by radar; a succession of small alterations of course and/or speed should be avoided.
> ㉢ Proper use shall be made of radar equipment if fitted and operational, including long-range scanning to obtain early warning of risk of collision and radar plotting or equivalent systematic observation of detected objects.
> ㉣ If necessary to avoid collision or allow more time to assess the situation, a vessel shall slacken her speed or take all way off by stopping or reversing her means of propulsion.

① 1개　　② 2개　　③ 3개　　④ 4개

해설 옳지 않은 것:
㉢ Rule 7 Risk of Collision(충돌의 위험) 조항에 해당하는 내용이다.

답 ❸

기출문제

19. 다음은 COLREG의 일부 내용이다. 빈칸에 들어갈 말로 가장 옳은 것은?

`22년 2차`

> Action taken to avoid collision with another vessel shall be such as to result in passing at ( ). The effectiveness of the action shall be carefully checked until the other vessel is finally past and clear.

① avoid of collision ② safe speed
③ a safe distance   ④ the port side

해설 다른 선박과의 충돌을 피하기 위한 동작은 안전한 거리(a safe distance)로 통과하는 결과를 갖는 것이어야 한다.

답 ❸

20. 다음 〈보기〉 중 COLREG RULE 8 규정상 'action to avoid collision'에 대한 내용으로 옳지 않은 것은 모두 몇 개인가?

`21년 상반기`

> ㉠ A succession of small alterations of course and/or speed should be ⓐ **avoided.**
> ㉡ If there is ⓑ **insufficient** sea room, alteration of course alone may be the most effective action to avoid a close-quarters situation provided that it is made in good time, is substantial and does not result in another close-quarters situation.
> ㉢ If necessary to avoid collision or allow more time to assess the situation, a vessel shall ⓒ **increase** her speed or take all way off by stopping or reversing her means of propulsion.
> ㉣ A vessel the passage of which is not to be impeded remains fully ⓓ **recommended** to comply with the rules of this part when the two vessels are approaching one an other so as to involve risk of collision.

① 없음   ② 1개
③ 2개   ④ 3개

해설 옳지 않은 것 :
- ㉡ 만일 ⓑ 충분한(sufficient) 해면이 있고 적시에 충분하게 행하고 다른 또 하나의 근접상태가 형성되지 아니한다면, 침로만의 변경도 근접 상황을 피하는 가장 유효한 동작이 될 수 있다.
- ㉢ 충돌을 피하기 위하여 또는, 상황을 판단하는 데 더 많은 시간을 얻기 위하여 필요하다면 선박은 ⓒ 감속(slacken her speed)을 하거나 또는 모든 타력을 없애기 위하여 기관을 정지하거나 역전하여야 한다.
- ㉣ 통항의 방해를 받지 아니하도록 되어 있는 선박은, 두 선박이 충돌의 위험을 안고 접근할 때는 이 장의 규정을 충실하게 이행할 ⓓ 의무가 있다(obliged).

답 ❹

Rule 9

Narrow Channels

ⓐ A vessel proceeding along the course of a narrow channel or fairway shall keep as near to the **outer limit** of the channel or fairway which lies on her **starboard side** as is safe and practicable.

ⓑ A vessel of **less than 20 metres** in length or a **sailing vessel** shall not impede the passage of a vessel which can safely navigate only within a narrow channel or fairway.

ⓒ **A vessel engaged in fishing** shall not impede the passage of any other vessel navigating within a narrow channel or fairway.

ⓓ A vessel shall **not cross** a narrow channel or fairway if such crossing impedes the passage of a vessel which can safely navigate only within such channel or fairway. The latter vessel may use the sound signal prescribed in Rule 34ⓓ if in doubt as to the intention of the crossing vessel.

ⓔ

(i) In a narrow channel or fairway when overtaking can take place only if the vessel to be overtaken has to take action to permit safe passing, the vessel intending to overtake shall indicate her intention by sounding the appropriate signal prescribed in Rule 34ⓒ(i). The vessel to be overtaken shall, if in agreement, sound the appropriate signal prescribed in Rule 34ⓒ(ii) and take steps to permit safe passing. If in doubt she may sound the signals prescribed in Rule 34ⓓ.

제 9 조

협 수 도

ⓐ 협수도나 항로를 따라 진행하고 있는 선박은 안전하고 실행가능하면 그 선박의 우현측에 위치한 수도 혹은 항로의 외연 가까이를 항행하여야 한다.

ⓑ 길이 20미터 미만인 선박이나 범선은 협수도나 항로내에서만 안전하게 항행할 수 있는 선박의 진로를 방해하여서는 아니된다.

ⓒ 어로에 종사하고 있는 선박은 협수도나 항로내에서 항행하는 타선의 통항을 방해하여서는 아니된다.

ⓓ 만일 자선의 횡단이 수도나 항로내에서만 안전하게 항행할 수 있는 선박의 통항을 방해한 다면 그 선박은 협수도나 항로를 횡단하여서는 아니된다. 후자는, 만약 횡단선의 의도가 의심스러울 때에는 34조ⓓ에 규정된 음향신호를 사용할 수 있다.

ⓔ

(ⅰ) 협수도나 항로에서, 피추월선이 안전한 통과를 허락하는 동작을 취하여야만 추월이 가능할 때는 추월하는 선박은 제34조ⓔ(ⅰ)에 규정한 적합한 음향신호에 의하여 자선의 의사를 표시하여야 한다. 동의하면, 피추월선은 제34조 ⓒ(ⅱ)에 규정된 적합한 음향신호를 하고 안전한 통과를 할 수 있도록 조치를 취하여야 한다. 만일 의 문이 있으면 피추월선은 제34조 ⓓ에 규정된 음향신호를 할 수 있다.

(ii) 이 조는 제13조에 규정된 추월선의 의무를 면제하지 아니한다.

(ii) This Rule does not relieve the overtaking vessel of her obligation under Rule 13.

ⓕ 중간에 개재하는 장애물 때문에 타선을 볼 수 없는 협수도나 항로의 만곡부 또는 구역에 접근하는 선박은 특별한 경계와 주의를 하여 항행하여야 하며 제34조ⓔ에 규정된 적합한 음향 신호를 하여야 한다.

ⓕ A vessel nearing a bend or an area of a narrow channel or fairway where other vessels may be obscured by an intervening obstruction shall navigate **with particular alertness and caution** and shall sound the appropriate signal prescribed in Rule 34ⓔ.

ⓖ 사정이 허락하는 한 모든 선박은 협수도 내에서 묘박을 피하여야 한다.

ⓖ Any vessel shall, if the circumstances of the case admit, **avoid anchoring** in a narrow channel.

기출문제

21. 다음은 COLREG(International Regulations for Preventing Collisions at Sea) RULE 9 Narrow Channels에 대한 것으로, 빈칸에 들어갈 단어로 가장 옳은 것은? `21년 하반기`

> A vessel of ( ) in length or a sailing vessel shall not impede the passage of a vessel which can safely navigate only within a narrow channel or fairway.

① less than 20 metres
② less than 24 metres
③ more than 20 metres
④ more than 24 metres

해설 길이 **20미터 미만의 선박** 혹은 범선은 좁은 수로나 좁은 항로에 안에서만 안전하게 항해할 수 있는 선박의 통항을 방해해서는 아니된다.

답 ❶

22. 다음은 〈COLREG(국제해상충돌예방규칙)〉상 "RULE 9 Narrow Channels"을 발췌해 온 것이다. 빈칸에 들어갈 단어로 가장 옳은 것은? `18년 일반직`

> A vessel of ( ) in length or a sailing vessel shall not impede the passage of a vessel which can safely navigate only within a narrow channel or fairway.

① less than 20 metres　　② more than 20 metres
③ less than 24 metres　　④ more than 24 metres

해설 위의 문제와 동일

답 ❶

기출문제

23. In a narrow channel every power-driven vessel when proceeding along the course of channel shall, when it is safe and practicable, keep to that side of the fairway of mid-channel which lies on the (   ) side of such vessel.   06년 3차

① bow   ② stern
③ starboard   ④ port

해설 협수로(a narrow channel)에서, 모든 동력선은 수로를 따라 침로를 유지하며 항해해야 한다. 이 때 안전하고 실행 가능한 한, 수로 중앙에서 <u>우측(starboard)</u>을 유지하면서 항해해야 한다.

답 ③

24. 다음 빈칸에 들어갈 말로 가장 적절한 것은?   15년 일반직

In a narrow channel, every power-driven vessel when proceeding along the course of channel shall, when it is safe and practicable, keep to that side of the fairway of mid-channel which lies on the (   ) side of such vessel.

① bow   ② stern
③ starboard   ④ port

해설 위 문제와 동일

답 ③

25. 다음 COLREG(International Rugulations for Preventing Collisions at Sea)상 빈칸에 가장 옳은 것은?   20년 1차

A vessel proceeding along the course of a narrow channel or fairway shall keep as near to the outer limit of the channel or fairway which lies on her (   ) as is safe and practicable.

① starboard side   ② port side
③ bow   ④ stern

해설 좁은 수로 또는 항로를 따라 항진하고 있는 선박은 안전하고 또 실행 가능한 한 자선의 <u>우현 쪽 (starboard side)</u>에 있는 수로 또는 항로의 외측한계에 접근하여 항행해야 한다.

답 ①

제 10 조
통항분리방식

ⓐ 이 조문은 본기구가 채택한 통항분리방식에 적용하며 어떤 선박에게도 다른 규정에 의한 의무를 면제하는 것은 아니다.

ⓑ 통항분리방식을 사용하는 선박은 :

(i) 적합한 통로 내에서 그 통로의 일반적인 교통방향을 따라서 진행하여야 한다;

(ii) 가능한 한 통항분리선 또는 분리대에서 멀리 떨어져야 한다;

(iii) 통상적으로 지정통로에 합류하거나 이탈할 때에는 통로의 시발점이나 종점에서 그렇게 하여야 한다. 그러나 한 측면에서 합류하거나 이탈할 때는 일반적인 교통방향에 대하여 가능한 한 소각도로 그렇게 하여야 한다.

ⓒ 선박은 가능한 한, 지정통로를 횡단하는 것을 피하여야 하지만 부득이 그렇게 하지 아니하면 아니되는 경우에는 일반적인 교통방향에 대하여, 자선의 선수방향이 가능한 한 직각에 가깝게 횡단하여야 한다.

ⓓ

(i) 가까이 있는 통항분리방식 내에 있는 적합한 통로를 안전하게 사용할 수 있는 선박은 연안 통항대를 사용하여서는 아니된다. 그러나 길이 20미터 미만의 선박, 범선 및 어로에 종사 중인 선박은 연안 통항대를 사용할 수 있다.

Rule 10

Traffic Separation Schemes

ⓐ This Rule Applies to traffic separation schemes adopted by the Organization and does not relieve any vessel of her obligation under any other rule.

ⓑ A vessel using a traffic separation scheme shall:

(i) proceed in the **appropriate traffic lane in the general direction of traffic flow for that lane;**

(ii) so far as practicable **keep clear of a traffic separation line or separation zone;**

(iii) normally join or leave a traffic lane at the termination of the lane, but when joining or leaving from either side shall do so at as **small** an angle to the general direction of traffic flow as practicable.

ⓒ A vessel shall so far as practicable **avoid crossing** traffic lanes, but if obliged to do so shall cross on a heading as nearly as practicable at **right angles** to the general direction of traffic flow.

ⓓ

(i) A vessel shall **not use an inshore traffic zone** when she can safely use the appropriate traffic lane within the adjacent traffic separation scheme. However, **vessels of less than 20 meters** in length, **sailing vessels** and **vessels engaged in fishing** may use the **inshore traffic zone.**

(ii) Notwithstanding subparagraph ⓓ (i), a vessel may use an inshore traffic zone when en route to or from **a port**, **offshore installation** or **structure**, **pilot station** or any **other place** situated within the inshore traffic zone, or to avoid immediate danger.

ⓔ A vessel, other than a crossing vessel, or a vessel joining or leaving a lane shall not normally enter a separation zone or cross a separation line except:

(i) **in cases of emergency** to avoid immediate danger;

(ii) **to engage in fishing** within a separation zone.

ⓕ A vessel navigating in areas **near the terminations** of traffic separation schemes shall do so **with particular caution.**

ⓖ A vessel shall so far as practicable **avoid anchoring** in a traffic separation scheme or in areas near its terminations.

ⓗ A vessel not using a traffic separation scheme shall avoid it by as **wide a margin** as is practicable.

ⓘ **A vessel engaged in fishing** shall not impede the passage of any vessel following a traffic lane.

ⓙ **A vessel of less than 20 meters in length or a sailing vessel** shall not impede the safe passage of a power-driven vessel following a traffic lane.

ⓚ **A vessel restricted in her ability** to manoeuvre when engaged in an operation for the maintenance of safety of navigation in a traffic separation scheme **is exempted** from complying with this Rule to the extent necessary to carry out the operation.

(ii) ⓓ항 (ⅰ)의 규정에도 불구하고 인접한 항구로 출입항 하는 선박, 연안 통항대 내에 위치하여 있는 기지, 구조물 또는 도선사 승하선 장소에 출입하는 선박이나 급박한 위험을 피하기 위한 선박은 연안 통항대를 사용할 수 있다.

ⓔ 통로를 횡단하는 선박 또는 통로에 진입하거나 통로를 떠나는 선박 이외의 선박은 아래의 경우를 제외하고는 통상적으로, 분리대 내에 들어가거나 분리선을 넘어서는 아니된다.

(ⅰ) 절박한 위험을 피하기 위한 긴급한 경우

(ⅱ) 분리대 내에서 어로에 종사하고자 하는 경우

ⓕ 통항분리방식의 종점부근을 항해하는 선박은 특별한 주의를 하며 항행하여야 한다.

ⓖ 선박은 통항분리방식 내 혹은 그 종점부근의 해역에서 가능한 한 묘박을 피하여야 한다.

ⓗ 통항분리방식을 이용하지 아니하는 선박은 가능한 한 넓은 여지를 두고 그것을 피하여야 한다.

ⓘ 어로에 종사 중인 선박은 통로를 따라 진행하는 모든 선박의 통행을 방해하여서는 아니된다.

ⓙ 길이 20미터 미만의 선박이나 범선은 통로를 따라 진행하는 동력선의 안전한 통행을 방해하여서는 아니된다.

ⓚ 통항분리대 내에서 항해의 안전을 유지하기 위한 작업에 종사 중이기 때문에 기동성이 제한되어 있는 선박은 그 작업을 수행하는데 필요한 범위 내에서 이 규칙의 준수가 면제된다.

① 통항분리대 내에서 해저전선의 부설, 보수 또는 인양작업에 종사 중이기 때문에 기동성이 제한되어 있는 선박은 작업을 수행하는데 필요한 범위 내에서 이 규칙의 준수가 면제된다.

① **A vessel restricted in her ability** to manoeuvre when engaged in an operation for the laying, servicing or picking up of a submarine cable, within a traffic separation scheme, **is exempted** from complying with this Rule to the extent necessary to carry out the operation.

기출문제

26. COLREG(국제해상충돌방지규칙)-TSS상 항법이 바르게 설명되지 않은 것은? 〔16년 일반직〕

① proceed in the appropriate traffic lane in the general direction of traffic flow for that lane
② so far as practicable keep clear of a traffic separation line or separation zone
③ normally join or leave a traffic lane at the termination of the lane, but when joining or leaving from either side shall do so at as small an angle to the general direction of traffic flow as practicable
④ so far as practicable, avoid crossing traffic lanes but if obliged to do so shall cross on a heading as nearly as practicable at as small an angle to the general direction of traffic flow.

해설 at as small an angle → at right angles
선박은 가능한 한, 지정통로를 횡단하는 것을 피하여야 하지만 부득이하게 해야 하는 경우에는 일반적인 교통방향에 대하여, 자선의 선수방향이 가능한 한 직각에 가깝게 횡단하여야 한다.

답 ④

27. 다음 중 COLREG상 아래 빈칸에 들어갈 단어로 가장 옳은 것은? 〔22년 2차〕

A vessel shall, so far as practicable, avoid crossing traffic lanes, but if obliged to do so shall cross on a heading as nearly as practicable at (   ) angles to the general direction of traffic flow.

① small   ② right   ③ large   ④ acute

해설 선박은 가능하다면 통항로(traffic lanes)를 횡단(crossing)하는 것은 피해야 하나, 만약 그럴 의무가 있다면 선수 방향이 일반적 교통흐름의 진행 방향에 가능한 한 직각(right angles)에 가깝게 횡단해야 한다.

답 ②

28. 빈칸에 들어갈 말로 가장 옳은 것은? 〔17년 1차〕

"A vessel using traffic separation scheme shall join or leave from the side (   )."

① only in areas near the terminations of traffic separation schemes
② by as wide a margin as is practicable
③ at as small an angle to the general direction of traffic flow as practicable
④ as nearly as practicable at right angles to the general direction of traffic flow

해설 통항분리방식을 사용하는 선박이 통상적으로 지정통로에 들어가거나 나오고자(join or leave) 할 때엔, 통로의 시발점이나 종점에서 그렇게 하여야 한다. 그러나 한쪽 측면에서 들어가거나 나오고자 할 때는 일반적인 교통방향에 대하여 가능한 한 소각도(small an angle)로 들어가거나 나와야 한다.

답 ③

SECTION II CONDUCT OF VESSELS IN SIGHT OF ONE ANOTHER

제 2 절 상호 시계 내에 있는 선박의 운항

Rule 11

Application

Rules in this Section apply to vessels in sight of one another.

제 11 조

적 용

이 절의 규정은 상호 시계 내에 있는 선박에 적용한다.

Rule 12

Sailing Vessels

(a) When two sailing vessels are approaching one another, so as to involve risk of collision, one of them shall keep out of the way of the other as follows;

(i) when each has the wind on a **different side**, the vessel which has the wind **on the port** side shall **keep out of the way** of the other;

(ii) when both have the wind on the **same side**, the vessel which is **to windward** shall **keep out of the way** of the vessel which is **to leeward**;

(iii) if a vessel with the wind **on the port side** sees a vessel to windward and cannot determine with certainty whether the other vessel has the wind on the port or on the starboard side, she shall keep out of the way of the other.

제 12 조

범 선

ⓐ 2척의 범선이 서로 접근하여 충돌의 위험이 있을 경우에는 그 중 한쪽의 범선이 다른 범선을 다음과 같이 피하여야 한다 :

(i) 각 선박이 서로 다른 현측에서 바람을 받고 있는 경우에는 좌현측에서 바람을 받고 있는 선박이 다른 선박의 진로를 피하여야 한다 ;

(ii) 두 선박이 같은 현측에서 바람을 받고 있는 경우에는 풍상측의 선박이 풍하측의 선박의 진로를 피하여야 한다;

(iii) 좌현측에 바람을 받고 있는 선박이 다른 선박을 풍상측에 보며 다른 선박이 바람을 좌현측에서 받고 있는지 우현측에서 받고 있는지 확실히 알 수 없는 경우에는 다른 선박의 진로를 피하여야 한다.

ⓑ 이 조문 규정의 적용에 있어서 풍상측이라 함은 주범을 펴고 있는 측의 반대측 또는 횡범선에 있어서는 최대의 종범을 펴고 있는 측의 반대측을 말한다.

제 13 조
추 월

ⓐ 추월선은 제2장 제1절에 있는 규칙의 여하한 규정에도 불구하고 추월당하는 선박의 진로를 피하여야 한다.

ⓑ 다른 선박의 정횡후 22.5도를 넘는 후방 즉, 추월당하는 선박과의 관계에 있어서 야간에는 그 선박의 선미등만을 볼 수 있고 현등을 볼 수 없는 선박은 추월선으로 보아야 한다.

ⓒ 다른 선박을 추월하고 있는지의 여부에 관하여 의문이 있는 선박은 자선이 추월하고 있는 경우로 생각하고 이에 합당한 동작을 취하여야 한다.

ⓓ 두 선박간의 방위가 그 후에 여하히 변경되더라도 추월선이 본규칙상의 의미에 있어서의 횡단선으로 되는 것은 아니며 또한 추월선은 완전히 앞질러 멀어질 때까지 추월당하는 선박의 진로를 피하여야 할 의무를 벗어나지 못한다.

ⓑ For the purposes of this Rule the windward side shall be deemed to be the side opposite to that on which the mainsail is carried or, in the case of a square-rigged vessel, the side opposite to that on which the largest fore-and-aft sail is carried.

Rule 13

Overtaking

ⓐ Notwithstanding anything contained in the Rules of Part B, Sections I and II any **vessel overtaking** any other shall **keep out of the way** of the **vessel being overtaken.**

ⓑ A vessel shall be deemed to be overtaking when coming up with another vessel from a direction more than **22.5 degrees** abaft her beam, that is, in such a position with reference to the vessel she is overtaking, that at night she would be able to see **only the sternlight** of that vessel but **neither of her sidelights.**

ⓒ When a vessel is in any doubt as to whether she is overtaking another, she shall **assume that** this is the case and **act accordingly.**

ⓓ Any **subsequent alteration** of the bearing between the two vessels shall **not** make the **overtaking vessel** a **crossing vessel** within the meaning of these Rules or relieve her of the duty of keeping clear of the overtaken vessel until she is finally past and clear.

기출문제

29. 다음 중 overtake vessel을 바르게 해석한 것은? `05년 2차`

① 흘수제약선　　② 피추월선
③ 추월선　　　　④ 기뢰제거선박

해설 추월선 = overtake vessel

답 ❸

30. 다음 중 아래의 상황을 가장 잘 표현한 것은? `19년 3차`

> When ship A is coming up with ship B from a direction more than two points abaft her beam at night, the only visual indication to those on board ship A of the presence of ship B will be the stern light of the latter.

① ship A and B are crossing each other.
② ship A and B are meeting on reciprocal courses.
③ ship A is overtaking ship B.
④ ship A is followed by ship B.

해설 *1point는 11.25°, 즉, 2point는 22.5°이다.*
　　선박 A가 선박 B의 정횡 후방 22.5도 이후의 방향에서 선박 B쪽으로 다가가고 있다. 그리고 선박 A에서 선박 B의 존재를 보았을 때, 선박 B의 선미등만 보이는 상태이다. 다시 말해, 선박 A가 선박 B를 추월하고 있는 상태라는 것을 '22.5도'라는 각도를 보고 알 수 있다.

답 ❸

31. 〈COLREG(국제해상충돌예방규칙)〉상 아래 빈칸에 들어갈 단어는? `16년 일반직`

> Any subsequent alteration of the bearing between the two vessels shall not make the overtaking vessel a crossing vessel within the meaning of these Rules or relieve her of the duty of keeping clear of the (　　　) vessel until she is finally past and clear.

① overtaken　　　② overtaking
③ crossing　　　 ④ each

해설 그 이후에 두 선박 사이의 방위가 변경(alteration)되더라도 추월하는 선박(overtaking vessel)은 이 규칙상의 의미에 있어서의 횡단선(crossing vessel)으로 바뀌는 것은 아니고, 또한 피추월선을 완전히 앞질러 지나가버릴 때까지 피추월선(overtaken vessel)을 피해야 할 의무(duty)에서 벗어나지 못한다.

답 ❶

제 14 조	Rule 14
정면으로 마주치는 상태	Head-on Situation

ⓐ 충돌의 위험이 내포되도록 2척의 동력선이 반대되는 방향 또는 거의 반대되는 방향으로 마주치는 경우에는 각 선박은 서로 다른 선박의 좌현측을 통과할 수 있도록 각기 우현측으로 변침하여야 한다.

ⓐ When two power-driven vessels are meeting **on reciprocal** or nearly reciprocal courses so as to involve risk of collision each shall alter her course to **starboard** so that each shall pass on the **port** side of the other.

ⓑ 서로 다른 선박을 선수방향 또는 거의 선수방향에서 보는 경우 즉, 야간에는 다른 선박의 두개의 마스트정부등을 일직선 또는 거의 일직선상에서 보며 동시에 양현등을 볼 수 있는 경우, 그러한 마스트정부등이나 또는 양현등만을 볼 수 있는 경우, 그리고 주간에 있어서는 다른 선박의 상응하는 면을 보는 경우에는 정면으로 마주치는 상태가 존재한다고 보아야 한다.

ⓑ Such a situation shall be deemed to exist when a vessel sees the other ahead or nearly ahead and by night she could see the **masthead lights** of the other **in a line** or nearly in a line and/or **both sidelights** and by day she observes the corresponding aspect of the other vessel.

ⓒ 그러한 상태가 존재하는가의 여부에 관하여 의문이 있는 선박은 정면으로 마주치는 상태에 있다고 생각하고 행동하여야 한다.

ⓒ When a vessel is **in any doubt** as to whether such a situation exists she shall **assume that** it does **exist and act accordingly.**

기출문제

32. COLREG(국제해상충돌방지규칙)상 아래 밑줄 친 부분이 의미하는 것은? 〈16년 일반직〉

<u>Such a situation</u> shall be deemed to exist when a vessel sees the other ahead or nearly ahead and by night she could see the masthead lights of the other in a line or nearly in a line and/or both sidelights and by day she observes the corresponding aspect of the other vessel.

① overtaking
② head-on situation
③ crossing situation
④ vessels in restricted visibility

해설 마주치는 상태(head-on situation)란, 다른 선박을 선수 방향 또는 거의 선수 방향에서 볼 때, 그리고 야간에는 다른 선박의 마스트 정부등을 일직선 또는 거의 일직선으로 보거나 양현등을 동시에 볼 수 있을 때, 주간에는 다른 선박의 그에 상응하는 측면을 관찰할 수 있을 때를 말한다.

답 ❷

Rule 15

Crossing Situation

When two power-driven vessels are **crossing** so as to involve risk of collision, the vessel which has the other on her own **starboard side** shall **keep out of the way** and shall, if the circumstances of the case admit, **avoid crossing ahead** of the other vessel.

제 15 조
횡단상태

두 척의 동력선이 서로 진로를 횡단할 경우에 충돌의 위험이 있을 때에는 다른 선박을 우현측에 두고 있는 선박이 다른 선박의 진로를 피하여야 하며, 사정이 허락하는 한, 다른 선박의 전방을 횡단하여서는 아니된다.

기출문제

33. When two power driven vessels are (   ), so as to involve risk of collision the vessel which has the other on her own starboard side shall keep out of the way of the other

`07년 2차 / 15년 일반직`

① head-on situation　　② crossing
③ proceeding　　④ meeting-end on

해설 횡단(crossing)상황에서 타선을 우측에 둔 선박이 피항선이 된다.

답 ❷

34. Choose the correct one for the blank

`13년 1차`

When two power driven vessels are crossing, so as to involve risk of collision the vessel which has the other on her own (   ) side shall keep out of the way of the other.

① starboard　　② port　　③ bow　　④ stern

해설 횡단상황에서 타선을 우측(starboard)에 둔 선박이 피항선이 된다.

답 ❶

35. Choose the correct one for the blank.

`18년 1차`

When two power-driven vessels are crossing so as to involve risk of collision, the vessel which has the other on her own (   ) side shall keep out of the way and shall, if the circumstances of the case admit, avoid crossing ahead of the other vessel.

① starboard　　② port　　③ bow　　④ stern

해설 횡단상황에서 타선을 우측(starboard)에 둔 선박이 피항선이 되며 피항 시 상황이 허락 하는 한 타선의 앞으로(ahead of the other vessel) 횡단하는 것은 피해야 한다.

답 ❶

기출문제

36. 다음은 COLREG(International Regulations for Preventing Collisions at Sea) RULE 15에 대한 것이다. 빈칸에 들어갈 말로 가장 옳은 것은?

`19년 1차`

> When two power-driven vessels are crossing so as to involve risk of collision, the vessel which has the other on her own (ⓐ) side shall keep out of the way and shall, if the circumstances of the case admit, avoid crossing (ⓑ) of the other vessel.

	ⓐ	ⓑ
①	starboard	ahead
②	port	astern
③	starboard	astern
④	port	ahead

해설 횡단상황에서 타선을 ⓐ<u>우측(starboard)</u>에 둔 선박이 피항선이 되며 피항 시 상황이 허락 하는 한 타선의 ⓑ<u>앞으로(ahead)</u> 횡단하는 것은 피해야 한다.

답 ❶

37. 다음의 그림이 나타내는 상황과 그에 대한 설명이 가장 옳은 것은?

`14년 2차`

(B, 20kts, 270°)

(A, 10kts, 055°)

① Crossing situation, 'A' is the give-way vessel
② Crossing situation, 'B' is the give-way vessel
③ Head on situation, 'A' is the stand-on vessel
④ Head on situation, 'B' is the stand-on vessel

해설 다음은 횡단하는 상태(Crossing situation)이다. 다른 선박을 우현(starboard) 쪽에 두고 있는 A선박이 피항선('A' is the give-wayvessel)이 된다.

답 ❶

Rule 16

Action by Give-way Vessel

Every vessel which is directed to keep out of the way of another vessel shall, so far as possible, take **early** and **substantial** action to keep well clear.

제 16 조

피항선의 동작

이 규칙에 의하여 다른 선박의 진로를 피하여야 할 선박은 타선을 확실하게 피할 수 있도록 가능한 한 조기에 충분한 동작을 취하여야 한다.

기출문제

38. COLREG(국제해상충돌방지규칙)상 아래 빈칸에 들어갈 단어는? [16년 일반직]

> Every vessel which is directed by these Rules to keep out of the way of another vessel shall, so far as possible, take (   ) and (   ) action to keep well clear.

① early, substantial
② hurry, good
③ early, good
④ slowly, substantial

해설 이 규칙에서 지시한 대로 다른 선박을 피항해야 하는 모든 선박은, 타선을 확실하게 피할 수 있도록 가능한 한 조기(early)에 충분한(substantial) 동작을 취해야 한다.

답 ❶

39. 다음은 COLREG의 일부 내용이다. 빈칸에 들어갈 단어로 가장 옳은 것은? [22년 2차]

> ⓐ When two power-driven vessels are crossing so as to involve risk of collision, the vessel which has the other on her own (㉠) shall keep out of the way and shall, if the circumstances of the case admit, avoid crossing ahead of the other vessel.
>
> ⓑ Every vessel which is directed by these Rules to keep out of the way of another vessel shall, so far as possible, take (㉡) action to keep well clear.

	㉠	㉡
①	port side	safe and properly
②	port side	early and substantial
③	starboard side	safe and properly
④	starboard side	early and substantial

해설 ⓐ 횡단 상황에선 타선을 ㉠우측(starboard side)에 둔 선박이 피항선이다.
ⓑ 규정에 의거해 다른 선박에게 길을 비켜줘야 하는 선박은 가능하다면 ㉡조기에 충분한(early and substantial) 동작을 취해야 한다.

답 ❹

| 제 17 조 | Rule 17 |

유지선의 동작

Action by Stand-on Vessel

ⓐ

(ⅰ) 두 선박 중의 한 선박이 다른 선박의 진로를 피하여야 할 경우 다른 선박은 그 침로 및 속력을 유지하여야 한다.

(ⅱ) 그러나 유지선은 진로를 피하여야 할 선박이 이 규칙에 따른 적절한 동작을 취하지 아니하고 있음이 분명하여지는 즉시로 자선의 조종만으로서 충돌을 피하기 위한 동작을 취할 수 있다.

ⓑ 이유는 불문하고 침로와 속력을 유지하여야 할 선박은, 양선이 아주 가까이 접근하였기 때문에, 피항선의 동작만으로 충돌을 피할 수 없다고 판단할 때에는 충돌을 피하기 위한 최선의 협력동작을 취하여야 한다.

ⓒ 횡단 상태에서 다른 동력선과 충돌을 피하기 위하여 이 조문 ⓐ항 (ⅱ)의 규정에 따라 동작을 취하는 선박은 상황이 허락하는 한, 자선의 좌현측에 있는 선박을 피하기 위하여 좌현측으로 변침하여서는 아니된다.

ⓓ 이 조문은 피항선에게 진로를 피하여야 할 의무를 면제하는 것은 아니다.

ⓐ

(i) Where one of two vessels is to **keep out of the way** the other shall **keep her course and speed.**

(ii) The latter vessel may however take action to avoid collision by her manoeuvre alone, as soon as it becomes apparent to her that the vessel required to keep out of the way is not taking appropriate action in compliance with these Rules.

ⓑ When, from any cause, the vessel required to keep her course and speed finds herself so close that collision cannot be avoided by the action of the give-way vessel alone, she shall take such action as will best aid to avoid collision.

ⓒ A power-driven vessel which takes action **in a crossing situation** in accordance **with sub-paragraph ⓐ(ii)** of this Rule to avoid collision with another power-driven vessel shall, if the circumstances of the case admit, **not alter course to port** for a vessel on her own port side.

ⓓ This Rule **does not relieve** the give-way vessel of her obligation to **keep out of the way.**

기출문제

40. One of the vessels approaching each other so as to involve risk of collision, which is directed by the Rules to keep her course and speed, is : 　　07년 3차

① a pilot
② a privileged vessel
③ fishing vessel
④ an overtaking vessel

해설 두선박이 충돌의 위험이 있을 때에 선박의 침로와 속도(course and speed)를 유지하는 선박은 <u>특권이 있는 선박(a privileged vessel)</u>이라고 볼 수 있다.

답 ❷

41. 다음은 COLREG(International Regulations for Preventing Collisions at Sea) 중 일부를 발췌한 것이다. 밑줄 친 (가)의 선박을 고르고, 빈 칸 (나)에 들어갈 말을 고르시오. 　17년 2차

ⓐ (1) Where by any of these Rules one of two vessels is to keep out of the way the other shall keep her course and speed.
(2) **(가) The latter vessel** may however take action to avoid collision by her manoeuvre alone, as soon as it becomes apparent to her that the vessel required to keep out of the way is not taking appropriate action in compliance with these Rules.
ⓑ A power-driven vessel which takes action in a crossing situation in accordance with subparagraph (a)(ii) of this Rule to avoid collision with another power-driven vessel shall, if the circumstances of the case admit, not alter course to (나)＿＿＿ for a vessel on her own port side.

① (가) : stand-on vessel 　　(나) : port
② (가) : give-way vessel 　　(나) : port
③ (가) : stand-on vessel 　　(나) : starboard
④ (가) : give-way vessel 　　(나) : starboard

해설 (가) 부분을 해석해보면 '그러나 유지선은 진로를 피하여야 할 선박이 이 규칙에 따른 적절한 동작을 취하지 아니하고 있음이 분명하여지는 즉시 자선의 조종만으로 충돌을 피하기 위한 동작을 취할 수 있다.'가 된다. 즉, (가)는 유지선을 의미한다.
(나) 부분을 해석해보면 '자선의 좌현측으로 변침하여서는 아니 된다.'가 된다. 두 선박이 횡단 중a(ii) 상황(피항선이 적절한 피항동작을 취하고 있지 아니하는 상황, 즉 유지선이 피항을 해야만 하는 상황.) 이 발생했다면 유지선은 좌현 쪽으로는 변침해서는 안 된다.
일반적으로 횡단 상황에서 선박들은 타선의 선수방향을 통과하지 않기 위해 선미 쪽으로 변침을 한다. 피항을 해야 할 상황이 된 유지선이 타선의 선미로 피항을 하기위해서는 좌현 변침을 하게 되는데 이 경우 적절한 동작을 취하고 있지 않던 피항선이 뒤늦게 우현변침을 해버린다면 충돌 할 가능성이 있다.

답 ❶

제 18 조	Rule 18
선박상호간의 책임한계	Responsibilities between Vessels

제9조, 제10조 및 제13조에서 달리 규정하는 경우를 제외하고 :

ⓐ 항행중인 동력선은 다음 선박의 진로를 피하여야 한다 :

(i) 운전이 자유롭지 못한 상태에 있는 선박 ;

(ii) 조종성능에 제한을 받고 있는 선박 ;

(iii) 어로에 종사하고 있는 선박 ;

(iv) 범선.

ⓑ 항행 중인 범선은 다음 선박의 진로를 피하여야 한다. :

(i) 운전이 자유롭지 못한 상태에 있는 선박 ;

(ii) 조종성능에 제한을 받고 있는 선박 ;

(iii) 어로에 종사하고 있는 선박.

ⓒ 어로에 종사하고 있는 선박이 항행 중에 있을 때에는 가능한 한 다음 선박의 진로를 피하여야 한다. :

(i) 운전이 자유롭지 못한 상태에 있는 선박 ;

(ii) 조종성능에 제한을 받고 있는 선박.

ⓓ

(i) 운전이 자유롭지 못한 상태에 있는 선박 또는 조종성능에 제한을 받고 있는 선박 이외의 선박은 상황이 허락하는 한 흘수에 제약을 받아 제28조의 신호를 표시하고 있는 선박의 안전한 통행을 방해하지 아니하도록 하여야 한다.

Except where Rules 9, 10 and 13 otherwise require:

ⓐ A power-driven vessel underway shall keep out of the way of:

(i) a vessel not under command;

(ii) a vessel restricted in her ability to manoeuvre;

(iii) a vessel engaged in fishing;

(iv) a sailing vessel.

ⓑ A sailing vessel underway shall keep out of the way of:

(i) a vessel not under command;

(ii) a vessel restricted in her ability to manoeuvre;

(iii) a vessel engaged in fishing.

ⓒ A vessel engaged in fishing when underway shall, so far as possible, keep out of the way of:

(i) a vessel not under command;

(ii) a vessel restricted in her ability to manoeuvre.

ⓓ

(i) Any vessel other than a vessel not under command or a vessel restricted in her ability to manoeuvre shall, if the circumstances of the case admit, avoid impeding the safe passage of a vessel constrained by her draught, exhibiting the signals in Rule 28.

(ii) A vessel constrained by her draught shall navigate with particular caution having full regard to her special condition.

(ii) 흘수의 제약을 받는 선박은 자선의 특수한 조건에 충분히 유의하고 특별히 조심하여 운항하여야 한다.

ⓔ A seaplane on the water shall, in general, keep well clear of all vessels and avoid impeding their navigation. In circumstances, however, where risk of collision exists, she shall comply with the Rules of this Part.

ⓔ 수면상에 떠있는 수상항공기는 원칙적으로 모든 선박으로부터 충분히 떨어져서 그들의 항행을 방해하지 아니하도록 하여야 한다. 다만, 충돌의 위험이 있는 경우에는 이 편의 항법규정에 따라야 한다.

ⓕ

ⓕ

(i) A WIG craft shall, when taking off, landing and in flight near the surface, keep well clear of all other vessels and avoid impeding their navigation;

(i) 이륙, 착륙 및 표면에 근접하여 비행시에, WIG선은 다른 모든 선박과 확실한 간격을 유지하여야 하며 그들의 항해를 방해하지 않도록 하여야 한다;

(ii) a WIG craft operating on the water surface shall comply with the Rules of this Part as a power-driven vessel.

(ii) 수면 위를 운항하는 WIG선은 동력구동 선박과 같이 이 편의 규칙을 준수하여야 한다.

기출문제

42. Choose the incorrect sentence to avoid risk of collision according to the COLREG. (Two vessels are in sight of one another) `14년 2차`

① Two sailing vessels approaching one another, Port gives way to Starboard. When each has the wind on a different side, the vessel which has the wind to port must give way.
② When two power-driven vessels are meeting head-on both must alter course to starboard so that they pass on the port side of the other.
③ When two power-driven vessels are crossing, the vessel which has the other on the starboard side must give way.
④ Except in narrow channels, traffic separation scheme, and when overtaking, a sailing vessel must give way to a power-driven vessel.

> **해설** 범선(sailing vessel)이 동력선(power-driven vessel)을 피항하는 것이 아닌, 동력선(power-driven vessel)이 범선(sailing vessel)을 피항해야 한다.
> ① 두 범선이 서로 접근 중일 때 서로 다른 현측에서 바람을 받는다면, 좌현에서 바람을 받는 선박이 피항선이 된다.
> ② 두 동력선이 서로 마주칠 때에는 좌현 대 좌현으로 피하기 위해 우현으로 변침해야 한다.
> ③ 두 동력선이 횡단하고 있을 때에는 타선을 자선의 우현 쪽에 두고 있는 선박이 피항선이 된다.
>
> 답 ④

43. COLREG(International Regulations for Preventing Collisions at Sea) RULE 18 "Responsibilities between vessels"에 대한 설명으로 가장 적절하지 않은 것은? `18년 1차`

① A power-driven vessel underway shall keep out of the way of a vessel not engaged in fishing when underway.
② A sailing vessel underway shall keep out of the way of a vessel not under command.
③ A vessel engaged in fishing when shall, so far as possible, keep out of the way a vessel not under command.
④ A vessel constrained by her draught shall navigate with particular caution having full regard to her special condition.

> **해설** 항해 중인 동력선은 항해 중인 어로에 종사 중인 선박을 피항해야 한다. 허나, 문제에서는 어로에 종사 중이지 않은 선박(a vessel not engaged in fishing)이라고 되어있기 때문에, 이는 동력선이 피항 해야 할 선박에 해당하지 않는다.
>
> 답 ①

Section III-Conduct of Vessels in Restricted Visibility

RULE 19

Conduct of Vessels in Restricted Visibility

ⓐ This Rule applies to vessels not in sight of one another when navigating in or near an area of restricted visibility.

ⓑ Every vessel shall proceed at a safe speed adapted to the prevailing circumstances and conditions of restricted visibility. A power-driven vessel shall have **engines ready** for immediate manoeuvre.

ⓒ Every vessel shall have due regard to the prevailing circumstances and conditions of restricted visibility when complying with the Rules of Section I of this Part.

ⓓ A vessel which detects by radar alone the presence of another vessel shall determine if a close-quarters situation is developing and/or risk of collision exists. If so, she shall take avoiding action in ample time, provided that when such action consists of an alteration of course, so far as possible the following **shall be avoided:**

(i) an alteration of course **to port** for a vessel **forward of the beam**, other than for a vessel being overtaken;

(ii) an alteration of course **towards a vessel abeam or abaft the beam.**

제 3 절 제한시계 내에서의 선박운항

제 19 조
제한시계 내에서의 선박운항

ⓐ 이 조문은 선박이 상호 시계 내에 있지 아니하고 시계가 제한된 상태 하에 놓여있는 수역 또는 그 부근에서 운항하는 경우에 적용된다.

ⓑ 모든 선박은 시계가 제한된 그 당시의 상태에 적합한 안전한 속력으로 항행하여야 한다. 동력선은 즉시 조작할 수 있도록 기관의 준비태세를 갖추어야 한다.

ⓒ 모든 선박은 이 장 제1절 항법규정을 이행함에 있어서 시계가 제한된 당시의 상황과 상태에 충분히 유의하여야 한다.

ⓓ 레이더만으로 다른 선박이 존재함을 탐지한 선박은 근접상태의 형성과 충돌의 위험 또는 충돌의 위험이 있는가의 여부를 결정하여야 한다. 그러한 위험이 있으면 충분한 시간을 두고 회피동작을 취하여야 한다. 다만, 그러한 동작이 변침만으로 이루어질 경우에는 가능한 한 다음과 같은 동작은 피하여야 한다 :

(ⅰ) 추월당하고 있는 선박에 대한 경우를 제외하고 자선의 정횡보다 전방에 있는 선박을 피하기 위하여 좌현측(左舷側)으로 변침하는 일 ;

(ⅱ) 정횡에 있는 선박 또는 정횡보다 후방에 있는 선박쪽으로 변침하는 일.

ⓔ 충돌의 위험이 없다고 인정되었을 경우를 제외하고, 자선의 정횡의 전방으로 믿어지는 곳에서 다른 선박의 무중신호를 듣거나 또는 그 정횡의 전방에 있는 다른 선박과 근접상태를 면할 수 없는 모든 선박은 자선의 침로를 유지함에 필요한 최저한도의 속력으로 감속하여야 한다. 필요하다면 모든 타력을 없이 하여야 하고 어떠한 경우에도 충돌의 위험이 사라질 때까지 극도로 조심하여 운항하여야 한다.

ⓔ Except where it has been determined that a risk of collision does not exist, every vessel which hears apparently forward of her beam the fog signal of another vessel, or which cannot avoid a close quarters situation with another vessel forward of her beam, shall reduce her **speed to the minimum** at which she can be kept on her course. She shall if necessary **take all her way off** and in any event navigate **with extreme caution** until danger of collision is over.

PART C-Lights and shapes

RULE 20
Application

ⓐ Rules in this Part shall be complied with in all weathers.

ⓑ The Rules concerning lights shall be complied with **from sunset to sunrise**, and during such times **no other lights shall be exhibited,** except such lights as cannot be mistaken for the lights specified in these Rules or do not impair their visibility or distinctive character, or interfere with the keeping of a proper look-out.

ⓒ The lights prescribed by these Rules shall, if carried, also be exhibited from sunrise to sunset **in restricted visibility** and may be exhibited in all other circumstances when it is deemed necessary.

ⓓ The Rules concerning **shapes** shall be complied with **by day.**

ⓔ The lights and shapes specified in these Rules shall comply with the provisions of Annex I to these Regulations.

제 20 조
적 용

ⓐ 이장의 규정은 모든 기싱 상태에서 적용한다.

ⓑ 등화에 관한 규정은 일몰시로부터 일출시까지 실시하며 그 동안은 규정된 등화로 오인되든가, 그 시인 또는 특성의 식별을 방해하든가, 또는 적당한 견시를 방해하는 것과 같은 타등화를 표시하여서는 아니된다.

ⓒ 이장에 규정된 등화는, 설치되어 있으면, 제한된 시계에 있어서는 일출시부터 일몰시 사이라 하더라도, 표시하여야 하고 그리고 기타 필요하다고 인정되는 경우에는 표시할 수 있다.

ⓓ 형상물에 관한 규정은 주간에 적용한다.

ⓔ 이 장의 규정된 등화 및 형상물은 이 규칙 부속서 I의 규정에 일치하여야 한다.

제 21 조

정의

ⓐ 마스트정부등이라 함은 선체 종방향중심선상에 있는 백등을 뜻하며 225°의 수평의 호를 고르게 비추고, 정선수로부터 각기 정횡후 22.5°까지 비추도록 설치되어 있는 등화이다.

ⓑ 현등이라 함은 우현의 녹등, 좌현의 홍등을 말하며 각기 112.5°의 수평의 호를 고르게 비추고, 그리고 정선수로부터 각현 정횡후 22.5°까지 비추도록 설치되어 있는 등화이다. 길이 20미터 미만의 선박에 있어서는 양현등은 선체 종방향 중심선상에 있는 하나의 등각에 합칠 수 있다.

ⓒ 선미등이라 함은 실행가능한 한 선미에 가깝게 놓여 있는 백등을 말하고, 135°의 수평의 호를 고르게 비추며 정선미로부터 각 현측에 67.5°를 비출 수 있도록 설치된 등화이다.

ⓓ 예인등이라 함은 이 조문 ⓒ항에 규정된 선미등과 똑같은 특성을 가진 황색의 등화를 말한다.

ⓔ 전주등이라 함은 360°의 수평의 호를 고르게 비추는 등화를 말한다.

ⓕ 섬광등이라 함은 매분 120 또는 그 이상의 회수로 규칙적인 섬광을 발하는 등화를 말한다.

Rule 21

Definitions

ⓐ **'Masthead light'** means a **white light** placed over the fore and aft centerline of the vessel showing an unbroken light over an arc of the horizon of **225 degrees** and so fixed as to show the light from right ahead to **22.5 degrees** abaft the beam on either side of the vessel.

ⓑ **'Sidelights'** means **a green light on the starboard side** and a **red light on the port side** each showing an unbroken light over an arc of the horizon of **112.5 degrees** and so fixed as to show the light from right ahead to **22.5 degrees** abaft the beam on its respective side. In a vessel of **less than 20 meters in length** the sidelights **may be combined** in one lantern carried on the fore and aft centreline of the vessel.

ⓒ **'Sternlight'** means **a white light** placed as nearly as practicable at the **stern** showing an unbroken light over an arc of the horizon of **135 degrees** and so fixed as to show the light **67.5 degrees** from right aft on each side of the vessel.

ⓓ **'Towing light'** means a **yellow light** having the same characteristics as the **'sternlight'** defined in paragraph ⓒ of this Rule.

ⓔ **'All round light'** means a light showing an unbroken light over an arc of the horizon of **360 degrees.**

ⓕ **'Flashing light'** means a light flashing at regular intervals at a frequency of **120 flashes or more per minute.**

기출문제

44. Choose the suitable answer in the blank

'Stern light' means a white light placed as nearly as practicable at the stern showing an unbroken light over an arc of the horizon of (   ) degree.

① 112.5
② 135
③ 180
④ 225

해설 선미등(Stern light)은 선미에 있으며 135도의 수평의 호를 비춘다.

답 ❷

45. Choose the correct one for the blank.

Red and green lights are used to mark the sides of the vessel, and the white lights are usually located on the vessel's centerline. Navigation lights are not used by the navigator to see by, as are the headlights of car, but rather to allow navigators and lookouts on other vessels to see the vessel. The red and green lights are called "(   )." A white light at or near the stern is called a "stern light". And one, and sometimes two, white lights on the vessel's superstructure, or on masts, are called "(   )"

① side light - running light
② position light - running light
③ side light - masthead light
④ position light - masthead light

해설 홍등과 녹등은 선박의 현측을 표시하기 위해 사용된다. 그리고 백등은 일반적으로 선박의 중심선상에 위치한다. 항해등은 항해사가 전방을 보기위해 사용되는 게 아니라 (마치 자동차의 전주등처럼)오히려 다른 선박의 항해사나 견시자들로 하여금 자선을 볼 수 있게 해주기 위해 사용된다. 홍등과 녹등은 "현등(side light)"이라고 불린다. 선미나 선미 근처의 백등은 "선미등(stern light)"이라고 불린다. 그리고 선박의 상부 구조물이나 마스트에 달리는 백등(한 개거나 간혹 두 개다)은 "정부마스트등(masthead light)"이라고 불린다.

답 ❸

46. 국제 해상 충돌 방지 규칙의 일부이다. 다음 빈칸에 들어갈 말로 가장 적절한 것은?

(   ) means a white light placed as nearly as practicable at the stern showing an unbroken light over an arc of the horizon of 135 degrees and so fixed as to show the light 67.5 degrees from right aft on each side of the vessel.

① Masthead light
② Towing light
③ Stern light
④ Side light

해설 선미등(Stern light)에 대한 설명이다.

답 ❸

COLREG(International Regulations for preventing Collision at Sea.) | **275**

기출문제

47. "COLREG" RULE 21 "Definitions"에 따를 때, 다음 빈칸에 들어갈 숫자를 고르시오.

17년 2차

"Masthead light" means a white light placed over the fore and aft centreline of the vessel showing an unbroken light over an arc of the horizon of (가)_____ degrees.
"Sidelights" means a green light on the starboard side and a red light on the port side each showing an unbroken light over an arc of the horizon of (나)_____ degrees.
"Sternlight" means a white light placed as nearly as practicable at the stern showing an unbroken light over an arc of the horizon of (다)_____ degrees.

① 112.5   225   135
② 225   135   67.5
③ 225   112.5 135
④ 112.5   135   225

답 ③

48. 다음은 COLREG(International Regulations for Preventing Collisions at Sea) RULE21에 대한 것이다. 빈칸에 들어갈 말로 가장 옳은 것은?

19년 1차

ⓐ (   ) means a white light placed over the fore and aft centreline of the vessel showing an unbroken light over an arc of the horizon of 225 degrees and so fixed as to show the light from right ahead to 22.5 degrees abaft the beam on either side of the vessel.

ⓑ (   ) means a light showing an unbroken light over an arc of the horizon of 360 degrees.

	ⓐ	ⓑ
①	Masthead light	Towing light
②	Masthead light	All round light
③	Stern light	Towing light
④	Stern light	All round light

해설 ⓐ "정부마스트등(Masthead light)"
ⓑ "전주등(All round light)"이라 함은 360°의 수평의 호를 고르게 비추는 등화를 말한다.

답 ②

I 기출문제

49. 〈COLREG〉상의 내용으로 다음 각각의 빈칸에 들어가는 숫자의 합은? `19년 3차`

"Masthead light" means a white light placed over the fore and aft centerline of the vessel showing an unbroken light over an arc of the horizon of (   ) degrees and so fixed as to show the light from right ahead to (   ) degrees abaft the beam on either side of the vessel.
"Sidelights" means a green light on the starboard side and a red light on the port side each showing an unbroken light over an arc of the horizon of (   ) degrees and so fixed as to show the light from right ahead to (   ) degrees abaft the beam on its respective side.
"Stern light" means a white light placed as nearly as practicable at the stern showing an unbroken light over an arc of the horizon of (   ) degrees and so fixed as to show the light (   ) degrees from right aft on each side of the vessel.

① 440
② 502.5
③ 585
④ 607.5

해설 각각 순서대로 225, 22.5, 112.5, 22.5, 135, 67.5 이다.

답 ❸

50. 다음 COLREG(International Regulations for Preventing Collisions at Sea)상 각각의 빈칸에 들어갈 숫자의 합은? `20년 1차`

"Masthead light" means a white light placed over the fore and aft centerline of the vessel showing an unbroken light over an arc of the horizon of (   ) degrees and so fixed as to show the light from right ahead to (   ) degrees abaft the beam on either side of the vssel.
"All-round light" means a light showing an unbroken light over an arc of the horizon of (   ) degrees.
"Sidelights" means a green light on the starboard side and a red light on the port side each showing an unbroken light over an are of the horixon of (   ) degrees and so fixed as to show the light from right ahead to (   ) degrees abaft the beam on its respective side.

① 742.5
② 885
③ 540
④ 602.5

해설 각각 순서대로 225, 22.5, 360, 112.5, 22.5이다.

답 ❶

제 22 조
등화의 시인거리

이 장에서 규정하는 등화는 다음 최저거리에서 보이도록 부속서 Ⅰ의 8절에 규정된 광도를 가져야 한다.

ⓐ 길이 50미터 이상의 선박 :
- 마스트정부등, 6해리 ;
- 현등, 3해리 ;
- 선미등, 3해리 ;
- 예인등, 3해리 ;
- 백색, 홍색, 녹색, 또는 황색의 전주등, 3해리.

ⓑ 길이 12미터 이상 50미터 미만인 선박 :
- 마스트정부등, 5해리 ; 20미터 미만의 선박에 있어서는 3해리 ;
- 현등, 2해리 ;
- 선미등, 2해리 ;
- 예인등, 2해리 ;
- 백색, 홍색, 녹색 또는 황색의 전주등, 2해리.

ⓒ 길이 12미터 미만의 선박 :
- 마스트 정부등, 2해리 ;
- 현등, 1해리 ;
- 선미등, 2해리 ;
- 예인등, 2해리 ;
- 백색, 홍색, 녹색 또는 황색의 전주등, 2해리.

ⓓ 눈에 잘 띄지 않고 부분적으로 잠수되어 끌어가고 있는 선박이나 물체 :
- 백색의 전주등, 3해리.

Rule 22
Visibility of Lights

The lights prescribed in these Rules shall have an intensity as specified in Section 8 Annex I to these Regulation so as to be visible at the following minimum ranges:

ⓐ In vessels of 50 metres or more in length:
- a masthead light, 6 miles;
- a sidelight, 3 miles;
- a sternlight, 3 miles;
- a towing light, 3 miles;
- a white, red, green or yellow all-round light, 3 miles.

ⓑ In vessels of 12 metres or more in length but less than 50 m in length:
- a masthead light, 5 miles; except that where the length of the vessel is less than 20 meters, 3 miles;
- a sidelight, 2 miles;
- a sternlight, 2 miles;
- a towing light, 2 miles;
- a white, red, green or yellow all-round light, 2 miles.

ⓒ In vessels of less than 12 metres in length:
- a masthead light, 2 miles,
- a sidelight, 1 mile,
- a sternlight, 2 miles,
- a towing light, 2 miles;
- a white, red, green or yellow all-round light, 2 miles.

ⓓ In inconspicuous, partly submerged vessels or objects being towed;
- a white all-round light, 3 miles.

Rule 23
Power-driven Vessels underway

ⓐ A power-driven vessel underway shall exhibit:

(i) a masthead light forward;

(ii) a second masthead light abaft of and higher than the forward one; except that a vessel of **less than 50 meters** in length shall not be obliged to exhibit such light but may do so;

(iii) sidelights;

(iv) a sternlight.

제 23 조

항해 중인 동력선

ⓐ 항해 중인 동력선은 다음 각 호를 표시하여야 한다 :

(i) 전부에 하나의 마스트정부등 ;

(ii) 전부의 마스트정부등보다 후방의 높은 위치에 하나의 제2의 마스트정부등 ; 길이 50미터 미만의 선박에서는 표시할 의무는 없으나 그렇게 하여도 좋다 ;

(iii) 현등 ;

(iv) 선미등 ;

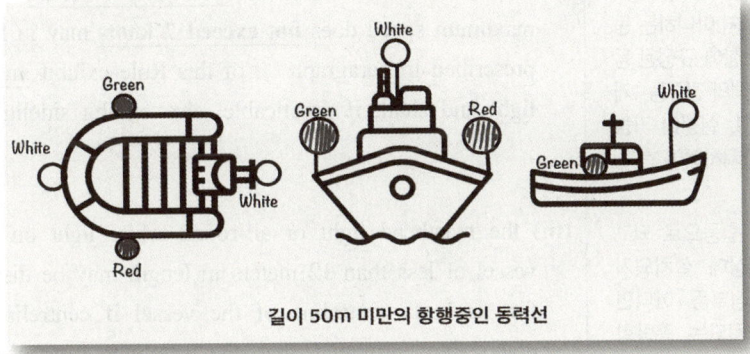

길이 50m 미만의 항행중인 동력선

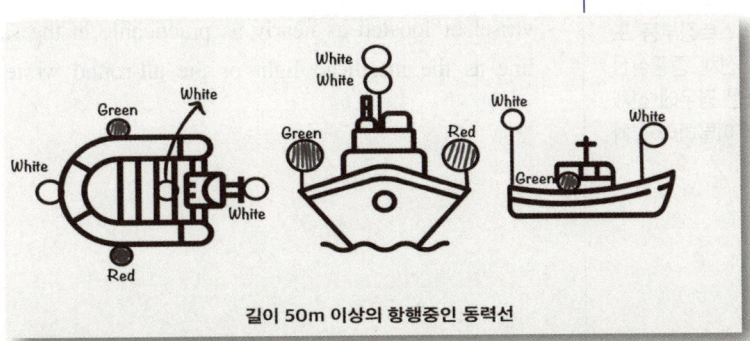

길이 50m 이상의 항행중인 동력선

ⓑ 수상활공선이 배수량이 없는 상태로 동작할 때에는, 이 조문의 ⓐ항에 규정된 등화에 추가하여 전주를 비추는 황색섬광등 하나를 표시하여야 한다.

ⓒ 이 규칙의 ⓐ항의 등화에 추가하여, 이륙, 착륙 및 표면에 근접하여 비행시에만, WIG선은 전주를 비추는 고강도 적색섬광등 하나를 표시하여야 한다.

ⓓ

(ⅰ) 길이가 12미터 미만인 동력선은 이 조문 ⓐ항에 규정된 등화에 대신하여 백색의 전주 등 1개와 현등을 표시할 수 있다.

(ⅱ) 길이가 7미터 미만이고 최대속력이 7노트를 초과하지 아니하는 동력선은 이 조문 ⓐ항에 규정된 등화에 대신하여 백색의 전주등 1개를 표시할 수 있고, 실행이 가능하다면, 현등을 표시하여야 한다.

(ⅲ) 현등이 하나의 복합등으로 되고 선체의 종중심선상에 설치되거나 또는 마스트정부등 아니면 백색전주등이 설치되는 종방향 선상에 가능한 한 가까이 설치된다는 조건으로 길이 12미터 미만의 동력선의 마스트정부등 또는 백색전주등은 선체 종중심선상 설치가 불가능한 경우에 선체 종중심선으로부터 이탈하여 설치될 수 있다.

ⓑ **An air-cushion vessel** when operating in the non-displacement mode shall, in addition to the lights prescribed in paragraph ⓐ of this Rule exhibit an **all-round flashing yellow light.**

ⓒ **A WIG craft** only when taking off, landing and in flight near the surface shall, in addition to the lights prescribed in paragraph ⓐ of this Rule, exhibit a high intensity **all-round flashing red light.**

ⓓ

(i) A power-driven vessel of **less than 12 meters** in length may in lieu of the lights prescribed in paragraph ⓐ of this Rule exhibit an **all-round white light and sidelights:**

(ii) a power-driven vessel of **less than 7 meters** in length whose maximum speed does **not exceed 7 knots** may in lieu of the lights prescribed in paragraph ⓐ of this Rule exhibit **an all-round white light** and shall, if practicable, also exhibit sidelights;

(iii) the masthead light or all-round white light on a power-driven vessel of less than 12 meters in length may be displaced from the fore and aft centreline of the vessel if centreline fitting is not practicable, provided that the sidelights are combined in one lantern which shall be carried on the fore and aft centreline of the vessel or located as nearly as practicable in the same fore and aft line as the masthead light or the all-round white light.

Rule 24
Towing and Pushing

ⓐ A power-driven vessel when towing shall exhibit:

(i) instead of the light prescribed in Rule 23ⓐ(i) or ⓐ(ii), **two masthead lights** in a vertical line. When the length of the tow, measuring from the stern of the towing vessel to the after end of the tow **exceeds 200 metres, three such lights** in a vertical line;

(ii) sidelights;

(iii) a sternlight;

(iv) **a towing light** in a vertical line **above the sternlight;**

(v) when the length of the tow **exceeds 200 metres,** a **diamond shape** where it can best be seen.

ⓑ When a pushing vessel and a vessel being pushed ahead are rigidly connected in a composite unit they shall be regarded as a power-driven vessel and exhibit the lights prescribed in Rule 23.

ⓒ A power-driven vessel when pushing ahead or towing alongside, except in the case of a composite unit, shall exhibit:

(i) instead of the light prescribed in Rule 23ⓐ(i) or ⓐ(ii), two masthead lights in a vertical line;

(ii) sidelights;

(iii) a sternlight.

제 24 조
끌고가는 선박 및 밀고가는 선박

ⓐ 예인 중인 동력선은 다음 각호를 표시하여야 한다.

(i) 제23조 ⓐ(i) 또는 ⓐ(ii)에 규정된 등화 대신에, 동일 수직선상에 2개의 마스트정부등, 예선의 선미로부터 피예물의 후부단까지 측정한 예인의 길이가 200미터를 초과할 때에는, 동일 수직선상에 3개의 그러한 마스트정부등 ;

(ii) 현등 ;

(iii) 하나의 선미등 ;

(iv) 선미등의 상부에 수직으로 단 하나의 예인등 ;

(v) 예인의 길이가 200미터를 초과할 때에는 가장 잘 보이는 장소에 하나의 다이아몬드 형상물

ⓑ 미는 선박과 앞으로 밀리고 있는 선박이 견고하게 연결되어 하나의 복합체를 이룰 때에는 한척의 동력선으로 취급되며 제23조에 규정된 등화를 표시하여야 한다.

ⓒ 앞으로 미는 또는 옆에 밀착시켜서 끌고 있는 동력선은 하나의 복합체의 경우를 제외하고는 다음 각호를 표시하여야 한다.

(i) 제23조 ⓐ(i) 또는 ⓐ(ii)에 규정된 등화 대신에, 하나의 수직선상에 2개의 마스트정부등 ;

(ii) 현등

(iii) 선미등

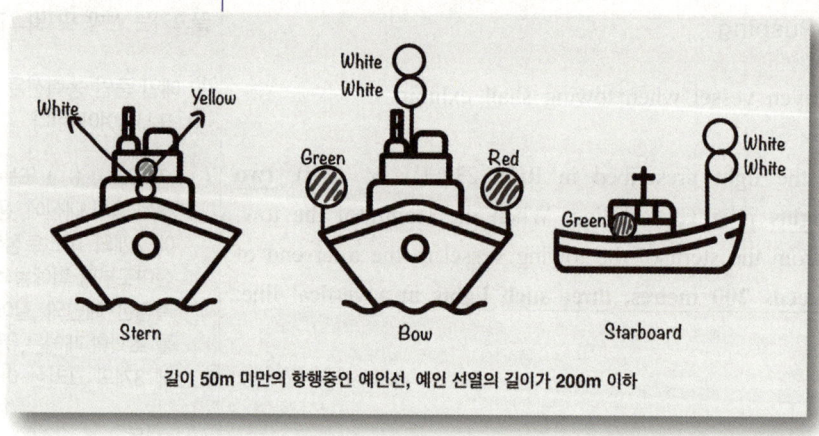

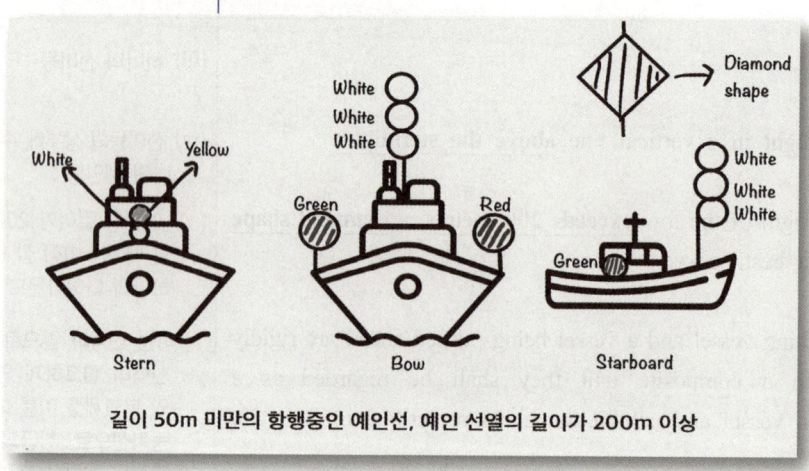

ⓓ 이조문의 ⓐ 또는 ⓒ항이 적용되는 동력선에는 제23조 ⓐ(ⅱ)도 적용된다.

ⓔ 피예선 또는 피예물은 이 규칙 ⓖ항에 언급한 경우를 제외하고는 다음 각호를 표시하여야 한다.

(ⅰ) 현등 ;

(ⅱ) 선미등 ;

(ⅲ) 예인의 길이가 200미터를 초과할 때에는 가장 잘 보이는 장소에 다이아몬드 형상물 1개

ⓓ A power-driven vessel to which paragraph ⓐ or ⓒ of this Rule applies shall also comply with Rule 23ⓐ(ⅱ).

ⓔ A vessel or object being towed, other than those mentioned in paragraph ⓖ of this Rule, shall exhibit:

(i) sidelights;

(ii) a sternlight;

(iii) when the length of the tow **exceeds 200 metres,** a **diamond shape** where it can best be seen.

ⓕ Provided that any number of vessels being towed alongside or pushed in a group shall be lighted as one vessel,

(i) a vessel being pushed ahead, not being part of a composite unit, shall exhibit at the forward end, sidelights;

(ii) a vessel being towed alongside shall exhibit a sternlight and at the forward end, sidelights.

ⓕ 만약 수척의 선박이 한 덩어리가 되어 현측에서 끌리거나 앞으로 밀릴 때에는 한척의 선박처럼 등화를 표시하여야 한다. 즉,

(ⅰ) 밀리고 있는 선박이 복합체가 아닐 때에는, 전부단에 현등을 표시하여야 한다.

(ⅱ) 현측에서 끌려가고 있는 선박은 선미등을 표시하여야 하고 그리고 전부단에 양현등을 표시하여야 한다.

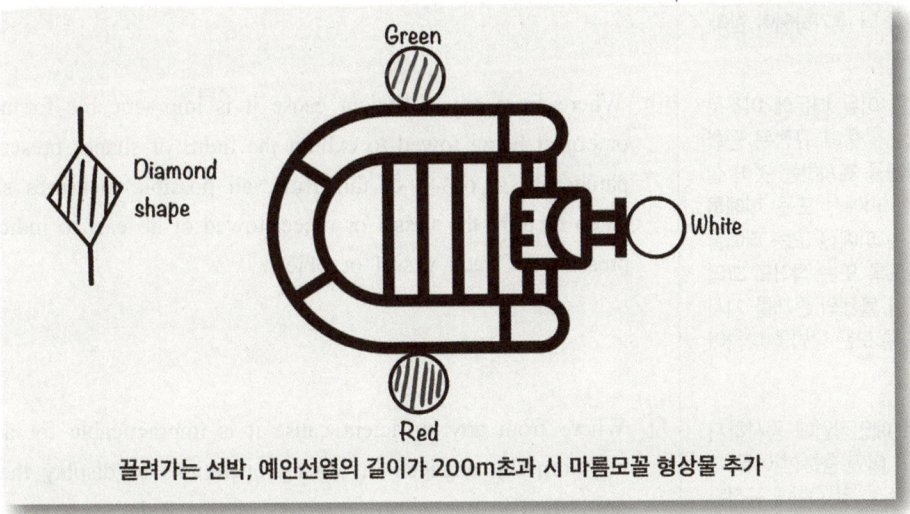

끌려가는 선박, 예인선열의 길이가 200m초과 시 마름모꼴 형상물 추가

ⓖ An inconspicuous, partly submerged vessel or object, or combination of such vessels or objects being towed, shall exhibit:

(i) if it is less than 25 metres in breadth, one all-round white light at or near the forward end and one at or near the after end except that dracones need not exhibit a light at or near the forward end;

(ii) if it is 25 metres or more in breadth, two additional all-round white lights at or near the extremities of its breadth;

ⓖ 눈에 잘 띄지않는 상태로 부분적으로 잠수되어 끌려가고 있는 선박이나 물체 또는 끌려가고 있는 선박들 또는 물체들은 다음 각호를 표시하여야 한다.

(ⅰ) 폭이 25미터 미만이면 전단이나 전단부근에 하나의 백색전주등과 후단이나 후단 부근에 하나의 백색전주등 단, dracone은 전단부 또는 그 부근에 등화를 표시할 필요가 없다. Dracone : 석유 또는 기타화물을 채워서 수상 수송에 사용되는 고무로 된 용기.

(ⅱ) 폭이 25미터 이상이면 폭의 양단 또는 그 부근에 2개의 백색전주등 추가.

(iii) 만약 길이가 100미터를 초과하면 (ⅰ) 및 (ⅱ)호에서 규정한 등화의 사이에 백색전주등을 추가 설치하되 등화간의 간격은 100미터를 초과하지 못한다.

(iv) 끌려가는 선박 또는 물체의 최후단이나 그 부근에 한개의 다이아몬드 형상물, 만약에 예인되는 길이가 200미터를 초과할 경우에는 실행이 가능한 한 전부의 가장 잘 보이는 장소에 다이아몬드 형상물 하나를 더 추가하여야 한다.

ⓗ 어떤 충분한 이유 때문에 이조문의 ⓔ 또는 ⓖ항에 규정된 등화 또는 형상물을 표시하는 것이 실행불가능한 피예선 또는 피예물에 대하여는 피예선 또는 피예물을 점등하도록 또는 적어도 그러한 선박이나 물체의 존재를 지시할 수 있도록 모든 방법을 다하여야 한다.

ⓘ 통상적으로 예인작업에 종사하지 않는 선박이 어떤 충분한 이유 때문에 이 조문 ⓐ 및 ⓒ항에 규정된 등화를 표시하는 것이 실행불가능한 경우 즉, 그러한 선박이 조난선 또는 구원을 요청하는 선박의 예인작업에 종사할 때는 이들 등화를 표시하지 아니하여도 된다. 이러한 경우에는 예선과 피예선의 관계를 나타내기 위하여 규칙 제36조에서 인정하는 모든 수단을 다하여야 하고 특히 예색을 비추어 주어서 그들의 관계를 나타내여야 한다.

(iii) if it exceeds 100 metres in length, additional all-round white lights between the lights prescribed in sub-paragraphs (i) and (ii) so that the distance between the lights shall not exceed 100 metres;

(iv) a diamond shape at or near the after most extremity of the last vessel or object being towed and if the length of the tow exceeds 200 metres an additional diamond shape where it can best be seen and located as far forward as is practicable.

ⓗ Where from any sufficient cause it is impracticable for a vessel or object being towed to exhibit the lights or shapes prescribed in paragraph ⓔ or ⓖ of this Rule, all possible measures shall be taken to light the vessel or object towed or at least to indicate the presence of such vessel or object.

ⓘ Where from any sufficient cause it is impracticable for a vessel not normally engaged in towing operations to display the lights prescribed in paragraph ⓐ or ⓒ of this Rule, such vessel shall not be required to exhibit those lights when engaged in towing another vessel in distress or otherwise in need of assistance. All possible measures shall be taken to indicate the nature of the relationship between the towing vessel and the vessel being towed as authorized by Rule 36, in particular by illuminating the towline.

Rule 25
Sailing Vessels underway and Vessels under Oars

ⓐ A sailing vessel underway shall exhibit:

(i) sidelights;

(ii) a sternlight.

ⓑ In a sailing vessel of **less than 20 metres** in length the lights prescribed in paragraph ⓐ of this Rule **may be combined in one lantern** carried at or near the top of the mast where it can best be seen.

ⓒ A sailing vessel underway may, in addition to the lights prescribed in paragraph ⓐ of this Rule, exhibit at or near the top of the mast, where they can best be seen, two all-round lights in a vertical line, **the upper being red** and the **lower green,** but these lights shall **not be exhibited in conjunction with the combined lantern** permitted by paragraph ⓑ of this Rule.

ⓓ

(i) A sailing vessel of **less than 7 metres** in length shall, if practicable, exhibit the lights prescribed in paragraph ⓐ or ⓑ of this Rule, but if she does not, she shall have ready at hand an electric torch or lighted lantern showing a white light which shall be exhibited in sufficient time to prevent collision.

제 25 조
항해 중인 범선 및 노도선

ⓐ 항해 중인 범선은 다음 각호를 표시하여야 한다 :

(ⅰ) 현등 ;

(ⅱ) 선미등.

ⓑ 길이 20미터 미만의 범선에 있어서는 이 조문 ⓐ항에 규정된 등화를 마스트의 꼭지 또는 그 부근 가장 잘 보이는 장소에, 하나의 등각에 합칠 수 있다.

ⓒ 항해 중인 범선은 이 조문 ⓐ항에 규정된 등화에 추가하여 마스트의 꼭지 또는 그 부근 가장 잘 보이는 장소에 2개의 전주등을 수직으로 달 수 있고, 위는 홍등 아래는 녹등이어야 하나, 이들 등화가 이 조문 ⓑ항에 허용된 복합등과 접속되어 표시되어서는 아니된다.

ⓓ

(ⅰ) 길이 7미터 미만인 범선은, 실행 가능하면, ⓐ 및 ⓑ항에 규정된 등화를 표시하여야 한다. 그러나 만약 표시하지 아니할 때에는, 백광의 전지등 또는 점화된 등화를 준비하여 두었다가 충돌을 방지할 수 있는 충분한 시간동안 비추어 주어야 한다.

(ii) 노도선은 이 조문에 규정된 범선의 등화를 달 수 있다. 그러나 그러하지 아니할 때에는 백광을 발하는 전지등 또는 점화된 등화를 준비하여 두었다가 충돌을 방지할 수 있는 충분한 시간동안 비추어 주어야 한다.

ⓔ 돛을 펴고 진행하지만 동시에 기관에 의하여 추진되고 있는 선박은 전부 가장 잘 보이는 장소에 정점을 하방으로 둔 원추형형상물 1개를 달아야 한다.

(ii) **A vessel under oars** may exhibit the lights prescribed in this Rule for sailing vessels, but if she does not, she shall have ready at hand an electric torch or lighted lantern showing a white light which shall be exhibited in sufficient time to prevent collision.

ⓔ A vessel proceeding under sail when also being propelled by machinery shall exhibit forward where it can best be seen a conical shape, apex down wards.

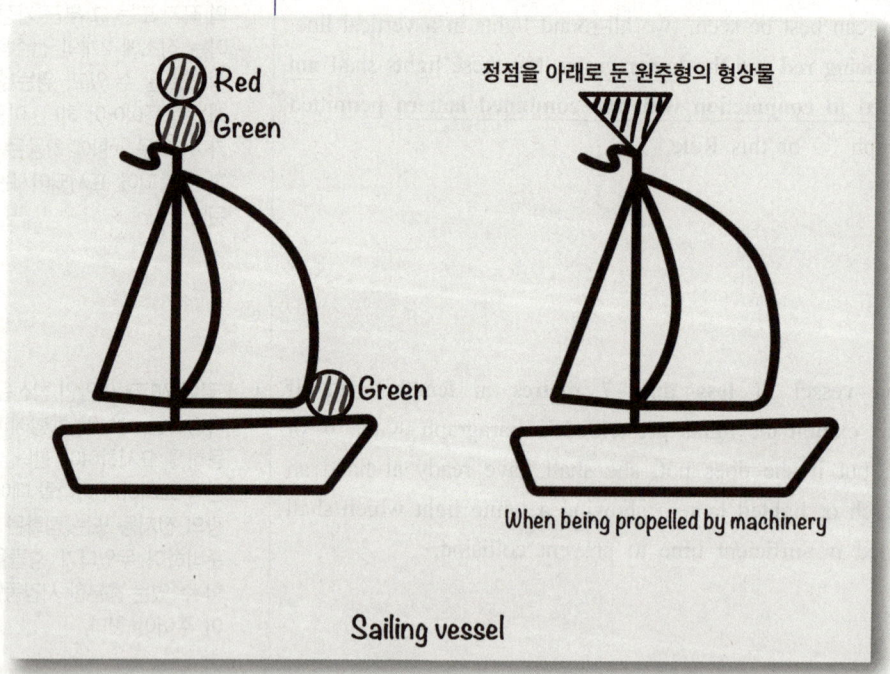

Rule 26
Fishing Vessels

ⓐ A vessel engaged in fishing, whether underway or at anchor, shall exhibit only the lights and shapes prescribed in this Rule.

ⓑ A vessel when engaged **in trawling,** by which is meant the dragging through the water of a dredge net or other apparatus used as a fishing appliance, shall exhibit:

(i) two all-round lights in a vertical line, the **upper being green** and the **lower white,** or a **shape consisting of two cones with their apexes together** in a vertical line one above the other ;

(ii) a masthead light abaft of and higher than the all-round green light; a vessel of less than 50 metres in length shall not be obliged to exhibit such a light but may do so ;

(iii) when making way through the water, in addition to the lights prescribed in this paragraph, sidelights and a sternlight.

제 26 조
어 선

ⓐ 어로에 종사 중인 선박은 항행 중이든 정박 중이든 간에 이 조문에 규정된 등화 및 형성물만을 표시하여야 한다.

ⓑ 저인망 또는 기타의 어구를 수중에서 끄는 트로올 어로에 종사하는 어선은 다음 각호를 표시하여야 한다 :

(i) 2개의 전주등을 수직으로 달되, 위의 것은 녹등이고 아래 것은 백등이어야 한다. 또는 2개의 원추형을 정점을 포개서 수직으로 달은 형상물 1개를 표시한다 ;

(ii) 전주를 비추는 녹색등화보다 후방 및 그보다 높은 장소에 표시되는 하나의 마스트정부등 ; 길이가 50미터 미만인 선박은 그러한 등화를 표시할 의무는 없으나 그렇게 하여도 좋다 ;

(iii) 대수속력이 있을 때에는 이항에 명시된 등화에 추가하여, 현등 및 선미등을 표시한다.

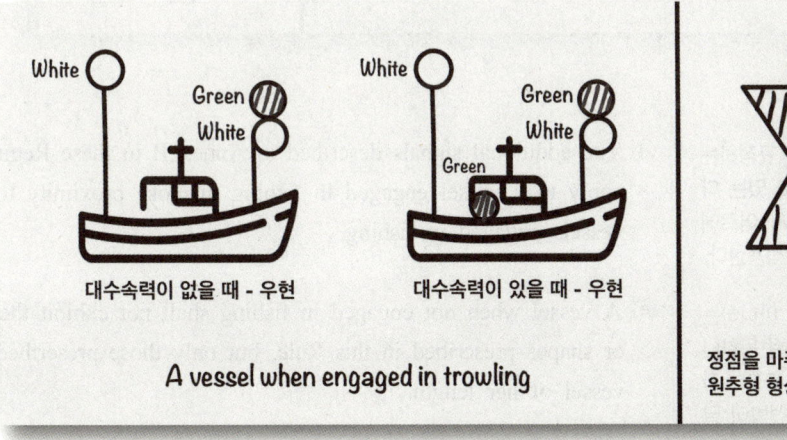

ⓒ A vessel engaged in fishing, other than trawling, shall exhibit:

ⓒ 트로올 이외의 어로에 종사하는 선박은 다음 각호를 표시하여야 한다.

(ⅰ) 2개의 전주등을 수직으로 달되, 위의 것은 홍등이고 아래 것은 백등이어야 한다. 또는 2개의 원추를 정점을 포개서 수직으로 달은 형상물 1개를 표시한다;

(ⅰ) two all-round lights in a vertical line, the **upper being red** and the **lower white,** or a shape consisting of two cones with apexes together in a vertical line one above the other;

(ⅱ) 어구가 선박으로부터 수평으로 150미터 이상 뻗어 있을 때에는 그 어구방향으로, 전주를 비추는 백등 1개 또는 하나의 원추를 정점으로 상방으로 하여 표시한다;

(ⅱ) when there is **outlying gear extending more than 150 metres** horizontally from the vessel, **an all-round white light** or **a cone apex upwards** in the direction of the gear;

(ⅲ) 대수속력이 있을 때에는 이항에 규정된 등화에 추가하여, 현등 및 선미등을 표시한다.

(ⅲ) when making way through the water, in addition to the lights prescribed in this paragraph, sidelights and a sternlight.

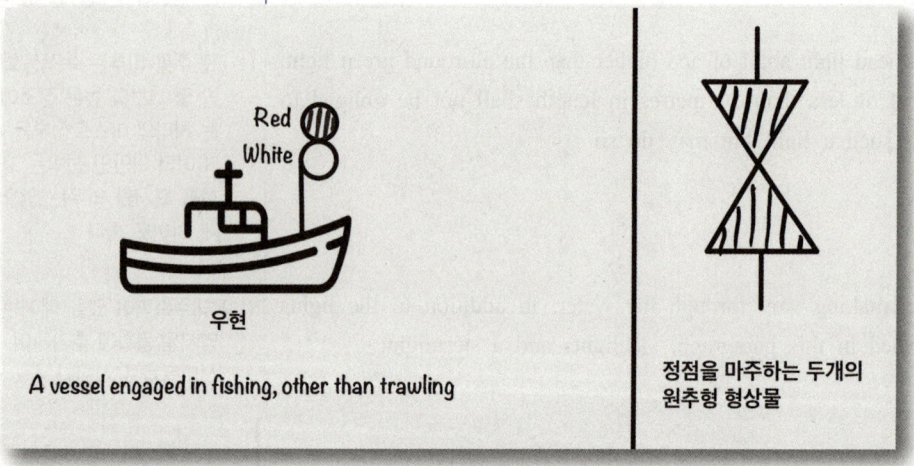

A vessel engaged in fishing, other than trawling

정점을 마주하는 두개의 원추형 형상물

ⓓ 이 규칙 부속서Ⅱ에서 규정하는 추가신호는 어로를 하고 있는 다른 선박의 지근거리에서 어로에 종사하고 있는 선박에 적용한다.

ⓓ The additional signals described in Annex II to these Regulations apply to a vessel engaged in fishing in close proximity to other vessels engaged in fishing.

ⓔ 어로에 종사하고 있지 아니하는 선박은 이 조문에 규정된 등화나 형상물을 달아서는 아니되고, 지선의 길이에 해당되는 선박이 달아야 할 등화 및 형상물만을 달아야 한다.

ⓔ A vessel when not engaged in fishing shall not exhibit the lights or shapes prescribed in this Rule, but only those prescribed for a vessel of her length.

Rule 27

Vessels not under Command
or Restricted in their Ability to Manoeuvre

ⓐ A vessel not under command shall exhibit:

(i) **two all-round red lights** in a vertical line where they can best be seen;

(ii) **two balls** or similar shapes in a vertical line where they can best be seen;

(iii) when making way through the water, in addition to the lights prescribed in this paragraph, sidelights and a sternlight.

제 27 조
운전이 자유롭지 못한 선박 또는 조종성능에 제한을 받는 선박

ⓐ 운전이 자유롭지 못한 선박은 다음 각호를 표시하여야 한다.

(ⅰ) 가장 잘 보이는 곳, 수직선상에 전주를 비추는 홍등 2개;

(ⅱ) 가장 잘 보이는 곳, 수직선상에 구 또는 이와 유사한 형상물 2개;

(ⅲ) 대수속력이 있는 경우에는 이항에 규정된 등화 이외에 현등 및 선미등.

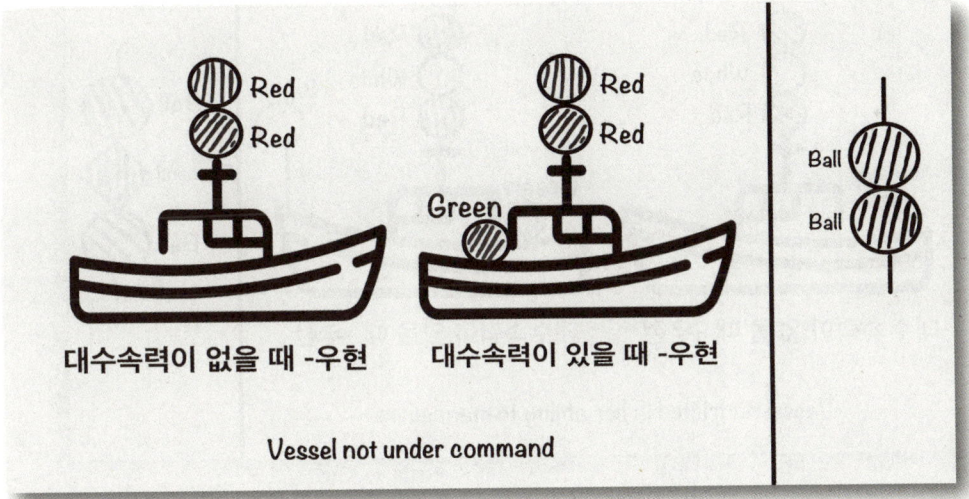

ⓑ A vessel restricted in her ability to manoeuvre, except a vessel engaged in mineclearance operations, shall exhibit:

(i) three all-round lights in a vertical line where they can best be seen. **The highest and lowest** of these lights shall be **red** and the **middle light** shall be **white**;

ⓑ 기뢰 제거작업에 종사하고 있는 선박을 제외하고, 조종성능에 제한을 받는 선박은 다음 등화를 표시하여야 한다.

(ⅰ) 가장 잘 보이는 곳, 수직선상에 전주를 비추는 등화 3개, 이들 등화중 상단 및 하단의 등화는 홍색이어야 하며, 중간의 등화는 백색이어야 한다.

(ii) 가장 잘 보이는 곳, 수직선상에 형상물 3개, 이들 형상물중 상단 및 하단의 형상물은 구형이어야 하며 중간의 형상물은 능형이어야 한다.

(ii) three shapes in a vertical line where they can best be seen. The **highest and lowest** of these shapes shall be **balls** and the **middle** one **a diamond**;

(iii) 대수속력이 있는 경우에는, 전호 (ⅰ)에 규정된 등화에 추가하여 하나 또는 그 이상의 마스트정부 등, 현등 및 선미등 ;

(iii) when making way through the water, **a masthead light** or lights, sidelights and a sternlight in addition to the lights prescribed in subparagraph (i);

(iv) 묘박중인 경우에는, 전호 (ⅰ) 및 (ⅱ)에 규정된 등화 또는 형상물에 부가하여 제30조 에규정된 등화 및 형상물.

(iv) when at anchor, in addition to the lights or shapes prescribed in sub-paragraphs (i) and (ii), the light, lights or shape prescribed in Rule 30.

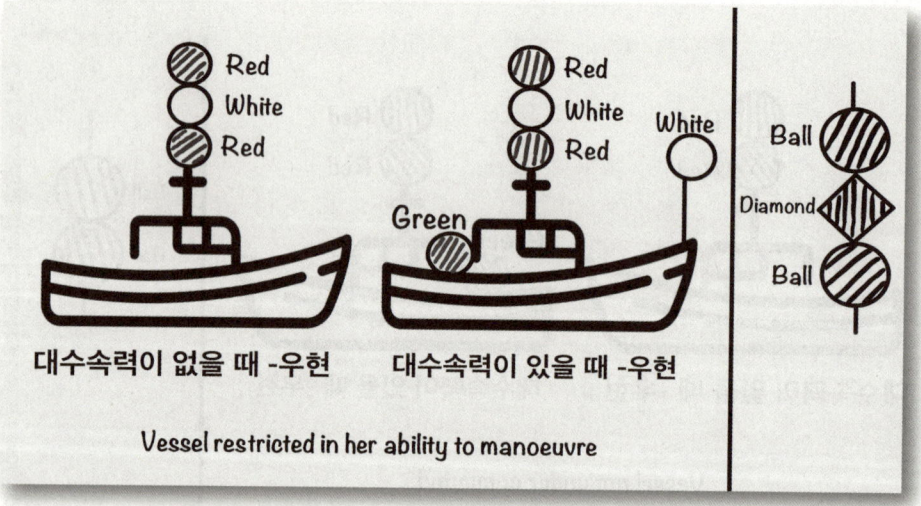

ⓒ 예선과 피예선이 그들의 침로에서 이탈하는 것을 심하게 제한하는 성질의 예인작업에 종사하는 동력선은 24조 ⓐ항에서 규정하는 등화 또는 형상물에 추가하여 이 조문 ⓑ항 (ⅰ) 및 (ⅱ)에 규정된 등화 또는 형상물을 표시하여야 한다.

ⓒ A power-driven vessel engaged in a towing operation such as severely restricts the towing vessel and her tow in their ability to deviate from their course shall, in addition to the lights or shapes prescribed in Rule 24ⓐ, exhibit the lights or shapes prescribed in sub-paragraphs ⓑ(i) and (ii) of this Rule.

ⓓ A vessel engaged in **dredging or underwater operations,** when restricted in her ability to manoeuvre, shall exhibit the lights and shapes prescribed in sub-paragraphs ⓑ (i),(ii) and (iii) of this Rule and shall in addition, when an obstruction exists, exhibit:

(i) **two all-round red lights** or **two balls** in a vertical line to indicate the side on which the **obstruction** exists;

(ii) **two all-round green lights** or **two diamonds** in a vertical line to indicate the side on which another **vessel may pass;**

(iii) when at anchor, the lights or shapes prescribed in this paragraph instead of the lights or shape prescribed in Rule 30.

ⓔ Whenever the size of a vessel engaged in **diving operations** makes it impracticable to exhibit all lights and shapes prescribed in paragraph ⓓ of this Rule, the following shall be exhibited:

(i) three all-round lights in a vertical line where they can best be seen. **The highest and lowest** of these lights shall be **red** and the **middle** light shall be **white;**

(ii) a rigid replica of the International Code **flag "A"** not less than 1 metre in height. Measures shall be taken to ensure its all-round visibility.

ⓓ 조종성에 제한을 받는 준설 또는 수중작업에 종사하고 있는 선박은, 이 조문ⓑ항(ⅰ), (ⅱ) 및 (ⅲ)에 규정된 등화 및 형상물을 표시하여야 하며, 장애물이 있는 경우에는 추가하여 다음 등화 및 형상물을 표시하여야 한다 ;

(ⅰ) 장애물이 있는 쪽을 가리키는 수직선상에 전주를 비추는 홍등 2개 또는 구형 형상물 2개 ;

(ⅱ) 타선이 항과할 수 있는 쪽을 가리키는 수직선상에 전주를 비추는 녹등 2개 또는 능형 형상물 2개 ;

(ⅲ) 정박 중인 때에는, 제30조에 규정하는 등화 또는 형상물에 대신하여 이 항에 규정하는 등화 또는 형상물을 표시하여야 한다.

ⓔ 잠수작업에 종사하는 선박이 그 크기로 인하여 이 조문 ⓓ항에서 규정하는 등화나 형상물을 표시하는 것이 불가능한 때는 다음을 표시하여야 한다.

(ⅰ) 가장 잘 보이는 곳의 수직선상에 전주를 비추는 세개의 등화. 최상단 및 최하단의 등은 홍등이고 중간등은 백등이어야 한다.

(ⅱ) 딱딱한 판에 새긴 높이가 1미터 이상되는 국제신호기 "A"자. 이것은 사방에서 보일 수 있도록 되어 있어야 한다.

ⓕ 기뢰 제거작업에 종사하고 있는 선박은 규칙 제23조에서 규정하고 있는 동력선의 등화 또는 규칙 제30조에서 규정하고 있는 정박선의 등화나 형상물에 추가하여 전주를 비추는 세개의 녹등 또는 세개의 구상 형상물을 표시하여야 한다. 이들 등화나 형상물 중 1개는 전부 마스트정부 부근에 표시되어야 하고 나머지 2개는 전부 야드(yard)의 양단에 각각 표시하여야 한다. 이들 등화나 형상물은 타선박이 기뢰 제거작업중인 선박의 1,000미터 범위 이내로 접근하는 것은 위험하다는 것을 표시한다.

ⓖ 길이 12미터 미만의 선박은 잠수작업에 종사하고 있는 경우를 제외하고, 이 조문에 규정된 등화 및 형상물을 표시하지 아니하여도 된다.

ⓗ 이 조문에 규정된 신호는 조난 및 구조를 필요로 하는 선박의 신호가 아니다. 그와 같은 신호는 이 규칙 부속서 Ⅳ에 포함되어 있다.

ⓕ **A vessel engaged in mineclearance operations** shall in addition to the lights prescribed for a power-driven vessel in Rule 23 or to the lights or shape prescribed for a vessel at anchor in Rule 30 as appropriate, exhibit **three all-round green lights** or **three balls**. One of these lights or shapes shall be exhibited near the foremast head and one at each end of the fore yard. These lights or shapes indicate that it is dangerous for another vessel to approach within **1000 metres** of the mineclearance vessel.

ⓖ Vessels of **less than 12 metres** in length, except those engaged in diving operations, shall **not be required** to exhibit the lights and shapes prescribed in this Rule.

ⓗ The signals prescribed in this Rule are not signals of vessels in distress and requiring assistance. Such signals are contained in Annex IV to these Regulations

Rule 28

Vessel constrained by their draught

A vessel constrained by her draught may, in addition to the lights prescribed for power-driven vessels in rule 23, exhibit where they can best be seen **three all-round red lights** in a vertical line, or a **cylinder.**

제 28 조

흘수로 인하여 제한을 받는 선박

흘수로 인하여 제한을 받는 선박은, 제23조에서 규정한 동력선의 등화에 추가하여, 가장 잘 보일 수 있는 곳, 수직선상에 전주를 비추는 홍등 3개 또는 원통형 형상물 1개를 표시할 수 있다.

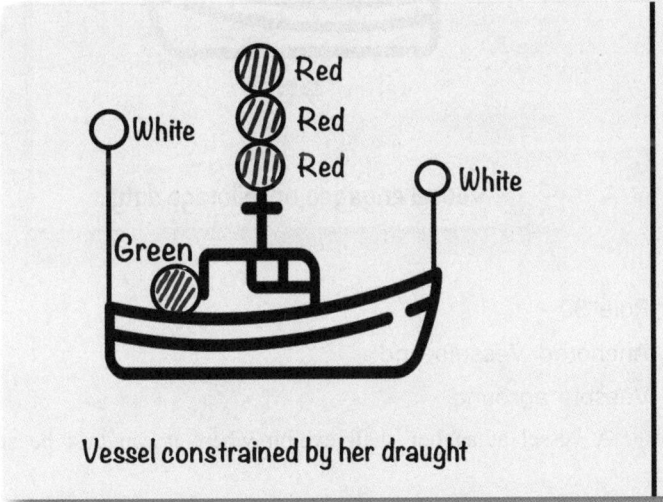 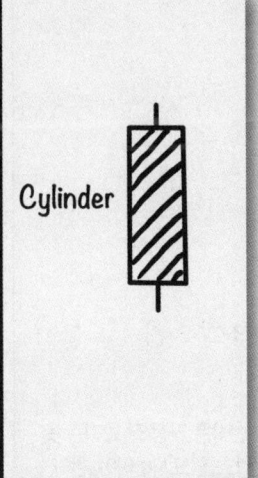

Rule 29

Pilot Vessels

ⓐ A vessel engaged on pilotage duty shall exhibit:

(i) at or near the masthead, two all-round lights in a vertical line, the **upper being white and the lower red;**

(ii) when underway, in addition, sidelight and a sternlight;

(iii) when at anchor, in addition to the lights prescribed in subparagraph (i), the light, lights or shape prescribed in Rule 30 for vessels at anchor.

제 29 조
도선선
ⓐ 도선업무에 종사하고 있는 선박은 다음 각호를 표시하여야 한다 :

(ⅰ) 마스트정부, 또는 그 부근 수직선상에 전주를 비추는 2개의 등화, 이 중 상부등은 백등이며 하부등은 홍등이다 ;

(ⅱ) 항해 중인 경우에는 현등 및 선미등을 추가한다;

(ⅲ) 묘박중인 경우, 전호 (ⅰ)에 규정한 등화에 추가하여 규칙 제30조에서 규정하는 정박선에 대한 등화나 등화군 또는 형상물을 표시한다.

ⓑ 도선업무에 종사하고 있지 아니하는 경우의 도선선은, 그 선박과 길이가 같은 선박에 대하여 규정한 등화 또는 형상물을 표시하여야 한다.

ⓑ A pilot vessel when not engaged on pilotage duty shall exhibit the lights or shapes prescribed for a similar vessel of her length.

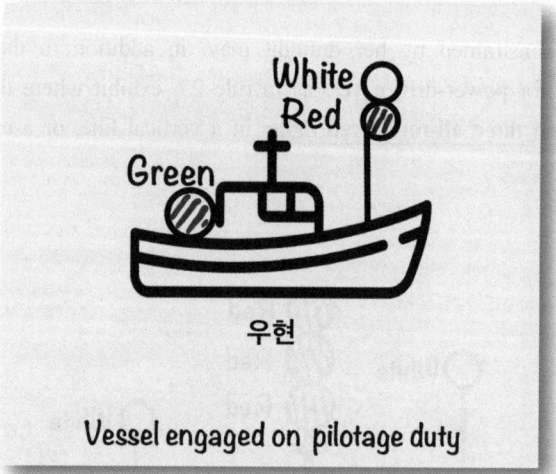

Vessel engaged on pilotage duty

제 30 조
정박선 및 좌초선

ⓐ 정박 중인 선박은 가장 잘 보이는 곳에 다음 각호를 표시하여야 한다.

(ⅰ) 전부에 전주를 비추는 백등 1개 또는 구형 형상물 1개,

(ⅱ) 선미 또는 그 부근에 전호 (ⅰ)에 규정한 등화보다 더 낮은 높이로 전주를 비추는 백등 1개,

ⓑ 길이 50미터 미만의 선박은 이 조문 ⓐ항에 규정한 등화 대신에 가장 잘 보이는 곳에 전주를 비추는 백등 1개를 표시할 수 있다.

ⓒ 정박 중인 선박은 갑판을 조명하기 위하여 이용할 수 있는 작업등, 또는 이와 동등한 등화를 사용할 수 있으며, 길이 100미터 이상의 선박은 이와 같은 등화를 사용하여야 한다.

Rule 30
Anchored Vessels and
Vessels aground

ⓐ A vessel at anchor shall exhibit where it can best be seen:

(i) in the **fore part**, **an all-round white light** or **one ball**;

(ii) **at or near the stern and at** a **lower level** than the light prescribed in sub-paragraph (i), **an all-round white light**

ⓑ A vessel of **less than 50 metres** in length may exhibit **an all-round white light** where it can best be seen instead of the lights prescribed in paragraph ⓐ of this Rule.

ⓒ A vessel at anchor may, and a vessel of **100 metres and more** in length shall, also use the available working or equivalent lights to **illuminate her decks.**

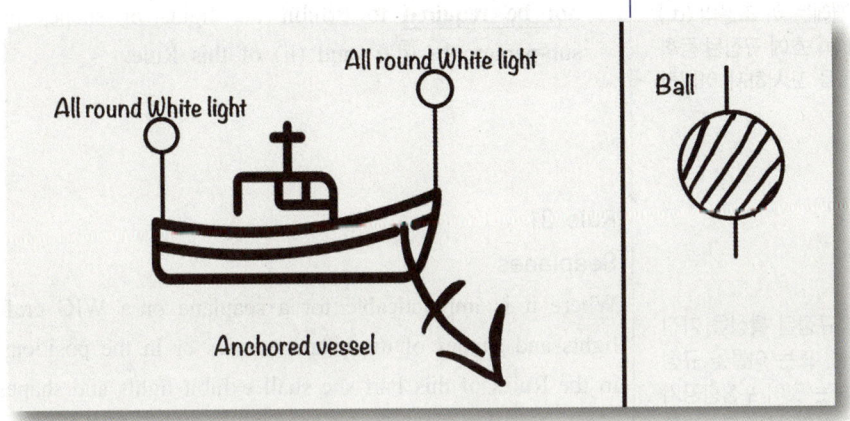

ⓓ A vessel aground shall exhibit the lights prescribed in paragraph ⓐ or ⓑ of this Rule and in addition, where they can best be seen:

(i) **two all-round red lights** in a vertical line;

(ii) **three balls** in a vertical line.

ⓓ 좌초선은 이 조문 ⓐ항, 또는 ⓑ항에 규정한 등화를 표시하여야 하며, 이에 추가하여 가장 잘 보이는 곳에 다음 등화 또는 형상물을 표시하여야 한다.

(i) 수직선상에 전주를 비추는 홍등 2개 ;

(ii) 수직선상에 구형 형상물 3개.

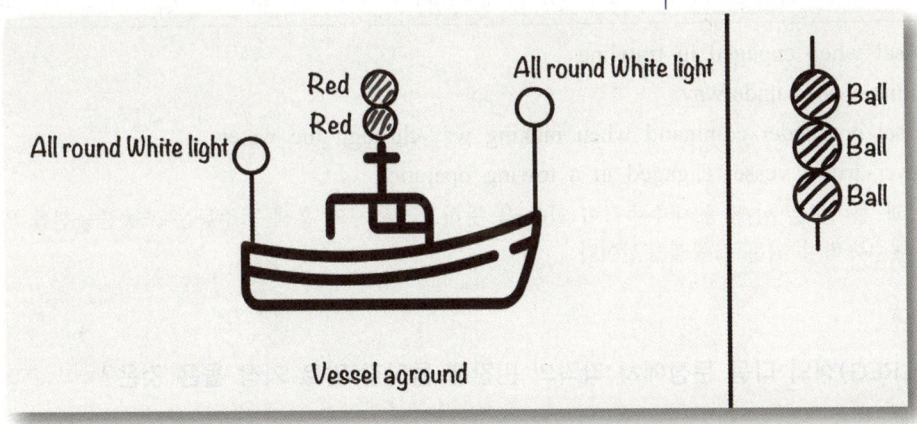

ⓔ A vessel of **less than 7 metres** in length, when at anchor, not in or near a narrow channel, fairway or anchorage, or where other vessels normally navigate, shall **not be required** to exhibit the lights or shape prescribed in paragraphs ⓐ , ⓑ of this Rule.

ⓔ 길이 7미터 미만의 선박이, 협수로, 항만 또는 묘박지 내나 또는 그 부근, 또는 타 선박이 통상 항해하는 곳 등에 묘박하지 아니할 때에는 그 선박은 이조문 ⓐ, ⓑ항에 규정한 등화 또는 형상물을 표시하지 아니하여도 된다.

ⓕ 길이 12미터 미만의 선박이 좌초되어 있을 때에는 이 조문의 (d)항 (ⅰ)호와 (ⅱ)호에 규정된 등화 또는 형상물을 표시하지 아니하여도 된다.

ⓕ A vessel of **less than 12 metres** in length, **when aground**, shall **not be required** to exhibit the lights or shapes prescribed in sub-paragraphs ⓓ(i) and (ii) of this Rule.

제 31 조
수상항공기

이 편의 규칙에 규정된 특성을 가진 등화 및 형상물을, 또는 이들을 규정된 위치에 표시하는 것이 수상항공기 또는 WIG선에 대하여 실현 불가능할 때에는 수상항공기 또는 WIG선은 가능한 한 이들 특성 및 위치에 가깝게 등화 및 형상물을 표시하여야 한다.

Rule 31
Seaplanes

Where it is impracticable for a seaplane or a WIG craft to exhibit lights and shapes of the characteristics or in the positions prescribed in the Rules of this Part she shall exhibit lights and shapes as closely similar in characteristics and position as is possible.

기출문제

51. 다음 중 COLREG(국제해상충돌방지규칙)상 등화를 표시하여야 하는 선박으로 가장 옳은 것은?

[18년 일반직]

A vessel exhibits sidelights and a sternlight in addition to two all-round red lights in a vertical line.

① A vessel when engaged in trawling
② A sailing vessel underway
③ A vessel not under command when making way through the water
④ A power-driven vessel engaged in a towing operation

해설 현등과 선미등은 항해 중(대수속력이 있음)을 뜻하고, 두 개의 홍색 전주등은 조종불능선을 의미한다. 즉, 대수속력이 있는 조종불능선이다.

답 ❸

52. 〈COLREG〉상의 다음 문장에서 각각의 빈칸에 들어갈 말로 가장 옳은 것은?

[19년 3차]

A vessel not under command shall exhibit : (   ) all round (   ) lights in a vertical line where they can best be seen.

① three, red
② two, red
③ two, white
④ three, white

해설 조종불능선: 2개의 홍색 전주등

답 ❷

기출문제

53. Which of the following day signals should be displayed for a vessel not under command?　　　　　　　　　　　　　　　　　　　　　　　　　　16년 2차

① Two black balls or similar shapes in a vertical line where they can best be seen.
② Three black balls or similar shapes in a horizontal line where they can best be seen.
③ Two red balls or similar shapes in a vertical line where they can best be seen.
④ Three red balls or similar shapes in a horizontal line where they can best be see.

해설 조종불능선의 주간 형상물 : 2개의 흑색 구형 형상물

답 ❶

54. 1972 국제해상충돌예방규칙의 일부이다. 보기들 중 아래에서 설명하는 등화를 표시하고 있는 선박은?　　　　　　　　　　　　　　　　　　　　　　　　　　14년 2차

> A vessel exhibits sidelights and a sternlight in addition to two all-round red lights in a vertical line.

① A vessel when engaged in trawling
② A vessel restricted in her ability to manoeuvre
③ A vessel not under command when making way through the water
④ A power-driven vessel engaged in a towing operation

해설 현등과 선미등은 항해 중(대수속력이 있음)을 뜻하고, 두 개의 홍색 전주등은 조종불능선을 의미한다. 즉, 대수속력이 있는 조종불능선이다.

답 ❸

55. 다음 그림이 나타내는 선박으로 가장 옳은 것은?　　　　　　　　　　14년 1차

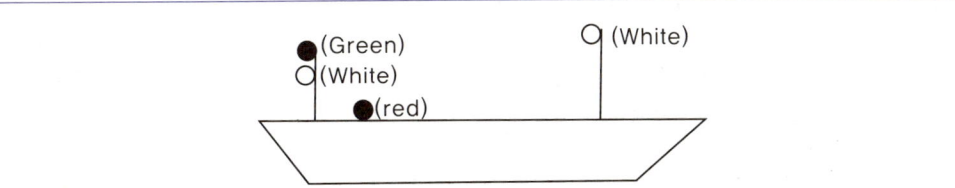

① vessel constrained by her draught
② pilot boat
③ vessel engaged in other than draught
④ vessel engaged in trawling

해설 녹색과 백색의 전주등이 수직상으로 달려있는 것을 보아, 트롤 어로를 하고 있는 어선임을 알 수 있다.

답 ❹

기출문제

56. 아래 지문은 COLREG 여러 조항 중 하나이다. 빈칸에 들어갈 말은? [18년 2차]

> _____ may, in addition to the lights prescribed for power-driven vessels in Rule 23, exhibit where they can best be seen three all-round red lights in a vertical line, or a cylinder.

① A vessel restricted in her ability
② A vessel constrained by her draught
③ A vessel not under command
④ A vessel aground

해설 3개의 홍색 전주등이나 원통형 형상물을 표시하는 것으로 보아, 흘수제약선임을 알 수 있다.

답 ❷

57. 다음은 COLREG(International Regulations for Preventing Collision at Sea) Rule 28에 대한 것이다. 빈칸에 들어갈 단어로 가장 옳은 것은? [20년 1차]

> A vessel constrained by her draught may, in addition to the lights prescribed for power-driven vessels in Rule 23, exhibit where they can best be seen (㉠) lights in a vertical line, or a (㉡).

	㉠	㉡
①	three all-round white	diamond
②	three all-round red	diamond
③	three all-round white	cylinder
④	three all-round red	cylinder

해설 흘수제약선은 야간에는 홍색 전주등 3개, 주간에는 원통형 형상물 1개를 표시한다.

답 ❹

기출문제

58. 다음은 〈COLREG〉상 등화에 대한 설명이다. ㉠, ㉡, ㉢에 해당하는 내용으로 가장 옳은 것은?

20년 3차

㉠ two all-round lights in a vertical line, the upper being red and the lower white, or a shape consisting of two cones with apexes together in a vertical line one above the other
㉡ two all-round red lights in a vertical line where they can best be seen
㉢ at or near the masthead, two all-round lights in a vertical line, the upper being white and the lower red

① ㉠ A vessel engaged in fishing
　㉡ A vessel not under command
　㉢ A vessel engaged on pilotage duty

② ㉠ A vessel engaged in fishing
　㉡ A vessel at anchor
　㉢ A vessel engaged on pilotage duty

③ ㉠ A vessel engaged in fishing, other than trawling
　㉡ A vessel not under command
　㉢ A vessel engaged on pilotage duty

④ ㉠ A vessel engaged in fishing, other than trawling
　㉡ A vessel engaged on pilotage duty
　㉢ A vessel not under command

해설 ㉠ 트롤링이 아닌 어로 종사중인 선박은 상부 홍등 하부 백등을 켠다.
㉡ 조종불능선은 수직의 선상에 홍색 등화 두 개를 켠다.
㉢ 도선 업무에 종사중인 선박은 상부 백등 하부 홍등을 켠다.

답 ③

기출문제

59. 다음 〈보기〉의 COLREG RULE상 아래에서 설명하는 선박으로 가장 옳은 것은? [21년 상반기]

> ㉠ Two all-round lights in a vertical line, the upper being green and the lower white, or a shape consisting of two cones with their apexes together in a vertical line one above the other
> ㉡ A masthead light abaft of and higher than the all-round green light; a vessel of less than 50 metres in length shall not be obliged to exhibit such a light but may do so

① A vessel not under command
② A vessel when engaged in trawling
③ A vessel restricted in her ability to manoeuvre
④ A vessel engaged in mineclearance operations

해설 ㉠ 상부 녹등 하부 백등(upper being green and lower white) 그리고 주간에는 꼭지점이 마주보는 원추형 형상물(a shape consisting of two cones with their apexes together)을 다는 선박은 트롤링에 종사 중인 선박이다.
㉡ 또한 선박의 정부마스트등을(masthead light)를 전방에 녹색 전주등보다 높이 선미 부근에 점등하나, 선박 길이가 50미터 미만인 경우 그러할 필요는 없다.

답 ❷

60. When deep draft vessel enter into the narrow channel, what light will be on? [11년 1차]

① one all-round red light
② two all-round red lights
③ three all-round red lights
④ two all-round white lights

해설 깊은 흘수의 선박이 좁은 수로로 들어갔기 때문에 흘수제약선(vessel constrained by her draught) 등화를 켜주는 것이 적합하다.
흘수 제약선의 등화는 세 개의 홍등이다(three all-round red lights).

답 ❸

PART D - Sound and light signals

Rule 32
Definitions

ⓐ The word 'whistle' means any sound signalling appliance capable of producing the prescribed blasts and which complies with the specifications in Annex III to these Regulations.

ⓑ The term **'short blast'** means a blast of about **one** second's duration.

ⓒ The term **'prolonged blast'** means a blast of from **four to six** seconds's duration.

Rule 33
Equipment for Sound Signals

ⓐ A vessel of **12 metres** or more in length shall be provided with a **whistle**, a vessel of **20 metres** or more in length shall be provided with **a bell** in addition to a whistle, and a vessel of **100 metres** or more in length shall, in addition, be provided with **a gong,** the tone and sound of which cannot be confused with that of the bell. The whistle, bell and gong shall comply with the specification in Annex III to these Regulations. The bell or gong or both may be replaced by other equipment having the same respective sound characteristics, provided that manual sounding of the required signals shall always be possible.

ⓑ A vessel of **less than 12 metres** in length shall **not be obliged** to carry the sound signalling appliances prescribed in paragraph ⓐ of this Rule but if she does not, she shall be provided with some other means of making an efficient sound signal.

제 32 조
정 의

ⓐ 「기적」이라 함은 규칙 부속서 Ⅲ에 명시되어 있는 음을 발할 수 있는 음향신호기구를 말한다.

ⓑ 「단음」이라 함은 약 1초간의 취명을 말한다.

ⓒ 「장음」이라 함은 4초 내지 6초간의 취명을 말한다.

제 33 조
음향신호장비

ⓐ 길이 12미터 이상의 선박은 기적 1개를 그리고 길이 20미터 이상의 선박은 기적1개 및 호종 1개를 장비하여야 하며, 길이 100미터 이상의 선박은 이에 부가하여 음조 및 음성이 호종과 혼동되지 아니하는 동라 1개를 장비하여야 한다. 기적, 호종 및 동라는 이 규칙 부속서Ⅲ에 명시된 것과 일치하여야 한다. 호종 또는 동라 또는 이들 양자는 각기 동일한 음향특성을 가진 다른 장비로 대치될 수 있다. 다만, 이들은 규정된 신호를 수동으로도 항시 낼 수 있어야 한다.

ⓑ 길이 12미터 미만의 선박은 이 조문 ⓐ항에 규정된 음향신호기구를 장비하지 아니하여도 되지만, 이와 같은 기구를 장비하지 아니할 경우에는 유효한 음향신호를 발하는 다른 수단을 가져야 한다.

Rule 34
Manoeuvring and Warning Signals

ⓐ When vessels are in sight of one another, a power-driven vessel underway, when manoeuvring as authorized or required by these Rules, shall indicate that manoeuvre by the following signals on her whistle:

- **one short** blast to mean 'I am altering my course **to starboard**';

- **two short** blasts to mean 'I am altering my course **to port**';

- **three short** blasts to mean 'I am operating **astern propulsion**'.

ⓑ Any vessel may supplement the whistle signals prescribed in paragraph ⓐ of this Rule by **light signals**, repeated as appropriate, whilst the manoeuvre is being carried out:

(i) these light signals shall have the following significance:

- one flash to mean 'I am altering my course to starboard';

- two flashes to mean 'I am altering my course to port';

- three flashes to mean 'I am operating astern propulsion';

(ii) **the duration** of each flash shall be about **one second**, **the interval between flashes** shall be about **one second**, and the **interval between successive signals** shall be not **less than ten seconds;**

(iii) the light used for this signals shall, if fitted, be an **all-round white light**, visible at a **minimum range of 5 miles** and shall comply with the provisions of Annex I to these Regulations.

ⓒ When in sight of one another in a narrow channel or fairway:

(i) a vessel intending to overtake another shall in compliance with Rule 9(e)(i) indicate her intention by the following signals on her whistle :

- **two prolonged blasts** followed by **one short blast** to mean 'I intend to **overtake you on your starboard side**';
- **two prolonged blasts** followed by **two short blasts** to mean 'I intend to **overtake you on your port side**';

(ii) **the vessel about to be overtaken** when acting in accordance with Rule 9(e)(i) shall indicate **her agreement** by the following signal on her whistle:

- **one prolonged, one short, one prolonged and one short blast**, in that order.

(d) When vessels in sight of one another are approaching each other and from any cause either vessel **fails to understand** the intentions or actions of the other, or is in doubt whether sufficient action is being taken by the other to avoid collision, the vessel in doubt shall immediately indicate such doubt by giving **at least five short and rapid blasts** on the whistle. Such signal may be supplemented by a light signal of at least five short and rapid flashes.

(e) **A vessel nearing a bend** or an area of a channel or fairway where other vessels may be obscured by an intervening obstruction shall sound **one prolonged** blast. Such signal shall be answered with **a prolonged blast** by any approaching vessel that may be within hearing around the bend or behind the intervening obstruction.

(ⅰ) 타선을 추월하고자 하는 선박은, 제9조 (e)(ⅰ)에 따라 기적으로 다음 신호를 하여 자선의 의사를 표시하여야 한다. :
- 장음 2발 단음 1발 '본선은 귀선의 우현측으로 추월하고자 함'을 뜻한다 ;
- 장음 2발 단음 2발 '본선은 귀선의 좌현측으로 추월하고자 함'을 뜻한다 ;

(ⅱ) 피추월 선박은 제9조 (e)(ⅰ)에 따라 행동을 할 때에는 기적으로 다음 신호를 하여 자선의 동의를 표시하여야 한다 :
- 장음, 단음, 장음 및 단음.

(d) 시계 내에 있는 선박이 서로 접근하고 있을 때, 어떠한 사유로 인하여 한 선박이 다른 선박의 의도 또는 행동을 알지 못하는 경우 또는 충돌을 회피하기 위하여 다른 선박이 충분한 조치를 취하고 있는지의 여부가 의심스러운 경우는, 의심을 하는 선박은 기적으로 적어도 5회의 짧고 급속한 음향을 취명하여 그와 같은 의문을 즉시 표시하여야 한다. 그와 같은 신호는 적어도 5회의 짧고 급속한 섬광의 발광신호로써 보충될 수 있다.

(e) 중간에 개재하는 장애물로 인하여 다른 선박을 볼 수 없는 만곡부 또는 협수로 또는 항로의 수역에 접근하는 선박은 1회의 장음을 취명하여야 한다. 반대편 만곡부 또는 중간 장애물 뒤에서 접근하는 선박은 그러한 신호를 들었을 때에는 동일한 장음 1회의 신호로 응답하여야 한다.

ⓕ 100미터가 넘는 거리에 둘 이상의 기적을 설치하고 있는 선박은 조종 및 경고신호를 울릴 때에는 기적 1개만을 사용하여야 한다.

ⓕ If whistles are fitted on a vessel at a distance apart of more than **100 metres**, **one whistle only** shall be used for giving manoeuvring and warning signals.

기출문제

61. When you are navigating vessel in thick fog, you heard two short blasts on the whistle your starboard. What this means?　　　05년 2차

① Unknown vessel is changing course to port.
② Unknown vessel is changing course to starboard.
③ Unknown vessel is using engine now.
④ Unknown vessel is stopping now.

[해설] 단음 2회는 좌현 변침 중(course to port) 사용하는 음향신호이다.

답 ❶

62. 우현변침 시 사용해야 하는 기적은?　　　07년 2차

① one short blast
② two short blast
③ three short blast
④ one prolonged blast

[해설] 우현 변침 시 1회 단음을 사용한다.

답 ❶

기출문제

63. 다음은 COLREG(International Regulations for Preventing Collisions at Sea) RULE 34에 대한 것으로, 빈칸에 순서대로 들어갈 단어로 가장 옳은 것은? [21년도 하반기]

> When in sight of one another in a narrow channel or fairway:
>
> (i) a vessel intending to overtake another shall in compliance with Rule 9ⓔ(i) indicate her intention by the following signals on her whistle:
>
> - ( ) prolonged blast(s) followed by ( ) short blast(s) to mean 'I intend to overtake you on your port side':
>
> (ii) the vessel about to be overtaken when acting in accordance with Rule 9ⓔ(i) shall indicate her agreement by the following signal on her whistle:
>
> - ( ) prolonged, ( ) short, ( ) prolonged and ( ) short blast, in that order.

① one - one - two - one - two - one
② two - one - one - two - one - two
③ one - two - one - two - one - two
④ two - two - one - one - one - one

해설 (i) 좌현 추월을 하는 경우 2회 장음에 이은 2회 단음을 사용한다.
(ii) 추월되려는 선박이 상대선박의 행동에 동의한다면 1회 장음 1회 단음 1회 장음 1회 단음으로 그 동의를 표시한다.

답 ❹

64. 다음은 COLREG(국제해상충돌방지규칙)상 일반적인 항법에 관한 설명이다. 빈칸에 들어갈 말이 순서대로 올바르게 배열된 것은? [18년 3차 / 16년 일반직]

> When vessels in sight of one another are approaching each other and from any cause either vessel fails to understand ( ) or actions of the other, or is in doubt whether ( ) is being taken by the other to avoid collision, the vessel in doubt shall immediately indicate such doubt by giving ( ) and rapid ( ).

가. blasts on the whistle
나. at least five short
다. sufficient action
라. the intentions

① 라 - 다 - 나 - 가
② 라 - 다 - 가 - 나
③ 라 - 나 - 다 - 가
④ 다 - 라 - 가 - 나

해설 서로 상호 시계 내에 있는 선박이 서로 접근하고 있을 때, 어떠한 사유로 인하여 한 선박이 다른 선박의 의도 또는 행동을 알지 못하는 경우 또는 충돌을 회피하기 위하여 다른 선박이 충분한 조치를 취하고 있는지의 여부가 의심스러운 경우는, 의심을 하는 선박은 기적으로 적어도 5회의 짧고 급속한 음향을 취명하여 그와 같은 의문을 즉시 표시하여야 한다.

답 ❶

기출문제

65. 다음은 COLREG(International Regulations for Preventing Collisions at Sea) RULE 34에 대한 것이다. 빈칸에 들어갈 단어로 가장 옳은 것은? `19년 1차`

> In a narrow channel, a vessel nearing a bend where other vessels may be obscured shall sound (   ).

① one prolonged blast
② one short blast
③ five short and rapid blasts
④ one prolonged and one short blast

해설 타선이 가려지는 만곡부(bend)의 선박은 1회의 장음을 울려준다.

답 ❶

66. 다음 빈 칸에 들어갈 말로 가장 적절한 것은? `15년 일반직`

> A vessel nearing a bend or an area of a channel or fairway where other vessels may be obscured by an intervening obstruction shall sound (   ) prolonged blast.

① one   ② two
③ four   ④ five

해설 위 문제와 동일

답 ❶

67. 다음 COLREG(International Regulation for Preventing Collision at Sear)상 문장의 빈칸에 들어갈 말로 가장 옳은 것은? `20년 1차`

> A vessel nearing a bend or an area of a channel or fairway where other vessels may be obscured by an intervening obstruction shall sound (   ). Such signal shall be answered with a prolonged blast by any approaching vessel that may be within hearing around the bend or behind the intervening obstruction.

① two prolonged blasts
② one short blast
③ one prolonged blast
④ two short blasts

해설 위 문제와 동일

답 ❸

Rule 35
Sound Signals in restricted Visibility

In or near an area of restricted visibility, whether by day or night, the signals prescribed in this Rule shall be used as follows:

ⓐ **A power-driven vessel making way through the water** shall sound at intervals of not more than **2 minutes one prolonged blast.**

ⓑ **A power-driven vessel underway but stopped and making no way through the water** shall sound at intervals of not more than 2 minutes **two prolonged blasts** in succession with an interval of **about 2 seconds** between them.

ⓒ A vessel not under command, a vessel restricted in her ability to manoeuvre, a vessel constrained by her draught, a sailing vessel, a vessel engaged in fishing and a vessel engaged in towing or pushing another vessel shall, instead of the signals prescribed in paragraphs ⓐ or ⓑ of this Rule sound at intervals of not more than 2 minutes three blasts in succession, namely **one prolonged** followed by **two short** blasts.

ⓓ A vessel engaged in fishing, when at anchor, and a vessel restricted in her ability to manoeuvre when carrying out her work at anchor, shall instead of the signals prescribed in paragraph ⓖ of this Rule sound the signal prescribed in paragraph ⓒ of this Rule.

ⓔ **A vessel towed** or if more than one vessel is towed the **last** vessel of the tow, if manned, shall at intervals of not more than 2 minutes sound four blasts in succession, namely **one prolonged** followed by **three short** blasts. When practicable, this signal shall be made immediately **after** the signal made by the towing vessel.

제 35 조
제한 시계 내에서의 음향신호

제한시계의 수역 내 또는 그의 부근에 있어서, 주야를 막론하고 이 조문에 규정된 신호는 다음과 같이 사용되어야 한다 :

ⓐ 대수속력이 있는 동력선은 2분을 초과하지 아니하는 간격으로 장음 1회를 울리어야 한다.

ⓑ 항해 중 정선하여 대수속력이 없는 동력선은, 장음간격을 약 2초로 하여 장음 2회를 2분을 초과하지 아니하는 간격으로 울리어야 한다.

ⓒ 운전부자유선, 조종성능이 제한된 선박, 자선의 흘수로 인하여 제한을 받는 선박, 범선, 어로에 종사하고 있는 선박 및 타선을 예인하거나 또는 밀고 있는 선박은 이 조문 ⓐ항 또는 ⓑ항에 규정된 신호 대신에, 2분간을 초과하지 아니하는 간격으로 연속 3음 즉, 장음 1회에 이어 단음 2회를 울리어야 한다.

ⓓ 어로에 종사하면서 닻을 내리고 있는 선박과 작업을 수행하면서 닻을 내리고 있어서 기동성에 크게 제한을 받는 선박은 이 조문의 ⓖ항에 규정된 신호대신에 이 조문 ⓒ항에 규정된 음향신호를 발하여야 한다.

ⓔ 피예인선박 또는 2척 이상의 선박이 피예인되는 경우에는 그 예인의 최후단 선박은, 승조원이 승선하고 있는 경우, 2분을 초과하지 아니하는 간격으로 4회의 연속음 즉, 장음 1회에 단 음 3회를 울리어야 한다. 실행가능한 경우, 본신호는 예인선이 신호를 한 직후 하여야 한다.

ⓕ 전방으로 밀고 있는 선박 및 밀리고 있는 선박이 견고하게 연결되어 복합체로 되어 있는 경우, 이들은 1척의 동력선으로 간주되며 이 조문 ⓐ 및 ⓑ항에 규정된 신호를 하여야 한다.

ⓖ 정박 중인 선박은 1분을 초과하지 아니하는 간격으로 약 5초 동안 급속히 호종을 울리어야 한다. 길이 100미터 이상의 선박에 있어서, 호종은 선박의 전부에서 울리어야 하며 이 호종을 울린 직후 선박의 후부에서 동라(징)를 약 5초 동안 급속히 울리어야 한다. 정박 중인 동력선은 이에 부가하여, 접근하는 선박에 대하여 자선의 위치 및 충돌의 가능성을 경고하기 위하여 연속된 3음 즉, 단음, 장음, 단음을 울릴 수 있다.

ⓗ 좌초선은 호종신호 및 요구되는 경우 이 조문 ⓖ항에 규정된 동라신호를 하여야 하며, 이에 부가하여, 급속히 울린 호종음의 직전 및 직후에 각각 분리되어 명확하게 3회 타종하여야 한다. 좌초선은 이에 부가하여 적절한 기적신호를 할 수 있다.

ⓘ 길이 12미터 이상 20미터 미만의 선박은 이 규칙의 제ⓖ 및 ⓗ항에 규정된 호종 신호를 울릴 필요는 없다. 그러나 그러한 선박이 호종 신호를 울리지 아니하면, 다른 유효한 음향 신호를 2분 이상의 간격으로 발하여야 한다.

ⓙ 길이 12미터 미만의 선박은 위의 신호를 의무적으로 할 필요는 없으나 이들 신호를 하지 아니하는 경우, 2분을 초과하지 아니하는 간격으로 기타 유효한 음향신호를 하여야 한다.

ⓚ 도선업무에 종사하고 있는 경우의 도선선은 이 조문 ⓐ항, ⓑ항 또는 ⓖ항에 규정된 신호에 부가하여, 단음 4회로 된 식별신호를 할 수 있다.

ⓕ When a pushing vessel and a vessel being pushed ahead are rigidly connected in a composite unit they shall be regarded as a power-driven vessel and shall give the signals prescribed in paragraphs ⓐ or ⓑ of this Rule.

ⓖ **A vessel at anchor** shall at intervals of not more than **one minute** ring the **bell** rapidly for about **5 seconds.** In a vessel of **100 metres** or more in length the bell shall be sounded in the forepart of the vessel and immediately after the ringing of the bell **the gong** shall be sounded rapidly for about **5 seconds** in the after part of the vessel. A vessel at anchor may in addition sound three blasts in succession, namely **one short, one prolonged and one short blast**, to give warning of her position and of the possibility of collision to an approaching vessel.

ⓗ A vessel aground shall give the bell signal and if required the gone signal prescribed in paragraph ⓖ of this Rule and shall, in addition, give three separate and distinct strokes on the bell immediately before and after the rapid ringing of the bell. A vessel aground may in addition sound an appropriate whistle signal.

ⓘ A vessel of 12 metres or more but less than 20 metres in length shall not be obliged to give the bell signals prescribed in paragraphs ⓖ and ⓗ of this Rule. However, if she does not, she shall make some other efficient sound signal at intervals of not more than 2 minutes.

ⓙ A vessel of less than 12 metres in length shall not be obliged to give the above-mentioned signals but, if she does not, shall make some other efficient sound signal at intervals of not more than 2 minutes.

ⓚ **A pilot vessel** when engaged on pilotage duty may in addition to the signals prescribed in paragraphs ⓐ, ⓑ or ⓖ of this Rule sound an identity signal consisting of **four short blasts.**

⟨ Signalling ⟩

●   Turning to starboard
●●   Turning to port
●●●   Astern
●●●●●   Unsure of your intentions

━━ ━━ ●   Overtaking starboard side
━━ ━━ ● ●   Overtaking port side
━━ ● ━━ ●   OK
━━   Approaching band or obstruction

⟨ FOG ⟩

━━   Power-driven vessel
━━ ● ●   Power-driven vessel; stopped
━━ ●   Other vessel
━━ ● ● ●   Towed vessel (in response)
● ━━ ●   Anchored; warning
● ● ● ●   Pilot vessel

Bell & Gong   Anchored

Ⅰ 기출문제

68. 다음 중 빈칸에 들어갈 단어로 가장 옳은 것은? `18년 일반직`

> In or near an area of restricted visibility, (　　　) making way through the water shall sound at intervals of not more than 2 minutes one prolonged blast.

① A vessel engaged in fishing　② A power-driven vessel
③ A vessel not under command　④ A vessel at anchor

해설 제한시계에서, 대수속력이 있는 동력선은 2분을 초과하지 않는 간격으로 장음 1회를 울려야 한다.

답 ❷

69. 다음 〈보기〉는 COLREG RULE 34(Manoeuvring and warning signals)와 RULE 35(Sound signals in restricted visibility)에 관한 설명이다. 빈 칸에 들어갈 말로 가장 옳은 것은? `21년 상반기`

> ㉠ Two prolonged blasts followed by two short blasts to mean 'I intend to overtake you on your (ⓐ)'.
> ㉡ If whistles are fitted on a vessel at a distance apart of more than (ⓑ), one whistle only shall be used for giving manoeuvring and warning signals.
> ㉢ A power-driven vessel (ⓒ) through the water shall sound at intervals of not more than 2 minutes one prolonged blast.
> ㉣ A vessel (ⓓ) shall sound at intervals of not more than 2 minutes three blasts in succession, namely one prolonged followed by two short blasts.

	ⓐ	ⓑ	ⓒ	ⓓ
①	port side	100 metres	making way	engaged in towing
②	port side	100 metres	making no way	towed
③	starboard side	50 metres	making way	towed
④	port side	50 metres	making no way	engaged in towing

해설
㉠ 2회 장음 2회 단음은 ⓐ좌현(port side) 추월 시 사용한다.
㉡ 만일 선박의 기적들이 ⓑ100미터를 초과한 거리에 설치돼 있다면 하나의 기적만이 조종이나 경고 신호를 위해 사용되어야만 한다.
㉢ 동력선이 ⓒ대수속력을 가지고(making way) 항해중인 경우 2분을 넘지 않는 간격으로 1회의 장음을 울려줘야 한다.
㉣ ⓓ예인작업중인(engaged in towing) 선박은 2분을 넘지 않는 간격으로 3회의 연속음을 울려준다 즉 1회의 장음에 이은 2회의 단음이다.

답 ❶

기출문제

70. A vessel loses her engine during fog. What fog signal would she sound?

11년 2차

① prolonged blast of whistle
② prolonged-short blasts of whistle
③ prolonged-short-short blasts of whistle
④ prolonged-short-short-short blasts of whistle

해설 무중에 기관이 꺼진 선박 즉 조종불능선(vessel not under command)은 <u>1회의 장음에 이은 2회의 단음</u>을 울려준다.

답 ❸

71. 다음은 〈COLREG(International Regulations for Preventing Collision at Sea)〉상 음향신호에 대한 설명이다. 옳지 않은 것은 모두 몇 개인가?

20년 3차

1. A power driven vessel underway but stopped and making no way through the water shall sound at intervals of not more than ⓐ <u>2 minutes</u> ⓑ <u>one prolonged blast</u> in succession with an interval about ⓒ <u>1 second</u> between them.
2. A vessel at anchor shall at interval of not more than ⓓ <u>2 minutes</u> ring the bell rapidly for about ⓔ <u>5 seconds</u>. In vessel of ⓕ <u>100meters</u> or more in length the bell shall be sounded in the forepart of the vessel and immediately after the ringing of the bell the gong shall be sounded rapidly for ⓖ <u>5 seconds</u> in the after part of the vessel.

① 1개　　　　　　　　② 2개
③ 3개　　　　　　　　④ 4개

해설
1. 항해 중 정선하여 대수속력이 없는 동력선은, 장음간격을 ⓒ약 2초로 하여 ⓑ장음 2회를 ⓐ2분을 초과하지 아니하는 간격으로 울려야 한다.
2. 정박 중인 선박은 ⓓ1분을 초과하지 아니하는 간격으로 약 ⓔ5초 동안 급속히 호종을 울려야 한다. 길이 ⓕ100미터 이상의 선박에 있어서, 호종은 선박의 전부에서 울려야 하며 이 호종을 울린 직후 선박의 후부에서 동라(징)를 약 ⓖ5초 동안 급속히 울려야 한다.
옳지 않은 것: ⓑ, ⓒ, ⓓ

답 ❸

기출문제

72. 다음은 COLREG(International Regulations for Preventing Collisions at Sea)의 제한시계 내에서의 음향신호이다. 빈칸에 알맞은 수를 모두 합한 값은?　　21년 하반기

㉠ A vessel at anchor shall at intervals of not more than ( ) minute ring the bell rapidly for about ( ) seconds.

㉡ In a vessel of ( ) metres or more in length the bell shall be sounded in the forepart of the vessel and immediately after the ringing of the bell the gong shall be sounded rapidly for about ( ) seconds in the after part of the vessel.

㉢ A vessel of less than ( ) metres in length shall not be obliged to give the above-mentioned signals but, if she does not, shall make some other efficient sound signal at intervals of not more than ( ) minutes.

① 125　　　　　　　　② 129
③ 137　　　　　　　　④ 141

해설　㉠ 정박선은 (1)분을 넘지 않는 간격으로 호종을 급속하게 약 (5)초간 울려야한다.
㉡ 길이 (100)미터 이상의 선박은 호종을 선수부에서 울리고 호종을 울린 바로 그 다음에 징(동라)을 약 (5)초간 울려야한다.
㉢ 길이 (12)미터 미만의 선박은 위에서 언급한 신호를 울릴 의무는 없지만, 만약 그렇지 않다면 다른 유효한 음향신호를 (2)분을 넘지 않는 간격으로 울릴 수 있다.
　　1+5+100+5+12+2= 125

답 ①

Rule 36
Signals to attract Attention

If necessary to attract the attention of another vessel any vessel may make light or sound signals that cannot be mistaken for any signal authorized elsewhere in these Rules, or may direct the beam of her searchlight in the direction of the danger, in such a way as not to embarrass any vessel. Any light to attract the attention of another vessel shall be such that it can not be mistaken for any aid to navigation. For the purpose of this Rule the use of high intensity intermittent or revolving lights, such as strove lights, shall be avoided.

Rule 37
Distress Signals

When a vessel is in distress and requires assistance she shall use or exhibit the signals described in Annex IV to these Regulations.

제 36 조
주의환기 신호

다른 선박의 주의를 환기할 필요가 있을 경우에는, 모든 선박은, 이 규칙의 다른 조항에서 정한 신호와 오인되지 아니하는 방법으로, 위험이 있는 쪽으로 탐조등을 비출 수 있다. 타 선박의 주의를 환기시키기 위한 어떤 등화도 항로표지 등으로 오인될 수 없는 것이어야 한다. 이 조문의 설치 목적에 비추어 볼 때 스트로브등화(갑자기 반짝하는 등화)와 같은 고광도의 간헐적인 등화 또는 회전등 등의 사용은 피하여야 한다.

제 37 조
조난신호

선박이 조난을 당하여 구조를 요청할 때에는 이 규칙 부속서 IV에 규정된 신호를 사용하거나 표시하여야 한다.

PART E – Exemptions

제 38 조
적용유보 규정

1960년의 국제해상충돌예방규칙의 요구조건에 일치된다는 조건하에 이 조약이 실시되기 이전에 용골이 놓였거나, 또는 건조단계에 있는 선박 [또는 유형의 선박]은 다음과 같이 적용에서 유보될 수 있다.

ⓐ 22조에 규정된 시인거리를 갖는 등화의 설치는 이 규칙을 시행한 날로부터 4년까지 유보 (시한 만료).

ⓑ 이 규칙 부속서 I 의 7절에 규정된 색조를 가진 등화의 설치는 이 규칙을 시행한 날로부터 4년까지 유보(시한 만료).

ⓒ 인치(inch)단위에서 미터(meter) 단위로 바꾸고 남은 끝 수치 때문에 생기는 등화의 재배치는 영구히 유보(유효).

ⓓ

(i) 이 규칙 부속서 I 의 3절 ⓐ항에 규정한 결과에 의하여, 길이 150 미터 미만의 선박의 마스트정부 등을 재배치 하는 것은 영구히 면제(유효).

(ii) 이 규칙 부속서 I 의 3절 ⓐ항의 규정에 의하여 길이 150미터 이상의 선박의 마스트정부등을 재배치하여야 하는 것은 이 규칙 시행 이후 9년까지 유보(시한 만료).

Rule 38
Exemptions

Any vessel (or class of vessels) provided that she complies with the requirements of the International Regulations for Preventing Collisions at Sea, 1960, the keel of which is laid or which is at a corresponding stage of construction before the entry into force of these Regulations may be exempted from compliance therewith as follows:

ⓐ The installation of lights with ranges prescribed in Rule 22, until four years after the date of entry into force of these Regulations.

ⓑ The installation of lights with colour specifications as prescribed in Section 7 of Annex I to these Regulations, until four years after the date of entry into force of these Regulations.

ⓒ The repositioning of lights as a result of conversion from Imperial to metric units and rounding off measurement figures, permanent exemption.

ⓓ

(i) The repositioning of masthead lights on vessels of less than 150 meters in length, resulting from the prescriptions of Section 3ⓐ of Annex I to these Regulations, permanent exemption.

(ii) The repositioning of masthead lights on vessels of 150 meters or more in length, resulting from the prescriptions of Section 3ⓐ of Annex I to these Regulations, until nine years after the date of entry into force of these Regulations.

ⓔ The repositioning of masthead lights resulting from the prescriptions of Section 2ⓑ of Annex I to these Regulations, until nine years after the date of entry into force of these Regulations.

ⓕ The repositioning of sidelights resulting from the prescriptions of Sections 2ⓖ and 3ⓑ of Annex I to these Regulations, until nine years after the date of entry into force of these Regulations.

ⓖ The requirements for sound signal appliances prescribed in Annex III to these regulations, until nine years after the date of entry into force of these Regulations.

ⓗ The repositioning of all-round lights resulting from the prescription of Section 9ⓑ of AnnexI to these Regulations, permanent exemption.

ⓔ 이 규칙 부속서Ⅰ의 2절 ⓑ항의 규정에 의하여 마스트정부등을 재배치하는 것은 이 규칙 시행일로부터 9년까지 유보(시한만료).

ⓕ 이 규칙 부속서Ⅰ의 2절 ⓖ항 및 3절 ⓑ항의 규정에 의하여 현등을 재배치하는 것은 이 규칙 시행일로부터 9년까지 유보(시한만료).

ⓖ 이 규칙 부속서Ⅱ에 규정한 음향 신호장치의 구비는 이 규칙 시행일부터 9년까지 유보(시한 만료).

ⓗ 이 규칙 부속서Ⅰ의 9절 ⓑ항의 규정에 의한 전주등의 재배치는 영구히 면제한다(유효).

해사영어 기본이론 임하람

PART 05 SOLAS (International Convention for the Safety of Life at Sea)

Chapter 1 Definitions 정의
Chapter 2 Exceptions 적용제외
Chapter 3 안전 증서
Chapter 4 SOLAS 규정
Chapter 5 SOLAS의 아직 출제되지 않은 규정

chapter 01 Definitions 정의

선박 및 일반용어	meaning	의미
Administration 주관청	the government of the State whose flag the ship is entitled to fly	선박이 국가의 국기를 게양할 자격을 가진 국가의 정부
International voyage 국제항해	a voyage from a country to which the present Convention applies to a port outside such country, or conversely	협약이 적용되는 한 국가에서 그 국외의 항에 이르는 항해 또는 그 반대의 항해
Passenger 여객	every person other than: (i) the master and the member of the crew or other persons employed or engaged in any capacity on board a ship and (ii) a child under one year of age	다음 이외의 자를 말한다: (i) 선장과 선원 또는 자격여하를 불문하고 승선하여 선박의 업무에 고용되거나 종사하는 기타의 자; 그리고 (ii) 1세 미만의 유아
Passenger ship 여객선	any ship which carries more than twelve passengers	12인을 초과하는 여객을 운송하는 선박을 말한다.
Cargo ship 화물선	any ship which is not a passenger ship	여객선이 아닌 모든 선박
Tanker 유조선	a cargo ship constructed or adapted for the carriage in bulk of liquid cargoes of an inflammable nature	인화성 액체화물의 산적운송을 위하여 건조되거나 개조된 화물선
New ship 신조선	a ship the keel of which is laid or which is at a similar stage of construction on or after 25 May 1980	1980년 5월 25일 이후에 용골을 거치하거나 동등한 건조 단계에 있는 선박
Existing ship 현존선	a ship which is not a new ship	신조선이 아닌 선박
구조 용어	meaning	의미
Weathertight 풍우밀	that in any sea conditions water will not penetrate into the ship	풍우밀이란 어떠한 해상상태에서도 선박에 물이 들어오지 않는 것을 말한다.
Watertight 수밀	having scantlings and arrangements capable of preventing the passage of water in any direction under the head of water likely to occur in intact and damaged conditions. In the damaged condition, the head of water is to be considered in the worst situation at equilibrium, including intermediate stages of flooding	비손상 및 손상상태에서 생길 수 있는 수두에서 어떠한 방향으로도 물이 통과하는 막을 수 있는 재료치수 및 배치를 말한다. 손상상태에서 수두는 침수의 중간과정을 포함하여 최악의 평형상태에 있는 것으로 간주하여야 한다.

Dead ship condition	the condition under which the main propulsion plant, boilers and auxiliaries are not in operation due to the absence of power.	동력이 공급되지 않아 주추진 장치, 보일러 및 보조기관이 작동하지 않는 상태를 말한다.
Main switchboard 주 배전반	a switchboard which is directly supplied by the main source of electrical power and is intended to distribute electrical energy to the ship's services.	주전원으로부터 직접 전력을 공급받아 선박의 여러 장치에 전력을 배급하는 배전반을 말한다.
Main source of electrical power 주전원	a source intended to supply electrical power to the main switchboard for distribution to all services necessary for maintaining the ship in normal operational and habitable condition.	선박을 정상적인 작동 및 거주상태로 유지하는데 필요한 모든 기능을 위하여 전력을 배급하는 주배전반에 전력을 공급하기 위한 전원을 말한다.
Emergency switchboard 비상 배전반	a switchboard which in the event of failure of the main electrical power supply system is directly supplied by the emergency source of electrical power.	주전원으로부터의 공급이 차단된 경우에 비상전원으로 공급되는 배전반을 말한다.
Emergency source of electrical power 비상전원	a source of electrical power, intended to supply the emergency switchboard in the event of failure of the supply from the main source of electrical power.	비상전원이란 주전원으로부터 공급이 차단된 경우에 비상배전반에 전력을 공급하기 위한 전원을 말한다.
조타기 용어	meaning	의미
Steering gear control system 조타장치제어계통	the equipment by which orders are transmitted from the navigating bridge to the steering gear power units. Steering gear control systems comprise transmitters, receivers, hydraulic control pumps and their associated motors, motor controllers, piping and cables.	명령이 선교로부터 조타장치의 동력장치에 전달되는 장치를 말한다. 조타장치제어 계통은 송신기, 수신기, 유압제어 펌프와 부속전동기, 전동기제어기, 관 및 전선으로 구성되어 있다.
Main steering gear 주조타장치	the machinery, rudder actuators, steering gear, power units, if any, and ancillary equipment and the means of applying torque to the rudder stock (e.g. tiller or quadrant) necessary for effecting movement of the rudder for the purpose of steering the ship under normal service conditions.	조타기계, 라다-액츄에이터, 조타장치의 동력장치, 보조설비 및 통상 항행상태에서 조선을 위하여 타를 유효하게 동작하는 데 필요한 회전력을 타두재에 주는 장치(예를 들면, 틸러 또는 쿼드란트)를 말한다.
Auxiliary steering gear 보조조타장치	the equipment other than any part of the main steering gear necessary to steer the ship in the event of failure of the main steering gear but not including the tiller, quadrant or components serving the same purpose.	주조타장치에 고장이 생긴 경우에 선박을 조종하는데 필요한 주조타 장치의 어느 부분과도 분리된 장치를 말한다. 다만, 틸러, 쿼드란트 또는 이와 같은 목적으로 사용되는 기기는 제외한다.

Steering gear power unit 조타장치의 동력장치	1. in the case of electric steering gear, an electric motor and its associated electrical equipment; 2. in the case of electrohydraulic steering gear, an electric motor and its associated electrical equipment and connected pump; or 3. in the case of other hydraulic steering gear, a driving engine and connected pump.	1. 전동조타장치에 대하여는 전동기 및 관련 전기설비 2. 전동유압 조타장치에 대하여는 전동기와 관련 전기설비 및 전동기에 연결된 펌프 3. 전동유압조타장치 이외의 유압조타장치에 대하여는 구동기관 및 이것에 연결된 펌프
구명	meaning	의미
Float-free launching 자유부양식 진수	method of launching a survival craft whereby the craft is automatically released from a sinking ship and is ready for use	Float free 진수 방식은 선박이 물에 잠긴 선박에서 자동으로 구명정을 진수시키는 방식이다.
Free-fall launching 자유낙하식 진수	method of launching a survival craft whereby the craft with its complement of persons and equipment on board is released and allowed to fall into the sea without any restraining apparatus	Free-fall 진수 방식은 수동으로 선박장치를 통해서 생존정을 선박에서 방출 시키고, 바다에 어떠한 억제 장치 없이 낙하시킨다.
Inflatable appliance 팽창식 설비	an appliance which depends upon non-rigid, gasfilled chambers for buoyancy and which is normally kept uninflated until ready for use	부력유지를 위하여 가스로 채워진, 딱딱하지 아니한 부력실에 의존하며, 사용 전까지는 팽창되지 아니한 상태로 유지되는 설비를 말한다.
Inflated appliance 팽창된 설비	an appliance which depends upon non-rigid, gasfilled chambers for buoyancy and which is kept inflated and ready for use at all times	부력유지를 위하여 가스로 채워진, 딱딱하지 아니한 부력실에 의존하며, 팽창되어 있는 상태로 언제든지 사용할 수 있도록 준비가 되어있는 설비를 말한다.
Embarkation ladder 승정사다리	the ladder provided at survival craft embarkation stations to permit safe access to survival craft after launching.	진수 후에 생존정에 안전하게 승정할 수 있도록 생존정 승정장소에 설치된 사다리
Anti-exposure suit	protective suit for use by rescue boat and marine evacuation system parties	Anti-exposure suit 는 구조정 멤버, 그리고 해양 탈출시스템 승조원 전용 보호 복이다.
Immersion suit 방수복	a protective suit which reduces the body heat loss of a person wearing it in cold water.	찬 수중에서 사람의 체열을 감소시키지 않도록 보온해주는 보호복을 말한다.
Thermal protective aid 보온복	a bag or suit made of waterproof material with low thermal conductivity	저온 전도성을 가진 방수물질 로 만들어진 포대기 또는 옷을 말한다.
Survival craft 생존정	a craft capable of sustaining the lives of persons in distress from the time of abandoning the ship *shall be stowed in a state of continuous readiness so that two crew members can carry out preparations for embarkation and launching in less than 5 min*	퇴선 시로 부터 조난 중에 있는 사람의 생명을 유지 시켜 줄 수 있는 배를 말한다. *두 사람이 5분 내에 승성 및 진수를 할 수 있어야한다.*

Rescue boat 구조정	a boat designed to rescue persons in distress and to marshal survival craft. *shall be stowed in a state of continuous readiness for launching in not more than 5min*	조난 중에 있는 사람을 구조하고 또한 생존정을 향도하기 위하여 설계된 보트를 말한다. *5분 이내에 진수할 수 있도록 계속 준비된 상태로 탑재되어야 한다.*
Marine evacuation system 해상탈출설비	an appliance for the rapid transfer of persons from the embarkation deck of a ship to a floating survival craft.	선박의 승정갑판부터 물위에 떠 있는 생존정으로 사람을 신속히 옮길 수 있게 하는 장치를 말한다.
Detection 탐지	the determination of the location of survivors or survival craft.	생존자 또는 생존정의 위치를 결정하는 것을 말한다.
Locating 발견	finding of ships, aircraft units or persons in distress.	조난에 빠진 선박이나 항공기 및 사람을 찾는 것
Recovery time 회수시간	for a rescue boat is the time required to raise the boat to a position where persons on board can disembark to the deck of the ship. Recovery time includes the time required to make preparations for recovery on board the rescue boat such as passing and securing a painter, connecting the rescue boat to the launching appliance, and the time to raise the rescue boat.	선박의 갑판 상에 사람들을 내려놓을 수 있는 위치까지 구조정을 올리는 데 필요한 시간을 말한다. 이 회수시간에는 페인터를 전달하여 고박 하는 시간, 진수설비에 구조정을 연결하는 시간, 구조정을 올리는데 필요한 시간이 포함되어야 한다.
Retrieval 회수	the safe recovery of survivors.	생존자를 안전하게 복귀시키는 것

기출문제

01. In SOLAS'83 a passenger ship is a ship which carries more than (   ) passengers.

15년 3차

① 12　　　　② 13
③ 14　　　　④ 15

해설 12인을 초과하는 여객을 운송하는 선박을 여객선(passengers ship)이라 말한다.

답 ❶

02. 다음 SOLAS(International Convention for the Safety of Life at Sea, 1974)상 빈칸에 들어갈 말로 가장 옳은 것은?

20년 1차

(　　　) means the condition under which the main propulsion plant, boilers and auxiliaries are not in operation due to the absence of power.

① Deadship condition　　　② Emergency condition
③ Distress　　　　　　　　④ Abandon vessel

해설 데드쉽 상태(Deadship condition)란 동력이 공급되지 않아 주추진 장치, 보일러 및 보조기관이 작동하지 않는(not in operation) 상태를 말한다.

답 ❶

03. Choose the best one for the blank.

12년 2차

"(　　　　　)" means that in any sea conditions water will not penetrate into the ship.

① Bulkhead deck　　　② Packing
③ Watertight　　　　　④ Uppermost deck

해설 풍우밀(Weathertight)이란 어떠한 해상상태에서도 선박에 물이 들어오지 않는 것을 말한다.
　　해당 기출 문제는 오류가 있다. 보기는 풍우밀(Weathertight)에 대한 설명이나 정답은 수밀(Watertight)이었다.

답 ❸

기출문제

04. 다음 중 SOLAS(International Convention for the Safety of Life at Sea)원문의 내용과 일치하지 않은 것은 모두 몇 개인가? 〔21년 하반기〕

㉠ "Free-fall Launching" is that method of launching a survival craft whereby the craft is automatically released from a sinking ship and is ready for use
㉡ "Dead ship condition" means the condition under which the main propulsion plant, boilers and auxiliaries are not in operation due to the absence of power
㉢ "Rescue boat" is a boat designed to rescue persons in distress and to marshal survival craft
㉣ "Retrieval"is the safe recovery of survivors

① 없음 ② 1개
③ 2개 ④ 3개

해설 옳지 않은 것:
㉠ 자유부양식 진수(Float-free Launching)에 대한 설명이다.

답 ❷

05. 다음 〈보기〉는 「SOLAS(International Convention for the Safety of Life at Sea)」의 내용이다. 빈 칸에 공통으로 들어갈 용어로 가장 옳은 것은? 〔22년 일반직〕

(   ) for a rescue boat is the time required to raise the boat to a position where persons on board can disembark to the deck of the ship.
(   ) includes the time required to make preparations for recovery on board the rescue boat such as passing and securing a painter, connecting the rescue boat to the launching appliance, and the time to raise the rescue boat.

① Recovery time ② Retrieval
③ Launching time ④ Embarkation time

해설 회수시간(Recovery time)에 대한 설명이다.

답 ❶

기출문제

06. 다음 〈보기〉는 「SOLAS(International Convention for the Safety of Life at Sea)」 상용어의 정의이다. 옳지 않은 것은 모두 몇 개인가?　　　22년 일반직

> ㉠ Steering gear control system : the equipment by which orders are transmitted from the navigating bridge to the steering gear power units.
> ㉡ Auxiliary steering gear : the machinery, rudder actuators, steering gear, power units, if any, and ancillary equipment and the means of applying torque to the rudder stock(e.g. tiller or quadrant) necessary for effecting movement of the rudder for the purpose of steering the ship under normal service conditions.
> ㉢ Steering gear power unit : the equipment other than any part of the main steering gear necessary to steer the ship in the event of failure of the main steering gear but not including the tiller, quadrant or components serving the same purpose.
> ㉣ Free-fall launching : method of launching a survival craft whereby the craft is automatically released from a sinking ship and is ready for use.

① 1개　　② 2개
③ 3개　　④ 4개

해설 옳지 않은 것:
　㉡ 주조타장치(Main steering gear)에 대한 설명이다.
　㉢ 보조조타장치(Auxiliary steering gear)에 대한 설명이다.
　㉣ 자유부양식진수(Float-free launching)에 대한 설명이다.

답 ③

chapter 02 Exceptions 적용제외

The present regulations, unless expressly provided otherwise, do not apply to:

① Ships of war and troopships
② **Cargo** ships of less than **500** tons gross tonnage
③ Ships **not** propelled by mechanical means
④ Wooden ships of primitive build
⑤ Pleasure yachts **not** engaged in trade
⑥ Fishing vessels

이 규칙은 별도의 명문규정이 없는 한 다음 선박에는 적용하지 아니한다.

① 전쟁 및 군인 수송선
② 총톤수 500톤이 넘지 않는 화물선
③ 기관을 사용하지 않는 선박
④ 원시적으로 만들어진 목선
⑤ 무역에 사용되지 않고 오락으로 사용되는 요트
⑥ 어선

기출문제

01. Which ship is exempted from installation of radiography and radio telephony equipment?

10년 2차

① A yacht engaged in trade
② A sailing boat of 500 tons of gross tonnage
③ A cargo ship of 400 tons of gross tonnage
④ A tanker of 1,000 tons of gross tonnage which navigates only in a lake and river.

해설 SOLAS적용 제외 선박 조건 중 500톤을 넘지 않는 화물선에 ③이 해당한다.(총톤수 400톤의 선박) ①의 경우 무역에 사용된다고 되어있기 때문에 SOLAS적용 선박이다.

답 ③

02. 다음 중 「SOLAS(The International Convention for the Safety of Life at Sea)」상 적용제외 선박은 모두 몇 개인가?

20년 3차

㉠ Wooden ships of primitive build.
㉡ Ships not propelled by mechanical means.
㉢ Passenger ships of less than 500 tons gross tonnage.
㉣ Ships of war and troopships.
㉤ Fishing vessels.
㉥ Pleasure yachts engaged in trade.

① 2개 ② 3개
③ 4개 ④ 5개

해설 옳지 않은 것:
㉢ Passenger ship은 톤수 상관없이 SOLAS적용 선박이다. Cargo ship이 500톤 미만인 경우 SOLAS적용이 제외 된다.
㉥ 여가용 요트는 무역에 종사하지 않는 경우 SOLAS적용 제외이다. Pleasure yachts **not** engaged in trade가 되어야 한다.

답 ③

chapter 03 안전 증서

Duration and validity of certificates

A Passenger Ship Safety Certificate shall be issued for a period **not exceeding 12months**. A Cargo Ship Safety Construction Certificate, Cargo Ship Safety Equipment Certificate and Cargo Ship Safety Radio Certificate shall be issued for a period specified by the Administration which shall **not exceed five years**. An Exemption Certificate **shall not be Valid** for longer than the period of the certificate to which it refers

증서의 유효기간 및 효력

여객선안전증서는 12개월을 초과하지 아니하는 기간에 대하여 발급하여야 한다. 화물선안전구조증서, 화물선안전설비증서 및 화물선 안전 무선증서는 주관청이 규정한 5년을 초과하지 아니하는 기간에 대하여 발급하여야 한다. 면제증서의 경우 관련증서의 유효기간을 초과하는 기간을 대하여서는 그 효력을 상실한다.

기출문제

01. 다음은 〈SOLAS(The international Convention for the safety of life at Sea)〉상 증서의 유효기간 효력에 관한 규정이다. 옳은 것은 모두 몇 개인가? `20년 3차`

> A Passenger ship safety certificate shall be issued for a period ⓐ not exceeding 12 months. A Cargo Ship Construction Certificate, Cargo Ship Safety Equipment Certificate and Cargo Ship Safety Radio Certificate shall be issued for a period specified ⓑ by the Administration which shall ⓒ not exceed five years. An Exemption Certificate ⓓ shall be valid for longer than the period of the certificate to which it refers

① 1개 ② 2개
③ 3개 ④ 4개

해설 옳지 않은 것
ⓓ 면제 증서(Exemption Certificate)의 유효기간은 해당 증서에 명시된 유효기간을 초과하여 유효해서는 안 된다. (shall <u>not</u> be valid)

답

chapter 04

SOLAS 규정

01
Drill 훈련

① 화재훈련 퇴선 훈련 규정 : 매달 1회 실시
Every crew member shall participate in at least **one abandon ship drill** and **one fire drill every month**.

모든 승무원은 한 달에 1번의 퇴선훈련과 1번의 화재 훈련에 참여해야 한다.

② 전달 훈련을 선원의 25%이상 받지 않은 경우 : 출항 후 24시간 이내 실시
The drills of the crew shall take place within **24h** of the ship leaving a port if more than **25%** of the crew have not participated in abandon ship and fire drills on board that particular ship in the previous month.

이 훈련은 전 달의 퇴선 훈련과 화재 훈련에 참여하지 않은 승무원의 수가 25퍼센트를 넘는다면 출항 후 24시간 안에 시행되어야 한다.

③ 주요개조, 새로운 선원 승선 시 : 출항 전 훈련실시
When ship enters service for the first time, after modification of a major character or when a new crew is engaged, these drills shall be held **before sailing**.

선박이 처음으로 운항을 하는 경우, 주요 개조가 이루어진 후 또는 새로운 선원이 승선한 경우 이러한 훈련을 항해 전에 실시해야한다.

④ 진수훈련 : 3개월 1회 실시
Each lifeboat **shall be launched, and manoeuvred in the water** by its assigned operating crew, at least once **every three months** during an abandon ship drill

각 구명정은 적어도 3개월에 한 번 퇴선훈련 시행중 진수되어 수면 위에서 지정된 작동요원에 의해 조종되어야 한다.

⑤ 여객선의 훈련 : 매주 실시
On **passenger ships**, an abandon ship drill and fire drill shall take place **weekly**.

여객선에 있어서는 퇴선훈련과 소화 훈련을 매주 실시하여야 한다.

⑥ 새로 승선한 여객들의 안전교육 : 출항 전 혹은 출항 직후
On a ship engaged on voyage, where passengers are scheduled to be on board for more than **24h**, musters of newly-embarked passengers shall take place **prior to or immediately upon departure**. Passengers shall be instructed in the use of the lifejackets and the action to take in an emergency.

여객을 24시간보다 초과하여서 이송하도록 되어있는 선박에 새로 승선한 여객들은, 출항 전, 혹은 출항 직후에 훈련을 받아야한다. 여객들은 구명조끼 사용과 비상시 취해야할 행동에 대해 교육받아야한다.

기출문제

01. Choose the best one for the blank. `15년 2차`

> According to SOLAS 83, each member of the crew shall participate in at least one abandon ship drill and one fire drill every month. The drills of the crew shall take place within (　) of the ship leaving a port if more than (　) of the crew have not been participated in abandon ship and fire drills on board in the previous month.

① 24h, 25%　　　② 48h, 50%
③ 48h, 25%　　　④ 24h, 50%

해설 모든 승무원은 한 달에 1번의 퇴선훈련과 1번의 화재 훈련에 참여해야 한다. 이 훈련은 전 달의 퇴선훈련과 화재 훈련에 참여하지 않은 승무원의 수가 <u>25퍼센트</u>를 넘는다면 출항 후 <u>24시간</u> 안에 시행되어야 한다.

답

02. 다음 빈칸에 들어갈 말로 가장 적합한 것은? `18년 1차`

> According to SOLAS 83, each member of the crew shall participate in at least one abandon ship drill and one fire drill every month. The drills of the crew shall take place within (　) of the ship leaving a port if more than (　) of the crew have not been participated in abandon ship and fire drills on board in the previous month.

① 24h, 15%　　　② 48h, 15%
③ 24h, 25%　　　④ 48h, 25%

해설 위 문제와 동일

답 ③

03. 다음 〈보기〉는 「SOLAS(International Convention for the Safety of Life at Sea)」상 훈련에 관한 규정이다. 밑줄 친 내용 중 옳지 않은 것은 모두 몇 개인가? `22년 일반직`

> The drills of the crew shall take place within ㉠ <u>24h</u> of the ship leaving a port if more than 25% of the crew ㉡ <u>have participated</u> in abandon ship and fire drills on board that particular ship in the previous month.
> When ship enters service for the first time, after modification of a major character or when a new crew ㉢ <u>is engaged</u>, these drills shall be held ㉣ <u>after sailing</u>.

① 1개　　　② 2개
③ 3개　　　④ 4개

해설 옳지 않은 것:
　㉡ have <u>not</u> participated 으로 고쳐줘야 한다.
　㉣ <u>before</u> sailing 으로 고쳐줘야 한다.

답 ②

Chapter 4. SOLAS 규정 | **329**

기출문제

04. 다음은 SOLAS의 일부 내용이다. 밑줄의 내용 중 가장 옳지 않은 것은? `22년 2차`

> Every crew member shall participate in at least one abandon ship drill and one fire drill ① every month.
>
> The drills of the crew shall take place within 24h of the ship leaving a port if more than 25% of the crew have not participated in abandon ship and fire drills on board that particular ship in the ② previous month.
>
> When a ship enters service for the first time, after modification of a major character or when a new crew is engaged, these drills shall be held ③ after sailing.
>
> Each lifeboat shall be launched with its assigned operating crew aboard and manoeuvred in the water at least once every ④ three months during an abandon ship drill

해설 ③ before sailing 이 되어야 한다.

답 ③

05. 다음은 SOLAS 내용 중 일부이다. 빈칸에 들어갈 알맞은 말은? `기출예상문제`

> On a ship engaged on voyage, where passengers are scheduled to be on board for more than 24h, musters of newly-embarked passengers shall take place (   ). Passengers shall be instructed in the use of the lifejackets and the action to take in an emergency

① weekly
② within 24h after their embarkation
③ prior to or immediately upon departure
④ before sailing

해설 여객이 24시간을 초과하여 항해하는 선박의 경우 새로운 승선여객의 소집이 출항 전 혹은 출항 직후에 이루어져야하며(prior to or immediately upon departure), 여객들은 구명 자켓 사용법과, 비상시에 해야 하는 행동에 대해 교육을 받아야한다.

답 ③

02
조타장치 규정

① Main steering gear
Capable of putting the rudder over from **35°** on one side to **35°** on the other side with the ship at its deepest seagoing draught and running ahead at maximum ahead service speed and, under the same conditions, from **35°** on either side to **30°** on the other side in not more than **28s**.

② Auxiliary steering gear
Capable of putting the rudder over from **15°** on one side to **15°** on the other side in not more than **60s** with the ship at its deepest seagoing draught and running ahead at one half of the maximum ahead service speed or 7 knots, whichever is the greater.

① 주 조타 장치
가장 깊은 항해 흘수에서 전속력 전진 시 타를 현측 35°에서 다른 현측 35°으로 전타하였을 때 현측 35°에서 다른 현측 30°까지 바뀌는데 28초를 넘겨서는 안 된다.

② 보조 조타 장치
가장 깊은 항해 흘수에서 전속력의 절반이나 7노트 중 더 빠른 속력으로 항해할 때, 타를 현측 15°에서 다른 현측 15°으로 전타하였을 때 60초를 넘겨서는 안 된다.

기출문제

06. SOLAS 규정에 따를 때, 다음 빈칸에 들어갈 숫자를 고르시오.　　　17년 2차

capable of putting the rudder over from 35° on one side to 35° on the other side with the ship at its deepest seagoing draught and running ahead at maximum ahead service speed and, under the same conditions, from 35° on either side to 30° on the other side in not more than (　) sec.

① 25　　　　　　　　② 28
③ 30　　　　　　　　④ 60

해설 가장 깊은 항해 흘수에서 전속력 전진 시 타를 현측 35°에서 다른 현측 35°으로 전타하였을 때 현측 35°에서 다른 현측 30°까지 바뀌는데 28초를 넘겨서는 안 된다.

답 ❷

07. 다음 SOLAS(International Convention for the Safety of Life at Sea, 1974)상 빈칸에 들어갈 말로 가장 옳은 것은?　　　20년 1차

The main steering gear rudder stock shall be capable of putting the rudder from 35° on either side 30° on the other side in not more than (　) seconds at its deepest seagoing draught and running ahead at maximum ahead service speed.

① 25　　　　　　　　② 28
③ 30　　　　　　　　④ 35

해설 가장 깊은 항해 흘수에서 전속력 전진 시 타를 전타하였을 때 현측 35°에서 다른 현측 30°까지 바뀌는데 28초를 넘겨서는 안 된다.

답 ❷

기출문제

08. 다음 〈보기〉는 「SOLAS(International Convention for the Safety of Life at Sea)」상 조타 장치에 대한 내용이다. 빈 칸에 들어갈 숫자들의 총합은? `22년 일반직`

> ㉠ The main steering gear shall be capable of putting the rudder over from ( )° on one side to ( )° on the other side with the ship at its deepest seagoing draught and running ahead at maximum ahead service speed and, under the same conditions, from ( )° on either side to ( )° on the other side in not more than ( )seconds;
>
> ㉡ The auxiliary steering gear shall be capable of putting the rudder over from ( )° on one side to ( )° on the other side in not more than ( ) seconds with the ship at its deepest seagoing draught and running ahead at one half of the maximum ahead service speed or ( ) knots, whichever is the greater;

① 250   ② 253
③ 260   ④ 263

해설 ㉠ 가장 깊은 항해 흘수에서 전속력 전진 시 타를 현측 (35)°에서 다른 현측 (35)°으로 전타하였을 때 현측 (35)°에서 다른 현측 (30)°까지 바뀌는데 (28)초를 넘겨서는 안 된다.
㉡ 타를 현측 (15)°에서 다른 현측 (15)°으로 전타하였을 때 (60)초를 넘겨서는 안 된다. 단, 가장 깊은 항해 흘수에서 전속력의 절반이나 (7)노트 중 더 빠른 속력으로 항해할 때.
35+35+35+30+28+15+15+60+7=<u>260</u>

답 ❸

09. 다음은 SOLAS의 일부 내용이다. 빈칸에 들어갈 숫자의 합은 무엇인가? `22년 2차`

> the Main steering gear shall be capable of putting the rudder over from 35° on one side to 35° on the other side with the ship at its deepest seagoing draught and running ahead at maximum ahead service speed and, under the same conditions, from ( )° on either side to ( )° on the other side in not more than ( ) seconds.

① 88   ② 93
③ 98   ④ 103

해설 가장 깊은 항해 흘수에서 전속력 전진 시 타를 현측 35°에서 다른 현측 35°으로 전타하였을 때 현측 (35)°에서 다른 현측 (30)°까지 바뀌는데 (28)초를 넘겨서는 안 된다.
35+30+28=<u>93</u>

답 ❷

03
Life Jacket 규정

① 일반요건

A lifejacket shall have buoyancy which is not reduced by more than **5%** after **24h** submersion in **fresh water**

② 어린이용 life Jacket

A number of lifejackets suitable for children equal to at least **10%** of the number of passengers on board shall be provided or such **greater number** as may be required to provide a **lifejacket for each child**.

③ 유아용 life jacket

- For passenger ship on voyage **less than 24h**, a number of infant life jackets equal to at least **2.5%** of the number of passengers on board shall be provided;

- For passenger ships on voyages **24h or greater**, infant lifejackets shall be provided for **each infant** on board

④ 당직요원을 위한 life jacket

A **Sufficient number** of lifejackets shall be carried **for persons on watch** and for use at **remotely located survival craft stations**. The lifejackets carried for persons on watch should be stowed on the **bridge, in the engine control room** and at any other **manned watch station;**

⑤ 여객선의 추가 life jacket

In addition to the lifejackets required by regulation 7.2, Every **passenger ship** shall carry life jackets for not less than **5%** of the total number of persons on board. These life jackets shall be stowed in conspicuous places on deck or at muster stations.

구명동의는 24시간 넘게 청수에 잠긴후에도 그 부양성이 5% 넘게 감소해서는 안된다.

여객정원의 적어도 10퍼센트에 해당하는 아동용 구명동의 또는 각 아동 당 1개에 해당하는 아동용 구명동의 수 중 큰 쪽의 수만큼을 비치해야 한다.

- 24시간미만 항해에 종사하는 여객선은, 승선한 여객 수의 적어도 2.5%와 동일한 개수의 유아용 구명동의가 제공되어야 한다.
- 24시간 이상 항해에 종사하는 여객선은, 탑승한 각각의 유아에 맞는 숫자의 구명동의가 제공되어야한다.

당직요원 및 멀리 떨어진 생존정 탑승 장소에서 이용할 수 있는 충분한 수의 구명동의를 배치하여야 한다. 당직선원용 구명동의는 선교, 기관실 등 당직이 필요한 모든 개소에 비치되어야 한다.

7.2규정에서 요구하는 것에 더하여서, 모든 여객선은 선내 총 승객의 수의 5퍼센트 이상 구명동의를 추가로 가지고 있어야 한다. 이 구명동의는 갑판의 잘 보이는 곳이나 집합장소에 적재되어야 한다.

기출문제

10. 다음은 SOLAS(해상에서의 인명안전을 위한 국제 협약)의 원문을 발췌해 온 것이다. 밑줄의 내용 중 가장 옳지 않은 것은?　　　　　　　　　　　　　　　　　　　　　　[18년 일반직]

- A number of lifejackets suitable for children equal to at least ① <u>10% of the number of passengers</u> on board shall be provided or such ② <u>lesser number</u> as may be required to provide a lifejacket for each child; and
- Every crew member shall participate in at least one ③ <u>abandon ship drill</u> and one ④ <u>fire drill</u> every month.

[해설] ② lesser number → greater number

답 ❷

11. 다음은 SOLAS(International Convention for the Safety of Life at Sea) chapter III Life-saving appliances and arrangements에 관한 내용이다. 빈칸에 알맞은 수를 모두 합한 값은?　　　　　　　　　　　　　　　　　　　　　　　　　　　　　　　[21년 하반기]

㉠ for passenger ships on voyages less than 24h, a number of infant lifejackets equal to at least (　　)% of the number of passengers on board shall be provided;
㉡ for passenger ships on voyages 24h or greater, infant lifejackets shall be provided for each infant onboard;
㉢ a number of lifejackets suitable for children equal to at least (　　)% of the number of passengers on board shall be provided or such greater number as may be required to provide a lifejacket for each child;

① 10　　　　　　　　　　　② 12.5
③ 15　　　　　　　　　　　④ 17.5

[해설] ㉠ 24시간미만 항해에 종사하는 여객선은, 승선한 여객 수의 적어도 (2.5)%와 동일한 개수의 유아용 구명동의가 제공되어야 한다.
㉢ 여객정원의 적어도 (10)퍼센트에 해당하는 아동용 구명동의 또는 각 아동 당 1개에 해당하는 아동용 구명동의 수 중 큰 쪽의 수만큼을 비치해야 한다.
2.5+10=12.5

답 ❷

04
항해선교의 시야 규정

① 조타위치에서의 해면 시야

The view of the sea surface from the conning position of ships of not less than **55m** in length shall not be obscured by more than two ship lengths, or **500m**, whichever is the less, forward of the bow to 10° on either side under all conditions of draught, trim and deck cargo.

SOLAS 협약에 따르면, 길이가 55m 보다 큰 선박은 조타 위치로부터 해면의 시야가 선박길이의 두 배 이상 혹은 500m이상보다 작은 값보다 가려져선 안 된다. 이는 흘수, 트림, 갑판적 화물의 모든 조건 하에서 선수에서 각 측면에 10도를 말한다.

② 맹목구간

- **No blind sector** caused by cargo, cargo gear or other obstructions outside of the wheelhouse forward of the beam which obstructs the view of the sea surface as seen from the conning position, shall exceed **10°**.

- The **total arc of blind sectors** shall **not exceed 20°**.

- The **clear sectors** between blind sectors shall be at least **5°.**

- However, in the view described in ①., each individual blind sector shall not exceed **5°**

- 조종 위치에서 바라볼 때 해면의 시야를 방해하는 선교의 정횡 보다 전방에 있는 화물, 외부의 하역 장치 또는 기타 방해물로 인한 단일 맹목 구간은 10°를 초과하여서는 아니 된다.
- 맹목 구간들의 총합계 각도는 20°를 초과하여서는 아니 된다.
- 맹목 구간 사이의 가시 구역은 5° 이상 이어야 한다.
- 그러나 제 ①항에서 기술 된 시야 내에서 각 맹목 구간은 5°를 초과하여서는 아니 된다.

③ 수평 시야

- The horizontal field of vision from the conning position shall extend over an arc of not less than 225°, that is from right ahead to not less than 22.5° abaft the beam on either side of the ship

- From each bridge wing the horizontal field of vision shall extend over an arc at least 225°, that is from at least 45° on the opposite bow through right ahead and then from right ahead to right astern through 180° on the same side of the ship

- From the main steering position, the horizontal field of vision shall extend over an arc from right ahead to at least 60° on each side of the ship.

- the ship's side shall be visible from the bridge wing

- 조종 위치에서 수평시야는 225° 이상이어야 한다. 즉 정 선수방향에서부터 정횡 후방 22.5° 이상이어야 한다(선박 양현으로).
- 양 윙 브릿지에서 수평 시야는 각각 225° 이상이어야 한다. 즉 정선수에서 반대 현 쪽 45°와 정선수에서 바로 선미까지 같은 현에서 180°이상이어야 한다.
- 주 조타위치에서 수평시야는 정 선수를 기준으로 최소한 좌우 60°의 범위에 달하여야 한다.
- 윙 브릿지에서 선체의 측면을 볼 수 있어야 한다.

기출문제

12. 다음 문장의 빈칸에 들어갈 가장 적절한 숫자들의 총합은? `18년 3차`

가. The exclusive economic zone shall not extend beyond (   ) nautical miles from the baselines from which the breadth of the territorial sea is measured.

나. "stern light" means a white light placed as nearly as practicable at the stern showing an unbroken light over an arc of the horizon of (   ) degrees and so fixed as to show the light (   ) degrees from right aft on each side of the vessel.

다. According to SOLAS Convention, The view of the sea surface from the conning position of ships of not less than (   ) m in length shall not be obscured by more than two ship lengths, or (   ) m, whichever is the less, forward of the bow to (   )° on either side under all conditions of draught, trim and deck cargo.

① 967.5　　　　　② 945
③ 1012.5　　　　　④ 1057.5

해설　가. 200
　　　나. 135, 67.5
　　　다. 55, 500, 10

답 ①

05

Line-throwing appliances 구명줄 발사기

모든 구명줄 발사기는 다음의 조건을 충족해야한다.

① 어느 정도는 정확한 발사가 가능해야한다.
② 잔잔한 날씨에서 적어도 230m 거리까지 줄을 이동시킬 수 있는 발사체가 4개 이상 있어야한다.
③ 파단 강도 2kN 이상인 줄이 각각 4개 이상 있어야한다.
④ 해당 발사기의 사용법에 대한 간단한 설명서나 도해도 등이 있어야한다.

Every Line-throwing appliances shall :

① be capable of throwing a line with **reasonable accuracy;**
② include not less than **four projectiles** each capable of carrying the line at least **230m** in clam weather;
③ include not less than **four lines** each having a breaking strength of no less than **2kN**; and
④ have brief instructions or diagrams clearly illustrating the use of the line-throwing appliance

---

기출문제

13. 다음은 SOLAS 협약 상 Line-throwing appliances에 관한 설명이다. 빈칸에 들어갈 말로 가장 옳은 것은?   `21년 상반기`

가. be capable of throwing a line with reasonable accuracy
나. include not less than ( )projectiles each capable of carrying the line at least ( )m in calm weather
다. include not less than ( )lines each having a breaking strength of not less than ( )kN,
라. have brief instructions or diagrams clearly illustrating the use of the line- throwing appliance

① three - 230 - three - 1
② four - 230 - four - 2
③ three - 300 - five - 1
④ four - 300 - six - 2

해설 나. 발사체가 (4)개 이상 있어야한다. (잔잔한 날씨에서 적어도 (230)m 거리까지 줄을 이동시킬 수 있는)
다. 줄이 각각 (4)개 이상 있어야한다. (파단 강도 (2)kN 이상인)

답

06
조난신호장비

① 구명정에서의 조난신호장비

The normal equipment of every lifeboat shall consist of
- **four rocket parachute flares** complying with the requirement of regulation
- **six hand flares** complying with requirements of regulation
- **two buoyant smoke signal** complying with the requirements of regulation.

> 구명정의 일반 장비는 다음으로 구성되야 한다.
> – 4개의 로켓낙하산화염신호 (규정에 맞는)
> – 5개의 신호흥염 (규정에 맞는)
> – 2개의 발연부 신호 (규정에 맞는)

② 선교에서의 조난신호장비

Not less than **12 rocket parachute flares**, complying with the requirement of the LSA Code, shall be carried and be stowed on or near the **navigation bridge.**

> LSA 코드에 부합하는 12개 이상의 로켓낙하산화염신호가 선교, 또는 그 근처에 비치되고 보관되어있어야 한다.

③ 자기점화등, 자기발연부신호를 갖춘 구명부환

Not less than **one half** of the total number of lifebuoys shall be provided with lifebuoy self-igniting lights complying with the requirements of paragraph 2.1.2 of the Code; not less than **two** of these shall also be provided with lifebuoy self-activating smoke signals complying with the requirements of paragraph 2.1.3 of the Code and be capable of quick release from the **navigation bridge**.

> 구명부환의 총 개수 중에 1/2 이상은 자기점화등을 갖춘 구명부환이어야 하고, 이 중 2개 이상은 자기발연부신호를 갖춘 구명부환이어야 한다. 그리고 이것은 항해 선교로부터 빠르게 사용 가능한 것이어야 한다.

│ 기출문제

14. 다음은 SOLAS상 선교 안전설비 규정이다. 빈칸에 들어갈 숫자로 옳은 것은? `기출예상문제`

> Not less than ( ) rocket parachute flares shall be carried and be stowed on or near the navigation bridge.

① 2　　　　　　② 4
③ 6　　　　　　④ 12

`해설` 로켓낙하산화염 신호는 선교에 12개 이상 구비해야 한다.

답 ④

chapter 05 SOLAS의 아직 출제되지 않은 규정

01

비상배치표 및 비상 지침

Muster list and Emergency instructions

이 규칙은 모든 선박에 적용 한다.

This regulation applies to all ships.

① 비상시 지켜야 할 명확한 지침이 모든 승선자에게 제공되어야 한다. 여객선에 있어서 이런 지침들은 선박의 기국에 의하여 요구되는 언어 또는 영어로 작성이 되어야 한다.

① Clear instructions to be followed in the event of an emergency shall be provided for every person on board. In the case of passenger ships these instructions shall be drawn up in the language or languages required by the ship's flag State and in the English language.

② 제 37규칙의 요건에 적합한 비상배치표와 비상지침서는 항해선교, 기관실과 선원 거주구역을 포함한 눈에 잘 띄는 장소에 게시 되어야 한다.

② Muster lists and emergency instructions complying with the requirements of regulation 37 shall be exhibited in conspicuous places throughout the ship including the navigation bridge, engine-room and crew accommodation spaces.

③ 적절한 언어로 된 아래사항의 도면이나 지침서가 여객이 알 수 있도록 여객실에 부착되거나 소집위치 기타의 여객 구역에 잘 보이도록 게시되어야 한다.

③ Illustrations and instructions in appropriate languages shall be posted in passenger cabins and be conspicuously displayed at muster stations and other passenger spaces to inform passengers of

- 소집 장소
- 비상시 여객들이 취하여야 하는 중요행동
- 구명동의 착용 법

- their muster station
- the essential actions they must take in an emergency
- the method of donning lifejackets.

02
Pilot transfer arrangements

① a pilot ladder requiring a climb of net less then 1.5m and not more than 9m above the surface of the water so positioned and secured

② an accommodation ladder in conjunction with the pilot ladder (i. e a combination arrangement), or other equally safe and convenient mean, whenever the distance from the surface of the water to the point of access to the ship is more than 9m

도선사 승선사다리
① 수면으로부터 1.5m 이상 9m 이하의 높이까지 올라가야 하는 경우, 설치되고 고정된 도선사용 사다리
② 수면으로부터 선박에의 출입을 위한 위치까지는 거리가 9m를 넘는 모든 경우, 도선사용 사다리와 결합된 현측사다리 (컴비네이션 사다리) 또는 이와 동등한 안전하고 용이한 다른 장치

03
생존자 소집 및 승정장치

① Lifeboats and liferafts for which approved launching appliances are required shall be stowed as **close to accommodation and service spaces** as possible.

② Muster stations shall be provided close to the embarkation stations. Each muster station shall have sufficient clear deck space to accommodate all persons assigned to muster at that station, but at least **0.35m²** per person.

③ **Muster and embarkation stations** shall be adequately **illuminated** by **lighting supplied** from the emergency source of electrical power required by regulation II-1/42 or II-1/43, as appropriate.

① 승인된 진수설비가 요구되는 구명정 및 구명뗏목은 거주구역 과 업무구역에 가능한 한 가깝게 탑재되어야 한다.

② 소집위치는 승정위치에 가까이 배치되어야 한다. 각. 소집위치에는 그 위치에 소집하도록 되어 있는 모든 사람을 수용할 수 있을 정도의 충분한 공간이 있어야 하며 그, 공간은 최소한 사람당 0.35m²가 되어야 한다.

③ 소집 및 승정위치는 제 장 2-1 의 제 규칙 42 또는 제 규칙의 43 해당 조항에서 규정하는 비상전원으로부터 공급되는 불빛에 의하여 충분히 조명되어야 한다.

04
기타 규정

① Manually operated call points
Manually operated call points complying with the Fire Safety Systems Code shall be installed throughout the accommodation spaces, service spaces and control stations. One manually operated call point shall be located at **each exit**. Manually operated call points shall be readily accessible in the corridors of each deck such that no part of the corridor is more than **20m** from a manually operated call point.

화재안전장치 코드에 만족하는 수동조작 콜 포인트를 거주구역, 업무구역 및 제어장소에 걸쳐 설치하여야한다 각출입구에는 하나의 수동조작 콜 포인트가 설치되어야한다 수동조작. 콜 포인트는 각 갑판의 통로에서 쉽게 접근할 수 있어야 하며 통로의 어느 부분도 수동조작 콜 포인트에 서 20m이상 떨어져서는 안 된다

② AIS(Automatic Identification System)
AIS shall provide automatically to appropriately equipped shore stations, other ships and aircraft information, including the ship's identity, type, position, course, speed, navigational status and other safety related information

AIS는 적절한 장비를 갖춘 육상국, 타선박 및 항공기에 선박의 식별, 종류, 위치, 침로, 항행상태 및 다른 안전관련 정보를 포함한 정보를 자동으로 제공하여야 한다.

③ 월간 구명 장비 점검
Inspection of the life-saving appliances, including lifeboat equipment, shall be carried out **monthly** using the **checklist** required by regulation.

구명정 장비를 포함한 구명설비점검은 협약에서 요구하는 체크리스트를 사용하여 매달 수행되어야 한다.

④ 여객선의 퇴선 추가규정
All survival craft required to provide for abandonment by the total number of persons on board shall be capable of being launched with their full complement of persons and equipment within a period of **30 min** from the time the abandon ship signal is given after all persons have been assembled, with lifejackets donned

총 승선인원을 퇴선 시키기 위하여 요구되는 모든 생존정은 모든 인원이 구명동의를 입고 집합이 완료된 후, 퇴선신호가 울린 시각으로부터 30분 이내에 총 정원과 의장품을 수용한 채로 진수될 수 있는 능력을 가지고 있어야 한다.

⑤ 화물선의 퇴선 추가규정
all survival craft required to provide for abandonment by the total number of persons on board shall be capable of being launched with their full complement of persons and equipment within a period of 10 min from the time the abandon ship signal is given.

총 승선인원을 퇴선 시키도록 되어있는 모든 생존정은 인원과 의장품을 만재한 상태로 퇴선신호가 울린 후 10분 이내에 진수될 수 있는 능력을 가져야 한다.

PART 06 ISPS (International Code for the Security of ships and of Port Facilities)

Chapter 1	ISPS의 목적과 용어
Chapter 2	SSAS(The Ship Security Alert System)
Chapter 3	보안에 대한 당사국의 조치
Chapter 4	Verification and Certification for Ship 선박의 검사 및 증명서
Chapter 5	ISPS 적용 선박

chapter 01 ISPS의 목적과 용어

01
ISPS의 목적

이 코드의 목적은:
국제 무역에 사용되는 선박 또는 항만시설에 위협이 되는 보안 위협에 대한 예방조치를 취하고 보안 위협을 탐지하기 위하여 당사국 정부, 정부기관, 지방관청과 해운 및 항만산업간의 상호 협조를 포함한 국제적 체계를 설정하기 위함이다.

The objectives of this code are:
to establish an international framework involving co-operation between Contracting Government agencies, local administrations and the shipping and port industries to detect security threats and take preventive measures against security incidents affecting ships or port facilities used in international trade;

02
용어

정의	meaning	의미
ISPS code	the International Code for the Security of Ships and of Port Facilities consisting of Part A (the provision of which shall be treated as mandatory) and Part B (the provision of which shall be treated as recommendatory), as adopted, on 12 December 2002, by resolution 2 of the Conference of Contracting Governments to the International Convention for the Safety of Life at Sea, 1974.	2002년 12월 12일 1974 SOLAS 협약의 당사국 정부회의에서 결의 2로 채택한 A편(강제사항)과 B편(권고사항)으로 구성된 선박과 항만시설의 보안을 위한 국제규칙을 말한다.
Port facility 항만시설	a location, as determined by the contracting Government or by the Designated Authority. where the ship/port interface takes place. This includes areas such as anchorages, waiting berths and approaches from seaward, as appropriate.	선박/항만 인터페이스가 발생하는 당사국 정부 또는 지정당국에 의해 결정된 장소를 말하며, 적절한 묘박지(anchorage), 대기선석(waiting berth) 및 해상으로부터의 진입수역(approach)을 포함한다.

Security incident 보안사건	any suspicious act or circumstance threatening the security of a ship, including a mobile offshore drilling unit and a high speed craft, or of a port facility or of any ship/port interface or any ship to ship activity.	이동식 해상 구조물과 고속선을 포함하여 선박 또는 항만시설 또는 선박/항만 인터페이스 또는 선박 대 선박 활동의 보안을 위협하는 의혹 행위 또는 상황을 말한다.	
Security level 보안등급	the qualification of the degree of risk that a security incident will be attempted or will occur.	보안사건이 시도되거나 발생할 수 있는 위험 정도를 정한 것을 말한다.	
Security level 1 보안등급 1	the level for which minimum appropriate protective security measures shall be maintained at all time.	최소한의 적절한 방어적 보안조치가 항상 유지되어야 하는 수준을 말한다.	
Security level 2 보안등급 2	the level for which appropriate additional protective security measures shall be maintained for a period of time as a result of heightened risk of a security incident.	증가된 보안사건 위험성의 결과로서 일정기간 동안 적절한 추가의 방어적 보안조치가 유지되어야 하는 수준을 말한다.	
Security level 3 보안등급 3	the level for which further specific protective security measures shall be maintained for a limited period of time when a security incident is probable or imminent, although it may not be possible to identify the specific target.	비록 구체적인 대상을 식별하는 것이 불가능할지라도 보안사건이 발생할 가능성이 있거나 긴급한 경우, 일정 기간 동안 보다 구체적인 방어적 보안조치가 유지되어야 하는 수준을 말한다.	

약어	meaning	의미
SSP	Ship Security Plan	선박 보안계획서
PFSP	Port Facility Security Plan	항만시설보안계획서
SSO	Ship Security Officer	선박보안책임자
CSO	Company Security Officer	회사보안책임자
PFSO	Port Facility Security Officer	항만시설보안책임자
AIS	Automatic Identification System	선박자동식별시스템
ISSC	International Ship Security Certificate	국제선박보안증서
SSAS	Ship Security Alert System	선박보안경보시스템
SSA	Ship Security Assessment	선박보안평가서
DOS	Declaration of security	보안선언서

기출문제

01. 다음은 ISPS(International Ship and Port Facility Security)에 관한 설명이다. 가장 적절하지 않은 것은?

18년 3차

① "ISPS code" means the international code for the Security of ships and of port Facilities consisting of part A(the provisions of which shall be treated as mandatory) and part B(the provisions of which shall be treated as recommendatory) as adopted, on 12 December 2002, by resolution 2 of the Conference of Contracting Governments to the international Convention for the Safety of Life at sea, 1974
② "Port facility" is a location, as determined by the Contracting Government or by the Designated Authority, where the ship/port interface takes place. This includes areas such as anchorages, waiting berths and approaches from seaward, as appropriate.
③ "Security incident" means the qualification of the degree of risk that a security incident will be attempted or will occur.
④ "Security level 1" means the level for which minimum appropriate protective security measures shall be maintained at all times.

해설 해당 내용은 Security level (보안 등급)에 대한 설명이다.
　　　보안등급이라 함은 보안사건이 시도되거나 발생할 수 있는 위험 정도를 정한 것을 말한다.

답 ③

02. Choose the best one for the blank.

12년 2차

(　　　　) means the qualification of degree of risk that a security incident will be attempted or will occur. (in the ISPS Code)

① Port facility　　　　② Security incident
③ Security level　　　④ Emergency phase

해설 보안등급(Security level)이라 함은 보안사건이 시도되거나 발생할 수 있는 위험 정도를 정한 것을 말한다.

답 ③

03. 다음 보기 중 약어의 설명이 옳지 않은 것은 모두 몇 개인가?

22년 일반직

AIS : Automatic Identification System
ISSC : International Ship Safety Certificate
SSAS : Ship Security Alert System
CSO : Chief Security Officer
PFSP : Port Facility Security Plan

① 1개　　② 2개　　③ 3개　　④ 없음

해설 옳지 않은 것:
　　ⓒ International Ship <u>Security</u> Certificate
　　ⓔ <u>Company</u> Security Officer

답 ②

Chapter 02 SSAS(The Ship Security Alert System)

The ship security alert system, when activated, shall :

ⓐ Initiate and transmit a **ship-to-shore** security alert to a competent authority designated by the Administration, which in these circumstances may include the Company, identifying the ship, its location and indicating that the security of the ship is under threat or it has been compromised.

ⓑ **Not send** the ship security alert to any other ships.

ⓒ **Not raise** any alarm on-board the ship.

ⓓ Continue the ship security alert **until deactivated and/or reset**.

ⓔ The ship security alert system shall be capable of being activated from the **navigation bridge** and in at least one other location.

ⓕ Conform to performance standards not inferior to those adopted by the Organization

ⓐ 선박 및 위치를 식별하고 선박의 보안이 위협 또는 침해되는 상황을 나타내는 선박 대(對) 육상보안경보를 발생시켜, 이를 주관청이 지정한 기관당국(동 상황에서는 회사가 포함될 수 있음)에 전송하여야 한다.

ⓑ 여타 선박에 선박보안경보가 송신되어서는 아니 된다.

ⓒ 선내에 어떠한 알람도 발생시키지 아니하여야 한다.

ⓓ 작동해제 그리고/또는 재설정 시까지 지속되어야 한다.

ⓔ 선박보안경보시스템은 항해선교로부터, 그리고 이외의 1개 이상의 장소에서, 작동 가능하여야 한다.

ⓕ 기구가 채택한 것보다 열등하지 아니한 성능기준에 따라야 한다.

기출문제

01. Choose the wrong answer in the below `11년 2차`

the ship security alert system, when activated. shall

① send the ship security alert to any other ship
② not raise any alarm on-board the ship
③ continue the ship security alert until deactivated and/or reset
④ initiate and transmit a ship to shore security alert to a competent authority designated by the Administration

해설 SSAS 작동 시 타선박에게는 경보를 송신해서는 안 된다.

답 ❶

02. 다음은 ISPS Code(International Ship & Port Facility Security Code)의 Ship security alert system에 관한 내용이다. 가장 옳지 않은 것은? `21년 하반기`

The ship security alert system, when activated, shall;
㉠ initiate and transmit a ship-to-ship security alert to a competent authority designated by the Administration, which in these circumstances may include the Company, identifying the ship, its location and indicating that the security of the ship is under threat or it has been compromised;
㉡ not send the ship security alert to any other ships;
㉢ not raise any alarm on board the ship; and
㉣ continue the ship security alert until deactivated and/or reset.

① ㉠ ② ㉡
③ ㉢ ④ ㉣

해설 ㉠ SSAS작동 시 선박과 육상 간(ship-to-shore) 송신이 이루어져야한다.

답 ❶

chapter 03 보안에 대한 당사국의 조치

01
보안등급 제공

① Administrations shall set **security levels** and ensure the provision of security level information to ships entitled to fly their flag. When changes in security level occur, security level information shall be updated as the circumstance dictates.

② Contracting Governments shall set **security levels** and ensure the provision of security level information to port facilities within their territory, and to ships prior to entering a port or whilst in a port within their territory. When changes in security level occur, security level information shall be updated as the circumstance dictates.

① 주관청은 보안등급을 책정하고 그 기국 선박에게 보안등급 정보의 제공을 보장하여야 한다. 보안등급의 변동이 발생했을 때, 보안등급 정보는 그 상황을 나타내어 최신화 되어야 한다.

② 당사국 정부는 보안등급을 책정하여, 영토(해) 내 항만시설과 항만에 입항하기 전 또는 항만에 정박해 있는 동안에 선박에게 보안등급 정보의 제공을 보장하여야 한다.

02
공격의 위험 식별

Where a risk of attack has been identified, the Contracting Government concerned shall advise the ships concerned and their Administrations of :

① the current security level.
② any security measures that should be put in place by the ships concerned to protect themselves from attack, in accordance with the provisions of part A of the ISPS Code.
③ security measures that the coastal state has decided to put in place, as appropriate.

공격위험이 식별된 경우, 해당 당사국 정부는 관련선박 및 그 주관청에 다음 사항을 통지하여야 한다.

① 현재의 보안등급
② ISPS 코드 A편에 따라, 선박을 공격으로부터 보호하기 위해 해당선박에 의해 취해져야하는 모든 보안조치
③ 연안국이 적절히 취하기로 결정한 보안조치

03
항만 내의 선박 통제.

Such control measures are as follows :

그러한 통제조치는 다음의 것들이 있다. :

① 선박의 임검
② 선박의 출항지연
③ 선박의 출항정지
④ 항만 내의 이동을 포함한 운항 제한
⑤ 항만으로부터의 추방

① inspection of the ship
② delaying the ship
③ detention of the ship
④ restriction of operations including movement within the port
⑤ expulsion of the ship from port.

chapter 04
Verification and Certification for Ship 선박의 검사 및 증명서

01
Verification

① Initial Verification

② Renewal Verification (not exceeding five years)
An International Ship Security Certificate (ISSC) shall be issued after the Initial or renewal Verification

③ at least one Intermediate Verification
If only one intermediate verification is carried out it shall take place between the second and third anniversary date of the certificate

02
Duration and validity of certificate

An International Ship Security Certificate shall be issued for a period specified by the Administration which shall not exceed **five years.**

01 검사

① 최초 검사

② 갱신검사 (5년이 넘지 않도록)
국제선박보안증서 (ISSC)는 최초검사 또는 갱신검사 이후에 발행되어져야 한다.

③ 적어도 한 번의 중간검사
만약 단지 한 번의 중간검사가 수행된다면, 그것은 증명서 날짜 이후 두 번째 해와 세 번째 해의 사이에 실시되어야 한다.

02 증서의 기간과 유효성

국제선박보안증서는 주관청에 의해 명시된 5년이 넘지 않는 기간으로 발행되어져야 한다.

│ 기출문제

01. 다음은 ISPS(International Ship & Port Facility Security Code)상 국제항해 선박의 Verification 종류이다. 가장 옳지 않은 것은? `20년 3차`

① Initial Verification
② Final Verification
③ Renewal Verification (not exceeding five years)
④ At least one Intermediate Verification

해설 Final Verification은 해석하면 최종검사이다 최종검사는 없는 검사이다.

답 ❷

chapter 05 ISPS 적용 선박

① 국제항해에 종사하는 다음의 선종
  - 고속여객선을 포함한 여객선
  - 총톤수 500톤 이상의 고속선을 포함한 화물선
  - 이동식 해상 시추선

② 국제항해에 종사하는 선박이 사용하는 항만시설

③ 본 규칙은 군함, 해군 보조함 또는 당사국 정부에 의해 운용 또는 소속되는 비상업용 선박에는 적용하지 아니한다.

① The following types of ships engaged on international voyages
  - passenger ships, including high-speed passenger craft
  - cargo ships, including high-speed craft, of 500 gross tonnage and upwards
  - mobile offshore drilling units

② Port facilities serving such ships engaged on international voyages

③ This Code does not apply to warships, naval auxiliaries or other ships owned or operated by a Contracting Government and used only on Government non-commercial service.

PART 07 STCW(International Convention on Standard of Training, Certification and Watchkeeping for Seafarers)

Chapter 1	용어
Chapter 2	승무원 자격
Chapter 3	당직임무에 대한 적합성
Chapter 4	Voyage planning 항해계획
Chapter 5	Watchkeeping at Sea 항해 중 당직근무
Chapter 6	여러 조건과 수역에서의 당직근무

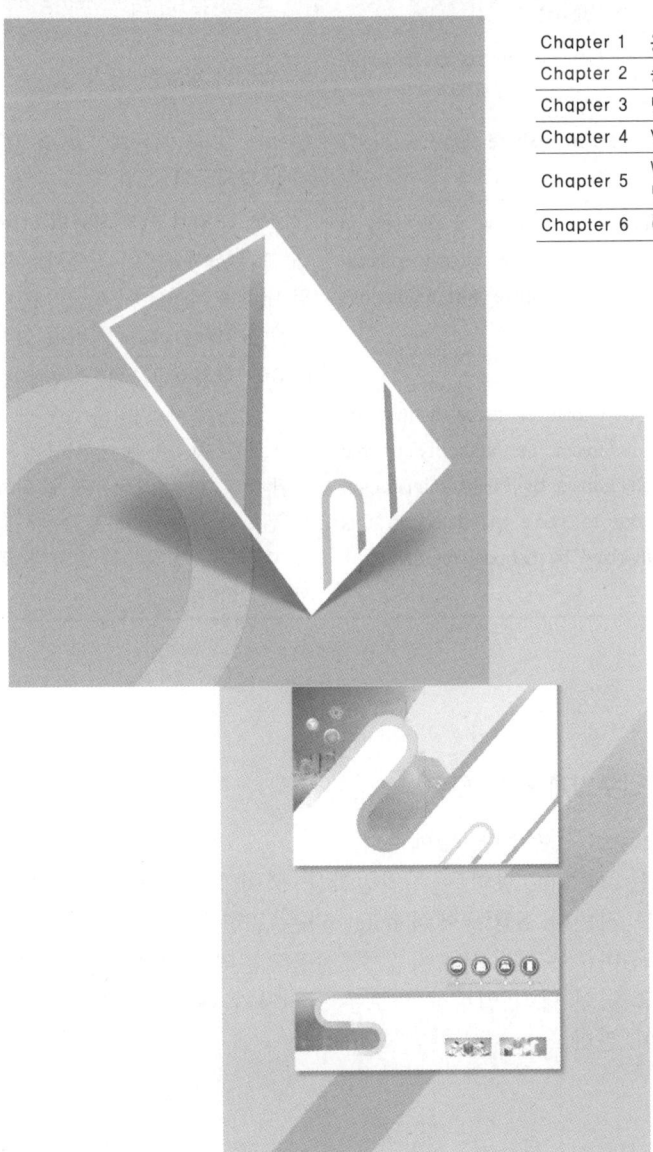

chapter 01 용어

01 정의

정의	meaning	의미
Party 당사국	a State for which the Convention has entered into force;	본 협약이 발효한 국가
Administration 주관청	The Government of the Party whose flag the ship is entitled to fly;	선박이 그 국기를 게양할 권리를 가진 당사국의 정부
Sea-going ship 항해선	a ship other than those which navigate exclusively in inland waters or in waters within, or closely adjacent to, sheltered waters or areas where port regulations apply;	내해를 운항하거나 차폐된 수역 내 또는 항만규칙이 적용되는 지역 내의 수역이나 이에 근접된 수역을 항행하는 선박 이외의 선박
Certificate 증명서	a valid document, by whatever name it may be known, issued by or under the authority of the Administration or recognized by the Administration authorizing the holder to serve as stated in this document or as authorized by national regulation;	어떠한 명칭으로든지 주관청 또는 그의 권한에 의거하여 발급되거나 그 소지자가 동 문서상에 기재된 대로 또는 국내규정에 의하여 권한이 부여된 대로 승무하도록 주관청이 인정하는 유효한 문서를 말한다.

02 당직 인수인계 관련 단어

① Relive : 덜어주다, 없애주다.

relive는 사전적 정의로 무엇인가를 덜어주거나 면제시켜준다는 의미를 지닌다. STCW에서 relieve라는 표현은 인수사관과 인계사관을 꾸며주는 형용사로써 많이 사용되는데, 기존의 당직자가 짊어지고 있던 당직 업무를 새로운 당직자가 대신 맡는다는 의미로 사용이 된다.

② Reliving officer : 인수 사관(인계받는 사관)
기존의 당직을 짊어지고 있던 사관으로부터 당직업무를 대신 져주는 사관이므로 **덜어주는(relieving)** 사관(Officer)이라 표현된다.

③ Officer relieved : 인계사관(인계하는 사관)
기존의 당직을 짊어지고 있다가 인수사관(relieving officer)로부터 덜어줌을 당하는 사관이므로 Officer **relieved**라고 표현된다.

④ Hand over : 인계하다.
당직 교대 시 인계사관(Officer relived)이 당직을 넘겨주는 행위
ex) Officer relived **hand over** the duty : 인계사관이 당직업무를 인계하다.

⑤ Take over : 인수하다(인계 받다)
당직 교대 시 인수사관(Relieving officer)가 당직을 넘겨받는 행위
ex) Relieving officer **take over** the duty : 인수사관이 당직업무를 인수했다(인계받았다).

⑥ Helmsperson : 조타수

chapter 02 승무원 자격

① 선장과 갑판부

총톤수 500톤 이상의 항해선에서 승무하는 항해당직을 담당하는 모든 사관은 적합한 증명서를 소지하여야 한다. 자격증명을 받고자 하는 모든 지원자는 다음 사항을 갖추어야 한다.

- ☐ 18세 이상일 것
- ☐ 선내훈련을 포함하는 승인된 훈련프로그램의 일부로서 1년 이상의 승인된 승무경력을 갖추어야 하며 선내훈련은 STCW 협약 제A-Ⅱ/1규칙의 요건을 충족하고 승인된 기록부로 문서화될 것. 그러하지 아니할 경우에는 3년 이상의 승인된 승무경력을 갖출 것

② 기관부

추진동력 750킬로와트 이상의 주추진기관에 의하여 추진되는 항해선의 유인기관실에서 기관당직을 담당하는 모든 기관사 또는 정기적 무인기관실의 모든 지정 당직기관사는 적합한 증명서를 소지하여야 한다. 자격증명을 받고자 하는 모든 지원자는 다음의 요건을 갖추어야 한다. :

- ☐ 18세 이상일 것
- ☐ STCW 협약 제A-Ⅱ/1규칙의 규정에 따라서 6월 이상의 기관부 승무경력을 갖추었을 것

① Master and department

Every officer in charge of a navigational watch serving on a seagoing ship of **500 gross tonnage** or more shall hold an appropriate certificate. Every candidate for certification shall :

- ☐ be not less than **18 years** of age.
- ☐ have approved seagoing service of not less than **one year** as part of an approved training programme which includes on-board training which meets the requirements of section A-Ⅱ/1 of the STCW Code and is documented in an approved training record book, or otherwise have approved seagoing service of not less than **three years**.

② Engine department

Every officer in charge of an engineering watch in a manned engine-room or designated duty engineer officer in a periodically unmanned engine-room on a seagoing ship powered by main propulsion machinery of **750KW** propulsion power or more shall hold an appropriate certificate. Every candidate for certification shall :

- ☐ be not less than **18 years** of age.
- ☐ have completed not less than **six months** seagoing service in the engine department in accordance with section A-Ⅱ/1 of the STCW Code.

기출문제

01. 다음은 STCW(International Convention on Standards of Training, Certification and Watchkeeping for Seafarers)의 원문을 발췌해 온 것이다. 내용 중 가장 옳지 않은 것은?

<small>19년 1차</small>

Certificate

Every officer in charge of a navigational watch serving on a seagoing ship of ① 500 gross tonnage or more shall hold an appropriate certificate. Every candidate for certification shall:
- be not less than 18 years of age;
- have approved seagoing service of not less than ② one year as part of an approved training programme which includes on-board training which meets the requirements of section A-II/1 of the STCW Code and is documented in an approved training record book, or otherwise have approved seagoing service of not less than three years;

Every officer in charge of an engineering watch in a manned engine-room or designated duty engineer officer in a periodically unmanned engine-room on a seagoing ship powered by main propulsion machinery of ③ 750KW propulsion power of more shall hold an appropriate certificate. Every candidate for certification shall:
- be not less than 18 years of age;
- have completed not less than ④ one year seagoing service in the engine department in accordance with section A-III/1 of the STCW Code;

해설 one year → six months

답 ④

chapter 03 당직임무에 대한 적합성

01
휴식

① 주관청은 특히 선박의 안전 및 보안 운항에 관련된 임무를 가진 선원의 피로에 의하여 야기되는 위험을 고려하여야 한다.

② 당직을 담당하는 해기사 또는 당직의 일부를 구성하는 부원으로서 안전 및 오염방지 그리고 보안업무에 관련된 임무가 부여된 모든 사람은 최소한 다음 이상의 휴식시간이 제공되어야 한다.
- 임의 24시간의 기간 내에 최소한 10시간의 휴식시간
- 매 7일의 기간 마다 적어도 77시간의 휴식시간

③ 이 휴식시간은 2회 이내로 나눌 수 있으며, 그 기간 중 하나는 적어도 6시간이어야 한다. 그리고 연속된 휴식시간간의 간격은 14시간을 초과할 수 없다.

④ 비상시 또는 그 밖의 우선되는 운항조건인 경우에는 제2항 및 제3항에 규정된 휴식시간에 대한 요건을 준수하지 아니할 수 있다. 소집, 소화 및 구명정 훈련 그리고 국내 법령 및 국제 규범에 규정된 훈련은 휴식시간에 대한 방해를 최소화하고 또한 피로를 유발하지 않는 방식으로 시행되어야 한다.

① Administrations shall take account of the danger posed by fatigue of seafarers, especially those whose duties involve the safe and secure operation of a ship.

② All persons who are assigned duty as officer in charge of a watch or as a rating forming part of a watch and those whose duties involve designated safety, prevention of pollution and security duties shall be provided with a rest period of not less than:

- a minimum of **10 hours** of rest in any **24-hour** period; and

- **77 hours** in any **7-day** period.

③ The hours of rest may be divided into **no more than two periods**, one of which shall be at least **6 hours** in length, and the intervals between consecutive periods of rest shall not exceed **14 hours**.

④ The requirements for rest periods laid down in paragraphs 2 and 3 need not be maintained in the case of an emergency or in other overriding operational conditions. Musters, fire-fighting and lifeboat drills, and drills prescribed by national laws and regulations and by international instruments, shall be conducted in a manner that minimizes the disturbance of rest periods and does not induce fatigue.

02 알콜 규정

The STCW code advice government to prescribe a maximum blood alcohol level of **0.05%** blood alcohol level (BAC) or **0.25 mg/l** alcohol in the breath for ship personnel during watchkeeping and to prohibit alcohol consumption within **4hours** prior to commencing a watch

STCW 코드 정부는 당직중인 선원의 최대 혈중 알코올 농도를 0.05%(BAC)로, 혹은 호흡의 최대 알콜 함유량을 0.25mg/l로 규정하고 당직 시작 4시간 전에 알코올 섭취를 금지할 것을 권고한다.

기출문제

01. 다음은 STCW의 일부 내용이다. 빈칸에 들어갈 숫자의 합은 무엇인가? [22년 2차]

> All persons who are assigned duty as officer in charge of a watch or as a rating forming part of a watch shall be provided with a rest period of not less than a minimum of ( ) hours of rest in any 24 hour period.
>
> The hours of rest may be divided into no more than two periods, one of which shall be at least ( ) hours in length, and the intervals between consecutive periods of rest shall not exceed ( ) hours

① 24 ② 26
③ 28 ④ 30

해설 당직 선원은 임의의 24시간의 기간 내에 최소한 (10)시간의 휴식시간을 가져야 하며 이 휴식시간은 2회 이내로 나눌 수 있으며, 그 기간 중 하나는 적어도 (6)시간이어야 한다. 그리고 연속된 휴식시간간의 간격은 (14)시간을 초과할 수 없다. 10+6+14=30

답 ④

chapter 04 Voyage planning 항해계획

매 항해 전에 본선의 선장은 예정항해에 필요한 적합한 해도와 제반 항로서지 등을 이용하여 출발항으로부터 최초의 도착항까지의 예정항로의 항해계획을 수립하여야 한다. 이때 이용되는 해도와 항로서지는 항구적 또는 예상 가능한 또한 선박의 안전항행에 관계되는 항행상의 한계 및 위험과 관련하여 정확하고 완전하며 최신의 정보를 담고 있어야 한다.

Prior to each voyage, the master of every ship shall ensure that the intended route from the port of departure to the first port of call is planned using adequate and appropriate charts and other nautical publications necessary for the intended voyage, containing accurate, complete and up-to-date information regarding those navigational limitations and hazards which are of a permanent or predictable nature and which are relevant to the safe navigation of the ship.

chapter 05
Watchkeeping at Sea 항해 중 당직근무

01
Principles applying to watchkeeping generally

The master of every ship is bound to ensure that watchkeeping arrangements are adequate for maintaining a safe navigational or cargo watch. Under the master's general direction, the officers of the navigational watch are responsible for navigating the ship safely during their periods of duty, when they will be particularly concerned with avoiding collision and stranding.

01 당직 근무의 원칙

모든 선박의 선장은 당직근무배치를 적절하게 하여 안전한 항해 당직이 유지되게 하여야 한다. 선장의 일반적인 지시에 따라, 항해당직을 담당하는 해기사는 당직 기간 중 선박을 안전하게 운항할 책임이 있으며, 충돌과 좌초를 피하는 데에 특별한 주의를 기울여야 한다.

02
Principles to be observed in keeping a navigational watch

The officer in charge of the navigational watch is the master's representative and is primarily responsible at all times for the safe navigation of the ship and for complying with the International Regulations for Preventing Collisions at Sea, 1972, as amended.

02 당직 중의 원칙

항해당직을 담당하는 해기사는 선장의 대행자이며, 항상 선박의 안전항해와 "1972 국제해상충돌방지규칙 및 개정규정"의 준수를 위한 일차적인 책임을 진다.

03 경계

경계자와 조타자의 임무는 분리되어야 하며, 조타자는 조타중에 경계자로 간주되어서는 아니된다. 단, 조타 위치에서 사방의 시야에 제한을 받지 않으며, 또한 야간경계의 장해 또는 기타 적절한 경계유지의 방해가 없는 소형선박의 경우는 예외로 한다. 다음 각 호의 경우, 항해당직을 담당하는 해기사는 주간에 단독으로 경계를 할 수 있다.

① 상황을 주의 깊게 검토하여, 그렇게 하여도 안전하다는 것이 의심 없이 확인되었을 경우

② 적어도 다음의 모든 관련 요소가 충분히 고려되었을 경우
- 기상상태
- 시정
- 해상교통량
- 항해위험물에 대한 근접도
- 통항분리제도 수역내 또는 그 부근을 항행중일 때 필요한 주의

③ 상황의 변화에 의하여 필요한 때에는 보조자가 즉시 선교에 호출될 수 있는 경우

04 당직의 인계

① 항해당직을 담당하는 해기사는 당직을 인계받을 해기사가 당직임무를 유효하게 수행할 수 없다고 믿을만한 이유가 있을 경우에는 그에게 당직을 인계하여서는 아니되며, 이러한 경우에 항해당직을 담당하는 해기사는 선장에게 보고하여야 한다.

03
Lookout

The duties of the lookout and helmsperson are **separate** and the helmsperson **shall not be considered** to be the lookout while steering, except in small ships where an unobstructed all-round view is provided at the steering position and there is no impairment of night vision or other impediment to the keeping of a proper lookout. The officer in charge of the navigational watch may be the sole lookout in daylight provided that, on each such occasion:

① the situation has been carefully assessed and it has been established without doubt that it is safe to do so;

② full account has been taken of all relevant factors, including, but not limited to:
- state of weather;
- visibility;
- traffic density;
- proximity of dangers to navigation; and
- the attention necessary when navigating in or near traffic separation schemes; and

③ assistance is immediately available to be summoned to the bridge when any change in the situation so requires.

04
Taking over the watch

① The officer in charge of the navigational watch **shall not hand over** the watch to the relieving officer if there is reason to believe that the latter is **not capable of carrying out the watchkeeping duties** effectively, in which case the **master shall be notified**.

② The relieving officer shall ensure that the members of the relieving watch are fully capable of performing their duties, particularly as regards their adjustment to **night vision**. Relieving officers shall **not take over the watch** until their vision is fully adjusted to the light conditions.

③ Prior to taking over the watch, relieving officers shall satisfy themselves as to the ship's estimated or true position and confirm its intended track, course and speed, and UMS controls as appropriate and shall note any dangers to navigation expected to be encountered during their watch.

Relieving officers shall personally satisfy themselves regarding the:

- **standing orders** and other special instructions of the master relating to navigation of the ship;
- **position, course, speed and draught** of the ship;
- prevailing and predicted **tides, currents, weather, visibility** and the effect of these factors upon course and speed;
- **procedures for the use of main engines** to manoeuvre when the main engines are on bridge control; and
- **navigational situation**

④ If any time the officer in charge of the navigational watch is to be relieved when a manoeuvre or other action to avoid any hazard is taking place, the relief of that officer **shall be deferred** until such action has been **completed**.

② 인계를 받는 해기사는 당직의 구성원이 자신의 임무를 충분히 수행할 수 있는지를 확인하여야 하며, 특히 어둠에 눈이 적응하는데에 주의하여야 한다. 인계를 받는 해기사는 자신의 눈이 조명상태에 완전히 적응할 때까지 당직을 인계받아서는 안된다.

③ 당직을 인계받기 전에 인계를 받는 해기사는 선박의 추정위치 또는 진위치를 스스로 확인하여야 하며, 선박의 예정항로, 침로와 속력 및 해당하는 경우에는 무인기관시스템(UMS) 제어상태를 확인하여야 하고, 당직 중에 조우할 것으로 예상되는 일체의 항해상의 위험물에 유의하여야 한다.

인계를 받는 해기사는 스스로 다음 사항을 확인하여야 한다.

- 선박의 항행과 관련한 선장의 당직지침 기타의 특별 지시사항
- 선박의 위치, 침로, 속력 및 흘수
- 현재 및 앞으로 예상되는 조석, 조류, 기상, 시정 및 이들 요소가 침로와 속력에 미치는 영향
- 주기관의 선교 조종시 선박을 조종하기 위한 주기관의 사용절차
- 항해상황

④ 교대될 시각에 선박의 조종 또는 어떠한 피항 조치가 진행 중인 경우, 항해당직을 담당하는 해기사의 교대는 그러한 조치가 완료될 때까지 연기되어야 한다.

기출문제

01. 다음 중 STCW(International Convention on Standards of Training, Certification and Watchkeeping for Seafarers) 협약상 항해당직 인계시, 인계를 받는 해기사가 확인해야 할 사항으로 가장 옳지 않은 것은? `21년 하반기`

① Course
② Speed
③ Draught of the ship
④ Gross tonnage

해설 총톤수(Gross tonnage)는 인계 시 인계를 받는 해기사가 확인할 사항이 아니다.

답 ④

02. Choose a proper word in blank `11년 2차`

> If any time the officer in charge of the navigational watch is to be relieved when a manoeuvre or other action to avoid any hazard is taking place, the relief of that officer shall be deferred until such action has been (   ).

① continued
② verified
③ finished
④ postponed

해설 STCW 본문 상 빈칸에는 완전히 끝나다를 의미하는 completed가 들어간다. '종료되다'를 의미하는 finished 또한 문맥상 들어갈 수 있는 단어이다.

답 ③

05
Radio operator

Radio operators are responsible for maintaining a continuous radio watch on appropriate frequencies during their periods of duty.

06
Performing the navigational watch

① The officer in charge of the navigational watch shall:

- keep the watch on the bridge;
- in no circumstances leave the bridge until properly relieved; and

- continue to be responsible for the safe navigation of the ship, despite the presence of the master on the bridge, until informed specifically that the master has assumed that responsibility and this is mutually understood.

- notify the master when in any doubt as to what action to take in the interest of safety

② During the watch, the course steered, position and speed shall be checked at sufficiently frequent intervals, using any available navigational aids necessary, to ensure that the ship follows the planned course.

③ The officer in charge of the navigational watch shall have full knowledge of the location and operation of all safety and navigational equipment on board the ship and shall be aware and take account of the operating limitations of such equipment.

---

05 무선통신사

무선통신사는 자신의 당직기간 중 적절한 주파수상에서 지속적으로 무선통신 청수당직을 유지할 책임이 있다.

06 당직의 수행

① 항해당직을 담당하는 해기사는 다음 사항을 준수하여야 한다.
- 선교에서 당직을 수행할 것
- 어떠한 상황하에서도 적절히 당직이 교대될 때까지 선교를 떠나지 말 것
- 선장이 선교에 있다고 하더라도 선장이 항해당직을 담당하는 해기사에게 책임을 맡겠다는 것을 특별히 통지하고 이것을 서로 이해할 때까지는 그 선박의 안전항해에 대하여 계속 책임을 질 것
- 선박 안전을 위하여 취할 행동에 대하여 의문이 있을 때에는 선장에게 보고 할 것

② 당직중에 선박이 계획항로를 따라 가고 있는지를 확인하기 위해, 필요하고 가능한 모든 항해장비를 이용하여 충분히 자주 조타침로, 선위 및 속력을 점검하여야 한다.

③ 항해당직을 담당하는 해기사는 선내의 모든 안전장치와 항해장치의 위치 및 작동에 관하여 숙지하여야 하며, 이들 장치의 작동상의 한계를 인지하고 고려하여야 한다.

④ 항해당직을 담당하는 해기사는 선박의 안전항해를 방해할 수 있는 어떠한 임무를 할당받거나 또는 수행하여서는 아니된다.

⑤ 레이더를 사용하고 있을 때, 항해당직을 담당하는 해기사는 발효중인 "1972 국제해상충돌방지규칙 및 개정규정"에서 규정하는 레이더의 사용에 관한 규정을 항상 준수하여야 할 필요성을 명심하여야 한다.

⑥ 필요한 경우 항해당직을 담당하는 해기사는 타(舵), 기관 및 음향신호장치의 사용을 주저하여서는 아니된다. 그러나, 관련 절차에 따라 선교에 설치된 무인기관실 제어장치의 사용이 가능하거나 효과적으로 사용할 수 있는 경우에는, 의도하는 기관속력의 변화를 적시에 통보하여야 한다.

④ The officer in charge of the navigational watch shall **not be assigned** or undertake any duties which would **interfere with** the safe navigation of the ship.

⑤ When using radar, the officer in charge of the navigational watch shall bear in mind the necessity to comply at all times with the provisions on the use of radar contained in the International Regulations for Preventing Collisions at Sea, 1972, as amended in force.

⑥ In cases of need, the officer in charge of the navigational watch shall not **hesitate** to use the helm, engines and sound signalling apparatus. However, timely notice of intended variations of engine speed shall be given where possible or effective use shall be made of UMS engine controls provided on the bridge in accordance with the applicable procedures.

기출문제

03. Select the best answer at blank 09년 2차

The officer of the watch should bear in mind that engines are at his disposal and he should not (　　) to use them in case of need.
However, timely notice of intended variations of engine speed should be given when possible

① memorize　　② notify
③ hesitate　　④ break off

해설 당직 항해사는 필요하다면 기관을 사용하는 것을 망설여서는(hesitate) 안 된다.

답 ③

⑦ Officers of the navigational watch shall know the **handling characteristics** of their ship, including its **stopping distances**, and should appreciate that other ships may have different handling characteristics.

⑧ A proper record shall be kept during the watch of the movements and activities relating to the navigation of the ship.

⑨ It is of special importance that at all times the officer in charge of the navigational watch ensures that a proper lookout is maintained. In a ship with a separate chartroom, the officer in charge of the navigational watch may visit the chartroom, when essential, for a short period for the necessary performance of navigational duties, but shall first ensure that it is safe to do so and that proper lookout is maintained.

⑩ Operational tests of shipboard navigational equipment shall be carried out at sea as frequently as practicable and as circumstances permit, in particular before hazardous conditions affecting navigation are expected. Whenever appropriate, these tests shall be recorded. Such tests shall also be carried out prior to port arrival and departure.

⑪ The officer in charge of the navigational watch shall make regular checks to ensure that:

㉠ the person steering the ship or the automatic pilot is steering the correct course;
㉡ the standard compass error is determined at least once a watch and, when possible, after any major alteration of course; the standard and gyro-compasses are frequently compared and repeaters are synchronized with their master compass;

⑦ 항해당직을 담당하는 해기사는 정선거리를 포함한 자선의 조종 특성을 숙지하고 있어야 하며, 조종 특성은 선박에 따라 다양하다는 것을 인지하고 있어야 한다.

⑧ 당직중 선박의 항해에 관계되는 이동과 활동을 적절히 기록하여야 한다.

⑨ 항해당직을 담당하는 해기사가 항상 적절한 경계가 유지되고 있는지를 확인하는 것은 매우 중요하다. 해도실이 분리된 선박에서는, 항해당직을 담당하는 해기사는 꼭 필요한 경우에 한하여 항해상 필요한 임무수행을 위해 잠시동안 해도실에 들어갈 수 있다. 그러나, 그렇게 하는 것이 안전하고 적절한 경계가 이루어지고 있음을 우선 확인하여야 한다.

⑩ 선내 항해장치의 작동시험은 실행 가능한 한 또한 상황이 허락하는 경우 특히 항해에 영향을 미치는 위험상태가 예견되면 자주 실시되어야 한다. 적절한 때에는 언제나 이러한 작동시험의 결과를 기록하여야 한다. 이러한 작동시험은 또한 입항 및 출항 전에 행하여야 한다.

⑪ 항해당직을 담당하는 해기사는 다음 사항을 확인하기 위해 규칙적으로 점검하여야 한다.

㉠ 조타하고 있는 자 또는 자동조타장치가 올바른 침로를 유지하는 것
㉡ 당직중에 적어도 한번, 그리고 가능한 경우 주요 변침 후 자기컴퍼스의 오차를 구하는 것, 자기컴퍼스와 자이로컴퍼스를 자주 비교하고 리피터가 주자이로컴퍼스와 일치하는 것

ⓒ 자동조타장치를 한 당직에 적어도 한번 수동으로 시험하는 것

ⓔ 항해등, 신호등 및 기타 항해장치가 적절히 작동하는 것

ⓕ 무선통신장치가 이 조 제86항에 따라 적절히 기능을 발휘하는 것

ⓗ 무인기관실시스템 제어장치, 경보장치 및 지시장치가 적절하게 기능하는 것

⑫ 항해당직을 담당하는 해기사는 탑재된 모든 전자항해장치의 성능과 한계를 포함한, 사용법을 철저히 숙지하여야 하며, 필요한 경우 이들 장비를 각각 이용할 수 있어야 하고, 음향측심기는 유효한 항해장비임을 명심하여야 한다.

⑬ 항해당직을 담당하는 해기사는 레이더 상에서 물표를 가능한 한 빨리 발견할 수 있도록 하기 위해 충분히 자주 탐지범위를 변경하여야 한다. 소형물표의 영상 또는 희미한 영상은 탐지되지 아니할 수 있음을 명심하여야 한다.

ⓒ the automatic pilot is tested manually at least once a watch;

ⓔ the navigation and signal lights and other navigational equipment are functioning properly;

ⓕ the radio equipment is functioning properly in accordance with paragraph 86 of this section; and

ⓗ the UMS controls, alarms and indicators are functioning properly.

⑫ Officers of the navigational watch shall be thoroughly familiar with the use of all electronic navigational aids carried, including their capabilities and limitations, and shall use each of these aids when appropriate and shall bear in mind that the echo-sounder is a valuable navigational aid.

⑬ The officer in charge of the navigational watch shall ensure that the **range scales** employed are changed at sufficiently frequent intervals so that echoes are detected as early as possible. It shall be borne in mind that small or poor echoes may escape detection.

기출문제

04. Choose best answer in the blank (10년 3차)

> The officer in charge of the navigational watch shall ensure that the (　) scales employed are changed at sufficiently frequent intervals so that echoes are detected as early as possible. It shall be borne in mind that small or poor echoes may escape detection.

① wind
② range
③ radar
④ navigation

해설 당직 항해사는 가능한 조기에 반사체를 탐지하기 위해 사용 중인 레이더의 range scale를 자주 바꿔가며 사용해야 한다.

답 ②

⑭ The officer in charge of the navigational watch shall notify the master immediately:

㉠ if restricted visibility is encountered or expected;

㉡ if the traffic conditions or the movements of other ships are causing concern;

㉢ if difficulty is experienced in maintaining course;

㉣ on failure to sight land, or a navigation mark or to obtain soundings by the expected time;

㉤ if, unexpectedly, land or a navigation mark is sighted or a change in soundings occurs;

㉥ on breakdown of the engines, propulsion machinery remote control, steering gear or any essential navigational equipment, alarm or indicator;

㉦ if the radio equipment malfunctions;

㉧ in heavy weather, if in any doubt about the possibility of weather damage;

㉨ if the ship meets any hazard to navigation, such as ice or a derelict; and

㉩ in any other emergency or if in any doubt.

⑭ 항해당직을 담당하는 해기사는 다음의 경우 즉시 선장에게 보고하여야 한다.
㉠ 시정이 제한되거나 또는 제한될 것이 예상될 경우
㉡ 선박의 통항상태 또는 다른 선박의 이동이 염려스러울 경우
㉢ 침로의 유지가 어려울 경우
㉣ 예정시각까지 육표와 항로표지를 발견하지 못하거나 또는 측심을 못하였을 경우
㉤ 예기치 아니한 육표 또는 항로표지를 발견하거나 또는 측심의 변화가 발생하였을 경우
㉥ 주기관, 추진기의 원격조정장치, 조타장치 또는 일체의 필수항해장치, 경보장치 또는 지시장치의 고장시
㉦ 무선통신장치의 오작동시
㉧ 황천속에서 기상으로 인한 선체손상이 우려되는 때
㉨ 선박이 유빙 또는 표류물 등 항행상의 위험물을 조우하였을 경우
㉩ 기타 모든 비상시 또는 의심이 가는 경우

| 기출문제

05. 다음은 항해 당직 및 업무와 관련한 내용이다. 가장 옳지 않은 것은 무엇인가?

① The intended voyage shall be planned in advance taking into consideration all pertinent information and any course laid down shall be checked.
② The safety and navigational equipment with which the ship is provided and the manner of the its operation shall be clearly understood; in addition its operational condition shall be fully taken into account.
③ On taking over the watch the ship's estimated or true position, intended track, course and speed shall be confirmed; any navigational hazard expected to be encountered during the watch shall be noted.
④ The officer in charge of the navigational watch shall be assigned or undertake any duties which would interfere with the safe navigation of the ship.

해설 당직 항해사는 선박의 안전항해에 방해가 되는 업무를 할당받거나 맡아서는 안 된다.(shall not be assigned)

chapter 06 여러 조건과 수역에서의 당직근무

01 제한시계

시정이 제한되었거나 제한될 것이 예상될 때, 항해당직을 담당하는 해기사의 일차적 책임은 "1972 국제해상충돌방지규칙 및 개정규정"의 관계 규정을 준수하는 것이며 특히 무중신호가 울리는 것에 주의하면서 안전한 속력으로 항행하고, 즉각적인 조선을 위해서 기관을 준비하여야 한다. 이에 부가하여 항해당직을 담당하는 해기사는 다음 조치를 취하여야 한다.

– 선장에게 보고할 것
– 적절한 경계자를 배치할 것
– 항해등을 켤 것
– 레이더를 작동하여 사용할 것

02 야간

경계임무를 할당할 때 선장과 항해당직을 담당하는 해기사는 사용가능한 선교 장치와 항해장비, 그 한계, 작동절차와 안전조치에 대해 상당한 주의를 하여야 한다.

01 Restricted visibility

When restricted visibility is encountered or expected, the first responsibility of the officer in charge of the navigational watch is to comply with the relevant rules of the International Regulations for Preventing Collisions at Sea, 1972, as amended with particular regard to the sounding of fog signals, proceeding at a safe speed and having the engines ready for immediate manoeuvre. In addition, the officer in charge of the navigational watch shall:

- inform the master;
- post a proper lookout;
- exhibit navigation lights; and
- operate and use the radar.

02 In hours of darkness

The master and the officer in charge of the navigational watch, when arranging lookout duty, shall have due regard to the bridge equipment and navigational aids available for use, their limitations, procedures and safeguards implemented.

03
Coastal and congested waters

① The largest scale chart on board, suitable for the area and corrected with the latest available information, shall be used. Fixes shall be taken at frequent intervals, and shall be carried out by more than one method whenever circumstances allow. When using ECDIS, appropriate usage code (scale) electronic navigational charts shall be used and the ship's position shall be checked by an independent means of position fixing at appropriate intervals.

② The officer in charge of the navigational watch shall positively identify all relevant navigation marks.

04
Navigation with pilot on board

① Despite the duties and obligations of pilots, their presence on board does not relieve the master or the officer in charge of the navigational watch from their duties and obligations for the safety of the ship. The master and the pilot shall exchange information regarding navigation procedures, local conditions and the ship's characteristics. The master and/or the officer in charge of the navigational watch shall co-operate closely with the pilot and maintain an accurate check on the ship's position and movement.

② If in any doubt as to the pilot's actions or intentions, the officer in charge of the navigational watch shall seek clarification from the pilot and, if doubt still exists, shall notify the master immediately and take whatever action is necessary before the master arrives.

---

03 연안 및 선박폭주 수역

① 최신의 정보에 의해 소개정된 당해 수역에 적합한 가장 큰 축적의 해도를 사용하여야 한다. 선위의 측정은 가능한 한 자주 행하여야 하며, 시정이 허락하는 한 한가지 이상의 방법으로 행하여야 한다. ECDIS 사용시 적절한 활용코드(축적) 전자항해해도를 사용하여야 하며, 선위는 적절한 간격으로 독립적인 선위측정 수단으로 확인하여야 한다.

② 항해당직을 담당하는 해기사는 모든 관련 항로표지를 적극적으로 확인하여야 한다.

04 도선사 승선시의 항해

① 도선사의 임무와 의무에도 불구하고, 도선사가 승선하여도 선박의 안전항해를 위한 선장과 항해당직을 담당하는 해기사의 임무와 의무가 면제되는 것은 아니다. 선장과 도선사는 항해절차, 지역적 조건 및 선박의 특성에 관한 정보를 교환하여야 한다. 선장 및/또는 항해당직을 담당하는 해기사는 도선사와 긴밀히 협력하여야 하며 선위와 선박의 이동에 관하여 계속 정확한 점검을 하여야 한다.

② 도선사의 조치 또는 의도가 의심스러울 경우, 항해당직을 담당하는 해기사는 도선사로부터 명확한 설명을 구하여야 하며, 그래도 여전히 의심스러울 때에는 선장에게 즉시 보고하여야 하며, 선장이 도착하기 전에 모든 필요한 조치를 취하여야 한다.

I 기출문제

01. 다음은 STCW중 도선사 승선시의 항해에 관한 사항이다. 옳지 않은 것은? 〔기출예상문제〕

① Despite the duties and obligations of pilot, his presence on board dose not relieve the master or officer in charge of the watch.
② The master and the pilot need to exchange information regarding navigation procedures, local conditions and the ship's characteristics.
③ The master and officer of navigational watch shall co-operate closely with the pilot and maintain an accurate check on the ships position and movement.
④ if in any doubt as to the pilot's action or intentions, the officer in charge of the navigational watch shall not seek clarification from the pilot.

해설
① 도선사(pilot)의 업무와 의무에 불구하고 도선사의 승선이 선장(master)과 당직항해사(officer in charge of the watch)를 당직의 의무로부터 면제시켜주지는 않는다.
② 선장(master)과 도선사(pilot)는 항해 절차, 지역의 상태 그리고 선박 성능에 관한 정보를 교환하여야 한다.
③ 선장(master)과 당직항해사(officer in charge of the watch)는 도선사(pilot)와 긴밀히 협업하여야하고 선위와 선박 움직임을 정확히 유지 해줘야한다.
④ 만일 파일럿의 동작이나 의도에 의심구심이 드는 경우, 당직항해사는 파일럿으로부터 그에 대한 해명을 요구할 수 있다(shall ~~not~~ seek clarification).

답 ④

PART 08 MARPOL(International Convention for the Prevention for Marine Pollution from Ship)

Chapter 1	MARPOL 부속서의 종류
Chapter 2	용어 정의
Chapter 3	기름(Oil)의 배출
Chapter 4	Oil filtering equipment & ODME
Chapter 5	유해액체물질(noxious liquid substances in bulk)의 배출
Chapter 6	하수(Sewage)의 배출
Chapter 7	폐기물(Garbage)의 배출
Chapter 8	각종 문서 및 기록부

chapter 01 MARPOL 부속서의 종류

부속서1 기름에 의한 오염방지를 위한 규칙	Annex 1 Prevention of pollution by oil & oily water
부속서2 산적 유해액체물질에 의한 오염규제를 위한 규칙	Annex 2 Control of pollution by noxious liquid substances in bulk
부속서3 포장된 형태로 선박에 의하여 운송되는 유해물질에 의한 오염방지를 위한 규칙	Annex 3 Prevention of pollution by harmful substances carried by sea in packaged form
부속서4 선박으로부터의 하수에 의한 오염방지를 위한 규칙	Annex 4 Prevention of pollution by sewage from ships
부속서5 선박으로부터의 폐기물에 의한 오염방지를 위한 규칙	Annex 5 Prevention of pollution by garbage from ships
부속서6 선박으로부터의 대기오염방지를 위한 규칙	Annex 6 Prevention of air pollution from ships

chapter 02 용어 정의

용어	meaning	의미
Oil 기름	petroleum in any form including crude oil, fuel oil, sludge, oil refuse and refined products (other than petrochemicals which are subject to the provisions of Annex II of the present Convention).	원유, 중유, 슬러지, 폐유 및 정제유를 포함한 모든 형태의 석유(이 협약 부속서 II의 규정에 따른 석유화학물질은 제외한다)를 말한다.
Oily mixture 유성혼합물	a mixture with any oil content.	유분을 함유한 혼합물을 말한다.
Oil fuel 연료유	any oil used as fuel in connection with the propulsion and auxiliary machinery of the ship in which such oil is carried.	당해 기름을 적재하는 선박의 추진기관 및 보조기관과 관련하여 연료로써 사용되는 모든 기름을 말한다.
Oil tanker 유탱커	a ship constructed or adapted primarily to carry oil in bulk in its cargo spaces and includes combination carriers and any "chemical tanker" as defined in Annex II of the present Convention when it is carrying a cargo or part cargo of oil in bulk.	주로 그의 화물창에 산적의 기름을 적재하도록 건조되거나 개조된 선박을 말하며, 겸용선과 산적의 기름을 화물 또는 화물의 일부로서 적재하고 있는 경우에는 이 협약의 부속서 II의 정의된 "케미컬 탱커"를 포함한다.
Combination carrier 겸용선	a ship designed to carry either oil or solid cargoes in bulk.	겸용선이라 함은 산적의 기름 또는 고체화물을 적재하도록 설계된 선박을 말한다.
Crude oil tanker 원유탱커	an oil tanker engaged in the trade of carrying crude oil.	원유를 운송하는 무역에 종사하는 유탱커를 말한다.
Product carrier 정제유운반선	an oil tanker engaged in the trade of carrying oil other than crude oil.	원유 이외의 기름을 운송하는 무역에 종사하는 유탱커를 말한다.
Nearest land 가장 가까운 육지	The term from the nearest land means from the baseline from which the territorial sea of the territory in question is established in accordance with international law	국제법에 따라 당해 영역의 영해를 설정하기 위한 기선으로부터를 말한다.
Special area 특별해역	a sea area where for recognized technical reasons in relation to its oceanographical and ecological condition and to the particular character of its traffic the adoption of special mandatory methods for the prevention of sea pollution by oil is required.	그 해양학상 및 생태학상의 조건과 교통의 특수한 성격으로부터 인정되는 기술적인 이유로 기름에 의한 해양오염 방지를 위한 특별한 강제조치의 채택이 요구되는 해역을 말한다.

Instantaneous rate of discharge of oil content 유분의 순간배출율	the rate of discharge of oil in litres per hour at any instant divided by the speed of the ship in knots at the same instant.	어느 순간에 있어서 시간당 리터 단위로 배출된 기름을 당해 순간에 있어서 노트 단위의 선박 속력에 의해 나눈 비율을 말한다.
Tank 탱크	an enclosed space which is formed by the permanent structure of a ship and which is designed for the carriage of liquid in bulk.	선박의 영구적인 구조로 형성되고 산적으로 액체를 운송하기 위하여 설계된 폐위구역을 말한다.
Wing tank 선측탱크	any tank adjacent to the side shell plating.	선측외판에 인접하는 탱크를 말한다.
Centre tank 중앙탱크	any tank inboard of a longitudinal bulkhead.	종통격벽의 내측의 탱크를 말한다.
Slop tank 슬롭탱크	a tank specifically designated for the collection of tank drainings, tank washings and other oily mixtures.	탱크배수, 탱크세정수 및 기타 유성혼합물을 모으기 위하여 특별히 지정된 탱크를 말한다.
Cofferdam 코퍼댐	the isolating space between two adjacent steel bulkheads or decks	인접한 두 금속 격벽사이, 혹은 갑판 사이의 분리된 공간
Clean ballast 청정평형수	the ballast in a tank which since oil was last carried therein, has been so cleaned that effluent therefrom if it were discharged from a ship which is stationary into clean calm water on a clear day would not produce visible traces of oil on the surface of the water or on adjoining shorelines or cause a sludge or emulsion to be deposited beneath the surface of the water or upon adjoining shorelines. If the ballast is discharged through an oil discharge monitoring and control system approved by the Administration, evidence based on such a system to the effect that the oil content of the effluent did not exceed 15 parts per million shall be determinative that the ballast was clean, notwithstanding the presence of visible traces.	최후에 기름이 운송된 후에 그곳으로부터의 배출액이 청명한 날 정지하고 있는 선박으로부터 맑고 잔잔한 해면에 배출된 경우에 눈으로 볼 수 있는 유막을 해면 또는 인접한 해안선에 생기게 하지 아니하거나, 해면하 또는 해안선상에 침전하는 슬러지 또는 에멀젼을 생기게 하지 아니할 정도로 세정된 탱크 내의 평형수를 말한다. 당해 평형수가 주관청에 의하여 승인된 기름배출감시제어장치를 통하여 배출될 경우에는 유출액 중의 유분이 100만분의 15를 넘지 아니한다는 것이 당해 장치에 의하여 입증되면 눈으로 볼 수 있는 유막이 생기는 것에 관계없이 당해 평형수는 청정평형수로 한다.
Segregated ballast 분리평형수	the ballast water introduced into a tank which is completely separated from the cargo oil and oil fuel system and which is permanently allocated to the carriage of ballast	화물유 계통 및 연료유 계통으로부터 완전히 분리되어 있으며 평형수를 적재하기 위하여 영구적으로 설치되어 있는 탱크에 적재된 평형수를 말한다.

Oil residue (sludge) 유성잔류물 (슬러지)	the residual waste oil products generated during the normal operation of a ship such as those resulting from the purification of fuel or lubricating oil for main or auxiliary machinery, separated waste oil from oil filtering equipment, waste oil collected in drip trays, and waste hydraulic and lubricating oils.	주기관 또는 보조 기기를 위한 연료유나 윤활유의 청정으로부터 발생하는 것, 기름 필터링장치로부터 발생하는 분리된·폐유, 기름받이에 모아지는 폐유, 그리고 폐유압유 및 폐유활유와 같이 선박의 통상 운항 중에 발생하는 잔존 폐유 물질을 말한다.

기출문제

01. MARPOL 73/78에서 OIL(기름)의 정의에 포함되지 않는 것은? 〔13년 2차 / 18년 2차〕

① Crude oil ② Oily water
③ Sludge ④ Refined products

해설 기름에 포함되는 것으로는 crude oil, fuel oil, sludge, oil refuse and refined products이 있고, Oily water (유성혼합물)는 기름이 포함된 물이기 때문에, 기름에 해당하지 않는다.

답 ❷

02. Choose the correct one for the blank. 〔13년 1차 / 18년 1차〕

(　　) means a tank specifically designated for the collection of tank drainings, tank washings and other oily mixtures according to MARPOL Convention.

① Slop tank
② Bilge tank
③ Sludge tank
④ Clean ballast tank

해설 슬롭탱크(slop tank)라 함은 탱크배수, 탱크세정수 및 기타의 유성혼합물을 모으기 위하여 특별히 지정된 탱크를 말한다.

답 ❶

기출문제

03. 다음은 「MARPOL(International Convention for the Prevention of Marine Pollution from Ship)」상 용어에 대한 설명이다 빈칸에 들어갈 단어로 가장 옳은 것은? `20년 3차`

( ) means a tank specifically designated for the collection of tank drainings, tank washings and other oily mixtures.

① Wing tank　　② Slop tank
③ Center tank　④ Tank

해설 위 문제와 동일

답 ❷

04. 다음 빈 칸에 들어갈 말로 가장 적절한 것은? `14년 1차`

In MARPOL 73/78, ( ) means the ballast water introduced into tank which is completely separated from the cargo oil and oil fuel system.

① segregated ballast　② clean ballast
③ slop ballast　　　　④ dirty ballast

해설 분리 발라스트(segregated ballast)라 함은 화물유 계통 및 연료유 계통으로부터 완전히 분리되어 있는 탱크에 적재된 발라스트 물을 말한다.

답 ❶

05. Choose a proper word in a blank `11년 2차`

In MAROP 73/78, "instantaneous rate of discharge of oil content" means the rate of discharge of oil in litres per ( ) at any instant divided by the speed of the ship in knots at the same instant.

① hour　　② minute
③ second　④ day

해설 유분의 순간 배출율(instantaneous rate of discharge of oil content)이란 어느 순간에 있어서 시간(hour) 당 리터 단위로 배출된 기름을 당해 순간에 있어서 노트 단위의 선박 속력에 의해 나눈 비율을 말한다.

답 ❶

기출문제

06. MARPOL(International Convention for the Prevention of Pollution from Ships)상 용어의 설명으로 가장 옳은 것은? 　　20년 1차

① "Tank" means an enclosed space which is formed by the permanent structure of a ship and which is designed for the carriage of liquid in bulk.
② "Center tank" means any tank adjacent to the side shell plating.
③ "Bilge tank" means any tank inboard of a longitudinal bulkhead.
④ "Wing tank" means a tank specifically designated for the collection of tank drainings, tank washings and other oily mixtures.

해설 옳지 않은 것:
② Wing tank에 대한 설명이다.
③ Center tank에 대한 설명이다.
④ Slop tank에 대한 설명이다.

답 ❶

07. 다음 〈보기〉는 MARPOL 협약상 용어의 정의에 대한 내용이다. 빈 칸에 들어갈 말로 가장 옳은 것은? 　　21년 상반기

> The term 'from the nearest land' means from the (　　) in accordance with international law except certain are as specified.

① coastline at high water
② coastline at low water
③ coastline at approximate highest high water
④ baseline from which the territorial seas is established

해설 가장 가까운 육지로부터(from the nearest land) 란 국제법에 따라 당해 영역의 <u>영해(territorial sea)</u>를 <u>설정하기 위한 기선</u>으로 부터를 말한다.

답 ❹

chapter 03 기름(Oil)의 배출

01
기관구역(Machinery spaces)에서의 기름 배출

총 톤수 400톤 이상의 선박으로부터 기름 또는 유성혼합물의 바다로의 배출은 다음의 모든 조건을 만족하는 경우를 제외하고 금지된다:

Any discharge into the sea of oil or oily mixtures from ships of 400 gross tonnage and above shall be prohibited except when all the following conditions are satisfied:

① 선박이 항행 중일 것;

① the ship is **proceeding** en route;

② 유성혼합물이 이 부속서의 제14규칙의 요건에 만족하는 기름필터링 장치를 통하여 처리될 것;

② the oily mixture is processed through an **oil filtering equipment** meeting the requirements of regulation 14 of this Annex;

③ 유출액 중의 유분이 희석되지 아니하고 15ppm을 초과하지 아니할 것;

③ the oil content of the effluent without dilution does **not exceed 15 parts per million;**

④ 유성혼합물이 유조선의 화물펌프실 빌지로부터 생성되지 않을 것; 그리고

④ the oily mixture does **not originate from cargo pump room bilges** on oil tankers; and

⑤ 유탱커의 경우, 유성혼합물이 기름 화물잔류물과 혼합되지 않을 것.

⑤ the oily mixture, in case of oil tankers, is **not mixed with oil cargo residues**.

02
유조선의 화물구역(Cargo area of oil tanker)에서의 배출

유탱커의 화물지역으로부터 기름 또는 유성혼합물의 바다로의 배출은 다음의 조건이 모두 충족되는 경우를 제외하고 금지된다:

any discharge into the sea of oil or oily mixtures from the cargo area of an oil tanker, shall be prohibited except when all the following conditions are satisfied:

① 탱커가 특별해역 내에 있지 아니할 것;

① the tanker is **not within a special area;**

② 탱커가 가장 가까운 육지로부터 50해리 밖에 있을 것;

② the tanker is more than **50 nautical miles from the nearest land;**

③ the tanker is **proceeding** en route;

④ the instantaneous rate of discharge of oil content does **not exceed 30 litres per nautical mile;**

⑤ the total quantity of oil discharged into the sea **does not exceed** for tankers delivered on or before 31 December 1979, as defined in regulation 1.28.1, **1/15,000** of the total quantity of the particular cargo of which the residue formed a part, and for tankers delivered after 31 December 1979, as defined in regulation 1.28.2, **1/30,000** of the total quantity of the particular cargo of which the residue formed a part; and

⑥ the tanker has **in operation** an **oil discharge monitoring and control system** and a **slop tank** arrangement as required by regulations 29 and 31 of this Annex.

③ 탱커가 항행 중일 것;

④ 유분의 순간배출율이 1해리 당 30리터를 초과하지 아니할 것;

⑤ 해역 내 배출되는 기름의 총량이 제1.28.1규칙에서 정의된 내로 1979년 12월 31일 이전에 인도된 유탱커에 있어서는 당해 잔류물이 일부로써 구성하고 있던 개별화물 총량의 15,000분의 1 이하이고, 그리고 제1.28.2규칙에서 정의된 대로 1979년 12월 31일 후에 인도된 탱커에 있어서는 당해 잔류물이 일부로써 구성하고 있던 개별화물총량의 30,000분의 1 이하일 것; 그리고

⑥ 탱커가 이 부속서의 제29 및 제31 규칙에 의하여 요구되는 기름배출 감시제어장치 및 슬롭탱크 장치를 작동시키고 있을 것.

기출문제

01. 다음은 MARPOL(International Convention for the Prevention of Marine Pollution from Ship) 73/78 협약상 기름 배출 내용이다. 가장 옳지 않은 것은? `21년 하반기`

> Any discharge into the sea of oil or oily mixtures from ships of 400 gross tonnage and above shall be prohibited except when all the following conditions are satisfied:

① the ship is proceeding en route;
② the oily mixture is processed through an oil filtering equipment;
③ the oil content of the effluent without dilution does exceed 15 parts per million;
④ the oily mixture, in case of tankers, is not mixed with oil cargo residues.

해설 유출액(effluent) 중의 유분(oil content)이 희석되지 아니하고 15ppm을 초과하지 아니할 것(not exceed);

답 ❸

기출문제

02. 다음은 「MARPOL(International Convention for the Prevention of Marine Pollution from Ship)」중 Regulation 9 (Control of discharge of oil) 일부를 발췌한 것이다. ㉠, ㉡, ㉢, ㉣ 중 옳은 지문은 모두 몇 개인가? `20년 3차`

(1) Subject to the provisions of regulations 10 and 11 of this Annex and paragraph (2) of this regulation, any discharge into the sea of oil or oily mixtures from ships to which this Annex applies shall be prohibited except when all the following conditions are satisfied :
(a) for an oil tanker, except as provided for in subparagraph ⓑ of this paragraph :
㉠ (i) the tanker is within a special area.
㉡ (ii) the tanker is more than 50 nautical miles from the nearest land.
㉢ (iii) the tanker is proceeding
㉣ (iv) the instantaneous rate of discharge of oil content does not exceed 30 liters per nautical mile.

① 1개　　　　　② 2개
③ 3개　　　　　④ 4개

해설 옳지 않은 것:
㉠ the tanker is <u>not</u> within a special area.

답 ③

chapter 04 Oil filtering equipment & ODME

01
Oil filtering equipment

① Any ship of **400 gross tonnage** and above but less than **10,000 gross tonnage** shall be fitted with oil filtering equipment

② Any ship of **10,000 gross tonnage** and above shall be fitted with **oil filtering equipment**. In addition, it shall be provided with **alarm arrangement** to indicate when this level cannot be maintained. The system shall also be provided with arrangements to ensure that any discharge of oily mixtures is **automatically stopped** when the oil content of the effluent exceeds **15 parts per million**.

02
Oil Discharge Monitoring and Control system (ODME)

Oil tankers of **150 gross tonnage** and above shall be equipped with an **oil discharge monitoring and control system** approved by the Administration.

① 총 톤수 400톤 이상 및 10,000톤 미만의 선박은 이 규칙의 6항에 따른 기름필터링장치를 설치하여야 한다.

② 총톤수 10,000톤 이상의 선박은 기름필터링장치를 설치하여야 한다. 추가적으로, 이 장치에는 이 기준이 유지될 수 없는 경우에 이를 표시하는 경보장치가 설치되어야 한다. 유출액의 유분농도가 15ppm을 초과하는 경우에는 유성 혼합물의 배출을 자동적으로 정지시키는 것을 확보하는 장치가 설치되어야 한다.

총 톤수 150톤 이상의 모든 유탱커는 주관청으로부터 승인된 기름배출감시제어장치를 갖춰야 한다.

기출문제

01. 다음은 MARPLO 원문을 발췌해 온 것이다. 빈칸에 들어갈 말로 가장 옳은 것은? `19년 1차`

> Any ship of ( ) gross tonnage and above shall be provided with oil filtering equipment, and with arrangements for an alarm and for automatically stopping any discharge of oily mixture when the oil content in the effluent exceeds 15 parts per million

① 150 ton   ② 400 ton
③ 10,000 ton   ④ 20,000 ton

해설 총톤수 10,000톤 이상의 선박은 유출액의 유분이 15ppm을 넘는 경우 알람을 울리고 자동으로 중지시키는 설비를 갖춰야한다.

답 ❸

chapter 05 유해액체물질(noxious liquid substances in bulk)의 배출

01
유해액체물질의 분류

① X류 - 탱크세정 또는 평형수 배출 작업에 의하여 해양에 배출된 경우, 해양자원이나 인체에 막대한 위해를 미치는 것으로 간주되므로, 해양환경으로 배출을 금지하는 것이 정당하다고 보는 유해액체물질.

② Y류 - 탱크세정 또는 평형수 배출 작업에 의하여 해양에 배출된 경우, 해양자원이나 인체에 위해를 미치거나 해양의 쾌적성 또는 기타의 적법한 이용에 해를 야기하기 하므로 해양환경으로의 배출물의 품질과 양에 대한 제한을 하는 것이 정당하다고 보는 유해액체물질.

③ Z류 - 탱크세정 또는 평형수 배출 작업에 의하여 해양에 배출된 경우, 해양자원이나 인체에 경미한 위해를 야기하기 하므로, 해양환경으로의 배출물의 품질과 양에 대한 완화된 제한을 하는 것이 정당하다고 보는 유해액체물질.

① Category X: Noxious Liquid Substances which, if discharged into the sea from tank cleaning or deballasting operations, are deemed to present **a major hazard** to either marine resources or human health and, therefore, justify the prohibition of the discharge into the marine environment;

② Category Y: Noxious Liquid Substances which, if discharged into the sea from tank cleaning or deballasting operations, are deemed to present a **hazard** to either marine resources or human health or cause harm to amenities or other legitimate uses of the sea and therefore justify a limitation on the quality and quantity of the discharge into the marine environment;

③ Category Z: Noxious Liquid Substances which, if discharged into the sea from tank cleaning or deballasting operations, are deemed to present a **minor hazard** to either marine resources or human health and therefore justify less stringent restrictions on the quality and quantity of the discharge into the marine environment;

④ Other Substances: substances indicated as OS (Other Substances) in the pollution category column of chapter 18 of the International Bulk Chemical Code which have been evaluated and found to fall **outside Category X, Y or Z** as defined in regulation 6.1 of this Annex because they are, at present, considered to present **no harm** to marine resources, human health, amenities or other legitimate uses of the sea when discharged into the sea from tank cleaning of deballasting operations. The discharge of bilge or ballast water or other residues or mixtures containing only substances referred to as "Other Substances" shall not be subject to any requirements of the Annex.

④ 기타 물질 : 기타물질이란 IBC 코드의 18장의 오염분류에서 OS(기타물질)로 표시된 것으로, 탱크세정 또는 평형수 배출 작업에 의하여 해양으로 배출시, 해양자원이나 인체에 경미한 위해를 미치거나 또는 해양의 쾌적성 기타 적법한 이용에, 지금 현재로는, 해가 없다고 간주되므로 이 부속서의 제6.1규칙에서 정의한 대로 평가되어 X류, Y류, Z류 범주를 벗어난 것으로 알려진 물질이다. "기타 물질"로 언급된 물질만을 포함하는 빌지 또는 평형수 또는 기타 잔류물 또는 혼합물의 배출은 부속서의 어떠한 요건에도 적용을 받지 아니 한다.

02
유해액체물질의 배출 기준

Where the provisions in this regulation allow the discharge into the sea of residues of substances in Category X, Y or Z or of those provisionally assessed as such or ballast water, tank washings or other mixtures containing such substances the following discharge standards shall apply:

이 규칙의 규정이 범주 X, Y 또는 Z로 지정된 물질, 그러한 것으로 잠정 평가된 물질의 잔류물 또는 이들 물질을 함유하는 선박평형수, 탱크세정수, 기타의 이들 혼합물의 해양 배출을 허용하는 경우, 다음의 배출 기준이 적용된다:

① the ship is **proceeding** en route at a speed of at least **7 knots** in the case of **self-propelled ships** or at least **4 knots** in the case of **ships which are not self-propelled;**

① 선박이 자항선의 경우는 7노트 이상, 비자항선의 경우는 4노트 이상의 속력으로 항행 중일 것 :

② the discharge is made **below the waterline** through the underwater discharge outlet(s) **not exceeding the maximum rate** for which the underwater discharge outlet(s) is (are) designed; and

② 수면하 배출이 설계된 최대 배출율을 넘지 아니하며 수면하 배출구를 통하여 수면하에서 배출할 것 ; 그리고

③ the discharge is made at a distance of not less than 12 nautical miles from the nearest land in a depth of water of **not less than 25 metres**.

③ 가장 가까운 육지로부터 12해리 이상 떨어진 수심 25미터 이상의 장소에서 배출할 것.

기출문제

01. MARPOL에 따라 산적 유해액체물질(noxious liquid substances in bulk)의 배출에 관련된 사항으로 옳지 않은 것을 고르시오. `기출예상문제`

① Discharging is made at a distance of not less than 12 nautical miles from the nearest land
② The ship is proceeding en route at a speed of at least 7 knots in the case of self-propelled.
③ Discharging is made in a place of which depth of water is not less than 25 meters.
④ Discharge is made above the waterline through the underwater discharge outlet.

해설 유해액체물질의 배출은 수면 아래(under)에서 이루어져야 한다. 'above'는 '위에' 라는 의미이다.

chapter 06 하수(Sewage)의 배출

01
Sewage의 정의

① drainage and other wastes from any form of toilets and urinals

② drainage from medical premises (dispensary, sick bay, etc.) via wash basins, wash tubs and scuppers located in such premises

③ drainage from spaces containing living animals

④ other waste waters when mixed with the drainages defined above.

① 모든 형태의 화장실 및 변소 배출구로부터의 배수 및 기타의 폐물

② 의료구역(의무실, 병실 등)으로부터 이들 구역 내에 있는 세면기, 세탁대야 및 하수구를 통하여 나오는 배수

③ 살아 있는 동물이 들어 있는 장소로부터의 배수

④ 위의 배수와 혼합된 기타 폐수

02
Sewage의 배출 규정

The discharge of sewage into the sea is prohibited, except when:

① The ship is discharging comminuted and disinfected sewage using a system approved by the Administration at a distance of more than **3 nautical miles** from the nearest land or

② sewage which is not comminuted or disinfected at a distance of more that **12 nautical miles** from the nearest land,

다음의 경우를 제외하고 해양에서의 오수 배출을 금지한다 :

① 선박이 가장 가까운 육지로부터 3해리를 넘는 거리에서 제9.1.2규칙에 따라 주관청이 승인한 장치를 사용하여 마쇄하고 소독한 오수를 배출하는 경우 또는

② 가장 가까운 육지로부터 12해리를 넘는 거리에서 마쇄하지 아니하거나 소독하지 아니한 오수를 배출하는 경우.

③ 다만, 어떠한 경우에도 저장탱크에 저장한 오수 또는 살아있는 동물이 들어있는 장소에서 발생하는 오수는 일시적으로 배출하여서는 아니되며 선박이 4노트 이상의 속력으로 항행 중에 적당한 비율로 배출하여야 한다. 이 배출율은 기구가 정하는 기준에 따라 주관청이 승인한 것이어야 한다.

③ provided that, in any case, the sewage that has been stored in holding tanks, or sewage originating from spaces containing living animals, **shall not be discharged instantaneously** but **at a moderate rate** when the ship is **en route and proceeding** at not less than **4 knots;** the rate of discharge shall be approved by the Administration based upon standards developed by the Organization

chapter 07 폐기물(Garbage)의 배출

01 Garbage의 정의

"Garbage" means all kinds of food wastes, domestic wastes and operational wastes, all plastics, cargo residues, incinerator ashes, cooking oil, fishing gear, and animal carcasses generated during the normal operation of the ship and liable to be disposed of continuously or periodically except those substances which are defined or listed in other Annexes to the present Convention. Garbage does not include fresh fish and parts thereof generated as a result of fishing activities undertaken during the voyage, or as a result of aquaculture activities which involve the transport of fish including shellfish for placement in the aquaculture facility and the transport of harvested fish including shellfish from such facilities to shore for processing.

"폐기물"이라 함은 이 협약의 타 부속서에 정의되어 있거나 열거된 물질을 제외하고 선박의 통상의 운항 중에 발생하고 연속적으로 또는 주기적으로 처분되는 모든 종류의 음식쓰레기, 생활 쓰레기, 운항 상 쓰레기, 모든 플라스틱, 화물 잔류물, 식용유, 어구 및 동물 사체를 말한다. 폐기물은 항해 중에 이루어지는 어업활동, 또는 양식 설비에 설치하기 위한 갑각류를 포함하여 어류의 이송 그리고 갑각류를 포함하여 수확한 어류의 처리를 위해 이러한 시설에서 육상으로 이송을 포함하는 양식 활동에 따라 발생하는 신선한 어류 및 그 일부는 포함하지 않는다.

02 Garbage의 배출 규정

① **Discharge of all garbage into the sea is prohibited**, except as provided otherwise in regulation 4, 5, 6 and 7 of this Annex and section 5.2 of part II-A of the Polar Code, as defined in regulation 13.1 of this Annex.

② **discharge into the sea of all plastics,** including but not limited to synthetic ropes, synthetic fishing nets, plastic garbage bags and incinerator ashes from plastic products is prohibited.

① 동 부속서의 제4, 5, 6 , 7 규칙 및 동 부속서 13.1규칙에 언급된 극지 운항선박 코드 Part II-A/5.2장의 요건을 제외하고, 해상으로의 모든 폐기물의 배출은 금지된다.

② 동 부속서의 제 7 규칙에 규정된 것을 제외하고, 합성로프, 합성어망, 플라스틱제의 쓰레기 봉지, 플라스틱 제품의 소각재를 포함한 모든 플라스틱류(그러나 이들에 한정된 것은 아님)의 해양에 처분은 금지한다.

03
특별해역 외에 있어서 폐기물의 배출

이 부속서의 제5규칙, 제6규칙 및 제7규칙의 규정에 따르는 것을 조건으로, 다음 폐기물의 해상으로의 배출은 선박의 항해 중에만 허용되어야 하며, 가장 가까운 육지로부터 가능한 한 멀리 떨어져 행하여야 하지만 어떠한 경우에도 다음의 거리에 미달하는 경우는 처분을 금지한다 :

Discharge of the following garbage into the sea outside special areas shall only be permitted while the ship is en route and as far as practicable from the nearest land, but in any case not less than:

① 분쇄기 또는 연마기를 통하여 배출된 음식쓰레기에 대하여 가장 가까운 육지로부터 3해리. 그러한 가루로 된 또는 분쇄된 음식찌꺼기는 25mm 이하의 구멍 뚫린 망을 통과할 수 있어야 한다.

① **3 nautical miles** from the nearest land for food wastes which have been passed through a comminuter or grinder. Such comminuted or ground food wastes shall be capable of passing through a screen with openings no greater than **25 mm**.

② 상기 ①에 따라서 처분되지 아니한 음식쓰레기는 가장 가까운 육지로부터 12해리.

② **12 nautical miles** from the nearest land for food wastes that have not been treated in accordance with subparagraph ① above.

③ 일반적으로 이용 가능한 하역방법을 통하여 회수될 수 없는 화물잔류물에 대하여 가장 가까운 육지로부터 12 해리. 이러한 화물잔류물은 동 부속서 부록 1에 명시된 기준에 따라 기구가 개발된 지침을 고려하여 해양환경에 해로운 것으로 분류된 어떠한 물질을 포함하지 않아야 한다.

③ **12 nautical miles** from the nearest land for cargo residues that cannot be recovered using commonly available methods for unloading. These cargo residues shall not contain any substances classified as harmful to the marine environment, in accordance with the criteria set out in appendix I of this Annex.

④ 동물 사체의 경우, 기구가 개발된 지침서를 고려하여, 배출은 가능한 한 가장 가까운 육지로부터 멀리 떨어진 곳에서 이루어져야 한다.

④ For animal carcasses, discharge shall occur as far from the nearest land as possible, taking into account the guidelines developed by the Organization.

chapter 08 각종 문서 및 기록부

01
Oil Record Book

① **Every oil tanker** of **150 tons gross tonnage** and above and **every ship** of **400 tons gross tonnage** and above other than an oil tanker shall be provided with an Oil Record Book, whether as part of this ship's official log book or otherwise in the form specified in Appendix 3 to this Annex.

② Each completed operation shall be signed by the officer or officers in charge of the operations concerned and each completed page or group of electronic entries shall be signed by the master of ship. The entries in the Oil Record Book Part I, for ships holding an International Oil Pollution Prevention Certificate, shall be at least in English, French or Spanish.

③ The Oil Record Book Part I shall be kept in such a place as to be readily available for inspection at all reasonable times and, except in the case of unmanned ships under tow, shall be kept on board the ship. It shall be preserved for a period of **three years** after the last entry has been made.

01 기름기록부

① 총 톤수 150톤 이상의 모든 유탱커 및 유탱커 이외의 총 톤수 400톤 이상의 모든 선박에는 기름기록부 제 I 부(기관구역에서의 작업)를 비치하여야 한다. 기름기록부는 공식항해일지의 일부로서, 기구가 개발한 지침서에 따라 승인되어야 하는 전자기록부로서, 또는 기타 형식으로서 이 부속서의 부록 II에 정해진 서식에 따라야 한다.

② 완료된 각 작업은 담당 사관 또는 당해 작업의 책임사관에 의해 서명되어야 하며, 기재된 각 면 또는 전자기록들의 무리는 선장에 의하여 서명되어야 한다. 국제기름오염방지증서를 비치하고 있는 선박에서는 기름기록부를 적어도 영어, 불어 또는 스페인어로 기재하여야 한다.

③ 기름기록부는 모든 합당한 경우에 점검하도록 쉽게 이용가능한 장소에 보관하여야 하며, 승무원이 없는 피예인선의 경우를 제외하고 선박 내에 보관하여야 한다. 기름기록부는 최후의 기록이 행해진 뒤로부터 3년간 보존하여야 한다.

02 선상기름오염비상계획서

총 톤수 150톤 이상의 모든 유탱커 및 총 톤수 400톤 이상의 유탱커 이외의 모든 선박은 주관청의 승인을 받은 선상기름오염비상계획서를 선내에 비치하여야 한다.

02 Shipboard oil pollution emergency plan

Every oil tanker of 150 gross tonnage and above and every **ship other than an oil tanker of 400 gross tonnage** and above shall carry on board a **shipboard oil pollution emergency plan** approved by the Administration.

03 국제오염방지증서

① 이 부속서 제 4규칙의 규정에 따른 검사가 종료한 때는 이 협약의 타 당사국의 관할권 하에 있는 항구 또는 해양터미널에의 항행에 종사하고 있는 150톤 이상의 유탱커 및 총톤수 400톤 이상의 유탱커 이외의 모든 선박에 대하여 국제기름오염방지증서가 발급된다.

② 국제기름오염방지증서는 5년을 초과하지 않는 범위에서 주관청이 정하는 기간 동안 발행되어야 한다.

03 International Oil Pollution Prevention Certificate

① An **International Oil Pollution Prevention Certificate** shall be issued, after survey in accordance with the provisions of Regulation 4 of this Annex, to any oil tanker of **150 tons gross tonnage** and above and any other ships of **400 tons gross tonnage** and above which are engaged in voyages to ports or off-shore terminals under the jurisdiction of other Parties to the Convention.

② An **International Oil Pollution Prevention Certificate** shall be issued for a period specified by the Administration, which shall not exceed **five years**.

04 기름배출감시제어장치 기록

이 기록은 일시를 판별할 수 있는 것이어야 하며, 적어도 3년간 보존하여야 한다.

04 Oil discharge monitoring and control system Record

This record shall be identifiable as to time and date and shall be kept for at least **three years**.

PART 09 항해, 일반

chapter 1 항해의 기초
chapter 2 Geo-Navigation (지문항법)
chapter 3 Bearing and Course (방위와 침로)
chapter 4 수로도지
chapter 5 Aids to navigation (항로표지)
chapter 6 Tide (조석)
chapter 7 RADAR
chapter 8 Navigation Equipment (항해 장비)
chapter 9 해양 기상
chapter 10 선박 개요
chapter 11 선박의 구조
chapter 12 선박 설비
chapter 13 선박에 작용하는 힘
chapter 14 Stability (복원성)
chapter 15 Turning circle (선회권)
chapter 16 Tonnage (톤수)
chapter 17 기관
chapter 18 선박 화재
chapter 19 기타 항해, 일반 문제 통암기

chapter 01 항해의 기초

01
항해의 종류

① Geo Navigation (지문 항법)
② Celestial Navigation (천문 항법)
③ Electronic Navigation (전파 항법)

02
지구상의 위치 용어

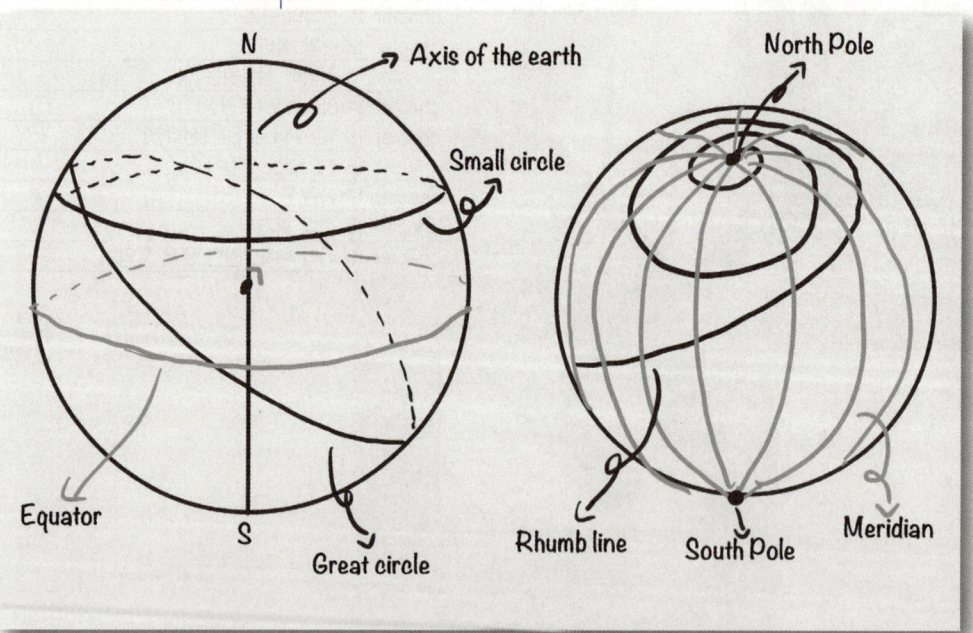

① Great Circle (대권) : 지구의 중심을 지나는 평면으로 구를 자를 때 구면 위에 생기는 원
② Small Circle (소권) : 지구의 중심을 지나지 않는 평면으로 구를 자를 때 구면 위에 생기는 원
③ Axis of the earth (지축) : 지구의 자전 축
④ Pole (지극) : 지축의 양쪽 끝으로 북극(North Pole)과 남극(South Pole)이 있다.
⑤ Equator (적노) : 지축에 직교하는 대권으로, 위도(Latitude)의 기준이 된다.
⑥ Parallel (거등권) : 적도에 평행한(parallel) 소권 또는 지축에 직교(right angle, perpendicular)하는 소권
⑦ Meridian (자오선) : 양극을 지나는 대권, 적도에 직교하는 대권
   - True meridian (진자오선) : 진북과 진남을 잇는 대권
   - Magnetic meridian (자기자오선) : 자북과 자남을 잇는 대권
⑧ Rhumb line (항정선) : 지구위의 모든 자오선과 같은 각(same angle)으로 만나는 곡선(an arc), 선박이 일정한 침로로 계속 항행하게 되면 나선형의 곡선을 그리며 점차 극에 가까워진다.
⑨ Distance (항정) : 출발지에서 도착지에 이르는 항정선상의 거리 또는 양 지점을 잇는 대권상의 호의 길이를 마일로 표시한 것이다.
⑩ Latitude, Lat. (위도) : 적도를 0도로 남북으로 90도 까지 측정
⑪ Longitude, Long. (경도) : 본초자오선을 0도로 동쪽 또는 서쪽으로 180도 까지 측정
⑫ Departure (동서거) : 거등권을 따라 재어진 두 자오선 사이의 길이를 마일로 표시한 것

기출문제

01. Choose best answer explained by belows   09년 3차

A method to obtain ship's position is by crossing-bearing of landmark aids to navigation etc. This can be useless when the weather gets poor

① celestial navigation   ② geo-navigation
③ electronic navigation   ④ meteorological navigation

해설 선박의 위치를 구할 때 육표를 통한 교차방위법, 표지 등을 사용한다. 날씨가 나빠지면 사용할 수 없다. : 지문항법(geo-navigation)

답 ②

I 기출문제

02. 다음 빈칸에 들어갈 단어를 고르시오. 〈기출예상문제〉

( ) are circles on a sphere whose planes pass through the center of the sphere

① Great Circle   ② Small Circle
③ Meridian   ④ Equator

해설 지구의 중심(center of the sphere)을 지나는 원을 대권(great circle)이라 한다.

답 ①

03. 다음 빈칸에 들어갈 단어를 고르시오. 〈기출예상문제〉

( ) is a great circle through the geographical poles of the earth.

① Great Circle   ② Small Circle
③ Meridian   ④ Equator

해설 자오선(meridian)은 지구의 지극을 통과하는 대권이다.

답 ③

04. A nautical mile is the average length of one minute of arc of ( ) of the earth. 〈07년 3차〉

① Great Circle   ② Small Circle
③ Meridian   ④ Equator

해설 해리는 지구위의 자오선(Meridian)상 호의 1분의 평균 길이이다.

답 ③

05. 다음 빈칸에 들어갈 단어를 고르시오. 〈기출예상문제〉

The distance between any two meridians measured along a parallel of latitude and expressed in miles is the ( ).

① departure   ② distance
③ meridian   ④ equator

해설 거등권(parallel)을 따라 재어진 두 자오선(meridian) 사이의 길이를 마일로 표시한 것을 동서거(departure)라 한다.

답 ①

I 기출문제

06. 다음 빈칸에 들어갈 단어를 고르시오.　　　　　　　　　　　　기출예상문제

(   ) is the diameter upon which the earth rotates diurnally from west to east. The north end of it is the north pole, and the south end of it is the south pole.

① Pole　　　　　　　　　② Meridian
③ Parallel　　　　　　　　④ Axis of the earth

해설　지축(Axis of the earth)은 지구가 매일 서쪽에서 동쪽으로 회전(rotate)할 때의 기준(standard) 축(axis)을 말한다. 이것의 북쪽 끝을 북극(north pole), 남쪽 끝을 남극(south pole)이라 한다.

답 ❹

07. Choose the correct answer for the blank　　　　　　　　　　　기출예상문제

(   ) is a curved line which cross all meridian at the same angle.

① Position lin　　　　　　② Meridian
③ Rhumb line　　　　　　④ Small circle

해설　항정선(Rhumb line)은 모든 자오선(meridian)을 같은 각(same angle)으로 가르는(cross) 곡선(curved line)이다.

답 ❸

Chapter 02 Geo-Navigation (지문항법)

01
Position (위치) 의 종류

① Actual Position, AP (실측위치) : 실제 물표를 관측하여 구한 선위

② Dead Reckoning Position, DR, DRP (추측위치) : 최근의 실측위치(AP)를 기준으로 하여 진침로(course)와 항정(distance)에 의하여 구한 선위.

③ Estimated Position, EP (추정위치) : 추측위치(DR)에 외력(leeway)의 영향 (풍압차(wind), 유압차(current))를 가감하여 구한 선위

02
Line of position, position line, LOP (위치선)

선박이 그 자취 위에 존재한다고 생각되는 특정한 선(imaginary line)으로 동시에 두 개의 위치선을 결정하면 그 교점이 선위가 된다.

① 방위(bearing)에 의한 위치선 : Compass bearing으로 구하며 직선(straight line)으로 표시

② 수평협각(Horizontal sextant angle)에 의한 위치선 : 육분의(sextant)로 구하며 원호(circle)로 표시

③ 중시선에 의한 위치선 : 두 물표가 일직선상에 겹쳐 보일 때 그들 물표를 연결한 직선.

④ 수평거리에 의한 위치선 : 레이더(radar)로 물표까지의 거리를 반지름으로 원을 그림

⑤ 수심에의한 위치선 : 음향 측심기(echo sounder)로 측정, 등심선(contour)사용

⑥ 천체(celestial) 고도 측정에 의한 위치선 : 태양 달 및 혹성, 항성의 고도를 육분의(sextant)로 측정

⑦ 무선방위(radio direction)에 의한 위치선 : Radio direction finder 로 측정, 직선으로 표시

03
선위 측정

① Cross bearing (교차방위법)
2개 이상의 뚜렷한 물표를 선정하여 동시에 각각의 방위를 재어 해도상에 교점을 표시하는 방법

② Fix by bearing and range (방위 거리법)
한 물표의 방위와 거리를 동시에 측정하여 그 방위에 의한 위치선과 수평거리에 의한 위치선의 교점을 선위로 측정하는 방법.

③ Horizontal sextant angle (수평협각법)
뚜렷한 3개의 물표를 육분의로 수평협각을 측정, 3간 분도기를 사용하여 협각의 각각의 원주각으로 하는 원의 교점을 구하는 방법

④ Running fix (격시관측법)
동시에 두 개 이상의 위치선을 구할 수 없을 때 시간차를 두고 위치선을 구한다.

| 기출문제

01. 다음 중 빈칸에 들어갈 단어로 가장 옳은 것은?   20년 3차

The position which is determined by only true course and distance without any other effect is ( ).

① Doubtful position   ② Estimated position
③ Actual position   ④ Dead reckoning position

해설 다른 외부 영향 없이 오직 진침로(true course)와 항정(distance)만을 통해서 구해진 위치는 <u>추측위치(Dead reckoning position)</u>이다.

답 ④

I 기출문제

02. Select the correct one for the blank

( ) is the determination of position by advancing a known position for courses and distances.

① Fix ② Crossing
③ Dead reckoning ④ Departure

해설 추측위치(Dead reckoning)란, 침로와 항정을 가지고 알려진 위치를 전진시킴으로써 위치를 결정하는 것이다.

답 ❸

03. Select the correct one for the blank

( ) is the position that can be obtained by calculation and estimation only. It is derived from the DR position with allowance made for the effects of currents and tidal streams

① Dead reckoning position ② Estimated position
③ Actual position ④ Line of Position

해설 추정위치(Estimated position)는 계산과 추정만으로 얻을 수 있는 위치이다. 이는 해류와 조류의 영향을 감안한 추측위치에서 구할 수 있다.

답 ❷

04. 다음 빈칸에 들어갈 말로 가장 옳은 것은? [20년 1차]

( ) is an imaginary line on which a ship at sea must lie to satisfy certain data obtained by the observations of terrestrial or celestial object.

① Cross bearing ② Position line
③ Gyro bearing ④ Dead Reckoning

해설 지상(terrestrial)과 천체(celestial)의 물표의 관찰로 얻어지는 특정한 정보를 만족시키는 선박의 가상의 선을 위치선(line of position)이라 한다.

답 ❷

05. 다음 밑줄 친 단어가 설명하고 있는 것이 무엇인지 고르시오.

This is a navigational position determined by the intersection of two or more lines of position taken at different times and then advanced to a common time

① Actual Position ② Estimated Position
③ Dead Reckoning ④ Running Fix

해설 서로 다른 시간에 취하여 공통 시간으로 나아가는 두 개 이상의 위치의 교차점에 의해 결정되는 항해 위치는 격시관측에 의한 위치(Running Fix)이다.

답 ❹

chapter 03 Bearing and Course(방위와 침로)

01
Course (침로)

- The intended direction of movement of a vessel through the water	수면을 기준으로 어느 선박이 이동하려는 방향
- The angle that the center line of a vessel or the vessel's keel, makes with the meridian	선박의 선수미선 또는 용골과 자오선이 이루는 각도
① True Course (진침로) the angel between the ship's track and the true meridian (or North)	선박의 항적과 진자오선(진북)사이의 각도
② Magnetic Course (자침로) the angle between the ship's track and the magnetic meridian (or North)	선박의 항적과 자기자오선(자북)사이의 각도
③ Compass course (나침로) the course steered by compass, or the angle between the ship's track and the compass needle	나침반에 의해 맞추는 침로, 또는 선박의 항적과 나침반의 바늘사이의 각도

02
Bearing (방위)

① Bearing (진방위) the angle between the great circle which cross the observer and the object and (true) meridian.	관측자와 물표를 지나는 대권(great cirlce)과 자오선(meridian)이 이루는 각으로 북쪽을 기준으로 시계방향으로 360도 까지 측정한 것
② Relative bearing (상대방위) it can be expressed in degree relative to the vessel's head	이것은 선수를 기준으로 표시된다.

03
Variation and Deviation (편차와 자차)

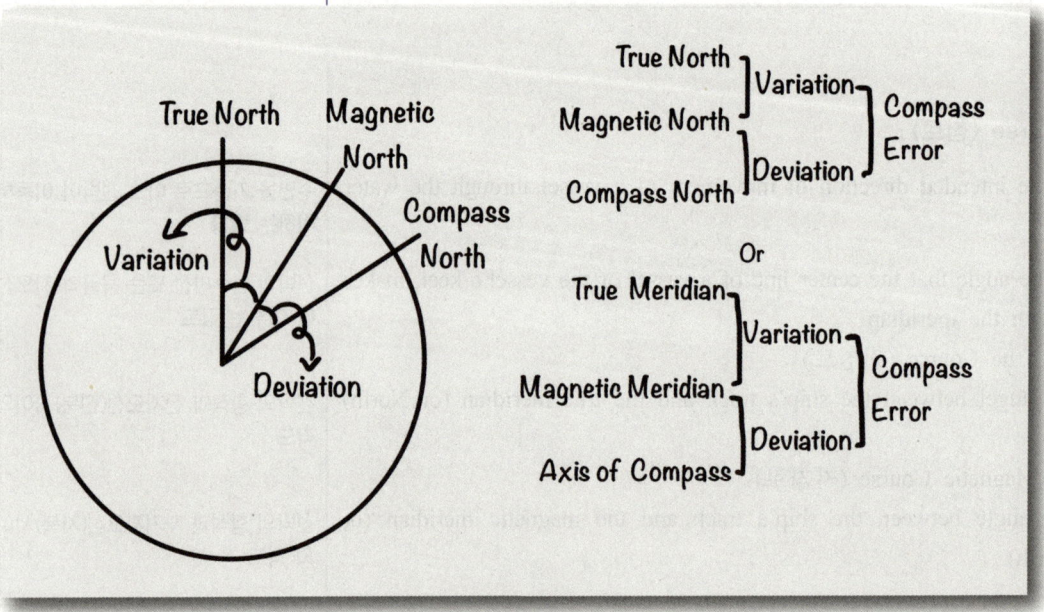

① Variation (편차)

편차란 나침반의 바늘이 지구의 북극 대신 자북을 가리켜서 생겨나게 되는 나침반의 오류이다.

Variation is an error of the compass caused by the fact that the magnetic needle point to the magnetic north pole instead of the geographic north pole.

② Deviation (자차)

컴퍼스의 축(나침의 남북선)과 자기 자오선의 축의 차이

The angle-caused between the axis of the compass and the magnetic meridian

③ Compass error (컴퍼스 오차)
  - Variation + Deviation = Compass error
  - The angle-caused between the True north and the Compass north

기출문제

01. 다음 빈칸에 들어갈 말로 가장 적합한 것은? `18년 1차`

( ) is the angle that the center line of a vessel, or the vessel's keel, makes with the meridian

① Course ② Draft
③ Deviation ④ Variation

해설 침로(Course)에 대한 설명이다.

답 ①

02. 다음 괄호 안에 들어갈 가장 알맞은 말은 무엇인가? `18년 3차`

( ) can be expressed in degrees relative to the vessel's head or head bow. More frequently this is in relation to the port or starboard bow.

① Position ② Bearing(s)
③ Course(s) ④ Relative bearing(s)

해설 선박 선수 기준으로 방위를 표현하는 상대방위(Relative bearing)에 대한 설명이다.

답 ④

03. 다음 설명에 해당하는 것을 고르시오. `17년 2차`

The angle-caused between the axis of the compass and magnetic meridian is called ;

① variation ② deviation
③ compass error ④ gyro error

해설 나침의 남북선과 자기자오선이 이루는 각은 자차(deviation)이다.

답 ②

04. Variation is caused by ; `04년 5차`

① worn gear in the compass housing
② magnetism from the earth's magnetic field
③ magnetism with in the vessel
④ lack of oil in the compass bearing

해설 지구의 자기장(magnetic field)으로부터의 자성(magnetism) 때문에 편차(variation)가 발생한다.

답 ②

chapter 04 수로도지

01
Nautical chart (해도)

① 도법에 따른 분류
- Plan projection (평면도법) : 지구 표면의 좁은 구역을 평면으로 간주하고 그린 축척이 큰 해도
- Mercator projection (점장도법) : 항정선(Rhumb line)이나 침로(course)를 직선(straight line)으로 나타내기 위하여 고안된 도법
- Great circle projection (대권도법) : 투영도법 또는 심사도법이라고도 하며, 지구표면의 한 점에 접하는 평면에 지구의 중심으로부터 지구의 점들을 투영한 해도. 대권(great circle)이 직선(straight line)으로 표현됨.

② 사용목적에 따른 분류
- Nautical Chart, General Chart (총도) : 1/400만 이하로 세계전도(world map)와 같이 극히 넓은 구역을 나타낸 소축척(small scale) 해도
- Sailing Chart (항양도) : 1/100만 이하로 긴 항해에 쓰이며 해안에서 떨어진 바다의 수심, 주요한 등대 등이 그려짐.
- Coastal Chart (항해도) : 1/30만 이하로 대개 육지를 바라보면서 항해할 때 사용되는 해도로, 육상의 물표를 측정하여 선위를 직접 해도 상에서 구함.
- Approach Chart (해안도) : 1/5만 이하로 연안항해에 주로 사용하는 것이며 연안의 상황을 자세하게 그린 대축척(large scale) 해도
- Harbour Plan (항박도) : 1/5만 이상으로 항만, 정박지, 협수로 등 좁은 구역을 상세히 그린 대축척(large scale) 해도

02
해도의 수심

- 해도에 표기된 수심은 항해사로 하여금 얕은 구역이나 위험물로부터 거리를 두고 안전하게 항해하게 하기위해 측심(sounding)된 것이다.
- 해도에 표기된 수심인 기본수준면(datum level)을 기준으로 기록된다.

03
Nautical publication (수로서지)

① Sailing direction (항로지)
수로의 지도 및 안내서로서 기상, 해류, 조류, 도선사, 검역, 항로표지 등의 일반기사 및 항로의 상황, 연안지형, 항만시설 등을 자세히 기록한 책자

② 특수서지
  - Light list (등대표)
  - Tide table (조석표)
  - Nautical Almanac (천측력)
  - Distance table (거리표)
  - Code of Signal, INTERCO (국제 신호서)
  - Chart symbol (해도도식)

04
Notice to mariner (NTM or N.M.)

해도(Chart)와 수로서지(Publication)의 수정사항을 항해자에게 통보하는 것

기출문제

01. which of the following chart is the largest scale?   07년 3차

① general chart
② coast chart
③ sailing chart
④ harbour plan

해설 해도 중 축척이 가장 큰 대축척(largest scale)지도는 항박도(Harbour plan)이다.

답 ④

02. The advantage of <u>this chart</u> is the fact that a vessel's course can be presented on it as a straight line. The underlined part means (   ).   12년

① plane chart
② mercator chart
③ polyconic chart
④ gnomonic chart

해설 점장도(mercator chart)의 가장 큰 이점은 선박의 침로가 직선(straight line)으로 표시된다는 점이다.

답 ②

기출문제

03. 다음 〈보기〉 중 해도의 분류에 대한 영문표기가 옳지 않은 것은 모두 몇 개인가? [22년 일반직]

㉠ 점장도법 : Great circle projection　㉡ 항양도 : Harbour plan
㉢ 항해도 : Coastal chart　㉣ 해안도 : Approach chart

① 1개　② 2개
③ 3개　④ 4개

해설 옳지 않은 것:
㉠ 점장도법 : mercator projection
㉡ 항양도 : Sailing chart

답 ❷

04. 다음 중 빈칸에 들어갈 말로 가장 적절한 것은? [16년 2차]

When sailing along a coast, to avoid sunken rocks, shoals, or dangerous obstructions at or below the surface of the water, and which are marked on the chart, the navigator may pass these at any desired distance by using what is known as (　　　).

① sounding　② cross bearing
③ danger　④ transit

해설 연안(coast) 항해 시 해도 상에 표기된 수면 또는 수면 하의 암초(rocks), 사주(shoals) 혹은 위험한 장애물(obstructions)을 피하기 위하여 측심(sounding)이라고 알려진 것을 이용하여 항해자는 원하는 거리만큼 떨어져 이런 위험들을 통과할 수 있다.

답 ❶

05. 다음 중 빈칸에 들어갈 내용으로 가장 옳은 것은? [21년 하반기]

Charted depth is the (　　　).

① vertical distance from the chart sounding to the ocean bottom, plus the height of tide
② vertical distance from the chart sounding datum to the ocean bottom
③ average height of water over a specified period
④ average height of all low waters at a place

해설 해도에 표기된 수심은 해도의 측심용 기본수준면(datum)으로부터 해저(ocean bottom)까지의 수직거리이다.

답 ❷

기출문제

06. 다음 빈칸에 들어갈 말로 가장 적합한 것은? [18년 1차]

"Chart and light lists should be checked to see that have been corrected through the latest (　　)."

① notice to mariners　　② guide to port entry
③ sailing directions　　④ chart correction table

해설 해도와 등대표는 최근의 항행통보(Notice to mariner)을 통해 제대로 수정되었는지 확인되어야 한다.

답 ❶

07. 다음 빈칸에 들어갈 문장으로 가장 적합한 것은? [기출예상문제]

On the mercator chart the rhumb line appears (　　).

① curved line　　② circle
③ straight line　　④ true course

해설 점장도(mercator chart)위에서 항정선(rhumb line)은 직선(straight line)으로 보인다.

답 ❸

08. Select the correct one for the blank [기출예상문제]

Publications with detailed descriptions of harbors and shore areas are called (　　).

① almanac　　② light lists
③ aids to navigation　　④ sailing direction

해설 항만(harbors)이나 연안(shore)에 대해 자세히(detailed) 서술(description)하고 있는 출판물(publication)은 항로지(sailing direction)라 불린다.

답 ❹

Chapter 05 Aids to navigation (항로표지)

01
용어

① Seamark (해상표지)

A navigation aid placed to act as a beacon, or warning

> ⟨IALA Seamark⟩
> ⓐ Lateral mark (측방위표지)
> ⓑ Cardinal mark (방위표지)
> ⓒ Isolated danger mark (고립장해표지)
> ⓓ Safe water mark (안전수역표지)
> ⓔ Special mark (특수표지)
> ⓕ Emergency wreck marking buoy (침선표지)

부표나 경고표지로 작동하도록 배치되는 항로표지

② Cardinal buoy (방위표지)

A seamark, i.e. a buoy, indicating the North, East South or West, i.e. the cardinal points from a fixed point such as a wreck, shallow water, banks, etc

침선, 천수구역, 사주와 같은 고정된 지점으로부터의 방위 - 북, 동, 남, 서를 가리키는 해상표지이다.

③ Cardinal point (방점)

The four main points of the compass: North, East, South, and West.

나침반의 주요 4방위 : 북, 동, 남, 서쪽

④ Half cardinal point (우점)

The four main points lying between the cardinal points: north east, south east, south west and north west

방점 사이에 있는 주요 4방위 - 북동, 남동, 남서, 북서

⑤ Off air (방송중지)

When the transmissions of a radion station etc., have broken down, been switched off or suspended

무선국의 송신이 고장 나거나, 꺼져 있거나 일시 중단되어 있는 상태

⑥ Unlit (소등)
When the light of a buoy or a lighthouse are inoperative

> 등대나 부표의 등화가 작동하지 않음

02
Visibility (광달거리)

해도나 등대표에 기재된 광달거리는 청천암야 기준 **안고(observer's eye) 5m(15ft)**를 기준으로 계산한 것.

① Geographic range (지리학적 광달거리)
지구의 만곡(curvature of the earth) 때문에 결정되는 광달거리.

② Luminous range (광학적 광달거리)
등화의 광력(intensity of the light)으로 결정되며 일정한 계산식에 의하여 구한 것.

③ Nominal range (명목적 광달거리)
주간 가시거리 10해리(meteorological visibility of 10mile)인 대기 상태에서 광학적 광달거리

▌기출문제

01. 항로표지는 다음 중 어느 것인가? 〔04년 2차〕

① Aids to navigation   ② Light list
③ Notice to mariner   ④ Sailing direction

해설 Aids to navigation : 항로표지
옳지 않은 것 :
② Light list : 등대표
③ Notice to mariner : 항행 통보
④ Sailing direction : 수로지, 항로지

답 ❶

02. 다음 중 빈칸에 들어갈 말로 가장 적절한 것은? 〔16년 2차〕

> All the distances given on the charts for the visibility of lights are calculated for (   ) of 5 meters.

① a minimum height of a light   ② a standard height of a light
③ a height of an observer's eye   ④ a height of a standard light

해설 해도 상에 표시되는 등대의 광달거리는 안고 5미터를 기준으로 계산한 것이다.

답 ❸

기출문제

03. 다음 중 빈칸에 들어갈 내용으로 가장 옳은 것은? `22년 2차`

"The (   ) is the maximum distance at which a light may be seen clear weather(meteorological visibility of 10 miles) expressed in nautical miles"

① nominal range   ② luminous range
③ visible range   ④ geographical range

해설 명목적 광달거리(nominal range)는 기상이 양호한 날 (주간 가시거리 10해리)등광을 볼 수 있는 최대거리를 의미한다.

답 ①

04. Choose the most suitable word for the blank `기출예상문제`

the (   ) range is the maximum distance at which the curvature of the earth permits a light to be seen from a particular height of eye without regard to the luminous intensity

① nominal   ② visible
③ geographic   ④ luminous

해설 지리학적광달거리(geographic range)는 광도(luminous intensity)에 상관없이 특정 안고(height of eye)에서 부터의 지구의 곡률(curvature) 상 빛의 가시거리를 말한다.

답 ③

05. 다음 빈칸에 들어갈 알맞은 말을 고르시오. `기출예상문제`

(   ) are generally used for well defined channels, in conjunction with a Conventional direction of Buoyage

① Lateral marks   ② Safe water marks
③ Special marks   ④ Cardinal marks

해설 측방위 표지(Lateral marks)는 전통적인 부표의 방향을 가지고 일반적으로 잘 정의된(well defined) 수로(channels)에서 사용된다.

답 ①

기출문제

06. 다음 보기중 IALA 해상부표식에 따른 표지의 영문표기가 옳지 않은 것은 모두 몇 개인가?

기출예상문제

ⓐ Lateral mark (측방위표지)
ⓑ Cardinal mark (방위표지)
ⓒ Isolated danger mark (안전수역표지)
ⓓ Safe water mark (고립장해표지)
ⓔ Special mark (특수표지)
ⓕ Emergency wreck marking buoy (침선표지)

① 1개　　　　　　② 2개
③ 3개　　　　　　④ 4개

해설 옳지 않은 것:
　　ⓒ Isolated danger mark (고립장해표지)
　　ⓓ Safe water mark (안전수역표지)

답 ❷

chapter 06 Tide(조석)

01 용어

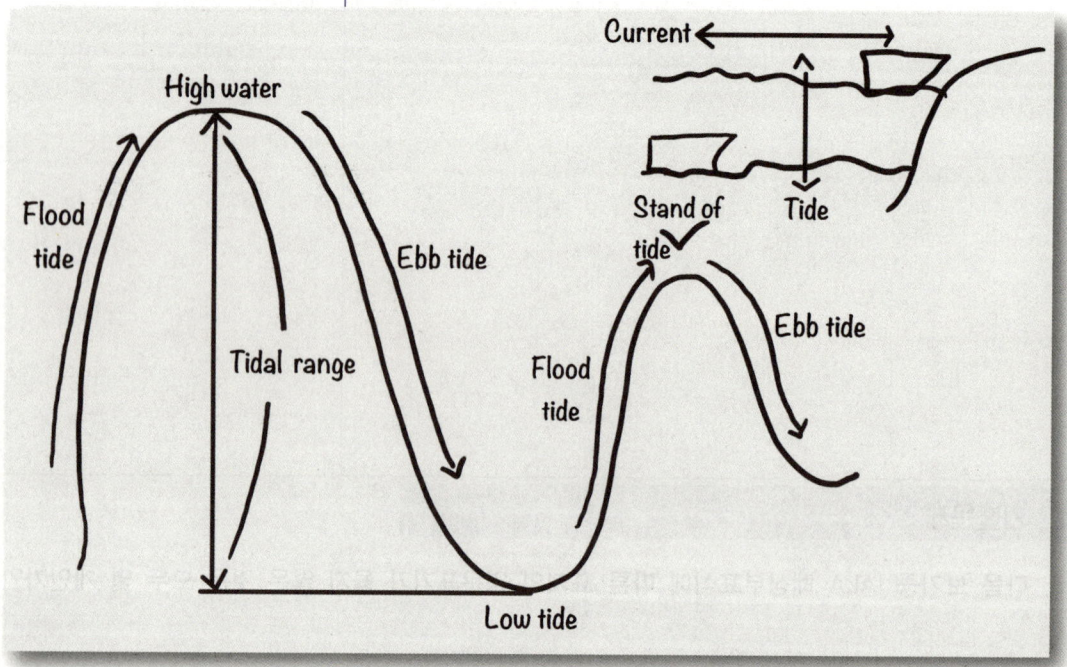

① Tide (조석) : 해면의 주기적인 상하운동으로 수직(vertical)방향의 운동이다.
② High water (고조) : 조석으로 인해 해면이 최고로 높아진 상태
③ Low water (저조) : 조석으로 인해 해면이 최하로 낮아진 상태
④ Flood tide (창조) : 저조에서 고조로 되기까지 해면이 높아지는 상태
⑤ Ebb tide (낙조) : 고조에서 저조로 되기까지 해면이 낮아지는 상태
⑥ Stand of tide (정조) : 고조나 저조시 해면의 승강운동이 순간적으로 거의 정지한 것과 같아 보이는 상태
⑦ Tidal range (조차) : 고조와 저조 때의 해면의 높이차
⑧ Spring tide (대조) : 삭과 망이 지난 뒤 1~2일만에 생긴 조차가 극대인 조석

⑨ Neap tide (소조) : 상현 및 하현이 지난 뒤 1~2일만에 생긴 조차가 극소인 조석
⑩ Tidal Current, Tidal stream (조류) : 조석에 의한 해수의 수평(horizontal) 방향의 주기적인 운동이다.
⑪ Flood current (창조류) : 저조에서 고조까지 흐르는 조류
⑫ Ebb current (낙조류) : 고조에서 저조까지 흐르는 조류
⑬ Slack water (게류) : 창조류에서 낙조류로 바뀔 때 흐름이 잠시 정지하는 것
⑭ Datum level, DL (기본수준면) : 해도 상 수심에 대한 정보의 기준이 되는 기준면이며 조석의 높이 또한 기본수준면이 기준면이 된다.
⑮ with tide (순조), against tide (역조)
⑯ ocean current (해류)

기출문제

01. 다음 중 빈칸에 들어갈 말로 가장 옳은 것은? [17년 1차]

( ) is the period between the flood and ebb or between the cessation of the tidal stream in one direction and its commencement in the opposite direction

① Tidal range　　② Slack water
③ Flood tide　　④ Ebb tide

해설 게류(Slack water)는 창조(flood) 시와 낙조(ebb) 시 사이 조류(tidal stream)의 흐름이 멈추고(cessation) 반대 방향에서 시작(commencement)되는 것을 말한다.

답 ②

02. The state of a tidal current when it's speed is near zero, especially the moment when a current changes direction and its speed is zero. What is the state? [기출예상문제]

① Tidal range　　② Stand of tide
③ Slack water　　④ Ebb

해설 조류(tidal current)의 속도가 0일 때, 특별히 조류의 방향이 바뀌는 순간의 그 속도가 0일 때 조류의 상태를 뭐라고 하는가? : 게류(Slack water)

답 ③

기출문제

03. 다음 중 빈칸에 들어갈 말로 가장 옳은 것은? `기출예상문제`

> The vertical distance on a given day between water surface at high and that at low water is called ( ).

① Tidal range ② Slack water
③ Flood tide ④ Ebb tide

해설 주어진 날에 고조면과 저조면 사이의 수직상의 높이 차이를 조차(tidal range)라 한다.

답 ❶

04. 다음 중 빈칸에 들어갈 말로 가장 옳은 것은? `기출예상문제`

> ( ) are tides that have lows lower than normal and highs higher than normal.

① Neap tide ② Spring tide
③ Hight water ④ Low water

해설 대조(Spring tide)란 평소보다 더 낮은 저조와 평소보다 더 높은 고조를 가지고 있는 조석을 의미한다.

답 ❷

05. 역조를 의미하는 표현은? `기출예상문제`

① The tide is setting ② The tide is with you
③ The tide is against you ④ The tide is ebb

해설 역조는 tide against이다.

답 ❸

06. The two most effective generating force of surface ocean currents are ; `10년 3차`

① water depth and underwater oceanography
② temperature and salinity difference in the water
③ wind and density difference in the water
④ rotation of the earth and continental interference

해설 바람(wind)과 해수의 밀도(density)차가 해류(ocean current)를 발생시키는 가장 큰 효과이다.

답 ❸

기출문제

07. 다음 중 빈칸에 들어갈 말로 가장 옳은 것은? `17년 1차`

The direction of the current is true, not (A), and is the direction (B) which the current is setting, while the wind given is in the direction (C) which it is blowing.

① relative, in, toward
② magnetic, toward, from
③ definite, through, on
④ relative, along, from

해설 조류의 방향은 자북(magnetic)이 아닌 진북(true)을 기준으로 하고, 그 방향은 조류가 흘러가는 (toward) 방향으로, 반면에 바람은 불어오는 (from) 방향으로 선정한다.

답 ❷

chapter 07 RADAR

01
Radar의 정의

RADAR는 Radio Detection And Ranging의 약어이며 마이크로파를 발사하고 반사파를 물체로부터 수신함으로서 물표의 거리와 방위를 얻는 장비이다.

RADAR is an abbreviation of Radio Detection And Ranging, and is a equipment to get **distance** and **bearing** by emitting an micro wave and getting reflective wave from an object

02
영상의 방해 현상

① Blind sector (맹목구간)

선박 상부 구조물, 마스트 등으로 인해 차폐되어 선박의 레이더로 탐지할 수 없는 구간

An area which **cannot be scanned** by the ship's radar because it is shielded by parts of the superstructure, masts, etc.

② Interference (간섭현상)

2개 이상의 전파가 동시에 한 곳에 도착하면 간섭현상이 일어난다.

If two more radio waves **arrive simultaneously** at the same point in space, interference results.

③ STC (Sensitive time control) : 해면반사 억제기

④ FTC (Fast time constant) : 우설반사 억제기

03
영상의 거짓상

① Specular reflection (경면반사)

경면 반사란 항해 시 안벽, 고층 빌딩과 같은 거울 면이 가까이 있을 경우에 실제 영상 이외에 거짓상이 생기는 현상을 말한다.

Specular may be caused by radiowaves reflected by **water surface or windows, buildings**

② Indirect reflection (간접반사)
Indirect reflection occurs when a part of the energy is **reflected to the antenna from a part of the ship's structure**.

| 간접반사란 선박의 선체 구조물에 반사되어 생기는 거짓상을 말한다.

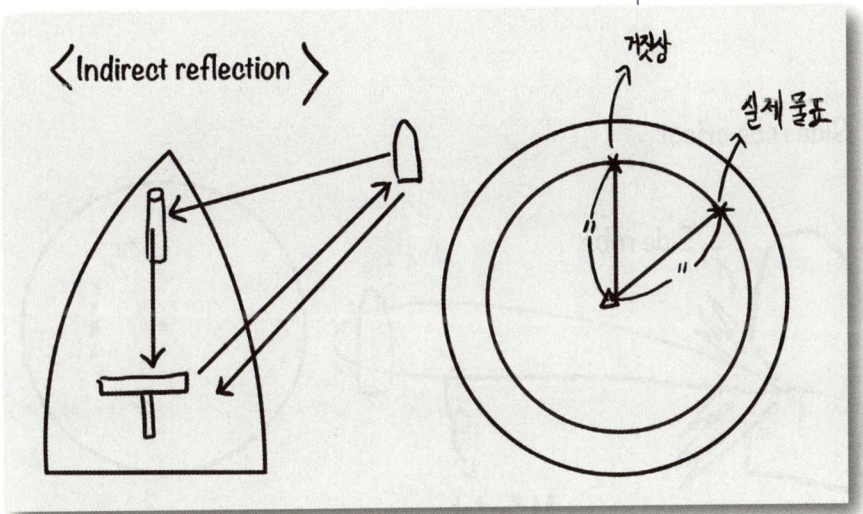

③ Multiple reflection (다중반사)
Multiple reflection is created by reflection between own ship and an object before the scanner finally collects its energy. we will see **a line of targets on the same bearing and with equal distance between them**.

| 다중 반사는 스캐너가 반사파를 마지막으로 수신하기 전에 자선과 목표 사이의 반사에 의해 생겨난다. 같은 방향의 동일 간격으로 이루어진 한 줄의 거짓상이 나타난다.

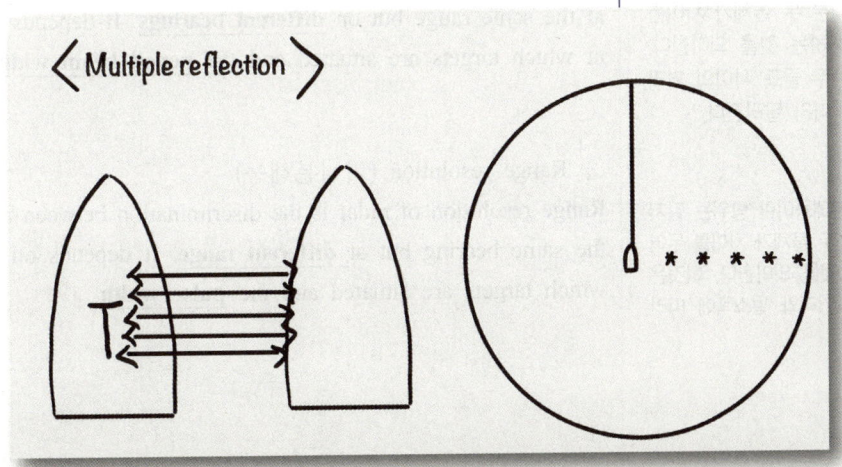

④ Side Lobe Effect (측엽효과)
When there is a large object close to the own ship, echo caused by the **side lobe** appears with the actual image caused by the main lobe. It appears in the form of **an arc**

본선과 가까운 거리에 큰 물체가 있는 경우 측엽에 의한 반사파가 주엽에 의한 실제 영상과 함께 나타나는 영상이다. 원호의 형태로 나타난다.

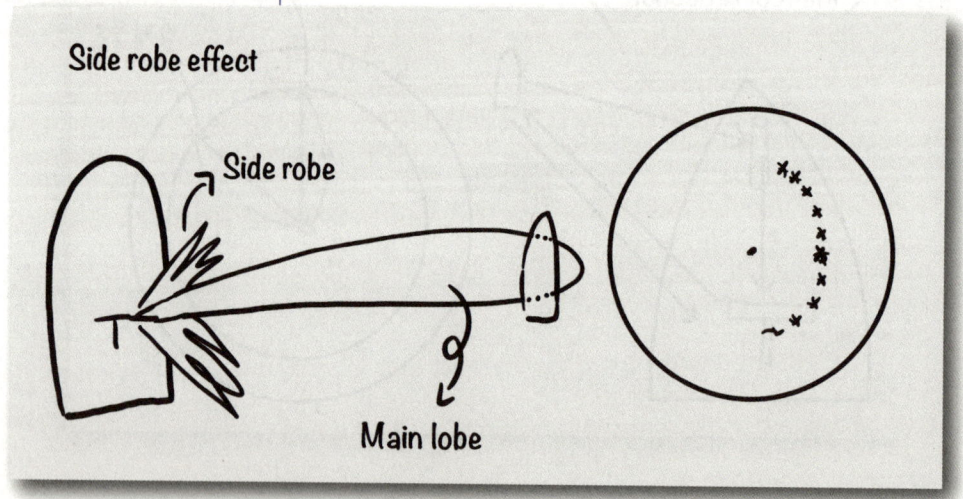

04
레이더 성능

① Bearing resolution (방위분해능)
Bearing resolution of radar is the discrimination between two objects at the same range but on **different bearings**. It depends on the range at which targets are situated and the **pencil beam width**.

레이더의 방위분해능이란 거리는 같지만 방위만 다른 두 물체가 차이를 두어 나타나게 하는 것을 의미한다. 이것은 위치한 두 목표 사이의 거리와 수평빔폭에 따라 달라진다.

② Range resolution (거리분해능)
Range resolution of radar is the discrimination between two object on the same bearing but at **different range**. It depends on the range at which targets are situated and the **pulse width**

레이더의 거리분해능이란 방위는 같지만 거리는 다른 두 물체가 차이를 두어 나타나게 하는 것을 의미한다. 이것은 두물표 사이의 거리와 펄스폭에 따라 달라진다.

05
레이더의 굴절현상

① Super refraction (초굴절)
If there is a marked **temperature inversion** or a sharp **decrease in water vapor content** with increased height, a horizontal radio duct may be formed.

고도의 증가에 따라 기온이 역전되고 상대습도가 감소하면서 일어난다. 도관현상이 발생한다.

② Sub refraction (아굴절)
If there is a rapid **fall in temperature or an increase in relative humidity** with increased height.

고도의 증가에 따라 기온이 급감하고 상대습도가 증가하면서 일어난다.

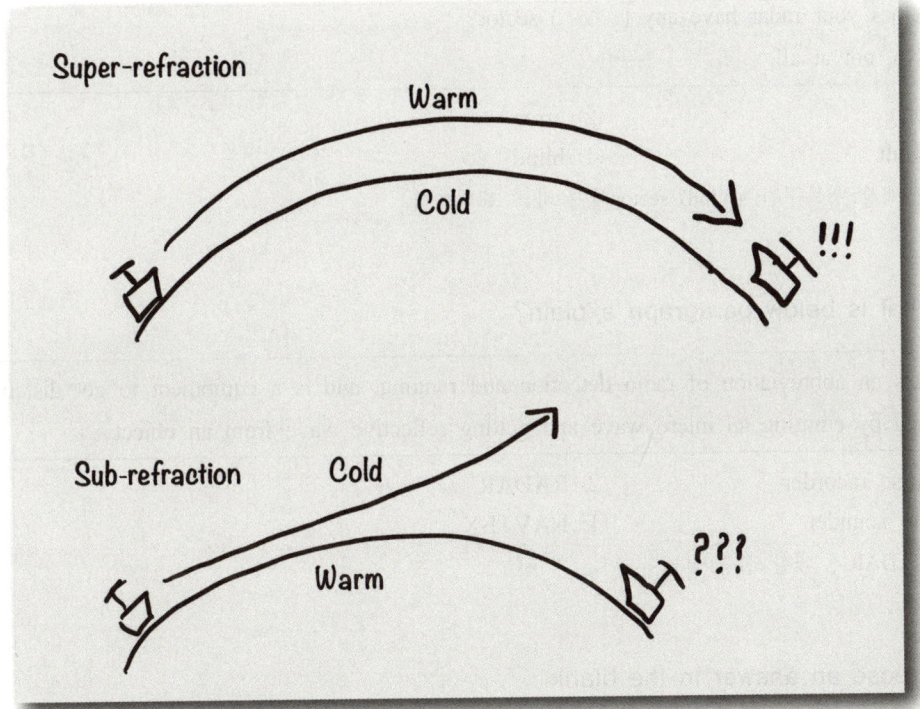

기출문제

01. 빈 칸에 들어갈 가장 적절한 단어는? `18년 2차 / 16년 2차 / 19년 3차`

If two more radio waves arrive simultaneously at the same point in space, ( ) results.

① radio beacon ② relay
③ refraction ④ interference

해설 간접 반사에 대한 설명이다.

답 ❹

02. Select the best answer at blank `09년 2차`

A : Does your radar have any ( ) sector?
B : No, not at all.

① detect ② error
③ default ④ blind

해설 문맥상 맹목구간, (blind) sector이 올바른 표현이다.

답 ❹

03. What is below paragraph explain? `10년 3차`

This is an abbreviation of radio detection and ranging, and is a equipment to get distance and bearing by emitting an micro wave and getting reflective wave from an object

① Course recorder ② RADAR
③ Echo sounder ④ NAVTEX

해설 RADAR에 대한 설명이다.

답 ❷

04. Choose an answer in the blank `11년 2차`

The characteristic on which bearing resolution is to distinguish an echo which is on the similar distance and different bearing, affected by ( )

① vertical beam width ② horizontal beam width
③ distance resolution ④ super- refraction

해설 비슷한 거리, 다른 방위에 있는 반사체(echo)를 구별해내는 방위분해능 특성은 수평빔폭(horizontal beam width)에 영향을 받는다.

답 ❷

기출문제

05. Which of the following does not limit the effective range of radar?   [17년 3차]

① signal
② horizontal beam width
③ fan beam width
④ peak power of the set

해설 수평의 빔폭(horizontal beam width)은 방위분해능(bearing resolution)에 영향을 준다.
*레이더 사거리에 영향을 주는 요소 *
① 신호
③ 수직빔폭
④ 첨두전력

답 ❷

06. Choose the correct one for the blank.   [13년 상반기 / 18년 1차]

If there is a marked temperature inversion or a sharp decrease in water vapor content with increased height, a horizontal radio duct may be formed. It is (　　　).

① super-refraction
② sub-refraction
③ radio-duct
④ super-saturation

해설 초굴절(super-refraction)에 대한 설명이다.

답 ❶

07. 다음 중 가장 옳은 것을 고르시오.   [18년 일반직]

① Blind sector is an area which can be scanned by the ship's radar because it is shielded by parts of the superstructure, masts, etc ...
② Radar interference can be created by reflection between own ship and an object before the scanner finally collects its energy, we will see a line of targets on the same bearing and with equal distance between them.
③ Specular reflections may be caused by radiowaves reflected by water surface or windows, buildings
④ Side Lobe Effect occurs when a part of the energy is reflected to the antenna from a part of the ship's structure.

해설 옳지 않은 것:
① can → cannot
② Radar interference → Multiple reflection
: 다중 반사란, 자선과 다른 물체 사이에서 반복적으로 생기는 반사로, 그 물표를 같은 방위에 물표 사이의 같은 거리로 여러 개의 물표가 일직선상으로 생기는 것을 볼 수 있다.
④ Side Lobe Effect → Indirect reflection

답 ❸

I 기출문제

08. 다음 〈보기〉는 RADAR(Radio Detection And Ranging)의 탐지 성능 및 거짓 영상에 관한 내용이다. 밑줄 친 단어 중 옳은 것은 모두 몇 개인가?

`22년 일반직`

- If there is a marked temperature ㉠ <u>inversion</u> or a sharp ㉡ <u>increase</u> in water vapor content with increased height, a horizontal radio duct may be formed. It is Super-refraction.
- If there is a rapid ㉢ <u>fall</u> in temperature or an ㉣ <u>decrease</u> in relative humidity with increased height. It is Sub-refraction.
- Multiple reflection is created by reflection between own ship and an object before the scanner finally collects its energy. we will see a line of targets on the ㉤ <u>same</u> bearing and with equal distance between them.

① 2개   ② 3개
③ 4개   ④ 5개

해설 옳지 않은 것:
㉡ increase → decrease
㉣ decrease → increase

답 ❶

09. 다음 〈보기〉 중 빈 칸에 들어갈 말로 가장 옳은 것은?

`21년 상반기`

The 3.2 cm radar as compared to a 10 cm radar with similar specifications will (   ).

① display small targets in a mass of dense sea clutter
② give better range performance in rain, hail, etc
③ display a more maplike presentation for inshore navigation
④ have less sea return in choppy rough seas

해설 X-band radar(3.2cm or 9G radar)는 동일 조건 S-band radar에 비해 <u>연안항해 시 좀 더 지도와 비슷한 화면을 보여준다</u>(display more maplike presentation for inshore navigation). 나머지는 S-band radar(10cm or 3G radar)에 대한 설명이다.

답 ❸

Chapter 08. Navigation Equipment(항해 장비)

01
종류

① Magnetic compass (자기 컴퍼스)
자석을 이용한 컴퍼스, **자차(Deviation)와 편차(Variation)**가 발생한다.

② Gyro compass (자이로 컴퍼스)
자이로컴퍼스는 자이로컴퍼스의 특성인 **회전관성 (rotational inertia)과 세차운동 (processional motion)**을 이용하고, **자전(daily rotation of the earth)과 중력(force of gravity)**을 이용해 북을 가리킨다.

③ Em-log
패러데이의 전자 유도 법칙(Faraday's Law)인 "도체와 자기장이 상대적인 운동 상태에 있을 때 도체에는 기전력이 유기 된다" 는 것을 응용한 것이다.

④ Doppler-log
항행중인 선박이 해저로 발사한 음파와 반사되어 수신한 **음파(sound wave)**는 주파수차(doppler 주파수차)가 생기고 이것은 선박의 속도에 비례한다는 원칙을 이용한다. 대지속력(SOG)과. **대수속력(Speed Trough the Water, STW)**을 측정 할 수 있다.

⑤ Echo sounder (음향 측심의)
선저에 해저로 쏜 짧은 펄스의 **초음파(sound wave)**가 해저에서 반사하여 되돌아오는 시간을 측정하여 **수심(depth of water)**을 측정한다.

⑥ Chronometer
정밀시계

⑦ Anemometer
풍속계

⑧ Barometer
기압계

⑨ Thermometer
온도계

⑩ VDR(Voyage Data Recorder)
선박의 운항 중 발생되는 각종 **항해정보(Voyage data)**를 **기록(Record)**, 유지 및 관리하여 해양사고 발생 시 항공기의 블랙박스와 같은 개념으로 회수하여 사고 원인 분석을 위해 사용된다.

⑪ AIS (Automatic Identification System)
선박의 **위치(position)**, **침로(course)**, **속력(speed)** 등 항해 정보를 실시간으로 제공하는 첨단 장비

⑫ GPS (Global Positioning System)
위성(satellite)로부터 전파의 도달시간으로 표시한 **거리(distance)**를 활용하여 위치를 구하는 위성합법체계. 일반적으로 대지속력(Speed Over the Ground, SOG)측정 시 사용된다.

⑬ ECDIS (Electronic Chart Display and Information System)
선박의 항해와 관련된 정보, 즉, 해도정보, 위치정보, 선박의 침로, 속력, 수심 자료 등을 종합하여 스크린에 도식하는 시스템. **Vector 방식**으로 제작된다.

⑭ Sextant (육분의)
the instrument used by navigator to measure the vertical angle between a heavenly body and horizon.
항해사가 천체와 수평선 사이의 수직 협각을 측정하기 위해 사용하는 장비이다.

기출문제

01. Choose the correct one for the blank． `10년 2차`

> Gyro compass is a device to indicate North constantly to use of rotational inertia of solid of revolution and precessional motion. Gyro compass also use of earth's (   ) and (   ) to indicate North

① precession - revolution
② gravity - revolution
③ gravity - rotation
④ precession - rotation

해설 자이로 컴퍼스는 영구적으로 북을 가리키는 장비로 회전관성과 세차운동을 사용한다. 자이로 컴퍼스는 또한 지북을 하기 위해 지구의 중력(gravity)과 자전(rotation)을 사용한다.

답 ③

02. Choose the correct one for the blank． `18년 1차`

> The basic principle of gyro compass pointing to the north is the combined effects of the force of (   ) and (   ) of the earth.

① gravity - the daily rotation
② the spinning vessel - the motion
③ heavy weight - the axis
④ revolution - annual rotation

해설 자이로 컴퍼스가 북쪽을 가리키는 기본 원리(basic principle)는 지구의 중력(force of gravity)과 자전(the daily rotation)의 힘의 영향을 결합한 것이다.

답 ①

03. 다음 중 빈칸에 들어갈 말로 가장 적절한 것은? `16년 2차`

> An instrument for measuring wind force or speed is (   ).

① an anemometer
② a thermometer
③ a hydrometer
④ a chronometer

해설 풍력과 풍속을 측정하는 장비는 풍속계(anemometer)이다.

답 ①

04. 다음 중 서로 관계없는 것끼리 짝지어진 것은? `04년 5차`

① barometer - air pressure
② thermometer - temperature
③ anemometer - wind speed
④ gyrocompass - water depth

해설 Gyrocompass 는 북쪽을 알려주는 장비이다. 수심(water depth)은 echo sounder로 알 수 있다.

답 ④

I 기출문제

05. 다음 보기가 설명하고 있는 항해 장비의 이름을 고르시오. 　　　기출예상문제

> This is an instrument in which the pressure of the air is measured. This instrument is based on a flexible metal compartment.

① Anemometer　　　　　② Aneroid barometer
③ thermometer　　　　　④ Chronometer

해설 공기의 압력 즉 기압을 측정하는 장비는 Aneroid barometer이다. 이 장비는 탄성(flexible)을 가진 금속 부품으로 이루어져 있다.
　　　elasticity 도 탄성을 의미한다.

답 ②

06. Choose the correct one for the blank 　　　기출예상문제

> "The GPS receiver makes time-of-arrival measurements of the satellite signals to obtain the (　　) between the user and satellite"

① time　　　　　　　　② distance
③ time-lag　　　　　　④ Gyro error

해설 GPS수신기는 관측자(user)와 위성(satellite)사이의 거리(distance)를 얻기 위해 위성신호의 도착 시간을 측정 한다.

답 ②

07. Choose the correct one for the blank 　　　기출예상문제

> The water depth is now made by means of the (　　　).

① EM log　　　　　　　② GPS
③ echo sounder　　　　④ doppler log

해설 수심은 음향측심기(echo sounder)로 측정한다.

답 ③

08. (　　) is the instrument used by navigator to measure the vertical angle between a heavenly body and horizon. 　　　04년 2차

① log　　　　　　　　　② sextant
③ radar　　　　　　　　④ compass

해설 육분의(sextant)는 항해사가 천체(heavenly body)와 수평선(horizon) 사이의 수직 협각을 측정하기 위해 사용하는 장비이다.

답 ②

chapter 09 해양 기상

01
고기압과 저기압

① Anticyclone, High pressure (고기압)
주위보다 상대적으로 기압이 높은 곳. 고기압 중심으로부터 저기압 쪽으로 바람이 불어나가며 북반구(Northen hemisphere) 기준으로 **시계방향(clockwise)**으로 불어나간다. 하강기류(descending air current)가 발생해 날씨가 좋다.

② Low pressure (저기압)
주위보다 상대적으로 기압이 낮은 곳. 북반부(Northen hemisphere)에서는 **시계반대방향(anticlockwise)**으로 불어 들어간다. 상승기류(ascending air current)가 발생해 날씨가 좋지 않다.

02
전선

① Warm front (온난전선)
Where a warm air mass moves on colder air mass.

따뜻한 공기가 찬 공기 위를 타고 올라가면 발생한다.

② Cold front (한랭전선)
Where a cold air mass moves under warmer air mass.

찬 공기가 따뜻한 공기 아래로 내려가면 발생한다.

03
각종 기상 용어들

① Advection fog (이류무)
The common type of fog formed when **warm moist air blows over a cold surface** and is cooled below its dew point; or, when **cold air blowing over a warm surface** as that the sea, absorbs and becomes "clouded" with excess moisture.

따뜻한 습기가찬 공기가 차가운 수면에 불 때, 이슬점 아래로 내려가 냉각되어 생기는 전형적인 안개;
찬 공기가 따뜻한 수면위로 불 때는 흡수하거나 습기를 머금은 구름이 된다

일정한 양의 공기와 습기에서 온도가 내려가는 경우, 습도는 상대적으로 높아지고, 공기 중의 수증기가 일정한 온도에서 액화되기 시작하는데, 이러한 온도를 이슬점(노점)이라 한다.

② Dew point (이슬점)
In case the temperature is decreasing at constant quantity of air and humidity, the humidity will be increased relatively and the moisture in the air shall begin to be liquefied at some point of temperature that is called as **dew point**.

기출문제

01. Select the best answer at blank `09년 2차`

Increasing wind and sea (　) again, Barometer falling fast

① shrinking   ② building up
③ weakening   ④ moving

해설 바람이 강해지고 파도가 높아진다(building up). 기압계(Barometer)는 급하게 떨어진다.

답 ❷

02. 다음 해상에서의 바람에 관한 다음의 보기 중 가장 옳은 것을 고르시오. `06년 2차`

① Wind is made mainly due to movement of clouds and evaporation of waterdrop
② Wind tend to move from low pressure to high pressure
③ Wind force is quoted according to the Beaufort scale
④ The bigger wind scale means the weaker the wind force

해설 옳지 않은 것 :
　① 구름과 수증기 증발로 만들어 지는 것은 비(rain)이다.
　② 바람은 고기압(high pressure)에서 저기압(low pressure)으로 부는 경향이 있다.
　④ 더 큰 풍력(wind scale)은 더 강한(stronger) 바람의 힘을 나타낸다.
　옳은 것 :
　③ 풍력(Wind force)은 뷰포트스케일(Beaufort scale)에 의해 매겨진다.
　* 뷰포트 스케일은 바람의 속도를 가지고 바람의 세기를 0~12단계까지 매겨놓은 것이다.*

답 ❸

기출문제

03. Choose the correct one for the blank [15년 2차]

In case the temperature is decreasing at constant quantity of air and humidity, the humidity will be increased relatively and the moisture in the air shall begin to be liquefied at some point of temperature that is called as (   ).

① relative humidity
② dew point
③ freezing point
④ absolute humidity

해설 일정한 양의 공기와 습기에서 온도가 내려가는 경우, 습도는 상대적으로 높아지고, 공기 중의 수증기가 일정한 온도에서 액화되기 시작하는데, 이러한 온도를 이슬점(dew point)이라 한다.

답 ❷

04. 다음 보기가 설명하는 것을 고르시오. [기출예상문제]

The common type of fog formed when warm moist air blows over a cold surface and is cooled below its dew point;

① radiation fog
② Advection fog
③ cumulus
④ cold front

해설 이류무(Advection fog)에 대한 설명이다.

답 ❷

05. Choose the correct one for the blank [기출예상문제]

Where a cold air mass moves under warmer air mass, it is known as the (   ).

① dew point
② advection fog
③ warm front
④ cold front

해설 찬 공기가 따뜻한 공기 아래로 내려가는 한랭전선(cold front)에 대한 설명이다.

답 ❹

Chapter 9. 해양 기상 | **429**

04

Typhoon (태풍)

① 정의
열대해상에서 발생하는 폭풍우를 동반하는 열대 저기압
② 열대 저기압의 발생 지역에 따른 이름
- Typhoon (태풍) : 우리나라, 일본, 중국, 북태평양
- Hurricane (허리케인) : 미국남동부, 북대서양 카리브해, 서인도제도, 멕시코
- Cyclone (사이클론) : 북인도양, 뱅골만, 아라비아해
- Willy Willy (윌리윌리) : 호주, 뉴질랜드, 피지, 사모아제도
③ 태풍 피항법
- 풍향이 시계방향(clockwise)으로 순전(veering)하면 본선은 태풍 진로의 우측(right)인 **위험반원(dangerous semicircle)**에 있는 것이다. 이 경우 우현(right) 선수로 바람을 받으며 피항 한다.
 (heave to 피항법) >> **RRR법칙**
- 풍향이 반시계방향(anticlockwise)으로 반전(backing)하면 본선은 태풍 진로의 좌측(left) **가항반원(Navigable semicircle)**에 위치하고 있는 것이다. 이 경우 좌현 선미로 바람을 받으며 피항 한다. (scudding 피항법) >> **LLS법칙**

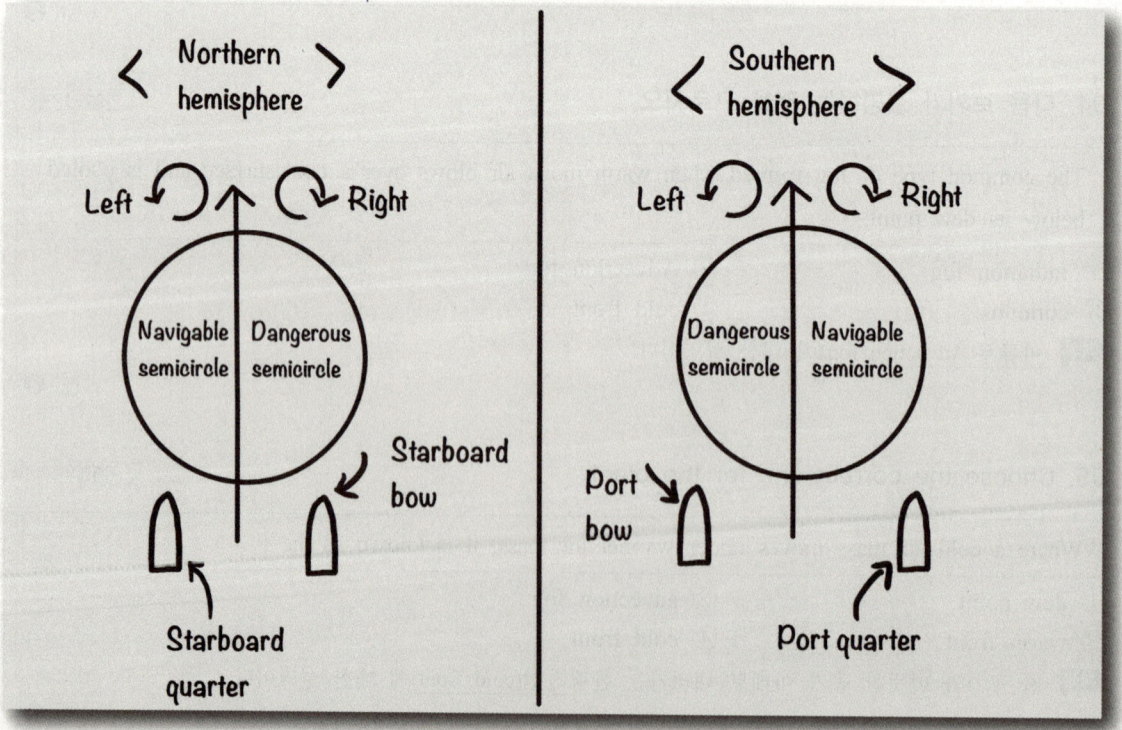

④ 바이스 밸럿의 법칙 (Buys Ballot)
- 북반구 기준 바람을 등지고 섰을 때 왼손이 향하는 쪽의 기압이 오른손에 비해 낮다. 그리하여 태풍의 중심은 **왼손 전방 20~30°**에 있다.
- 남반구 기준 바람을 등지고 섰을 때 오른손이 향하는 쪽의 기압이 왼손에 비해 낮다. 그리하여 태풍의 중심은 **오른손 전방 20~30°**에 있다.

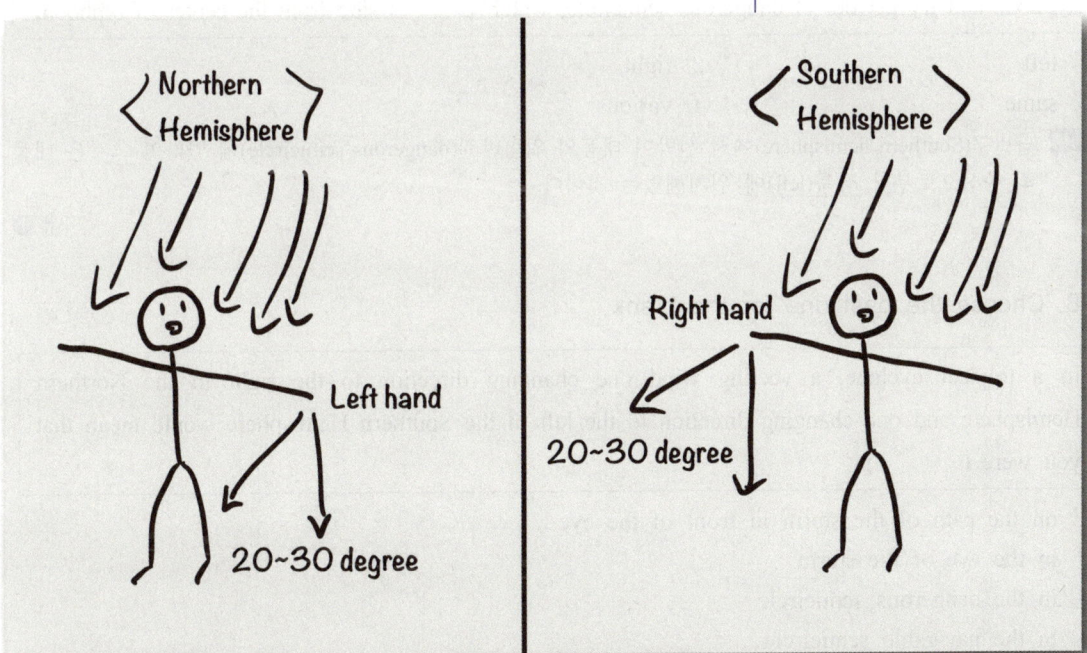

기출문제

06. The local name of the tropical storm in north pacific ocean is ( ). 07년 3차

① hurricane ② cyclone
③ willy-willy ④ typhoon

해설 북태평양(north pacific ocean)에서 발생하는 열대성 저기압은 태풍(typhoon)이다.

답 ④

I 기출문제

07. Choose best answer in the blank   　10년 2차

> When vessel encounter a typhoon at Southern hemisphere, master should check the center of typhoon and try get out of dangerous semicircle, which is (　) side from the center of typhoon.

① left　　　　　　　　　② right
③ same　　　　　　　　④ various

해설 남반구(Southern hemisphere)에서 선박이 태풍의 위험반원(dangerous semicircle)에 있다면 그것은 태풍의 중심으로부터 좌측(left)에 위치해있는 것이다.

답 ❶

08. Choose the best one for the blank.   　15년 2차

> In a tropical cyclone, a veering wind one changing direction to the right in the Northern Hemisphere and one changing direction to the left in the Southern Hemisphere would mean that you were (　　).

① on the path of the storm in front of the eye
② in the eye of the storm
③ in the dangerous semicircle
④ in the navigable semicircle

해설 북반구의 열대성 저기압(tropical cyclone)에서 바람이 순전(veering), 즉 바람이 오른쪽으로 변하고 남반구에서 풍향이 왼쪽으로 변하면 귀선은 위험반원(dangerous semicircle)에 있게 된다.

답 ❸

09. 다음 중 빈칸에 들어갈 말로 가장 옳은 것은?   　18년 일반직

> Hove to in the northern hemisphere under tropical cyclone conditions, a veering wind one changing direction to the (a) would mean that you were in the dangerous semicircle. The vessel should keep the wind on the (b).

① right, starboard bow　　　② right, starboard quarter
③ right, port bow　　　　　④ left, port quarter

해설 북반구에서 태풍상황일 때 풍향이 순전하면(방향이 오른쪽(right)으로 바뀌면)본선은 태풍 진로의 우측 위험 반원에 위치하고 있고, 그 때엔 풍랑을 우현 선수(starboard bow)에 받고 침로를 유지하며 피항해야 한다.

답 ❶

기출문제

10. When the wind is blow from southwest at North Hemisphere, where is the low pressure it is?

06년 3차

① southwest to sout
② southeast to east
③ northwest to north
④ northeast to north

해설 북반구에서 남서풍이 불고 있을 때 바람을 등지고 서면 왼손의 전방은 북서쪽에서 북쪽(northwest to north) 부근이 된다.

답 ❸

11. 다음 〈보기〉는 태풍의 중심 위치를 추정하는 바이스 밸럿의 법칙(Buys Ballot's Law)에 대한 설명이다. 빈 칸에 들어갈 말로 가장 옳은 것은?

21년 상반기

A rule in synoptic meteorology, announced in 1857 by Buys Ballot, of Utrecht, which states that if, in the northern hemisphere, one stands with one's back to the wind, pressure is lower on one's (㉠) hand than on one's (㉡), whilst in the southern hemisphere the converse is true.
This law implies that, in the northern hemisphere, winds blow (㉢) round a depression, and (㉣) round an anticyclone; the converse is true in the southern hemisphere.

	㉠	㉡	㉢	㉣
①	right	left	anticlockwise	clockwise
②	left	right	anticlockwise	clockwise
③	right	left	clockwise	anticlockwise
④	left	right	clockwise	anticlockwise

해설 1857년 Buys Ballot에 의해 발표된 기상학 법칙의 내용은 북반구에서 바람을 등지고 서 있는 경우 ㉡(오른손)보다 ㉠(왼손)에 압력이 낮지만 남반구에서는 그 반대라는 사실이다.
이 법칙은 북반구에서는 바람이 저기압을 중심으로 ㉢(반시계방향으로) 불고, 고기압을 중심으로 ㉣(시계방향으로) 분다는 것을 암시한다.

답 ❷

12. What is the underlined means?

09년 2차

Our ship passed over eye of hurricane, and encountered a <u>lull</u>, rain stopped and wind became weak for a short time

① trade wind
② calm interval
③ high pressure
④ isobar

해설 선박이 태풍의 눈을 지나고 있고 소강상태(lull)를 마주했다, 잠시 동안 비가 멈추고 바람은 약해졌다. 소강상태를 다른 말로 calm interval이라고 할 수 있다.

답 ❷

chapter 10 선박 개요

01
선박 치수

① Length Over All, LOA (전장)
선수 최전단부터 선미 최후단까지의 수평 길이

② Length Between Perpendiculars, LBP (수선간장)
계획 만재흘수선(load line)상 선수재 전면에서 러더포스트 후면까지의 수평 길이 혹은 전부수선 (FP)에서 후부수선 (AP)까지의 수평거리

③ Length On Load Water line, LWL (수선장)
계획만재흘수선(load line)상에서 물에 잠긴 선체의 길이

④ Registered Length (등록장)
상갑판 보(beam)상 선수재 전면에서 선미재 후면까지를 잰 수평거리

⑤ Extreme Breadth (전폭)
외판(shell plating)의 외면에서부터 맞은편 외판의 외면까지의 수평거리

⑥ Moulded Breadth (형폭)
늑골(frame)의 외면에서부터 맞은편 늑골의 외면까지의 수평거리

02
Trim (트림)

> 트림의 변화는 무게중심을 앞이나 뒤쪽으로 이동시켜서, 혹은 무게를 **부면심의(center of floatation)** 앞이나 뒤쪽에 더하거나 제거해서 생겨난다.
>
> 선수 흘수가 선미흘수보다 클 때

Change of trim is caused either by shifting weight forward or aft, or by adding or removing weight before or abaft the ship's center of floatation

① Trim by the head (선수 트림)
When draft froward is greater than draft after

② Trim by the stern (선미 트림)
When draft after is greater than draft forward

선미 흘수가 선수흘수보다 클 때

③ Even keel (등흘수)
When the keel is horizontal or her draft is the same at bow and stern

용골이 수평이거나 흘수가 선수선미에서 같을 때

기출문제

01. Choose the correct one for the blank. `18년 1차`

A vessel is said to be ( ) when her draft is the same at bow and stern.

① On a even keel　　② In ballast
③ On free surface　　④ Trim by the stern

해설 선박의 흘수가 선수와 선미에서가 같을 때 그 선박은 등흘수(even keel)이라고 불린다.

답 ❶

02. 다음 빈칸에 들어가기에 가장 적합한 단어를 고르시오. `기출예상문제`

Fill the fore peak tank to ( ) the stern trim.

① increase　　② decrease
③ maintain　　④ fill

해설 선미 트림을 줄이기(decrease) 위하여 선수 탱크를 채우시오. (선수 탱크를 채우면 선박 선수가 무거워져 선미부가 들리게 된다.)

답 ❷

03. Select the correct one for the blank `22년 2차`

Change of ( ) is caused either by shifting weight forward or aft, or by adding or removing weight before or abaft the ship's center of floatation

① center of gravity　　② center of buoyancy
③ trim　　④ metacenter

해설 트림(trim)의 변화는 무게중심을 앞이나 뒤쪽으로 이동시켜서, 혹은 무게를 부면심의(center of floatation) 앞이나 뒤쪽에 더하거나 제거해서 생겨난다.

답 ❸

chapter 11 선박의 구조

수면에서부터 선체의 가장 높은 지점까지의 높이	① Air draft The height from the waterline to the highest point of the vessel
물에 뜨는 선박의 깊이	② Draught or draft (흘수) Depth in water at which a vessel floats
선체 중앙부에서 수면에서 메인갑판까지 측정한 높이	③ Freeboard (건현) The distance measured amidships from the water line to the main deck of the vessel
선저 아래에 남아있는 깊이	④ UKC (Under Keel Clearance) Depth remaining under a vessel's bottom
선박의 주된 부분	⑤ Hull (선체) The main body of a ship
선박의 가장 중요한 뼈대의 부분은 선체 최하부의 중심선에 있는 중심선으로 용골로 알려져 있다.	⑥ Keel (용골) The most important part of the frame of a ship is the bottom center line, known as the keel
늑골은 가로 방향으로 용골로 용접되거나 이어진 갈비뼈이다.	⑦ Frame (늑골) Frames are ribs that are transverse bolted or welded to the keel

⑧ Shell Plating (외판)
The plates forming the outer side and bottom skin of the hull

외판은 선박의 외측이나 선저의 껍질을 형성한다.

⑨ Camber
Deck slope from center to both side, permit drainage to the scuppers

갑판의 구부러진 것으로 선박의 중심에서부터 양 현측으로 이루어진다. 스쿠퍼(배수구)로 배수가 이루어지게 해준다.

⑩ Tumble home
In the ship side slope inward, the amount of the slope is called tumble home

선박 외측이 안쪽으로 구부러진 경우, 그 구부러진 정도를 텀블홈이라 한다.

⑪ Flare
In the ship side slope outward, the amount of the slope is called flare.

선박 외측이 바깥쪽으로 구부러진 경우, 그 구부러진 정도를 플레어라고 한다.

⑫ Bilge
The bottom plating and side plating are joined by a curve which completes an approximate right angle

선저와 선측을 연결하는 만곡부

⑬ Bilge keel (빌지용골)
The bilge keel is fitted at the bilge turn in order to reduce rolling

빌지 킬은 빌지 만곡부 부분에 횡동요를 줄이기 위해 설치된다.

⑭ Bulkhead (격벽)
Vertical partitions of walls, watertight division. Reduce the danger of sinking

수직의 칸막이 벽, 또는 수밀 벽이다. 침수의 위험을 감소시켜준다.

⑮ Collision bulkhead (충돌격벽)
The first water tight bulkhead in the ship.

첫 번째 수밀 격벽을 의미한다.

이 선저는 두 개의 수밀 벽으로 되어 있다. 이 두 선저 사이의 공간은 평형수 탱크로 자주 사용된다.

⑯ Double bottom (이중저)
The bottom of the ship has two complete layers of watertight hull surface. The space in between the two bottoms is often used as storage tanks for Ballast water.

화물이나 잡은 물고기는 선창에 보관한다.

⑰ Hold (화물창)
The cargoes or fish catched are stowed in the hold

선원들이나 여객이 사용하는 선실로 구성된 장소

⑱ Accommodation (거주구)
A term for a cabin fitted out for the use of crew, passengers

혹의 형상처럼 둥근 것으로 선수에 위치해있다. 조파저항을 줄여준다.

⑲ Bulbous bow (구상선수)
A bulb like a shape of lump which is located ship's bow. This can reduce wave resistance

기출문제

01. Choose the best one for the blank. 12년

( ) is vertical distance from the uppermost deck to the center of the disc which marked on the vessel's sides and which indicates the position of the load water line in ( ).

① Draught - mark ② Summer - draught mark
③ Mean - draft ④ Freeboard - summer

해설 건현(Freeboard)은 상갑판에서부터 선체의 하기(summer)만재흘수선을 표시하는 원판 중간까지의 수직 높이를 말한다.

답 ④

기출문제

02. Choose best answer explained by below `09년 3차`

Crew and passengers can stay this place of vessel and rest and eat. Some vessel equipped with swimming pool or basket ball station

① Recreation space ② Seaman's club
③ Accommodation space ④ Crew's messroom

해설 선원과 여객은 선박의 이 공간에 있을 수 있고 쉬고, 먹을 수 있다. 어떤 선박에는 수영장이나 농구장이 설치되어 있기도 하다. : 거주구(Accommodation space)

답 ❸

03. The main body of as ship is called the (   ) `04년 3차`

① bow ② stern
③ hull ④ upside

해설 선박의 주된 부분인 hull에 대한 설명이다.

답 ❸

04. 다음 중 빈칸에 들어갈 단어로 가장 옳은 것은? `16년 2차 / 18년 1차`

(   ) are vertical partitions of walls. All ships must have a specified number of (   ) depending on their length. By dividing the ship into watertight divisions, they reduce the danger of sinking if one compartment is holed.

① Tanks ② Compartments
③ Bulkheads ④ Rails

해설 격벽(bulkheads)은 벽면의 수직칸막이이다. 모든 선박은 반드시 길이에 따라 격벽(bulkheads)을 일정한 개수 가지고 있어야 한다. 수밀 격벽은 선박을 나눔으로서 한 구획에 구멍이 뚫려도 침몰의 위험을 줄일 수 있다.

답 ❸

05. Choose the best one for the blank. `12년`

(   ) is the first water tight bulkhead in the ship.

① Bulkhead ② Collision bulkhead
③ Watertight ④ uppermost deck

해설 충돌격벽(Collision bulkhead) 선박의 첫 번째 수밀 격벽을 의미한다.

답 ❷

I 기출문제

06. What is right explanation regarding "bulbous bow"?

10년 3차

A. A bulb like a shape of lump which is located ship's bow
B. This can reduce wave resistance

① A only ② B only
③ Both A and B ④ neither A nor B

해설 A. bulbous bow는 혹의 형상처럼 둥근 것으로 선수에 위치해있다.
B. 조파저항을 줄여준다.
A와 B 둘 다 구상선수(bulbous bow)에 대한 설명이다.
  *- A only : 오직 A만
  - Both A and B : A와 B 둘 다
  - Neither A nor B : A도 B도 둘 다 아니다.*

답 ③

chapter 12 선박 설비

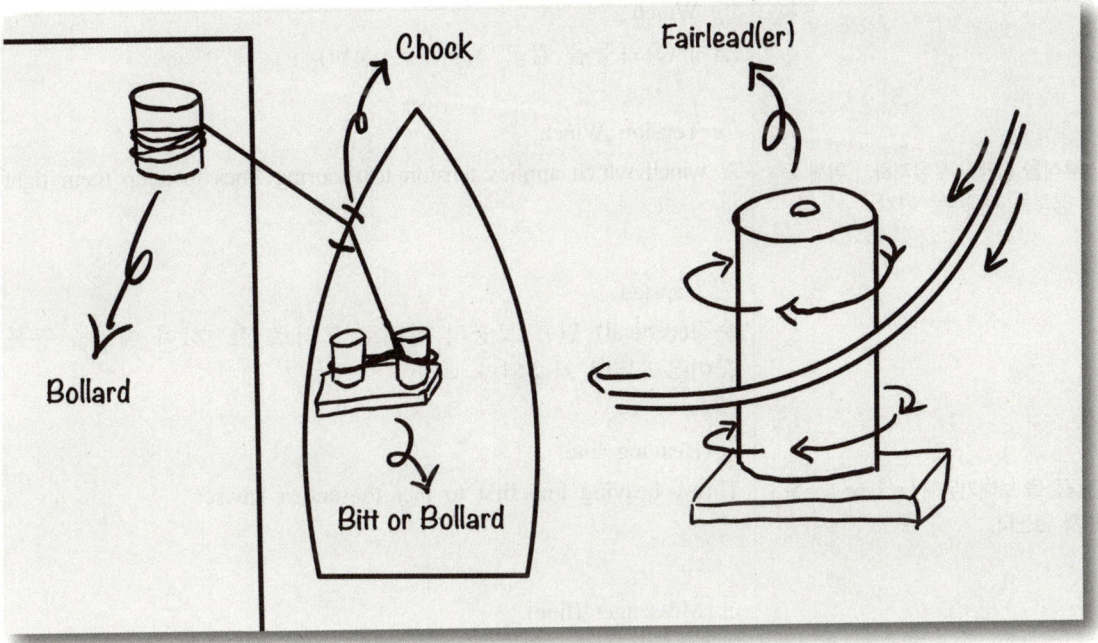

① Fairlead
- The fitting on the deck of a ship which guides the ropes when the ship is being moored. To ensure the best route for a line, it pass through a **fair lead** at the vessel's side

갑판상의 설비로 계류줄이 계류되는 동안에 줄을 잘 빠져나가게(guide)해 준다. 계류 줄이 통과하는 최고의 방법은 선측의 페어리더를 통과하는 것이다.

② Chock
선측으로 계류줄이 빠져나가게 해주는 부분

이것은 주로 chocks의 주변에서 발견되며 어떤 것들은 그 안에 설치되기도 한다. 이것들은 무거운 수직의 원통형이며 계류삭들이 chock를 통해 빠져나가는 동안에 줄을 묶기 위해 사용된다.

③ Bitt and Bollard
Which are usually found in the neighborhood of chocks and somewhat inboard of them. They are heavy vertical cylinders and often used for making fast lines that have been led through the chock.

④ Windlass
양묘기

⑤ Winch
윈치 (로프등을 감고 풀어주는 설비)

계류삭을 팽팽하게 유지하기 위해 줄에 장력을 가해주는 윈치.

⑥ Tension Winch
A winch which applies tension to mooring lines to keep them tight

⑦ Capstan
수직(vertical) 원통 모양의 설비로 모터로 회전하며 예인줄 등을 끌어올리는데 사용된다.

계류줄을 보내기위해 heaving line을 먼저 던진다.

⑧ Heaving line
Throw heaving line first to pier to send a hawser

무거운 줄을 보내기 위해 보내는 더 가벼운 줄을 메신저라고 한다.

⑨ Messenger (line)
A light line sent ashore or elsewhere to enable a heavier line to be hauled out is messenger

기출문제

01. 다음 박스의 실문에 가장 적절한 것은?   `16년 2차`

> What is the fitting on the deck of a ship which guides the ropes when the ship is being moored?

① Fairway 　　　② Bitt
③ Fair leader 　④ Bollard

해설 갑판상의 설비로 계류줄이 계류되는 동안에 줄을 잘 빠져나가게(guide)해주는 것은 Fair leader이다.

답 ❸

02. To ensure the best route for a line, it pass through a (　　) at the vessel's side   `07년 3차`

① pipe 　　　② winch
③ hole 　　　④ fairlead

해설 계류 줄이 통과하는 최고의 방법은 선측의 페어리더(fiarlead)를 통과하는 것이다.

답 ❹

03. Choose the best one for the blank.   `14년 2차`

> Approaching a dock, you will throw (　　) first to pier to send a hawser.

① heaving line 　　② towing line
③ mooring line 　　④ spring line

해설 접안시 가장먼저 던져주는 줄은 heaving line이다.

답 ❶

04. 다음 빈칸에 들어갈 말로 옳은 것은?   `기출예상문제`

> A light line sent ashore or elsewhere to enable a heavier line to be hauled out is (　　)

① messenger 　　② painter
③ preventer 　　④ runner

해설 무거운 줄을 보내기 위해 보내는 더 가벼운 줄을 메신저(messenger)라고 한다.

답 ❶

기출문제

05. 다음에서 설명하는 것으로 가장 옳은 것은?   15년 2차 / 22년 2차

( ) are usually found in the neighborhood of chocks and somewhat inboard of them. They are heavy vertical cylinders and often used for making fast lines that have been led through the chock.

① fairlead
② bitts
③ mooring buoy
④ capstan

해설 bitts나 bollard는 주로 chocks의 주변에서 발견되며 어떤 것들은 그 안에 설치되기도 한다. 이것들은 무거운 수직의 원통형이며 계류삭들이 chock를 통해 빠져나가는 동안에 줄을 묶기 위해 사용된다.

답 ②

chapter 13 선박에 작용하는 힘

01
종방향의 힘

① Hogging
A stress which a ship's hull or keel experiences that the middle of the ship is pushed to bend upward.

선체가 중앙부가 위쪽으로 휘는 현상으로 선체나 선박 용골이 받게되는 충격이다.

② Sagging
Sagging is brought about when the ship is supported fore and aft by two waves, so that the middle of the vessel is strained in the opposite direction.

새깅이란 두 개의 파에 의해서 선수미가 받쳐질 때 선박의 중간 부분이 힘을 받아 반대방향으로 작용하는 힘이다.

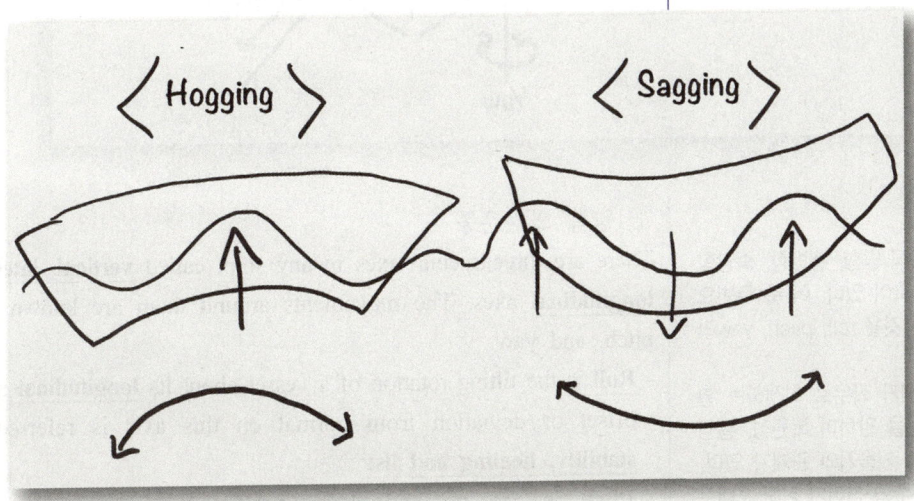

02
횡방향의 힘

① Heeling, List
횡경사

② Racking
선박의 우현 좌현의 흘수차이 발생으로 선체가 변형되는 것

03
선체 6자유 운동

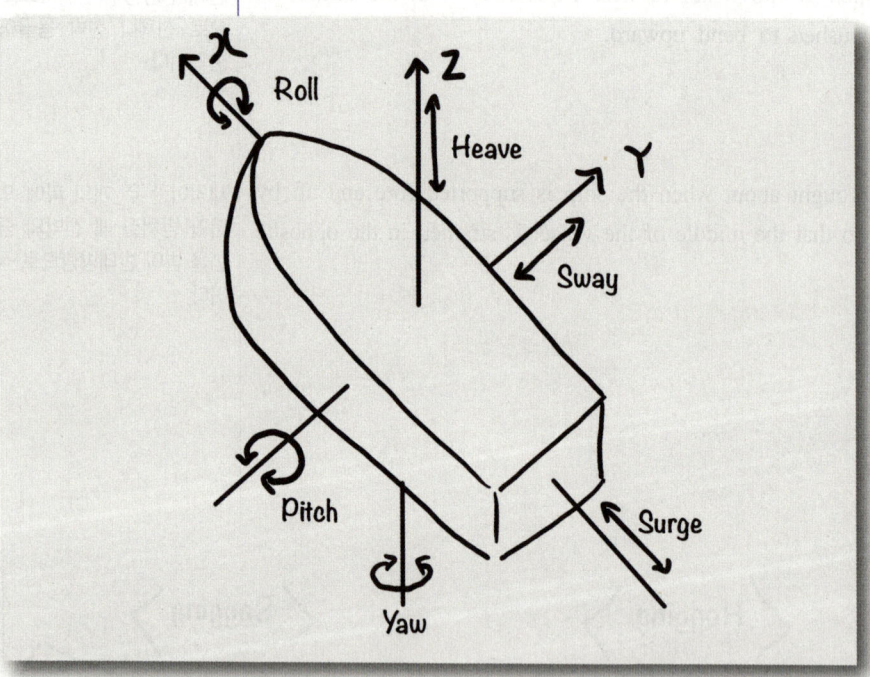

선박에는 수직 방향, 횡방향, 종방향의 세 가지 축이 있다. 이 축 주변으로 움직이는 것을 roll, pitch, yaw라 한다.
- Roll : 선체가 좌우로 회전하는 횡경사 운동을 말하며 복원성, 횡경사 그리고 기울기와 관계가 있다.
- Pitch : 선수와 선미가 상하 교대로 회전하는 종경사 운동으로 트림과 관계가 있다.

① 왕복 회전운동
There are three special axes in any ship, called **vertical, lateral, and longitudinal** axes. The movements around them are known as roll, pitch, and yaw.
- **Roll** is the tilting rotation of a vessel about its **longitudinal** axis. An offset or deviation from normal on this axis is referred to as **stability, heeling and list**
- **Pitch** is the up and down rotation of a vessel about its **lateral(transverse)** axis. An offset or deviation from normal on this axis is referred to as **trim**.

- **Yaw** is the turning rotation of a vessel about its **vertical** axis. An offset or deviation from normal on this axis is referred to as **course keeping ability**.

― Yaw : 선수가 좌우 교대로 선회하려는 왕복 운동으로 침로안정성과 관계가 있다.

② 왕복 직선운동
- **Surge** is the linear **longitudinal** motion
- **Sway** is the linear **transverse** motion
- **Heave** is the linear **vertical** motion

― Surge는 종방향의 직선 운동이다.
― Sway는 횡방향의 직선 운동이다.
― Heave는 수직의 직선 운동이다.

기출문제

01. Choose the correct one for the blank. 〔18년 1차〕

( ) is brought about when the ship is supported fore and aft by two waves, so that the middle of the vessel is strained in the opposite direction.

① Pounding ② Hogging
③ Sagging   ④ Pitching

해설 선수 선미가 파도에 의해 지지되어 중심부가 그 반대방향으로 구부러지는 Sagging에 대한 설명이다.

답 ❸

Chapter 13. 선박에 작용하는 힘 | **447**

l 기출문제

02. Choose the most appropriate group of words for the blank.　14년 2차

(A) is a stress which a ship's hull or keel experiences that the middle of the ship is pushed to bend upward.
When a ship's bow is pushed first to port and then to starboard, she is said to be (B).

① A : Rolling　　　　　　B : pitching
② A : Sagging　　　　　　B : swaying
③ A : Hogging　　　　　　B : yawing
④ A : Surging　　　　　　B : heaving

해설　A는 선체의 중간부분이 위로 휘어지는 Hogging에 대한 설명이다.
　　　B는 선수가 왼쪽 오른쪽으로 밀리는 Yawing에 대한 설명이다.

답 ❸

03. 다음 중 빈칸에 들어갈 단어로 가장 옳은 것은?　21년 하반기

- If there is a marked temperature inversion or a sharp decrease in water vapor content with increased height, a horizontal radio duct may be formed. It is (㉠).
- (㉡) is brought about when the ship is supported fore and aft by two waves, so that the middle of the vessel is strained in the opposite direction.

　　　　　　　㉠　　　　　　　　㉡
① super-refraction　　　　Hogging
② super-refraction　　　　Sagging
③ sub-refraction　　　　　Hogging
④ sub-refraction　　　　　Sagging

해설　㉠ super refraction
　　　㉡ Sagging

답 ❷

기출문제

04. Choose the most appropriate group of words for the blank.   17년 2차

> There are three special axes in any ship, called vertical, lateral, and longitudinal axes. The movements around them are known as roll, pitch, and yaw.
> - Roll is the tilting rotation of a vessel about its longitudinal axis. An offset or deviation from normal on this axis is referred to as (A).
> - Pitch is the up and down rotation of a vessel about its lateral axis. An offset or deviation from normal on this axis is referred to as (B).
> - Yaw is the turning rotation of a vessel about its vertical axis. An offset or deviation from normal on this axis is referred to as (C).

① stability - trim - course keeping ability
② stability - course keeping ability - trim
③ trim - stability - course keeping ability
④ trim - course keeping ability - stability

해설 A : Roll은 선박 복원성(stability)과 관련이 있다.
　　　B : Pitch는 선박 트림(trim)과 관련이 있다.
　　　C : Yaw는 선박 침로안정성(course keeping ability)와 관련이 있다.

답 ①

기출문제

05. 다음 〈보기〉 중 용어의 정의가 가장 올바르게 짝지어진 것은? `22년 일반직`

> ㉠ Rolling : The tilting rotation of a vessel about its longitudinal axis. An offset or deviation from normal on this axis is referred to as list or heel.
> ㉡ Pitching : The up and down rotation of a vessel about its transverse axis. An offset or deviation from normal on this axis is referred to as trim.
> ㉢ Hogging: A stress which is brought about when the ship is supported fore and aft by two waves, so that the middle of the vessel is strained in the opposite direction.
> ㉣ Sagging : A stress which a ship's hull or keel experiences that the middle of the ship is pushed to bend upward.

① ㉠, ㉣
② ㉢, ㉣
③ ㉠, ㉡
④ ㉡, ㉣

해설 옳지 않은 것:
㉢ Hogging → Sagging
㉣ Sagging → Hogging
옳은 것:
㉠, ㉡

답 ❸

06. 다음 중 용어의 설명이 맞는 것은? `05년 3차`

① racing - 상하동요
② yawing - 선수동요
③ rolling - 종요
④ pitching - 횡요

해설 ① racing - 선미가 들리면서 프로펠러가 수면 밖에서 공회전 하는 현상
③ rolling - 횡요
④ pitching - 종요

답 ❷

Chapter 14 Stability (복원성)

01
용어

① Stability (복원성)
선박이 물위에서 외부의 힘을 받아 경사하려 할 때의 원래 상태로 돌아오려고 하는 힘

② Center of Gravity, G (무게중심)
선체의 전체 중량이 한 점에 모여 있다고 생각되는 점

③ Center of Buoyancy, B (부심)
수면 아래 선체 용적의 기하학적 중심

④ Metacenter, M (메타센터, 경심)
횡경사가 일어날 때의 축이 되는 지점

⑤ Center of Floatation (부면심)
Trim의 축이 되는 지점 부면심을 중심으로 앞뒤로 무게이동이 일어나면 트림변화가 발생한다.

⑥ Free surface effect (자유표면효과)
선체내의 액체들은 선박이 횡요운동을 할 때 탱크의 좌우로 이동하여 선체에 손상을 입히거나 선체의 중심을 상승시키는 효과를 낳아 복원성을 나쁘게 한다. 이와 같이 유동하는 액면을 자유 표면이라고 하며 유동수에 의해 중심이 상승하는 효과를 자유표면효과라 한다.

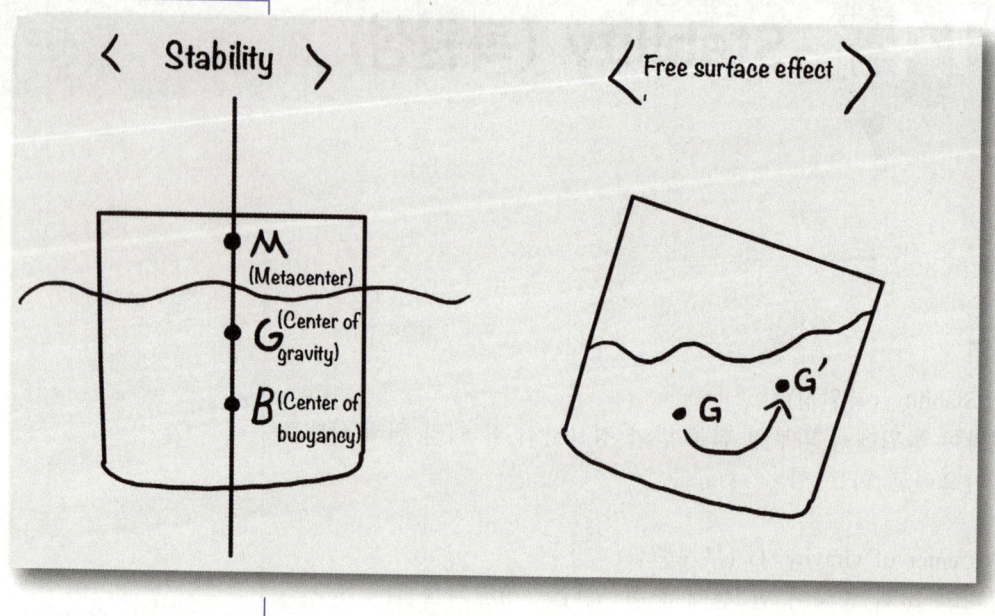

기출문제

01. Choose best answer in the blank

<기출예상문제>

If a ship's center of gravity is higher and higher, it can cause (   ).

① stability lose
② buoyancy bigger
③ stability raise
④ stranding

해설 선박의 무게 중심(center of gravity)이 점점 높아지면 복원성의 감소(stability lose)를 야기할 수 있다.

답 ❶

02. What is the below paragraph explain?

<09년 2차>

This is caused that water or oil is not fully loaded at cargo hold or other tanks and moves randomly according to ship's movement like rolling and pitching. This make a negative effect to stability, and cause ship's capsize down

① free surface reaction
② half liquid effect
③ random liquid effect
④ free surface effect

해설 화물창이나 탱크에 물이나 기름이 가득 차지 않아서 이것은 야기되며 이것은 선박의 롤링이나 피칭에 따라서 예기치 못하게 발생한다. 이것은 선박 복원성(stability)에 좋지 않은 영향을 주고 선박 전복(capsize down)을 야기한다. : 자유표면 효과 (free surface effect)

답 ❹

기출문제

03. 탱크 내의 물이 탱크 벽을 충격함에 따라 발생하는 손상을 무엇이라고 부르는가? `07년 2차`

① crashing   ② free surface
③ free surface effect   ④ surface crashing

해설 위 문제와 동일

답 ③

04. Choose a proper word to a blank each `09년 2차`

when ship's balance between gravity and (　) is broken, ship will lose her (　) and be capsized in a result.

① reaction – movement   ② attraction - hull
③ buoyancy – stability   ④ density – pitching

해설 중력(gravity)과 부력(buoyancy) 사이의 선박 균형이 깨질 때 선박은 복원성(stability)을 잃고 그 결과로 전복(capsized)된다.

답 ③

05. 다음 중 빈칸에 들어갈 단어로 가장 옳은 것은? `17년 1차`

(　) can be defined as the ability of the ship to return to the upright when slightly inclined.

① Ship capability   ② Ship maneuverability
③ Ship stability   ④ Ship navigability

해설 복원성(stability)는 선박이 약간 경사(inclined)했을 때 똑바로(upright) 돌아오는 능력으로 정의된다.

답 ③

06. Select the correct one for the blank `22년 2차`

Change of (　) is caused either by shifting weight forward or aft, or by adding or removing weight before or abaft the ship's center of floatation

① center of gravity   ② center of buoyancy
③ trim   ④ metacenter

해설 트림(trim)의 변화는 무게중심을 앞이나 뒤쪽으로 이동시켜서, 혹은 무게를 부면심의(center of floatation) 앞이나 뒤쪽에 더하거나 제거해서 생겨난다.

답 ③

기출문제

07. Choose the correct one for the blank
18년 1차

If a vessel goes from fresh water to salt water, (   )

① her draft will not be changed
② her draft will be increased
③ her freeboard will be decreased
④ her freeboard will be increased

해설 해수는 담수에 비해 액체의 비중이 높다(해수 1.025, 담수 1.00) 때문에 선박은 해수에서 더 큰 부력을 받아 더욱 떠오르게 되고 그로인해 흘수(draft)는 비교적 감소(decrease)하고 건현(freeboard)은 증가(increase)하게 되는 것이다.

답 ④

chapter 15 Turning circle(선회권)

01
선회권 용어

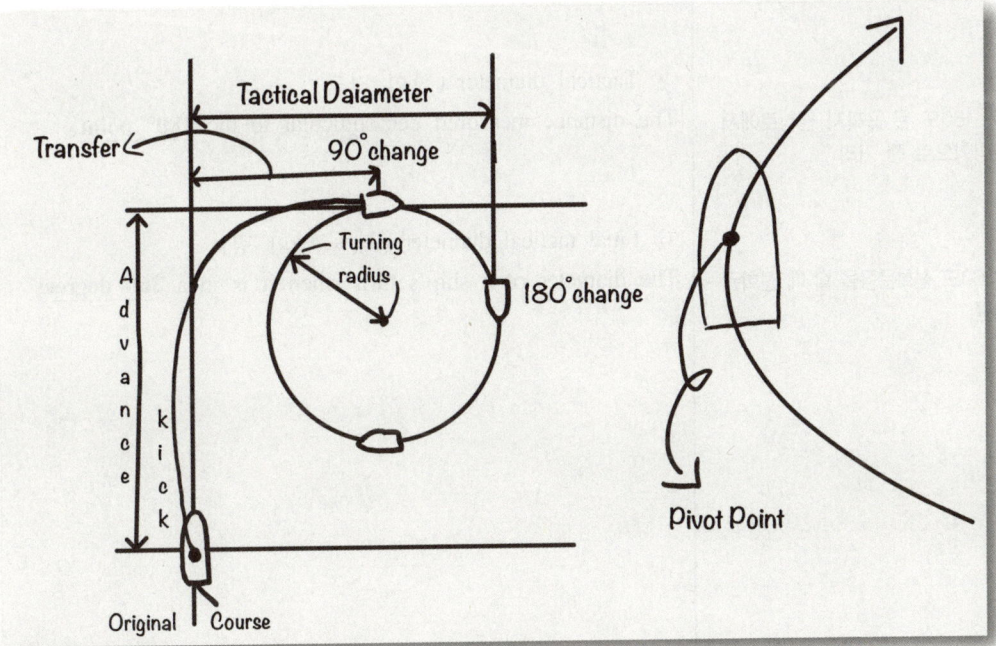

① Turning circle (선회권)
The path followed by the ship's pivot point (or center of gravity) when making a 360°

360도 선회운동 중에 선체의 전심(또는 무게중심)이 그리는 항적

② Pivot Point (전심)
A point on the centerline about which the ship turn when the rudder is put over

선박의 중심선상의 지점으로, 최대전타 하였을 때 선박이 이를 중심으로 회전한다.

전타 시 원침로와 평행한 방향으로 선박의 무게중심이 이동한 거리로 선수방위가 90도만큼 돌아갔을 때를 말한다.

③ Advance (선회 종거)
This is the distance travelled by the ship's center of gravity in a direction **parallel to the ship's initial(original) course** after the instant the rudder is put over

전타 시 원침로와 직각 방향으로 선박의 무게중심이 이동한 거리로 선수방위가 90도 바뀌었을 때 측정된다.

④ Transfer (선회 횡거)
This is the distance travelled by the ship's center of gravity in a direction **perpendicular (right angle) to the ship's initial course**. It is usually quoted for a 90° change of heading

회두가 180도 된 곳까지 원침로에서 직각 방향으로 잰 거리

⑤ Tactical diameter (선회 지름)
The distance measured perpendicular to the **180° point**

배가 360도 선회운동을 할 때 선회권의 지름

⑥ Final tactical diameter (최종 선회 경)
The diameter of a ship's turn when it is in a **360 degrees**

chapter 16
Tonnage(톤수)

01
Volume Tonnage (용적톤수)

① Gross Tonnage, G/T (총톤수)
선박의 크기를 나타내는 지표로 이용된다.

② Net Tonnage, N/T (순톤수)
선박의 용적중에서 직접 상행위에 사용되는 용적 즉 화물이나 여객을 수용하는 장소의 용적을 톤수로 나타낸 것이다.

③ Stowage factor (적화계수)
적화계수는 특정 화물 1톤이 얼마나 많은 큐빅미터를 차지하는가를 나타내는 것으로 ft^3로 나타낸다.

02
Weight Tonnage (중량톤수)

① Displacement Tonnage (배수톤수)
선박이 물위에 떠 있을 때 선체 수면 아래 부분의 배수용적(displacement)에 상당하는 물의 부피를 무게톤수로 환산한 선박 중량

② Full load displacement Tonnage (만재배수톤수)
선박의 배수톤수 중에서 만재상태(full load condition) 혹은 하기만재흘수선(load line in summer)까지 잠긴 상태에서의 배수톤수

③ Light load displacement Tonnage (경하배수톤수)
선박의 경하상태(light load condition)의 흘수에 대한 배수톤수

④ Deadweight Tonnage, DWT (재화중량톤수)
만재상태의 흘수에 대한 하기 만재 배수량과 경하상태의 흘수에 대한 경하 배수량의 차이 (즉 만재배수톤수 - 경하배수톤수= 재화중량톤수) 선박이 적재할 수 있는 최대 중량을 나타냄

기출문제

01. 다음 보기 중 톤수의 영문 표기명의 연결이 올바르지 않은 것을 고르시오 `기출예상문제`

① 총톤수 : Gross Tonnage, G/T
② 재화중량 톤수 : Net Tonnage, N/T
③ 만재 배수톤수 : Full load displacement Tonnage
④ 배수톤수 : displacement Tonnage

해설 재화중량 톤수는 Dead Weight Tonnage, DWT이다. Net Tonnage는 순톤수 이다.

답 ❷

02. 다음 중 괄호 안에 총톤수의 의미로 들어갈 말로 올바른 것은? `05년 3차`

what is your type of vessel and (   )?

① net tonnage
② deadweight tonnage
③ displacement tonnage
④ gross tonnage

해설 총톤수는 gross tonnage (G/T)이다.

답 ❹

03. Which of the following best indicates how many tones of cargo a vessel can carry? `07년 3차`

① bale cubic
② dead weight ton
③ loaded displacement ton
④ gross ton

해설 얼마나 많은 화물을 선박이 실을 수 있는지를 나타내주는 최적의 톤수는 재화중량톤수(dead weight ton)이다.

답 ❷

04. 다음 빈 칸에 들어갈 말로 가장 적절한 것은? `14년 1차`

In shipping, the (   ) indicate how many cubic meter of space one tonnage (or cubic feet of space one long ton) of a particular type of cargo occupies in a hold of a cargo ship

① deadweight
② stowage factor
③ cargo rate
④ measurement

해설 적화계수(stowage factor)는 특정 화물 1톤이 얼마나 많은 큐빅미터를 차지하는가를 나타내는 것으로 ft^3로 나타낸다.

답 ❷

chapter 17 기관

01
용어

① Manoeuvring speed (조종속력)
A vessel's reduced speed in circumstances where it may be required to use the engines at short notice.

| 기관을 즉시 사용하게 될 수도 있는 상황에서도 감소된 선박 속력 |

② Sea speed (항해속력)
Full speed sailing after the Rung up engine.

| Rung up engine 이후 전속력으로 항해하는 속력 |

③ Pitch
Distance that a propeller will move the vessel in one revolution.

| 프로펠러 한 바퀴 회전당 선박이 이동한 거리 |

④ Slip
The difference between the pitch of the propeller and the actual advance of the ship on one revolution is called **slip**. If the pitch is greater than the actual advance per revolution, this is positive ; If the pitch is less than the actual advance of the ship this is said to be negative

| 피치와 프로펠러 한 바퀴 회전당 실제 전진거리 사이의 차이를 Slip이라고 한다. 피치가 회전당 실제 전진거리보다 크다면 +(positive)이고 작다면 -(negative)이다. |

⑤ Hours underway
- Hours spent on voyage after departure from 'Up and down anchor' to 'Let go anchor'
- Hours from 'Last line let go' to 'First line to pier'.

| - 업앤다운 앵카 이후부터 투묘 시점까지의 항해 시간
- 마지막 줄을 풀어주는 시점부터 첫 줄을 거는 시점까지의 시간 |

⑥ Hours propelling
Hours from 'Rung up engine' to 'S.B.E' prior to entering next port

| Rung up 순간부터 다음 항구에 입항 전의 S.B.E까지의 시간 |

⑦ RPM
Resolution Per Minute

| 분당 엔진의 회전수 |

기출문제

01. 다음 괄호 안에 들어갈 말의 순서가 가장 옳게 연결된 것은 무엇인가?　　20년 1차

> ㉠ (　　) means the hours spent on voyage from up and down anchor to let go anchor.
> ㉡ (　　) means the distance that a propeller will move the vessel in one revolution.
> ㉢ (　　) of radar is the discrimination between two objects at the same range but on different bearings. It depends on the range at which targets are situated and the pencil beam width.

	㉠	㉡	㉢
①	Hours propelling	R.P.M.	Range resolution
②	Hours underway	Pitch	Bearing resolution
③	Hours propelling	Slip	Range resolution
④	Hours underway	Slip	Bearing resolution

해설　㉠ Up&Down부터 Let go anchor(투묘) 까지는 항해 중(underway)의 시간(Hours)이다.
　　　㉡ 프로펠러 한 바퀴 회전(one revolution)당 선박이 이동한 거리를 Pitch라고 한다.
　　　㉢ Bearing resolution : 방위분해능
　　　＊Range resolution : 거리분해능＊

답 ❷

02. The difference between the pitch of the propeller and the actual advance of the ship on one revolution is called (　　). If the pitch is greater than the actual advance per revolution, this is positive ; If the pitch is less than the actual advance of the ship this is said to be negative　　18년 1차

① slip　　　　　　　　② cavitation
③ gain　　　　　　　　④ speed

해설　피치와 프로펠러 한 바퀴 회전당 실제 전진거리 사이의 차이를 Slip이라고 한다. 피치가 회전당 실제 전진거리보다 크다면 +(positive)이고 작다면 -(negative)이다.

답 ❶

03. The (　　) is responsible for the engine department　　06년 3차

① master　　　　　　　② chief engineer
③ first engineer　　　　④ watch officer

해설　기관부의 Chief engineer는 한국에서의 기관장을 의미하며 기관부서를 총괄한다..

답 ❷

chapter 18 선박 화재

01
화재의 3요소

① Oxygen (산소)

② Fuel (연료원)

③ Heat or spark (열 혹은 불꽃)

02
소화

① Fuel removal (연료원 제거)

② Temperature reduction (냉각)

③ Oxygen Exclusion or dilution (산소의 차단, 혹은 희석)

④ Chemical Inhibition (화학 작용 억제소화)

03
화재의 종류

① A급 화재(일반 화재)
연소 후 재가 남는 고체물질의 화재로 목재, 종이, 의류, 로프 등의 화재

② B급 화재(유류 화재)
연소 후 재가 남지 않는 가연성 액체화재로, 페인트, 윤활유 등의 유류화재

③ C급 화재(전기 화재)
전기에 의한 화재

④ D급 화재(금속 화재)
가연성 금속 물질의 화재로 나트륨, 마그네슘, 알루미늄 등의 화재

04
Fire fighting equipment (소화 설비)

① Fire detector (화재탐지기)
   - Heat detector (열 탐지기)
   - Smoke detector (연기 탐지기)
   - Flame detector (불꽃 탐지기)

② Portable fire extinguisher (휴대용 소화기)
   - Foam extinguisher (포말소화기)
   - CO_2 extinguisher (이산화탄소소화기)
   - Dry powder extinguisher (분말소화기)
   - Halogen extinguisher (할론소화기)

③ Fire hydrant (소화전)
물을 분사하는 설비로 소화호스와 연결해서 사용한다.

④ Fixed fire extinguisher (고정식 소화기)
기관실 화물창 등에서 발생한 대형화재 진압용 소화기.

기출문제

01. Choose suitable case in the blank   〔10년 2차〕

Battery rooms are ventilated to rid them of (   )

① flammable gas   ② water vapor
③ carbon dioxide   ④ sulfur dioxide

해설 가연성 가스(flammable gas)를 제거(rid)하기 위하여 배터리 룸을 환기(ventilation)시켰다.

답 ①

기출문제

02. B급 화재에 사용하는 소화재는? 07년 2차

① CO_2 ② Foam
③ halogen gas ④ all of them

해설 B급 화재를 진화할 수 있는 소화재는 CO_2(이산화탄소), Foam(폼 약재), halogen gas(할론) 모두이다.

답 ❹

03. 다음 중 화재 소화방법으로 가장 옳지 않은 것은? 21년 하반기

① Fuel removal
② Temperature reduction (uner flash point)
③ Chemical Inhibition
④ Oxygen inclusion

해설 Oxygen inclusion은 산소 포함을 의미한다. 화재 진압을 위해서는 오히려 산소를 제거해야한다.

답 ❹

chapter 19 기타 항해, 일반 문제 통암기

I 기출문제

01. 다음 빈 칸에 들어갈 말로 가장 적절한 것은? _{14년 1차}

The result of chemical reaction with acids that are formed the products of combustion is (   )

① corrosion ② erosion
③ scuffing ④ abrasion

해설 부식(corrosion)은 산성(acids)에 의한 화학반응(chemical reaction)의 결과. 연소생성물질(products of combustion)을 만들어낸다

답 ❶

02. which of the following correction corrects a sighted sextant angle from the visible to the sensible horizon? _{13년 1차}

① dip ② index error
③ main body correction ④ refraction

해설 다음 중 어떤 수정법이 시수평으로부터의 육분의 각도와 거소수평으로부터의 육분의 각도를 수정해주는 개정인가? : 안고차(dip)

답 ❶

기출문제

03. All of the following statements concerning an urgency signal are correct except

<small>12년 2차</small>

① The signal may be sent on the distress frequencies only on the authority of the person responsible for the vessel.
② The urgency signal and message may be addressed to all stations or to a specific station.
③ The signal implies that the ship is in imminent danger or requires immediate assistance.
④ The urgency signal may be used when the master desires to issue a warning that circumstances may become necessary for him to send out a distress signal at a later stage.

해설 긴급신호에 관한 사항 중 옳지 않은 것을 고르는 문제이다.
③ 선박이 긴박한 위험에 빠졌거나 즉각적인 도움이 필요한 상태에서 사용하는 것은 조난 신호(distress signal)이다.
옳은 것 :
① 이 신호는 선박의 책임이 있는 자의 권한 하에서만 조난 주파수를 통해 송신될 수 있다.
② 긴급 신호와 메시지는 모든 국 또는 특정 국에게 보내질 수 있다.
④ 긴급 신호는 그 다음 단계에 조난 신호를 보내야 할 필요가 있는 상황에서 선장이 경고를 보내고자 할 때에 사용될 수 있다.

답 ③

04. "In case of ordinary leakage it should be remembered that the ship should not be given up till she shows evident signs of foundering." The underlined part means

<small>12년 2차</small>

① seeking   ② capsizing
③ sinking   ④ sounding

해설 일반적인 누수 발생 시 이것을 기억하라. 선박이 침몰의 명확한 사인을 보여줄 때까지 선박을 버려서는 안 된다는 것을.

답 ③

05. 다음 밑줄 친 빈칸에 가장 알맞은 것은?

<small>11년 3차</small>

A helicopter (   ) is a point at which it is safe for a helicopter to land. It is marked by H painted on the ship's deck.

① hover point   ② arriving point
③ contact point   ④ landing point

해설 헬기 착륙지점(landing point)은 헬기를 착륙해도 안전한 지점이다. 이 지점은 선박 갑판상에 페인트로 H가 표시되어있다.

답 ④

I 기출문제

06. Choose best description below paragraph   `10년 2차`

> This is signal flag of blue with a white square at the centre, display by a vessel about to leaving port

① leaving flag
② blue and white flag
③ quarantine flag
④ blue peter

해설 파란색 신호기이며 가운데에 흰색 사각형이 있다. 출항하려는 선박이 계양한다. PAPA기를 Blue peter라고도 한다.

답 ④

07. Choose best describe below paragraph   `10년 2차`

> This indicate that custom officers try to find out contraband or smuggling. Sometimes this can make crew's room and personal belongings messed up, but it is necessary to prevent possibility of smuggling

① rummage
② fumigation
③ stowaway
④ confiscation

해설 뒤지기(rummage)는 세관 관리인이 밀수품이나 밀반입품을 찾아내려 하는 것을 의미한다. 가끔 이것은 선원의 방이나 개인 용품을 어지르기도 한다. 하지만 이것은 밀수의 가능성을 방지하기 위해서는 필수적인 것이다.

답 ①

08. Put the anchor in order by arriving big size   `10년 2차`

① kedge anchor - bower anchor - kedge anchor
② bower anchor - kedge anchor - stream anchor
③ bower anchor - stream anchor - kedge anchor
④ stream anchor - bower anchor - kedge anchor

해설 단순 암기.

답 ③

기출문제

09. the similar word with underlined one 〔10년 2차〕

when a vessel is in **foundering**, first of all master should make a roll call for all crew to ensure all crew's safety and then try to contact search and rescue station, muster all crew to life boat station, block all openings to prevent any possible marine pollution and operate EPIRB.

① stranding ② collision
③ not under command ④ sinking

해설 *foundering : 가라앉다*
선박 침몰(sinking)시 우선적으로 선장은 전 선원과 그들의 안전을 확인하기 위해 인원 점검을 해야 하고 그 후 수색구조 본부에 연락을 해야 한다. 모든 선원들을 구명정 승정위치에 집합 시키고 가능한 해양 오염을 막기 위해 모든 개구를 차단해야한다. 그리고 EPIRB도 작동 시킨다.

답 ④

10. Before a vessel arrives this position, she should check all crew's health condition and sanitary condition all over the ship to get free pratique. 〔09년 3차〕

① Quarantine anchorage ② Outer anchorage
③ Inner anchorage ④ Special anchorage

해설 선박이 Quarantine anchorage(검역묘박지)에 들어가기 전에 검역증을 받기위해 모든 선원의 건강상태와 선박의 전반적인 위생상태를 확인해야한다.

답 ①

11. Looking (   ) from the monkey island, you can see the maindeck and forecastle. 〔07년 3차〕

① aft ② right aft
③ forward ④ forward of

해설 monkey island (마스트 위의 공간을 의미)에서 정면(forward)을 바라보면, 상갑판과 선수부가 보인다.

답 ③

12. Stevedore and supercargo left her. 여기서 Stevedore의 뜻은? 〔07년 2차〕

① 조리사 ② 하역인부
③ 검수인 ④ 선박검사관

해설 하역인부(Stevedore)와 화물감독관(supercargo)이 하선했다.

답 ②

기출문제

13. The ( ) is called sometime the navigation officer

① chief officer
② second officer
③ third officer
④ petty officer

[해설] 항해를 담당하는 사관은 2등 항해사(second officer)다.

답 ❷

14. 다음 중 선박의 life boat 외판에 표시하는 것으로는 선명과 ( )가 있다.

① port of registry
② destination
③ DP
④ gross tonnage

[해설] port of registry (기국)을 표시한다.

답 ❶

기출문제

09. the similar word with underlined one `10년 2차`

when a vessel is in **foundering**, first of all master should make a roll call for all crew to ensure all crew's safety and then try to contact search and rescue station, muster all crew to life boat station, block all openings to prevent any possible marine pollution and operate EPIRB.

① stranding ② collision
③ not under command ④ sinking

해설 *foundering : 가라앉다*
선박 침몰(sinking)시 우선적으로 선장은 전 선원과 그들의 안전을 확인하기 위해 인원 점검을 해야 하고 그 후 수색구조 본부에 연락을 해야 한다. 모든 선원들을 구명정 승정위치에 집합 시키고 가능한 해양 오염을 막기 위해 모든 개구를 차단해야한다. 그리고 EPIRB도 작동 시킨다.

답 ④

10. Before a vessel arrives this position, she should check all crew's health condition and sanitary condition all over the ship to get free pratique. `09년 3차`

① Quarantine anchorage ② Outer anchorage
③ Inner anchorage ④ Special anchorage

해설 선박이 Quarantine anchorage(검역묘박지)에 들어가기 전에 검역증을 받기위해 모든 선원의 건강상태와 선박의 전반적인 위생상태를 확인해야한다.

답 ①

11. Looking (　) from the monkey island, you can see the maindeck and forecastle. `07년 3차`

① aft ② right aft
③ forward ④ forward of

해설 monkey island (마스트 위의 공간을 의미)에서 정면(forward)을 바라보면, 상갑판과 선수부가 보인다.

답 ③

12. Stevedore and supercargo left her. 여기서 Stevedore의 뜻은? `07년 2차`

① 조리사 ② 하역인부
③ 검수인 ④ 선박검사관

해설 하역인부(Stevedore)와 화물감독관(supercargo)이 하선했다.

답 ②

기출문제

13. The (　) is called sometime the navigation officer　　07년 2차

① chief officer　　　　② second officer
③ third officer　　　　④ petty officer

해설　항해를 담당하는 사관은 2등 항해사(second officer)다.

답 ❷

14. 다음 중 선박의 life boat 외판에 표시하는 것으로는 선명과 (　)가 있다.　　06년 2차

① port of registry　　② destination
③ DP　　　　　　　④ gross tonnage

해설　port of registry (기국)을 표시한다.

답 ❶

PART 10 부 록

Chapter 1   2022 2차 채용 해경필기시험 해사영어 기출

chapter 01 해경필기시험 해사영어 기출

2022년 2차 채용

01 다음은 COLREG의 일부 내용이다. 빈칸에 들어갈 말로 가장 옳은 것은?

> Action taken to avoid collision with another vessel shall be such as to result in passing at (　). The effectiveness of the action shall be carefully checked until the other vessel is finally past and clear.

① avoid of collision　② safe speed
③ a safe distance　④ the port side

02 다음중 COLREG상 아래 빈칸에 들어갈 단어로 가장 옳은 것은?

> A vessel shall, so far as practicable, avoid crossing traffic lanes, but if obliged to do so shall cross on a heading as nearly as practicable at (　) angles to the general direction of traffic flow.

① small　② right
③ large　④ acute

03 다음 UNCLOS에서 통과통항(transit passage)중인 선박의 의무로 가장 옳지 않은 것은?

① Foreign ships, including marine scientific research and hydrographic survey ships, shall be carry out any research or survey activities without the prior authorization of the States bordering straits.
② refrain from any activities other than those incident to their normal modes of continuous and expeditious transit unless rendered necessary by force majeure or by distress;
③ comply with generally accepted international regulations, procedures and practices for safety at sea, including the International Regulations for Preventing Collisions at Sea;
④ comply with generally accepted international regulations, procedures and practices for the prevention, reduction and control of pollution from ships.

04 다음 중 UNCLOS상 무해 통항(Innocent passage)조항에서 외국선박이 연안국의 평화, 공공질서 또는 안전을 해치는 활동으로 규정한 것은 모두 몇 개 인가?

ⓐ any threat or use of force against the sovereignty, territorial integrity or political independence of the coastal State, or in any other manner in violation of the principles of international law embodies in the charter of the United Nations;
ⓑ any exercise or practice with weapons of any kind;
ⓒ any act aimed at collecting information to the prejudice of the defence or security of the coastal state;
ⓓ any act of propaganda aimed at affecting the defence or security of the coastal State;
ⓔ any act of negligent pollution contrary to this Convention;
ⓕ the carrying out of research or survey activities;

① 없다.
② 1개
③ 2개
④ 3개

05 다음은 COLREG의 일부 내용이다. 빈칸에 들어갈 단어로 가장 옳은 것은?

ⓐ When two power-driven vessels are crossing so as to involve risk of collision, the vessel which has the other on her own (㉠) shall keep out of the way and shall, if the circumstances of the case admit, avoid crossing ahead of the other vessel.
ⓑ Every vessel which is directed by these Rules to keep out of the way of another vessel shall, so far as possible, take (㉡) action to keep well clear.

	㉠	㉡
①	port side	safe and properly
②	port side	early and substantial
③	starboard side	safe and properly
④	starboard side	early and substantial

06 다음 IAMSAR MANUAL 상 Parallel Track(Sweep) Search에 대한 설명 중 가장 옳지 않은 것은?

① Used to search a large area when survivor location is certain.
② Usually used when a large search area must be divided into sub-areas for assignment to individual search facilities on-scene at the same time.
③ Search legs are parallel to each other and to the long sides of the sub-area.
④ Searching speed is the maximum speed of the slowest searching vessel.

07 다음은 SOLAS의 일부 내용이다. 빈칸에 들어갈 숫자의 합은 무엇인가?

> The Main steering gear shall be capable of putting the rudder over from 35° on one side to 35° on the other side with the ship at its deepest seagoing draught and running ahead at maximum ahead service speed and, under the same conditions, from ( )° on either side to ( )° on the other side in not more than ( )seconds.

① 88
② 93
③ 98
④ 103

08 다음 중 ISPS상 아래 내용에서 설명하는 보안등급으로 가장 옳은 것은?

> The level for which appropriate additional protective security measures shall be maintained for a period of time as a result of heightened risk of a security incident.

① Security level 1
② Security level 2
③ Security level 3
④ Security level 4

09 다음 빈칸에 들어갈 단어로 가장 옳은 것은?

> She is said to have (   ) when her speed is sufficient for her rudder to take effect

① headway
② steerageway
③ underway
④ advance

10 다음은 STCW의 일부 내용이다. 빈칸에 들어갈 숫자의 합은 무엇인가?

> All persons who are assigned duty as officer in charge of a watch or as a rating forming part of a watch shall be provided with a rest period of not less than a minimum of ( ) hours of rest in any 24 hour period.
> The hours of rest may be divided into no more than two periods, one of which shall be at least ( ) hours in length, and the intervals between consecutive periods of rest shall not exceed ( ) hours

① 24
② 26
③ 28
④ 30

11 다음은 SOLAS의 일부 내용이다. 밑줄의 내용 중 가장 옳지 않은 것은?

> Every crew member shall participate in at least one abandon ship drill and one fire drill ① every month.
> The drills of the crew shall take place within 24h of the ship leaving a port if more than 25% of the crew have not participated in abandon ship and fire drills on board that particular ship in the ② previous month.
> When a ship enters service for the first time, after modification of a major character or when a new crew is engaged, these drills shall be held ③ after sailing.
> Each lifeboat shall be launched with its assigned operating crew aboard and manoeuvred in the water at least once every ④ three months during an abandon ship drill

12 다음 빈칸에 들어갈 단어로 가장 옳은 것은?

> "In SMCP ( ) means a vessel damaged or impaired in such a manner as to be incapable of proceeding on its voyage"

① disabled
② derelict
③ wrecked
④ hampered

13 다음 중 빈칸에 들어갈 내용으로 가장 옳은 것은?

"The ( ) is the maximum distance at which a light may be seen clear weather (meteorological visibility of 10 miles) expressed in nautical miles"

① nominal range   ② luminous range
③ visible range   ④ geographical range

14 다음 중 빈칸에 들어갈 내용으로 가장 옳은 것은?

"Change of ( ) is caused either by shifting weight forward or aft, or by adding or removing weight before or abaft the ship's center of floatation."

① center of buoyancy   ② center of gravity
③ trim   ④ metacenter

15 다음에서 설명하고 있는 내용으로 가장 옳은 것은?

A routing measure aimed at the separation of opposing streams of traffic by appropriate means and by the establishment of traffic lanes.

① Separation zone or line   ② Inshore traffic zone
③ Traffic separation scheme   ④ Traffic lane

16 다음에서 설명하는 것으로 가장 옳은 것은?

These are usually found in the neighborhood of chocks and somewhat inboard of them. They are heavy vertical cylinders and often used for making fast lines that have been led through the chock.

① fairlead   ② bitts
③ mooring buoy   ④ capstan

17 다음 중 접안부터 이안까지의 작업 순서를 가장 옳게 나열한 것은?

> ㉠ Made fast fore and aft ㉡ R/up Eng.
> ㉢ Single up. ㉣ First Line to pier

① ㉣ → ㉠ → ㉢ → ㉡
② ㉡ → ㉢ → ㉠ → ㉣
③ ㉠ → ㉡ → ㉢ → ㉣
④ ㉢ → ㉡ → ㉠ → ㉣

18 다음 밑줄 친 This가 설명하는 것으로 가장 옳은 것은?

> This is used for the exchange of data in ship to ship communications and also in communication with shore-based facilities. The purpose of this is to help identify vessels; assist in target tracking; simplify information exchange (eg. reduce verbal reporting); and provide additional information to assist situation awareness.
> This may be used together with VHF voice communications.

① Maritime Safety Information (MSI)
② Digital Selective Calling (DSC)
③ Enhanced Group Calling (EGC)
④ Automatic Identification System (AIS)

19 다음 중 빈칸에 들어갈 단어를 가장 옳게 나열한 것은?

> How much cable is (㉠)?
> 닻줄은 몇 절 풀려나가 있는가?
> The windlass is (㉡) gear.
> 양묘기의 기어가 연결되었음.
> Attention! Turn (㉢) cable.
> 주의하시오! 닻줄이 꼬였음.
> How much weight is (㉣) the cable?
> 닻줄에 중량이 얼마나 걸려있는가?

	㉠	㉡	㉢	㉣		㉠	㉡	㉢	㉣
①	in	on	in	of	②	in	in	out	on
③	out	on	on	of	④	out	in	in	on

20 다음 중 해사영어의 약어의 설명으로 옳은 것은 모두 몇 개인가?

㉠ M/V : Motor Vessel
㉡ W/H : Wheel House
㉢ C.O.W : Crude Oil Washing
㉣ Q.M : Qurantine Master
㉤ O/B : On Board
㉥ D.W.T : Dead Weight Tonnage
㉦ G.T : Great Tonnage
㉧ L.S.T : Local Separate Time
㉨ D.R. : Dead Reckoning
㉩ F/H : Full Ahead

① 5개 ② 6개
③ 7개 ④ 8개

정답 및 해설

1	2	3	4	5	6	7	8	9	10
③	②	①	②	④	①	②	②	②	④
11	12	13	14	15	16	17	18	19	20
③	①	①	③	③	②	①	④	④	③

01 ③

해설

다른 선박과의 충돌을 피하기 위한 동작은 안전한 거리(a safe distance)로 통과하는 결과를 갖는 것이어야 한다.

02 ②

해설

선박은 가능하다면 통항로(traffic lanes)를 횡단(crossing)하는 것은 피해야 하나, 만약 그럴 의무가 있다면 선수 방향이 일반적 교통흐름의 진행 방향에 가능한 한 직각(right angles)에 가깝게 횡단해야 한다.

03 ①

해설

과학조사, 수로측량 등을 하는 외국 선박들은 해협을 끼고 있는 국가들의 우선적 허가 없이 조사활동이나 측량 활동을 수행할 수 없다.(may not carry out)

04 ②

해설

옳지 않은 것 :
ⓔ any act of wilful and serious pollution(의도적이고 심각한 오염) contrary to this Convention;
negligent는 '느긋한, 태만한'이라는 의미를 갖는다.

05 ④

해설

ⓐ 횡단 상황에선 타선을 ㉠ 우측(starboard side)에 둔 선박이 피항선이다.
ⓑ 규정에 의거해 다른 선박에게 길을 비켜줘야 하는 선박은 가능하다면 ㉡ 조기에 충분한(early and substantial) 동작을 취해야 한다.

06 ①

해설

certain → uncertain

07 ②

해설

가장 깊은 항해 흘수에서 전속력 전진 시 타를 현측 35°에서 다른 현측 35°으로 전타하였을 때 현측 (35)°에서 다른 현측 (30)°까지 바뀌는데 (28)초를 넘겨서는 안 된다.
35+30+28=93

08 ②

해설

보안등급2 (Security level 2)에 대한 설명이다.

09 ②

해설

선박이 타를 사용 했을 때 타효가 생길 수 있는 최소한의 속력을 말하며 SMCP상 Steerageway(최소타효속력)이라고 한다.

10 ④

해설

당직 선원은 임의의 24시간의 기간 내에 최소한 (10)시간의 휴식시간을 가져야 하며 이 휴식시간은 2회 이내로 나눌 수 있으며, 그 기간 중 하나는 적어도 (6)시간이어야 한다. 그리고 연속된 휴식시간간의 간격은 (14)시간을 초과할 수 없다. 10+6+14=30

11 ③

해설

③ before sailing 이 되어야 한다.

12 ①

해설

손상되고 파손되어서 항해를 할 수 없는 선박은 Disabled(파손선박)이다.

13 ①

해설

명목적 광달거리(nominal range)는 기상이 양호한 날 (주간 가시거리 10해리)등광을 볼 수 있는 최대거리를 의미한다.

14 ③

해설

트림(trim)의 변화는 무게중심을 앞이나 뒤쪽으로 이동시켜서, 혹은 무게를 부면심의(center of floatation) 앞이나 뒤쪽에 더하거나 제거해서 생겨난다.

15 ③

해설

마주 오는 두 개의 교통흐름을 통항로 등의 수단으로 나누는 통항분리대(Traffic Separation Scheme)에 대한 설명이다.

16 ②

해설

bitts나 bollard는 주로 chocks의 주변에서 발견되며 어떤 것들은 그 안에 설치되기도 한다. 이것들은 무거운 수직의 원통형이며 계류삭들이 chock를 통해 빠져나가는 동안에 줄을 묶기 위해 사용된다.

17 ①

해설

- ㄹ 첫줄을 부두에 연결하였습니다.
- ㄱ 선수미 줄을 모두 부두에 연결하였습니다.
- ㄷ 한 개의 계류줄을 두고 나머진 모두 거두어 들였습니다.
- ㄴ 전속 항주를 시작 하였습니다.

18 ④

해설

자동인식시스템(Automatic Identification System, AIS)에 대한 설명이다.

19 ④

해설

- ㄱ How much cable is out?
- ㄴ The windlass is in gear.
- ㄷ Attention! Turn in cable.
- ㄹ How much weight is on the cable?

20 ③

해설

- ㄹ Q.M : Quarter Master
- ㅅ G.T : Gross Tonnage
- ㅇ L.S.T : Local Standard Time

해사영어 기본이론 임하람